Tcl/Tk

PROGRAMMER'S REFERENCE

Christopher Nelson

Osborne/**McGraw-Hill**

Berkeley ▪ New York ▪ St. Louis ▪ San Francisco
Auckland ▪ Bogotá ▪ Hamburg ▪ London
Madrid ▪ Mexico City ▪ Milan ▪ Montreal
New Delhi ▪ Panama City ▪ Paris ▪ São Paulo
Singapore ▪ Sydney ▪ Tokyo ▪ Toronto

Osborne/**McGraw-Hill**
2600 Tenth Street
Berkeley, California 94710
U.S.A.

For information on translations or book distributors outside the U.S.A.,
or to arrange bulk purchase discounts for sales promotions, premiums, or
fund-raisers, please contact Osborne/**McGraw-Hill** at the above address.

Tcl/Tk Programmer's Reference

Publisher   Brandon A. Nordin
Associate Publisher,
Editor-in-Chief   Scott Rogers
Acquisitions Editor   Megg Bonar
Project Editor   Nancy McLaughlin
Editorial Assistant   Stephane Thomas
Technical Editor   Clifton Flynt
Copy Editor   William McManus
Proofreaders   Carol Burbo, Valerie Perry
Indexer   Jack Lewis
Computer Designers   Jani Beckwith, Gary Corrigan
Illustrator   Brian Wells
Cover Design   Matthew Willis

1234567890 DOC DOC 019876543210

ISBN 0-07-212004-5

This book was composed with Corel VENTURA™ Publisher.

To my beautiful daughters, Heather and Jennifer,
with all my love.

About the Author ...

Christopher Nelson is a Senior Software Engineer at Pinebush Technologies, Inc., where he uses Tcl/Tk to help create HyperPlot and HyperXpress high-performance raster image processing software. He has over 15 years experience developing software on systems from personal computers to mainframes. He first became interested in computers and electronics as the next best thing to magic, and holds a B.S. in Electrical Engineering and an M.S. in Computer Science from RPI.

Chris is a member of Interex (the International Association of Hewlett-Packard Computing Professionals), and a former member of its board of directors. He has been recognized for outstanding contributions to the HP 1000 Contributed Software Library. A frequent contributor to *PC Techniques*, *HP Professional*, *TC Interface*, and *Interact* magazines, Chris has also written for *The Office* and *Paradox Informant*. He lives with his two daughters near Albany, New York, where he enjoys reading, refinishing furniture, biking, and all aspects of community theatre.

CONTENTS @ A GLANCE

CONTENTS

x   Contents

TABLE OF TABLES

TABLE OF FIGURES

ACKNOWLEDGMENTS

Everyone always says, "I don't know where to start. I'm sure I'll forget someone important." Now I know how that feels. But here goes....

Thanks to my parents for getting me started. Thanks to Ellen, through whom I vicariously studied technical communication. Thanks to Adriane Dedic, Connie Wright, and the crew at Interex for giving me a place to practice. Thanks to Jeff Duntemann for kind words and encouragement along the way.

Thanks to John Ousterhout for inventing Tcl/Tk. Thanks for my friends at Pinebush for giving me a reason to learn and practice it, and to the folks on the **comp.lang.tcl** newsgroup for helping me to do that. Thanks especially to Cameron Laird, who helped me feel welcome in the Tcl community. Thanks to Jeffery Hobbs, Brian Oakley, Paul Duffin, and numerous others who share so readily in that community.

Thanks to those whose books have come before this one and cover their material so well, leaving me to fill in this particular gap. There are so many, but my copies of Brent Welch's *Practical Programming in Tcl and Tk* (Prentice Hall, 1997) and Mark Harrison and Michael McLennan's *Effective Tcl/Tk Programming* (Addison-Wesley, 1998) are well-thumbed.

Thanks to Larry Virden, who got me into this mess and provided much appreciated feedback, Clif Flynt, who kept me honest, and Jim Ingham and Steve Ball, who filled in Macintosh details. Thanks to my sister, Tina, for the music. Thanks to Megg Bonar and the folks at Osborne/McGraw-Hill for their patience in preparing this book. And thanks, finally, to you for buying it.

Welcome to the Tcl Community!

Tcl (the "tool command language," pronounced "tickle")
is an open-source, cross-platform scripting language created by
John K. Ousterhout at the University of California at Berkeley in
1988. Originally conceived as a reusable, embeddable language
core for tools being developed by Dr. Ousterhout and his
colleagues, Tcl has come to be much more.

One of the most significant technical additions has been Tk, a
high-level toolkit for building graphical applications. Tk is so
powerful and easy to use that it has found use with other
languages, but it remains most powerful and best suited for work
with Tcl, the language that gave it its genesis. Indeed, the two are
so closely associated that they are often referred to as a single
entity with the name *Tcl/Tk*.

Tcl is easy to write and easy to read. It works well for short, one-off
scripts, and scales well to projects with tens of thousands of lines
of code or more. It has extensive text-processing facilities, with full
internationalization support—including strong regular expressions—
as well as provisions for handling binary data. Tcl has strong ties to
several databases, including Oracle and Sybase, and is more easily
extensible than Perl or Java.

Tcl exists at several levels. To a programmer implementing an
application in C or another compiled language, Tcl/Tk provides the
ready-made core of an application scripting language (like REXX,
AppleScript, or Visual Basic for Applications), which is easily
extended with application-specific commands. To a programmer
looking for a rapid application development (RAD) environment,
Tcl shells provide a rich feature set that can be easily enhanced
with extensions written in Tcl or a compiled language, such as
C, C++, or even Fortran.

Write Once, Run Anywhere

Originally implemented on UNIX-like operating systems, Tcl/Tk has
been ported to various other platforms. The mainstream ports are
to Microsoft Windows and Macintosh systems. Other interesting

ports include Open/VMS, IBM OS/390, OS/2, and VxWorks. There has been recent talk of porting Tcl/Tk to Microsoft Windows CE and various handheld computers.

On these many platforms, Tcl/Tk delivers on a promise of "write once, run anywhere" for almost any general programming problem. Tk abstracts platform-specific user interface elements, with their native look and feel, to a platform-independent programming interface. Still, Tcl provides access to platform-specific features, such as Microsoft Windows DDE (dynamic data exchange) and AppleScript.

Tcl/Tk brings the strong networking heritage of UNIX to its new platforms, allowing easy development of peer-to-peer networking and client/server systems. A simple client can be implemented in a few dozen lines of Tcl. A very capable server can be written in a few hundred lines. Tcl has strong support of HTML and XML and is embedded in a number of Web server products.

One of Tcl/Tk's unique strengths is found in using its networking and other communications channels (such as DDE, AppleScript, CORBA, and COM) to make integrated applications from other, preexisting components and programs—effectively using Tcl as "glue." The resulting "hypertools" become more than the sum of their parts, with significant code reuse and minimal new development.

What's In This Book?

This book is a language reference for anyone who wants to write applications or extensions in Tcl/Tk. Interfaces to C and other languages are not covered here, nor is this a guide to building applications in Tcl/Tk—that ground is covered well elsewhere. But, if you are writing that killer app in Tcl/Tk and can't seem to remember the syntax of a command, look here for the details.

Part 1 introduces the Tcl language syntax and conventions, and the Tk graphical toolkit. Part 2, the bulk of the book, is an alphabetical reference to all the Tcl/Tk commands and the important global variables that control their behavior. An appendix summarizes configuring Tk widgets and the standard Tk widget options.

The long examples from the book, any errata, and other material relevant to the book can be found at **www.purl.org/net/TclTkProgRef**.

What's in a Name?   Tcl doesn't exist in a vacuum; you probably picked up this book knowing at least one other language. To help get you up to speed with Tcl, the index includes commands from several other languages, such as C++ and UNIX shells, with pointers to equivalent Tcl/Tk commands. For example, you may be accustomed to delaying program execution with **wait** or **sleep**, whereas Tcl calls that **after**.

Throughout the book, names of commands and variables that you type as shown appear in **bold**. Placeholders for variables or values that you supply are shown in *italic*. Where needed, emphasis is added with underlines. Code snippets and examples are shown in monospaced type, like this:

```
# This is an example.
```

Throughout this book, each basic Tcl command is marked with a feather icon, and each Tk command is marked with a genie's lamp.

What Versions of Tcl/Tk Are Covered Here?

As this book goes to press, version 8.2.0 of Tcl/Tk has just been released. The descriptions and examples in this book are based on 8.1.1, with some consideration to backward-compatibility with version 8.0. Changes in 8.2 are largely internal and should not affect what you see here.

I hope you enjoy the simplicity and power of programming in Tcl/Tk as much as I do. And, again, welcome!

Chris Nelson
nelson@pinebush.com

Part 1
Getting Started with Tcl and Tk

Tcl Basics

Tcl is a very simple language. Really. It has almost no syntax, no
reserved words, and only a few characters with special meaning.
If you are fairly new to programming, you should find that
remembering Tcl's rules is less burdensome than remembering
those of other languages. If you are an experienced programmer,
you may have to keep reminding yourself, "It really *is* that simple."
Still, entire books have been written on exploring the nuances
of Tcl's simplicity, and the rest of this section may leave you
wanting more. There are a number of tutorials available at
http://tclconsortium.org that may help fill in the gaps.

Tcl is an interpreted language, sometimes called a *scripting*
language. Compiled languages such as C, Fortran, and COBOL
require separate compiling, linking, and executing steps to move
from a human-readable source file to a machine-executable
program. Interpreted languages such as Tcl replace these distinct
steps with more closely tied stages of *parsing* (breaking up the
script into meaningful chunks) and *evaluation* (doing something
with the chunks).

NOTE: Starting with version 8.0, Tcl includes a just-in-time, or
on-the-fly, compiler that "compiles" Tcl scripts into bytecodes for
more efficient reevaluation. However, this process is internal to the
interpreter and exists only as an optimization.

Tcl interpreters come in various forms. Tcl comes with two
interpreters bound into *shells*: **tclsh** and **wish**. These shells
interpret commands much like **command.com** on MS-DOS, **cmd**
on Microsoft Windows NT, and **csh, ksh,** and so forth on UNIX.
tclsh (the Tcl shell) includes just basic Tcl commands. **wish** (the
windowing shell) includes all the basic commands in **tclsh**, as well
as all the graphical commands in the Tk extension.

The input to the Tcl interpreter is a *script*. A script may be read
from a source file or typed interactively into a shell. Scripts are

parsed into *commands*. Each command is evaluated independently of those before and after it, and returns a result string (which may be empty) and a status (indicating success or failure). The overall result of a script is the result of the last command evaluated in the script.

Generally, commands are executed as they are encountered in a script, but some commands set up event handlers to execute at a later time, when a specified event occurs. Events include such things as a specified amount of time passing, data becoming available on a network socket, and a user clicking a button in a dialog box.

For events to be processed, the interpreter must enter an *event loop*. **wish** always has an event loop active to handle graphical interaction with the user, but scripts running in **tclsh** must take special care to make sure events can be processed (see **vwait** for more information).

The Rules

A Tcl *script* consists of one or more command invocations separated by newlines or semicolons. Assuming that **analyze** and **report** are valid commands, the following are all valid scripts:

```
analyze
```

```
analyze;report
```

```
analyze
report
```

A Tcl *command invocation* consists of one or more *groups* separated by *whitespace* characters (excluding newlines). Whitespace characters depend on locale; the ASCII whitespace characters are space (blank), tab, vertical tab, carriage return, newline, and formfeed. Most scripts use only space and tab; other characters can cause problems, including having different interpretations on different platforms.

The first group of a command invocation is the command name, and the remaining groups, if any, are arguments to the command. For example, the predefined command **puts** ("put string") is used to output values like this:

```
puts Hello!
```

but not like this:

```
puts
Hello!
```

The latter script here tries to invoke the commands **puts** (with no arguments) and **Hello!** (which likely doesn't exist).

NOTE: Words like **if**, **exit**, **puts**, and **while** seem to have special meaning only because they are the names of predefined commands. They may be redefined by an application or extension script, and are recognized as command names only at the beginning of a command.

Commands may have many arguments. The following one-line script invokes **myCommand** and passes it six arguments:

```
myCommand foo bar baz stuff and nonsense
```

NOTE: The interpreter processes each word *exactly* once before passing it on to the command, which may interpret it further. This is significantly different from common UNIX shells, such as **csh** and **bash**, which often require extra quotes around variable references and command invocations, to maintain grouping as the shell reprocesses the script.

Variables

For the most part, Tcl is a typeless language at the script level. For example, quotes around a string of digits don't make it into text and prevent you from using the digits in arithmetic. At the source level, everything is a string (a sequence of characters), but Tcl interprets certain patterns of characters as certain types of values behind the scenes. These include numeric formats, logical values, and lists. (The Appendix goes into some detail about a number of other special interpretations used by Tk options.)

Tcl supports simple variables (single values, including lists) and arrays (groups of values accessed by index). Variables are not declared, and are created by assignment. The predefined command **set** creates a new variable and assigns it a value. Here is an example:

```
set pi 3.14159
```

Array indices are included in parentheses:

```
set constants(pi) 3.14159
set constants(e) 2.71828
```

Programmer's Tip: *Tcl arrays are one-dimensional—only one index is allowed—but multidimensional arrays can be faked with complex indices. The common practice is to separate parts of the index by commas, such as a(1,2) or b(foo,bar,baz).*

Variables are local in scope unless declared global. See **global**, **namespace**, **proc**, and **variable** in Part 2 for more information.

Tcl recognizes numbers in several formats. Integers can be represented in decimal (using digits 0 to 9), octal (using digits 0 to 7), and hexadecimal (using digits 0 to f).

- A *decimal integer* is any sequence of digits 0 through 9 that does not start with a 0, such as 123.

- An *octal number* is marked by a leading 0. For example, 077 is sixty-three (7 × 8 + 7 × 1), not seventy-seven. This leads to a common error when parsing formatted strings. For example, if you have a date represented as 1999-08-11 that you break at the dashes and try to increment the second field (08), you will get an error, because 08 starts with a 0 (indicating an octal number), but 8 is not a valid octal digit.

- A *hexadecimal number* is marked by a leading 0 followed by a letter **x**. For example, 0x55 is eighty-five (5 × 16 + 5 × 1), not fifty-five. The **x** and the hexadecimal digits a through f may be upper- or lowercase.

Floating-point numbers can be represented in scientific notation with or without an exponent.

Many languages use only integers to represent logical or Boolean values, with zero being false and non-zero integers being true. In many cases, Tcl is much more flexible in how it interprets logical or Boolean values. In addition to zero, the words **false**, **off**, and **no** are all interpreted as false, and non-zero integers, **true**, **on**, and **yes** are all interpreted as true.

NOTE: These flexible interpretations are limited to places where a single Boolean value is expected—they cannot be used in logical expressions, such as **true && on** (true and on) or ! **false** (not false).

Lists are an important data type in Tcl. While represented externally as formatted strings, Tcl internals provide special structures and functions to make list handling natural and efficient.

## 1

A script can be viewed as a list of commands, a command can be viewed as a list of words, and so on.

A Tcl list is one or more elements separated by whitespace, as in this example:

```
fe fi fo fum
```

Here we have a list of four elements. Braces ({}) are used to include elements with whitespace characters in them. For example, the following is also a list of four elements:

```
Alice {Tweedle Dee} {Mad Hatter} {Cheshire Cat}
```

Lists may be nested to an arbitrary depth. The following is a list of lists:

```
{{a b c d e f} {1 2 3 4 5 6}}
```

The first element here is {a b c d e f}, and the second element is {1 2 3 4 5 6}.

Grouping

Words may be *grouped* with double quotes ("") or braces ({}). If a word begins with a double quote, it begins a group that continues up to the next double quote. Semicolons, close brackets (]), and all whitespace characters have no special meaning and are made part of the group. Substitution is performed on the group. (See the following section for an explanation of substitution.) The double quotes are not retained as part of the group. For example:

```
puts "This is a 'group';
it includes a newline."
```

outputs

```
This is a 'group';
it includes a newline.
```

NOTE: The group must begin with the double quote for the double quote to have meaning; it is not necessary for quotes to balance. For example, **puts weird**" is valid and outputs **weird**".

If a word begins with an open brace ({), it begins a group that continues up to a matching close brace (}). Braces may be nested within the group. Substitution is not performed on the group, except that a backslash followed by a newline and any number of whitespace characters is replaced by a single space. Other than that, the group includes <u>exactly</u> the characters between the braces. The braces are <u>not</u> retained as part of the group. For example, the following script

```
puts {foo
  bar}
puts {foo {} bar}
```

produces this output:

```
foo
  bar
foo {} bar
```

However, the following script is incomplete.

```
puts {foo { bar}
```

Here, the second close brace matches the second open brace, and the first open brace is unmatched.

The following example is valid and complete, because the open bracket is within a quoted string:

```
puts "foo { bar"
```

Finally, the following script is probably not what you'd expect.

```
puts {foo { bar}
puts "foo } bar"
```

Here, the first open brace from the first line matches the close brace in the second line, giving the following three groups:

```
puts
foo { bar}\nputs "foo
bar"
```

Note that **\n** represents the newline after the first close brace.

Programmer's Tip   *Generally speaking, putting braces in strings in the manner just described is dangerous. See the following section for a discussion of backslash substitution.*

Substitution

When quoting with braces ({}) does not suppress substitution, the characters in a group may be *substituted* in one of three ways:

command substitution, variable substitution, or backslash substitution.

If a group contains an open bracket ([), then *command substitution* is performed. The characters up to a matching close bracket (]) are treated as a script and parsed and evaluated recursively. The brackets and all characters in between are replaced in the group by the return value of the script. Command substitutions may be nested, and a group may contain multiple command substitutions. For example, assuming that the commands **toupper** and **tolower** change the case of a string they are passed, the following script

```
puts "[toupper foo] bar [toupper [join {b a z} ""]]"
```

produces this output:

```
FOO bar BAZ
```

If a group contains a dollar sign ($), then *variable substitution* is performed. The dollar sign and the characters that follow it are replaced by the value of the variable. A variable substitution may take one of the following forms:

Form	Substitution
$*name*	*name* is any sequence of one or more letters, digits, and underscores.
${*name*}	*name* is any sequence of one or more characters, except the close brace.
$*name*(*index*)	*name* is the name of an array, and *index* is an index into that array. *name* is any sequence of letters, digits, and underscores.[1] *index* is a string; it may be a literal string, or it may include command, variable, and backslash substitutions.

A group may contain multiple variable substitutions. Here is an example:

```
puts "$a, $b!"
```

---

[1]Versions 8.0 and 8.1 require at least one character in an array name. Version 8.2 (and some earlier versions) allow zero characters. This has special uses for some particular programming problems and is <u>not</u> recommended practice.

Assuming that variable **a** has the value **Hello** and variable **b** has the value **world**, this script would output the following:

```
Hello, world!
```

The ${*name*} form is useful not only when *name* contains characters other than letters, digits, and underscores, but also when the variable substitution has a letter, digit, or underscore following it. For example, this script

```
puts "$a_$b"
```

tries to output the value of a variable named **a_**, while

```
puts "${a}_$b"
```

outputs the values of **a** and **b** with an underscore in between.

Once an array variable reference is parsed, the index part is processed for command, variable, and backslash substitution. For example, the following loops through the elements in a pseudo-two-dimensional array:

```
for {set r 0} {$r < 10} {incr r} {
    for {set c 0} {$c < 10} {incr c} {
        puts "array($r,$c)=$array($r,$c)"
    }
}
```

If a group contains a backslash (\), then *backslash substitution* is performed. The following table lists characters that receive special handling during backslash substitution. In all other cases, the character following the backslash is just included in the group. This allows characters that might otherwise have special meaning—such as braces, quotes, dollar signs, and brackets—to be safely included in a word.

Character	Substitution
\a	Alert ("bell"), the character whose ASCII code is 7.
\b	Backspace, the character whose ASCII code is 8.
\f	Formfeed, the character whose ASCII code is 12.
\n	Newline, the character whose ASCII code is 10.
\r	Carriage return, the character whose ASCII code is 14.
\t	Tab, the character whose ASCII code is 9.
\v	Vertical tab, the character whose ASCII code is 11.

Character	Substitution
\\	Backslash.
ooo	The Unicode character whose upper bits are 0 and whose lower 8 bits are represented by the octal digits *ooo*, which may be one, two, or three digits long.
\x*hh*	The Unicode character whose upper 8 bits are 0 and whose lower 8 bits are represented by the hexadecimal digits *hh*, which may include any number of digits, but only the last two are used.
\u*hhhh*	The Unicode character whose bits are represented by the hexadecimal digits *hhhh*, which may be one to four digits long; unspecified leading digits are treated as 0's.

One additional special interpretation of backslash exists. If a backslash is the last character on a line, it is treated as a continuation character. The backslash, the following newline, and all the whitespace characters at the start of the next line are replaced by a single space.

NOTE: This special substitution is done before parsing, and takes place even within words quoted with braces.

Comments

Tcl comments cause more confusion than is really warranted. They are really as simple as the rest of the language. You just have to remember one rule: If a number sign (#) appears where the parser expects a new command, it is treated as a comment delimiter, and the rest of the line is ignored. The number sign has no special significance anywhere else in a script. For example, the following script

```
puts #
```

outputs a number sign, whereas

```
puts
#
```

is an invalid **puts** (which lacks anything to output), and an empty comment on the next line.

Also note that because # has special meaning only at the beginning of a command, putting special characters, especially braces, in comments can lead to unexpected behavior. For example, **if** is a predefined command, <u>not</u> a feature of the Tcl language. In its simplest form, **if** takes two arguments: an expression, and a script to be evaluated if the expression evaluates to true. Here is an example of such a script:

```
if {$x<0} {puts "x is negative"}
```

It is common for the script to have multiple lines:

```
if {$x<0} {
    puts "x is negative"
    puts "Isn't that nice?"
}
```

It's important to realize that the top-level parser only sees three groups in the preceding script: **if**, the condition (**{$x<0}**), and the script (everything between the second open brace on the first line and the close brace on the last line). The following is valid:

```
if {$x<0} {
    # This is a comment
    puts "x is negative"
}
```

Here the top-level parser sees three properly formed groups, and when **if** evaluates the third group as a script, the # is where a command would start. However, the following is invalid:

```
if {$x<0} {
    # This looks like a comment. } but it isn't.
    puts "x is negative"
}
```

Here, when the top-level parser encounters the #, it is not expecting a new command (it's in the middle of processing **if**), and when it encounters the close brace in the second line, it matches it with the open brace on the first line. The **if** command would be passed the following groups:

```
$x<0
\n    # This looks like a comment.
but
it
isn't.
```

Because processing of a backslash as a continuation character is done before parsing, comments may be continued on multiple lines:

```
# A comment on two lines \
Line two of the comment
puts "This is now a command."
```

The Conventions

With so few rules, Tcl would be chaos without conventions. The *Tcl Style Guide* (available at **www.scriptics.com/doc/styleGuide.pdf**) has some good general rules for formatting programs. Some of its recommendations contribute mostly to readability of programs, whereas others help you to avoid making mistakes. But, there is a lot that is not covered by the *Tcl Style Guide*. The following sections summarize some important points from the *Guide* and some things not covered there.

Names
Command and variable names may contain any character. However, dealing with command or variable names like "my command" or "{!}" would require more quoting than it's worth. Generally, only letters, digits, and underscores are used in names.

NOTE: Tcl is case-sensitive, so **myCommand** and **MyCommand** are two different names. (The *Tcl Style Guide* prescribes a convention of using initial capital letters for private or internal routines, such as **MyCommand**, and lowercase initial letters for public routines, such as **myCommand**.)

Subcommands
Some Tcl commands group together related functionality. For example, **file** can be used to build filenames, break down filenames, test whether a file exists, and determine what type a file is. It decides which to do based on its first argument, which is called a *subcommand*. Here is an example:

```
file dirname $filename
file exists $filename
file size $filename
```

This script shows the **dirname**, **exists**, and **size** subcommands of the **file** command. However, other related functions are implemented in separate commands, such as the list-handling commands **lindex**, **lrange**, and **lsearch**. Generally, a single command with subcommands seems to be preferred.

Options

Some Tcl commands take *switches* or *options* that control their actions. For example, the **puts** command usually adds a newline after the data it is to output, but an option is available to suppress the newline:

```
puts -nonewline "Type something:"
```

Options always start with a dash or hyphen, as shown in the preceding line. Options may take values. For example, **button** allows a command to be associated with the button it creates. The option name is **-command**, and the value that follows is a script to be evaluated when the button is clicked:

```
button .b -text "Exit" -command exit
```

Generally, options may be specified in any order. Often, options must be grouped together at the start or end of a command. Many commands that require options before any nonoption arguments allow nonoption arguments to start with a dash, by recognizing a double dash (--) as a final option to divide options from nonoption arguments. For example, the following example safely copies a file that might have dash at the start of its name:

```
file copy -- $fromFile $toFile
```

Command Grouping

It is generally considered bad style to put multiple commands on a single line, like this:

```
analyze;report
```

Braces are used around scripts. For example, the third argument to an **if** command is a script that may contain multiple commands:

```
if {$x<0} {
    puts "x is negative"
}
```

The braces and newlines are used even when, as in this case, they are not needed to group multiple commands.

NOTE: The opening brace for the script must be on the first line.

The End

When accessing counted things, such as the items in a list or characters in a string, the last one is often referred to with the special index **end**. For example, the following

```
puts "The last character in \"$s\" is\
      [string index $s [string length $s]]"
```

can be shortened to

```
puts "The last character in \"$s\" is\
      [string index $s end]"
```

Tk Basics

Tk is a simple but powerful, somewhat object-oriented Tcl
extension. It includes a number of *widgets*, including the basic
**button, checkbutton, entry, frame, label, listbox, menu,
menubutton, message, radiobutton, scale, scrollbar,** and **toplevel**
widgets, and the complex **canvas** and **text** widgets. These widgets
can be combined to create *megawidgets*. Each widget has a
corresponding command to create new widgets of that *class*. Those
commands and the capabilities of the widgets are discussed in
detail in Part 2.

Part of the object-oriented nature of Tk is demonstrated by the
fact that a new widget inherits many default values from its class.
For example, you usually don't need to specify the colors for a
widget—the widget is created with colors that are consistent with
the rest of the system or application. The values that control how
a widget appears are detailed in Appendix A.

X Windows, and Beyond

The term *widget* derives from Tk's origin on UNIX and X Windows.
Other systems call these basic user-interface elements *controls* or
gadgets. Tk shows its UNIX heritage in other ways, as well.
Microsoft Windows users are accustomed to referring to the left-
and right-mouse buttons, and a Macintosh mouse has only one
button. Users of UNIX and X Windows, however, generally have
three mouse buttons, and no preconception exists about which
mouse button is on the left and what it should do.

X Windows and Tk number mouse buttons and allow the user to
determine which button is 1, 2, and 3. Usually, MB1 (mouse button
1) is the closest to the keyboard (the right-mouse button for
left-handed users, the left-mouse button for right-handers), MB2 is

the middle mouse button, and MB3 is the farthest button from the keyboard.

The Widget Hierarchy

The interface of a Tk application consists of widgets of various kinds arranged to suit the needs of the application. The widgets are arranged in a tree, or hierarchy, that usually (but not always) indicates how the widgets are visually contained within one another.

The highest-level widget is a *toplevel*; this is what you usually think of as a *window* with a border, title bar, and various decorations. The default toplevel widget in each application is named "." ("dot"). More can be created with **toplevel**. As widgets are created, they are specified by the path through the widget hierarchy from . to the new widget, with each level of the hierarchy separated by a dot. This example creates a new frame within the default toplevel:

```
frame .f
```

And the following creates a button within that frame:

```
button .f.b
```

In this case, the frame **.f** is said to be the *parent* of the button, and the button **.f.b** is said to be a *child* of the frame.

The dialog box shown here

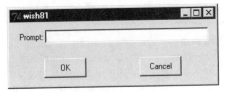

is created with the following code:

```
frame .f1
frame .f2
pack .f1 .f2 -side top -padx 3m -expand 1 -fill x

label .f1.l -text "Prompt:"
entry .f1.e -textvariable "value" -width 40
pack .f1.l -side left -pady 3m
```

```
pack .f1.e -side left -pady 3m -expand 1 -fill x

button .f2.b1 -text OK      -width 8
button .f2.b2 -text Cancel -width 8
pack .f2.b1 .f2.b2 -side left -expand 1 -pady 3m
```

The Tk widget heirarchy for this dialog can be sketched out as
follows:

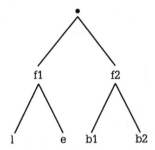

Usually, widgets are placed only within toplevel or frame widgets,
but it is possible to make an interactive widget—like a button—a
child of an entry or some other widget not usually used as a
container for other widgets. Also, the canvas and text widgets
have a very powerful mechanism for embedding any other type of
widget within their borders.

Widget Commands
When a widget is created, a command of the same name is also
created. This *widget command* can be used to manipulate the
widget by changing its options. For example, the following creates
a button with all default options and then uses the button's widget
command to reconfigure the label on the button:

```
button .f.b
.f.b configure —text "A Label"
```

Tk Coordinates

Tk uses a left-handed coordinate system as shown in Figure 1-1.
The origin is in the upper-left corner of the screen, the X axis
increasing to the right, and the Y axis increasing down the screen.

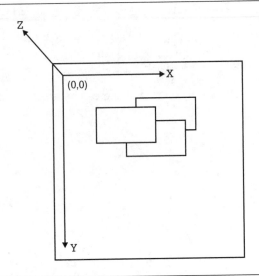

Figure 1-1. Tk coordinate system

A virtual Z axis comes out of the screen toward the user. The Z axis does not have coordinates associated with it; it is used for logically ordering widgets to determine which is drawn first. Widgets higher in the Z order obscure widgets lower in the Z order. The last-drawn widget is said to be "in front of" or "on top of" those drawn before it.

Screen Coordinates
The size and placement of widgets onscreen are specified in *screen coordinates*. A screen coordinate is a floating-point number followed by an optional one-character unit specifier from the following table:

Letter	Units
none	Pixels
c	Centimeters
i	Inches
m	Millimeters
p	Points (1 point = 1/72")

Window Coordinates
Each widget has its own coordinate system, with (0,0) in the upper-left corner. The *window coordinates* used within widgets

differ from screen coordinates only in the placement of the origin. All the screen coordinate unit specifiers listed in the preceding table still apply.

View Coordinates

Many Tk widgets support scrolling, so that only part of their contents is visible at any given time. Scrollbars can be associated with these widgets, so that manipulating the scrollbar updates the widget, and updating the widget causes the scrollbar to show its new state. Scrollable widgets all communicate with scrollbars with the same "protocol" implemented with the scrollbar's **set** command and the widget's **xview** and **yview** commands. These commands all operate on *view coordinates*.

The current view is described by a *view coordinate list,* a list of two real numbers between 0 and 1.0 indicating the range of the widget's content that is visible. For example, {.1 .7} indicates that the portion of the widget's content that is visible in the current view is from 10 percent to 70 percent of the content. In other words, the first 10 percent and last 30 percent of the content is out of view.

When setting the view, remember that only one view coordinate is needed; the second is determined by the size of the widget.

Part 2
Tcl/Tk Commands

Syntax

Many Tcl commands have options or parameters which may or may not be specified. For example, **puts** has an option to suppress output of a newline character at the end of the string, and an optional argument to specify the channel to write to. Optional arguments are denoted with question marks like this:

puts *?*-**nonewline***? ?channel? string*

In this case, both the -**nonewline** option and the *channel* parameter may be omitted. Thus the following are all valid forms of **puts**:

```
puts foo
puts -nonewline stdout "Type something:"
puts $fid $x
```

Many commands also allow an argument or pattern of arguments to be repeated an arbitrary number of times. For example, when creating a button widget, you can specify any number of options and option values. This is noted with an ellipsis, as shown here:

button *pathName ?option value ... ?*

after

The **after** command delays script execution, schedules a script for execution at a later time, and manages scheduled scripts. (See also **bgerror**; **concat**; **update**; **vwait**.) It takes the following forms:

> **after** *ms*
>
> **after** *ms arg arg arg ...*
>
> **after idle** *arg arg arg ...*
>
> **after cancel** *id*
>
> **after cancel** *arg arg arg ...*
>
> **after info** *?id?*

The arguments are as follows:

arg
Part of script to handle the **after** event. When multiple *args* are specified, they are combined as if passed to **concat**.

id
Event identifier returned from a previous call to **after**.

ms
Integer number of milliseconds to delay.

after *ms*

Delays script execution for approximately the specified number of milliseconds. No events will be processed during the delay.

after *ms arg arg arg ...*

Sets a timer to go off after at least *ms* milliseconds, and sets the script resulting from concatenating *args* as the event handler for that timer.

RETURNS   An event identifier that may be used to cancel or get information about the event.

after idle *arg arg arg ...*

Creates a low-priority event to be serviced when the event loop is otherwise idle, and sets the script resulting from concatenating *args* as the event handler for that timer.

RETURNS   An event identifier that may be used to cancel or get information about the event.

after cancel *id*

Cancels an event scheduled with **after idle** or **after ms**.

after cancel *arg arg arg ...*

Cancels an event whose event handler matches the script resulting from concatenating *args*.

after info

Retrieves a list of existing after events.

RETURNS   A list of IDs of events scheduled with **after**.

after info *id*

Determines the type and handler for after event *id*.

RETURNS   A two-element list consisting of the event handler script, and the keyword **timer** or **idle** indicating the type of the event.

ERROR   Raises an error if the specified event does not exist.

Example

```
# Make asynchronous request for data. Response is
# received by setting global variable myVar
requestData myVar
# Time-out after 5 seconds
after 5000 [list set myVar "TIMEOUT"]
# Wait for response or timeout
vwait myVar
# Check for timeout
if {[string match "TIMEOUT" $myVar]} {
    error "Timeout waiting for response"
} else {
    after cancel $id
}
```

Programmer's Tip: *The script must enter an event loop for the scheduled scripts to be executed. In Tcl-based scripts, you must use* **vwait** *or* **update** *to allow event processing. In Tk-based scripts, there is always an event loop, but it may be blocked by* **after ms**.

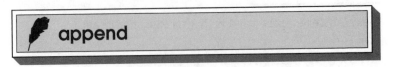

The **append** command appends one or more values to a variable. (See also **binary**; **lappend**; **string**.) It takes the following form:

> **append** *varName ?value value value ... ?*

The arguments are as follows:

value
Value to append to the variable. *value* may be a string (e.g., "foo"), a number (e.g., 2.4), a list (e.g., "{a b c}"), or the binary data, such as that returned by **binary format**.

varName
Name of a variable to append to. This variable is created if it doesn't exist.

Most Tcl commands accept a value rather than the name of a variable, and manipulate a copy of the data value. The **append** command is different in that it accepts the name of a variable and modifies the value of that variable.

RETURNS   The new value of the variable named by *varName*.

Example

```
# Create a string from three words
set w baz
append s "foo" bar $w
# Add a fourth word to the end
append s "blat"
# Append binary data, y ends up with the value
# "ffff"
set x [binary format h2 ff]
append x $x
binary scan h4 $x y
```

Programmer's Tip: *The values are combined without spaces between them. The preceding string example produces "foobarbazblat", not "foo bar baz blat".*

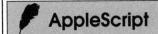

AppleScript

The **AppleScript** command allows Tcl to communicate with the AppleScript OSA component to run AppleScripts. (See also **exec**.) It takes the following forms:

AppleScript compile *?options? script ?script ... ?*

AppleScript decompile *scriptName*

AppleScript delete *scriptName*

AppleScript execute *?options? script ?script ... ?*

AppleScript info *what ?pattern?*

AppleScript load *?-rsrcname name? ?-rscrid id? fileName*

AppleScript run *?-context contextName? scriptName*

AppleScript store *?-rsrcname name? ?-rscrid id? scriptName fileName*

The arguments are as follows:

contextName
A context created by **AppleScript compile**.

filename
File whose resource should be accessed.

id
Resource ID for the script. If **-rsrcid** is not specified, *id* defaults to 128.

name
Resource name for the script. If **-rsrcname** is not specified, *name* defaults to **scpt**.

options
Compilation options. (See the following description of the
AppleScript compile command for details.)

pattern
A **glob**-style pattern used to match context or script names.

script
A string containing an AppleScript script.

scriptName
The name returned by **AppleScript compile**.

what
What information to return: **contexts** or **scripts**.

AppleScript compile
?options? script ?script ... ?

Combines all *script* arguments as if passed to **concat**, and then
passes the result to the AppleScript compiler with *options*.

RETURNS If **-context** is specified, the name of the new context. If
-context is not specified, the name of the compiled script.

The Applescript compile options are listed in Table 2-1.

ERROR Raises an error if there is a problem compiling the script.

AppleScript decompile *scriptName*

Decompiles *scriptName* into its AppleScript source string.

RETURNS A string containing the source for *scriptName*.

ERROR Raises an error if *scriptName* does not exist.

AppleScript delete *scriptName*

Deletes *scriptName* and frees all of its resources.

Option	Purpose
-augment *augment*	Specifies that *script* should augment the current contents of *contextName*. If *augment* is false, the contents of the context are replaced. If **-augment** is not specified, *augment* defaults to true.This option has no effect if *context* is false.
-context *context*	Specifies that *script* should be compiled into a context rather than a script. (AppleScript contexts are somewhat like Tcl namespaces.) The new context is executed immediately. If **-context** is not specified, *context* defaults to false.
-name *name*	Specifies the name for the script or context. If *context* is false and script *name* exists, it is replaced. If *context* is true and context *name* exists, it is replaced, unless *augment* is true.
-parent *contextName*	Specifies the parent context for *name*. *contextName* must be the name of an existing context. This option has no effect if *context* is false.

Table 2-1.   AppleScript compile options

AppleScript execute
?options? script ?script ... ?

Combines all *script* arguments as if passed to **concat**, and then passes the result to the AppleScript compiler with *options*, runs the script, and deletes it. This is like invoking **compile**, and then **run**, and then **delete**. *options* are the same as for **compile**. (See Table 2-1 for the AppleScript compile options.)

RETURNS   The result of running the script.

AppleScript info *what ?pattern?*

Retrieves a list of scripts or contexts. If *pattern* is not specified, it defaults to "*" to list all scripts or contexts.

RETURNS A list of scripts or contexts matching *pattern*.

AppleScript load
?-rsrcname name? ?-rscrid id? fileName

Loads the script data in the *name* or *id* resource of *fileName*.

RETURNS A token that may be used as a *scriptName* to **run**, **delete**, etc.

AppleScript run
?-context contextName? scriptName

Runs *scriptName* in *contextName*. *scriptName* and *contextName* must have been previously compiled with **compile**.

RETURNS The return value of *scriptName* as a string.

ERROR Raises an error if *scriptName* causes an error.

AppleScript store *?-rsrcname name?*
?-rscrid id? scriptName fileName

Stores *scriptName* in the *name* or *id* resource of *fileName*.

Example

```
# Prompt the user for a file name and have
# SimpleText open the file
set fileName [tk_getOpenFile]
if {[string length $fileName] != 0} {
    AppleScript execute "
        tell application \"SimpleText\"
            open \"$fileName\"
        end tell"
}
```

Compatibility

AppleScript is available only on Macintosh systems.

argv0

The **argv0** global variable is a string that contains the name of the script passed to the interpreter (if specified), or the name of the interpreter, if no script was specified. (See also **info nameofexecutable**; **info script**.)

Programmer's Tip: *Test code can be put in library scripts and triggered only when the script is run from a command line by testing* **argv0** *against the value returned by* **info script**:

```
# The test code executes only if the script is
# invoked with a command line like `tclsh
# script.tcl` but NOT when the script is
# sourced by another script for use in an
# application
if { [string compare [info script] $argv0] \
        == 0} {
    # Test code here
}
```

argc

The **argc** global variable is a number that contains the number of elements in the **argv** list. (See also **argv**; **argv0**.)

argv

The **argv** global variable is a list that contains command-line arguments to a script. (See also **argv0**; **source**.)

Example

```
# Process and remove an option before proceeding
set index [lsearch $argv "-myoption"]
if { $index != -1 } {
    doMyThing
    set argv [lreplace $argv $index $index]
}
```

Programmer's Tip: *The **argv** and **argc** variables are not read-only. It is sometimes helpful to set them before sourcing another script:*

```
# Set command line arguments for another script
set argv [list Fred Wilma Barney Betty]
# argc is not automatically updated, so set it
set argc [llength $argv]
set argv0 myscript.tcl
# Call that script
source $argv0
```

array

Programmer's Tip: *Tcl arrays are really "associative arrays" or "hash tables." The order of elements is not preserved. When the order of data items is important, use a list.*

The **array** command creates, accesses, and manipulates array variables. (See also **set**; **list**; **parray**; **glob**.) It takes the following forms:

> **array exists** *arrayName*
> **array names** *arrayName ?pattern?*
> **array size** *arrayName*
>
> **array get** *arrayName ?pattern?*
> **array set** *arrayName list*
>
> **array startsearch** *arrayName*
> **array nextelement** *arrayName searchID*

array anymore *arrayName searchID*
array donesearch *arrayName searchID*

The arguments are as follows:

arrayName
Name of array to create or access.

list
A list used to initialize elements of the array. The list has an even number of elements. The first, third, fifth, etc. elements of the list are array indices. The second, fourth, sixth, etc. elements of the list are corresponding values for those indices.

pattern
A **glob**-style pattern used to match array indices (for example, "a*").

searchID
Search identifier returned by **array startsearch**.

Programmer's Tip: *Processing all elements of an array with the search commands (**startsearch**, etc.) is slower, but uses less memory than processing with **array names**.*

array exists *arrayName*

Tests to see whether an array by the specified name exists.

RETURNS   1 if an array by that name exists; 0 otherwise.

array names *arrayName ?pattern?*

Retrieves a list of indices of the array that match *pattern*. If *pattern* is not specified, all indices are returned.

RETURNS   An unordered, possibly empty, list of all indices for the array.

array size *arrayName*

Determines the size of an array.

RETURNS   The number of elements in the array, or 0 if the name does not refer to an array variable.

array get *arrayName ?pattern?*

Retrieves a list of indices and values from the array. If *pattern* is
specified, retrieves values only for elements whose indices match
the **glob**-style pattern. If *pattern* is not specified, retrieves values
of all elements in the array. This list may be used with the **array
set** command.

RETURNS   A list like that passed to **array set**. (See the preceding
description of arguments for details.). If the array is empty or
pattern is supplied but does not match any elements, the list may
be empty (length 0).

array set *arrayName list*

Initializes or changes the value of one or more array elements.
Other elements of the array retain their values.

ERRORS   Raises an error if the name refers to an existing,
nonarray variable or if the list has an odd number of elements.

array startsearch *arrayName*

Initializes a search of all elements of an array.

NOTE: This isn't a "search" based on any criteria but rather a
means to process all the array elements. The elements will be
returned by **array nextelement** *in an unspecified order.*

RETURNS   A search identifier to be used with **array nextelement,
array donesearch**, and **array anymore**.

array nextelement *arrayName searchID*

Retrieves the next element for an array search.

RETURNS   The index of the next element in the search, or an
empty string if all elements have been processed.

array anymore *arrayName searchID*

Determines whether more elements are in the search.

RETURNS   0 if no more elements exist for an array search; 1 otherwise.

array donesearch *arrayName searchID*

Terminates a search started with **array startsearch** and cleans up state and resources associated with the *searchID*.

ERROR   Raises an error if *searchID* is invalid or not for the named array.

Example

```
# Create an array
array set a {first Bugs last Bunny}
# Add an element
array set a {type rabbit}
# Add another
set a(food) hamburgers
# Change the value of one element
array set a {food carrots}
# Process all elements in the array
foreach e [array names a] {
    puts "$e:\t$a($e)"
}
```

auto_execok

The **auto_execok** command searches for an executable program on your path (stored in **env(PATH)**), similar to the **which** command in UNIX. (See also **exec**; **auto_reset**.) It takes the following form:

auto_execok *program*

The arguments are as follows:

program
Executable program to search for.

RETURNS   The fully qualified name of the first program on the path that matches the specified name, or an empty string if the program can't be found.

Example

```
# Search for foo on the path, and run it
# if it is found
set fullName [auto_execok foo]
if {[string length $fullName]} {
    eval exec $fullName
}
```

Compatibility

On Microsoft Windows systems, **auto_execok** searches in platform-specific directories, including the directory pointed to by the **windir** environment variable, before searching directories in the **PATH** environment variable.

Programmer's Tip: *When a program is found, its path is cached for future reference, so that only the first **auto_execok** incurs the delay of accessing the disk. The cache can be cleared with the **auto_reset** command.*

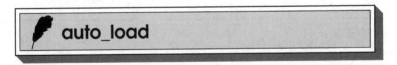

auto_load

The **auto_load** command attempts to find and load the definition of a command. (See also **auto_mkindex**; **auto_reset**; **package**; **unknown**.) It takes the following forms:

> **auto_load** *commandName*

The arguments are as follows:

commandName
The name of the command to search for and load.

Programmer's Tip: *Use of **auto_load** in scripts is rare. The functionality of **auto_load** is included in the default implementation of **unknown** that automatically loads unknown commands the first time that they are referenced.*

The **auto_load** command searches each directory on the *auto-load path* for a file named tclIndex, which should contain Tcl code that describes one or more commands and specifies a script to evaluate to load or define each of the commands. (tclIndex files are usually created with the **auto_mkindex** command.)

2

The *auto-load path* is the contents of the **auto_path** global variable, if it exists. If no **auto_path** exists, the value of **env(TCLLIBPATH)** is used, if it exists. If neither **auto_path** nor the **TCLLIBPATH** environment variable exist, the Tcl library directory is used.

RETURNS   1 if *commandName* is successfully loaded; 0 if no tclIndex entry was found or if the definition did not load the command.

ERROR   Errors from the command definition script are passed through.

Example

```
# Prepend personal library directory to auto_path
set auto_path [linsert $auto_path 0 ~/tcllib]
# Try to find myCmd
auto_load myCmd
```

Programmer's Tip: *The information in the tclIndex files is read only once and cached. The **auto_reset** command may be used to remove the cached information so that the next use of **auto_load** reads the tclIndex files again.*
    *Auto-loading is fully supported in current versions of Tcl/Tk, but the newer **package** command provides more flexible support for loading commands.*

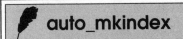

auto_mkindex

The **auto_mkindex** command prepares tclIndex files for **auto_load**. (See also **auto_load**; **glob**; **package**; **pkg_mkIndex**; **unknown**.) It takes the following form:

> **auto_mkindex** *dir ?pattern pattern ...?*

The arguments are as follows:

dir
Directory to search for files.

pattern
Pattern to match filenames to. Filenames are tested against the pattern using the same rules as **glob**. If no pattern is specified, *.tcl is the default.

The **auto_mkindex** command searches *dir* for files matching any of the specified *patterns* and generates an index of all the commands found in those files.

Example

```
# Index all *.tcl files in the current directory
auto_mkIndex .
```

Programmer's Tip: *Prior to version 8.1,* **auto_mkindex** *did not source the scripts to see what commands were defined. Rather, it read through the file, looking for the word* **proc** *at the start of a line, and assumed that the next word was the name of a command. Files that do not follow this strict format, such as those that use* **OptProc** *to define commands with variable arguments, will not index properly with earlier versions of Tcl. To work around this, you can include an empty* **proc** *definition before each* **proc** *that does not fit* **auto_mkindex**'s *pattern. Here is an example:*

```
# Make auto_mkindex happy
proc someProc { } { }
# Really create the proc
::tcl::OptProc someProc {
```

```
    ...proc arguments...
} {
    ...proc body...
}
```

*The original version of **auto_mkindex** is available in Tcl 8.1 as*
***auto_mkindex_old**.*

*Auto-loading is fully supported in current versions of Tcl/Tk, but
the newer **package** and **pkg_mkIndex** commands provide more
flexible support for loading commands.*

2

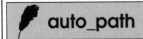

auto_path

The **auto_path** global variable contains a list of directories that will
be searched by **auto_load** to load command definitions. (See also
auto_load; **auto_mkIndex**.)

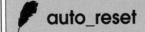

auto_reset

The **auto_reset** command removes information cached by
auto_execok and **auto_load**. The information will be re-read the
next time one of those commands is invoked. (See also **auto_load**;
auto_mkIndex; **auto_execok**.) It takes the following form:

   auto_reset

The arguments are as follows:

None.

beep

The **beep** command plays Macintosh sound resources. (See also
bell.) It takes the following form:

> **beep** *?-volume* *volume? snd*

The arguments are as follows:

snd
The name of a sound resource.

volume
A 32-bit integer representing the volume at which to play *snd*. The high word (most significant 16 bits) of *volume* controls the left channel, and the low word (least significant 16 bits) controls the right channel. Each word may have a value between 0 (no sound) and 256 (full volume). For example, 0x01000100 is full volume on both channels, and 0x00800000 is half volume on the left channel and no sound on the right.

beep -list

Lists all **snd** resources.

RETURNS   An unordered list of **snd** resources.

beep ?-volume *volume? snd*

Plays *snd* at a volume determined by *volume*.

Example

```
# A proc to play a sound at a specified volume
proc playSound { snd {volume 100}} {
    # Scale the total volume from 0-100 to 0-256
    set volume [expr {(256 * $volume) / 100}]
    set lvolume $volume
    set rvolume $volume
    # Compose 32-bit volume setting
    set volume [expr {(0xffff * $lvolume) + \
                                        $rvolume}]

    # Use it
    beep -volume $volume $snd
}
# Test it
foreach snd [beep -list] {
    playSound $snd 50
}
```

Compatibility

beep is available only on Macintosh systems.

Programmer's Tip: *Kåre Sjölander has created a very capable sound-playing extension, called Snack, for use with other platforms. Look for it at* ***www.speech.kth.se/snack.***

🪔 bell

The **bell** command rings a display's bell. It takes the following form:

    bell *?-***displayof** *window?*

The options are as follows:

-displayof *window*
Specifies a window whose display's bell should be rung. If not specified, the display of the application's main window (.) is used.

Description

Rings the bell on the display for the specified window, and resets the screen saver for that display. Some screen savers ignore the reset, whereas others restore the screen's normal visibility.

NOTE: On UNIX systems, **bell** uses the current bell-related settings for the display. Those settings may be modified with programs such as **xset**. On Microsoft Windows systems, **bell** uses the "Default sound," as configured with the Sounds application from the Control Panel.

🪶 binary

The **binary** command formats and parses binary strings. (See also **fconfigure -translation**; **format**; **scan**; **tcl_platform**.) It takes the following forms:

> **binary format** *formatString ?arg arg ... ?*

> **binary scan** *arg formatString ?varName varName ... ?*

The arguments are as follows:

arg
Value to be formatted into a binary string according to *formatString*.

formatString
Specifies how the data is to be converted. The format is one or more field specifiers separated by zero or more spaces. Each field specifier is a type character that identifies the data type, followed by an optional *count,* which may be an integer or an asterisk (*). If *count* is an asterisk, the rest of *arg* is converted. If no *count* is specified, it defaults to 1.

varName
Name of the variable to take value according to *formatString*.

binary format *formatString ?arg arg ... ?*

Encodes one or more *args* into binary data according to *formatString*. For example, the format string "h2" would interpret the first two characters in the next *arg* as hexadecimal digits, and format them into 1 byte of the binary data.

RETURNS   The formatted binary data.

ERROR   Raises an error if the number of field specifiers in *formatString* does not match the number of *args*.

Table 2-2 lists the format type characters and their effects.

Type Character	Purpose
a	Interprets *arg* as printable characters and copies the first *count* characters to the formatted binary data, padding on the right with null bytes if *arg* is less than *count* characters long.
A	Same as **a**, but pads on the right with blanks instead of nulls.
b	Interprets *arg* as a string of binary digits (1s and 0s), with the lowest-order bit first. Each binary digit in *arg* is converted to a bit in the formatted binary data. If *arg* has fewer than *count* characters, 0s are used for the remaining bits. If *arg* has more than *count* characters, the extra characters will be ignored. If the formatted output does not end at a byte boundary, 0 bits will be used to fill up to the byte boundary.
B	Same as **b**, but *arg* is interpreted as having the highest-order bit first.
h	Interprets *arg* as a string of hexadecimal digits (0-9, a-f, and A-F), with the lowest-order digit first. Each hexadecimal digit is converted to a nibble in the formatted binary data. If *arg* has fewer than *count* characters, 0s are used for the remaining digits. If *arg* has more than *count* characters, the extra characters are ignored. If the formatted output does not end on a byte boundary, 0 bits will be used to fill up to the byte boundary.
H	Same as **h**, but *arg* is interpreted as having the highest-order digit first.
c	Interprets *arg* as a list of integers. The low-order 8 bits of each integer are stored as a byte in the formatted binary output. If *arg* has fewer than *count* values, an error is raised. If *arg* has more than *count* values, the extra values are ignored.

Table 2-2.   Binary Format Type Characters

Type Character	Purpose
s	Same as **c**, but the low-order 16 bits of each element of *arg* are stored in the formatted binary output in little-endian byte order.
S	Same as **s**, but output is in big-endian byte order.
i	Same as **c**, but the low-order 32 bits of each element of *arg* are stored in the formatted binary output in little-endian byte order.
I	Same as **i**, but output is in big-endian byte order.
f	Interprets *arg* as a list of numbers. Each number is stored as a single-precision floating-point number in native format in the formatted binary output.[1] If *arg* has fewer than *count* values, an error is raised. If *arg* has more than *count* values, the extra values are ignored.
d	Same as **f**, but each element from *arg* is stored as a double-precision floating-point number.[1]
x	Stores *count* null bytes in the formatted binary output.
X	Backs up *count* bytes in the formatted binary output. If *count* is * or larger than the current length of the output, moves to the beginning of the output.
@@	Moves to byte *count* in the formatted binary output.

[1]The **f** and **d** formats are not portable across platforms and should not be used for moving floating-point data across systems or networks.

Table 2-2.   Binary Format Type Characters *(continued)*

binary scan *arg formatString ?varName varName ... ?*

Decodes a binary value into one or more variables according to *formatString*. Decoding stops when all variables have been assigned a value or *arg* has been exhausted.

RETURNS   The number of fields scanned.

Table 2-3 lists the scan type characters and their effects.

Type Character	Purpose
a	Moves *count* characters from *arg* to the next variable.
A	Same as **a**, but trailing blanks and null bytes are trimmed from the value stored in the variable.
b	Moves the next *count* bits from *arg* to the next variable as binary digits (1s and 0s). The lowest-order bit in *arg* will be first in the output variable. Extra bits in the last byte of *arg* are ignored.
B	Same as **b**, but the highest-order bit in *arg* will be first in the output variable.
h	Moves the next *count* nibbles from *arg* to the next variable as hexadecimal digits (0-9 and a-f). The lowest-order nibble will be first in the output variable.
H	Same as **h**, but the highest-order nibble will be first in the output variable.
c	Interprets the next *count* bytes in *arg* as 8-bit integers and sets the next variable to a list of those integer values.
s	Same as **c**, but interprets each pair of bytes in *arg* as a 16-bit integer in little-endian order.
S	Same as **s**, but interprets each pair of bytes in *arg* as a 16-bit integer in big-endian order.
i	Same as **c**, but interprets each 4 bytes in *arg* as a 32-bit integer in little-endian order.
I	Same as **i**, but interprets each 4 bytes in *arg* as a 32-bit integer in big-endian order.
f	Interprets bytes in *arg* as single-precision floating-point numbers and converts enough bytes to form *count* floating-point numbers. Sets the next variable as a list of those numbers.[1]
d	Same as **f**, but interprets bytes in *arg* as *count* double-precision floating-point numbers.[1]
x	Skips over the next *count* bytes in *string*.
X	Backs up *count* bytes in *string*.
@@	Moves to byte *count* in *string*.

[1]The **f** and **d** formats are not portable across platforms and should not be used for moving floating-point data across systems or networks.

Table 2-3.   Binary Scan Type Characters

Example

```
# Pack a binary data string that corresponds to
# the C structure:
#     struct {
#         uchar i;
#         float x;
#         float y;
#         int len;   /* The length of tag */
#         char tag;
#     }
# with consideration for the fact that x has to be
# aligned on a 4-byte boundary.
proc packBuf { i x y tag } {
    set packed [binary format "c x3 f f i a*" \
        $i $x $y [string length $tag] $tag]
    return $packed
}


# The opposite of packBuf
proc unpackBuf { buf iName xName yName tagName } {
    upvar $iName i;
    upvar $xName x;
    upvar $yName y;
    upvar $tagName tag;
    if {[binary scan $buf "c1 x3 f f i a*" \
                          i x y len tag] != 5} {
        error "Wrong number of fields scanned."
    }
    if {[string length $tag] != $len} {
        error "Tag length incorrect."
    }
}


# Test it.
unpackBuf [packBuf 1 3.14159 2.82 \
        "This is a test of the binary command"] \
        i x y tag

foreach v {i x y tag} {
    puts "$v:[set $v]"
}
```

Programmer's Tip: The *byteOrder* element of the **tcl_platform**
*global array can be used to determine the native byte order for
the machine that the script is running on, and to choose between **h**
and **H**, etc. to control the order of bytes in the binary data. Here is
an example:*

```
if {[string compare \
            $tcl_platform(byteOrder) \
            littleEndian] == 0} {
    set type i
} else {
    set type I
}
# x is a string of digits, an integer to Tcl
set x 1234
# y is a 4-byte binary integer which may be
# used in binary network protocols, etc.
set y [binary format $type $x]
# z is a string again, the same as x
binary scan $y $type z
```

bind

The **bind** command associates Tcl scripts with widget events. (See
also **bgerror**; **bindtags**; **event**.) It takes the following forms:

   bind *tag*

   bind *tag sequence*

   bind *tag sequence script*

The arguments are as follows:

script
Tcl script to execute when *sequence* is matched.

sequence
The sequence of events to match. The events may be separated by
white space, which is ignored.

tag

Binding tag to process. If *tag* begins with a dot (such as .button1), it must be a valid path for an existing widget. Otherwise, *tag* may be a widget class (such as Button), the keyword **all**, or an arbitrary string (a user-defined binding tag).

Events

There are three types of event specifications:

- Simple characters
- Physical events
- Virtual events

Simple character event specifications are any sequence of printable characters, such as "x" or "!". The simple character event specification "x" is translated to the physical event specification "<KeyPress-x>".

NOTE: " " (space) and "<" cannot be specified as simple character events.

Each physical event specification consist of zero or more modifiers (these are listed in Table 2-4), an event type (these are listed in Table 2-5), and/or an event detail. The modifiers, type, and detail are all surrounded by angle brackets ("<" and ">") and may be separated by white space or dashes. Here is an example:

```
<Control-Double-ButtonPress-1>
<Alt Shift comma>
```

Virtual event specifications refer to user-defined, virtual events created with **event add** or generated with **event generate**. Each virtual event specification must start with two left angle brackets and end with two right angle brackets, e.g., "<<Paste>>".

The event types listed in Table 2-5 show Tk's UNIX heritage. Many of the event types are not meaningful on other platforms.

bind *tag*

Lists the sequences with bindings for *tag*.

RETURNS   A list of all sequences with bindings for *tag*.

ERROR   Raises an error if *tag* is a widget path and the specified widget does not exist.

Example
```
# Get a list of events bound for the Button class.
bind Button
```

This code returns a list like the following:

```
<ButtonRelease-1> <Button-1> <Leave> <Enter>
<Key-space>
```

Modifier	Meaning
Alt	The ALT key must be pressed when the event occurs.
Button1, B1	Mouse button 1 must be pressed when the event occurs. This is usually the left-mouse button for right-handed mice, but may be reassigned with the UNIX **xmodmap** utility or the Microsoft Windows Control Panel.
Button2, B2	Mouse button 2 must be pressed when the event occurs. This is usually the middle mouse on three-button mice. Some two-button mouse drivers map this to both buttons being pressed simultaneously.
Button3, B3	Mouse button 3 must be pressed when the event occurs. This is usually the right-mouse button for right-handed mice.
Button4, B4	Mouse button 4 must be pressed when the event occurs.
Button5, B5	Mouse button 5 must be pressed when the event occurs.
Control	The CTRL key must be pressed when the event occurs.
Double	The event must be repeated twice in quick succession with minimal mouse movement. This is usually used for mouse clicks, but may be used for any event.[1]
Lock	The CAPS LOCK key must be pressed when the event occurs.

Table 2-4.   Event Modifiers

Modifier	Meaning
Meta, M	The META key must be pressed when the event occurs.
Mod1, M1	Modifier key 1 must be pressed when the event occurs.[2]
Mod2, M2	Modifier key 2 must be pressed when the event occurs.[2]
Mod3, M3	Modifier key 3 must be pressed when the event occurs.[2]
Mod4, M4	Modifier key 4 must be pressed when the event occurs.[2]
Mod5, M5	Modifier key 5 must be pressed when the event occurs.[2]
Shift	The SHIFT key must be pressed when the event occurs.
Triple	The event must be repeated three times in quick succession with minimal mouse movement. This is usually used for mouse clicks, but may be used for any event.[1]

[1] The event <Double-Button-1> is different from the event sequence <Button-1><Button-1>. When the Double or Triple modifier is used, the clicks must be rapid and close together. When two Button-1 events are specified, the sequence will be matched even if a long time passes or the mouse is moved a great distance between clicks.

[2] Mod1 through Mod5 refer to extra modifier keys, like ALT and CTRL, that exist or can be created through keyboard mappings on some systems.

Table 2-4. Event Modifiers *(continued)*

Type	Description
Activate	The widget's toplevel window becomes the active window. (Valid only on Microsoft Windows and Macintosh systems.)
ButtonPress, Button	The mouse button specified in the *detail* field is pressed.
ButtonRelease	The mouse button specified in the *detail* field is released.

Table 2-5. Event Types

Type	Description
Circulate	The Z order of the widget is changed. (Valid only on UNIX systems.)
Colormap	The color map for the widget is changed. (Valid only on UNIX systems.)
Configure	The size, position, or Z order of the widget is changed.
Deactivate	The widget's toplevel window is no longer the active window. (Valid only on Microsoft Windows and Macintosh systems.)
Destroy	The widget is destroyed.
Enter	The mouse pointer enters the widget.
Expose	All or part of the widget is exposed after being obscured by another widget.
FocusIn	The widget gains keyboard focus.
FocusOut	The widget loses keyboard focus.
Gravity	The widget moves because its parent is resized. (Valid only on UNIX systems.)
KeyPress, Key	The key specified in the *detail* field is pressed.
KeyRelease	The key specified in the *detail* field is released.
Leave	The mouse pointer leaves the widget.
Map	The widget is displayed—for example, when its top level is deiconified.
Motion	The mouse moves within the widget.
MouseWheel	The scrolling wheel on the mouse was moved. (Valid only on Microsoft Windows systems.)
Property	A property of the widget is changed. (Valid only on UNIX systems.)
Reparent	The parent of the widget is changed. (Valid only on UNIX systems.)
Unmap	The widget is removed from the display, such as when its top level is iconified.
Visibility	The visibility of the widget changes.

Table 2-5.   Event Types *(continued)*

bind *tag sequence*

Retrieves the script bound to *sequence* on *tag*.

RETURNS   The script bound to *sequence* on *tag*.

ERROR   Raises an error if *tag* is a widget path and the specified widget does not exist.

bind *tag sequence script*

Binds *script* to execute when the event *sequence* occurs on a widget with *tag* in its list of binding tags.

If *script* starts with a plus sign (+), the rest of *script* is added to the existing binding for *tag* and *sequence*; otherwise, *script* replaces the current binding. If *script* is {} (an empty list), the binding for *tag* and *sequence* is destroyed.

script may include placeholders for fields that describe the event that occurred. These fields consist of "%" (a percent sign) followed by a letter specifying what should be substituted in the field. The substitutions are listed in Table 2-6.

If *script* invokes the **continue** command, the rest of the script is bypassed, but other bindings will be processed for the triggering event.

If *script* invokes the **break** command, the rest of the script is bypassed and no other bindings for the triggering event will be processed.

ERROR   Raises an error if *tag* is a widget path and the specified widget does not exist.

Programmer's Tip: *The %A and %K substitutions can vary from system to system. The following Tk script lets you see what the values are on your system:*

```
entry .e
label .l
bind .e <KeyPress> \
        [list .l configure \
              -text "%%A %A   %%K:%K"]
pack .e .l -side top
```

Character	Substituted Value
%	A literal percent sign.
#	The number of the last client request processed by the server. Valid for all event types.
a	The *above* field, formatted as a hexadecimal number. Valid only for **Configure** events.
b	The number of the button that was pressed or released. Valid only for **ButtonPress** and **ButtonRelease** events.
c	The *count* field from the event. Valid only for **Expose** events.
d	The *detail* field from the event. Valid only for **Enter**, **Leave**, **FocusIn**, and **FocusOut** events. The substituted string will be one of **NotifyAncestor**, **NotifyDetailNone**, **NotifyInferior**, **NotifyNonlinear**, **NotifyNonlinearVirtual**, **NotifyPointer**, **NotifyPointerRoot**, or **NotifyVirtual**.
f	The *focus* field from the event (0 or 1). Valid only for **Enter** and **Leave** events.
h	The *height* field from the event. Valid only for **Configure** and **Expose** events.
k	The *keycode* field from the event. Valid only for **KeyPress** and **KeyRelease** events.
m	The *mode* field from the event. Valid only for **Enter**, **Leave**, **FocusIn**, and **FocusOut** events. The substituted string will be one of **NotifyNormal**, **NotifyGrab**, **NotifyUngrab**, or **NotifyWhileGrabbed**.
o	The *override_redirect* field from the event. Valid only for **Map**, **Reparent**, and **Configure** events.
p	The *place* field from the event. Valid only for **Circulate** events. The substituted string will be one of **PlaceOnTop** or **PlaceOnBottom**.
s	The *state* field from the event. For **ButtonPress**, **ButtonRelease**, **Enter**, **Leave**, **KeyPress**, **KeyRelease**, and **Motion** events, the substituted string is a decimal value. For **Visibility** events, the substituted string is one of **VisibilityUnobscured**, **VisibilityPartiallyObscured**, or **VisibilityFullyObscured**.

Table 2-6. Event Substitution Fields

Character	Substituted Value
t	The *time* field from the event. Valid only for events that contain a *time* field.
w	The *width* field from the event. Valid only for **Configure** and **Expose** events.
x	The *x* field from the event. Valid only for events that contain an *x* field. This is the widget-relative *x* coordinate of the event.
y	The *y* field from the event. Valid only for events that contain a *y* field. This is the widget-relative *y* coordinate of the event.
A	The ASCII character corresponding to the event, or an empty string if the event doesn't correspond to an ASCII character (such as a function or modifier key). Valid only for **KeyPress** and **KeyRelease** events.
B	The *border_width* field from the event. Valid only for **Configure** events.
D	The *delta* value from a **MouseWheel** event. The *delta* value represents the number of units the mouse wheel has been moved. The sign of *delta* represents the direction the mouse wheel was scrolled; positive values should scroll up, negative values should scroll down. Valid only for **MouseWheel** events.
E	The *send_event* field from the event. Valid for all event types.
K	The *keysym* corresponding to the event as a text string. Valid only for **KeyPress** and **KeyRelease** events.
N	The *keysym* corresponding to the event as a decimal number. Valid only for **KeyPress** and **KeyRelease** events.
R	The *root* window identifier of the event. Valid only for events that contain a *root* field.
S	The *subwindow* identifier from the event, formatted as a hexadecimal number. Valid only for events that contain a *subwindow* field.
T	The *type* field from the event. Valid for all event types.
W	The *window* field from the event. (The path name of the window receiving the event.) Valid for all event types.

Table 2-6.   Event Substitution Fields *(continued)*

Character	Substituted Value
X	The *x_root* field from the event. Valid only for **ButtonPress**, **ButtonRelease**, **KeyPress**, **KeyRelease**, and Motion events. This is the screen-relative *x* coordinate of the event.
Y	The *y_root* field from the event. Valid only for **ButtonPress**, **ButtonRelease**, **KeyPress**, **KeyRelease**, and **Motion** events. This is the screen-relative *y* coordinate of the event.

Table 2-6.   Event Substitution Fields *(continued)*

Multiple Matches

An event may match multiple sequences with bindings. For
example, each click in a double-click of a mouse button is a
single click, and could thus match a button-click binding. If an
event matches multiple bindings, the most specific match for
each binding tag is invoked in the order of the binding tags.
The following tests are used to determine which is the most
specific match:

- An event sequence that specifies a specific button or key is
  more specific than one that doesn't. For example,
  <KeyPress-a> is more specific than **<KeyPress>**.

- A longer sequence is more specific than a shorter sequence.
  For example, "xyzzy" is more specific than **<KeyPress-y>**.

- An event with more modifiers is more specific than one with
  fewer modifiers. For example, **<Shift-Control-x>** is more
  specific than **<Control-x>**.

- A virtual event is less specific than a physical event with the
  same sequence. For example, if **<<Paste>>** were associated
  with **<Control-v>**, and **<<Paste>>** and **<Control-v>** both had
  bindings, the **<Control-v>** binding would be invoked and the
  <<Paste>> binding would not.

NOTE: If a sequence matches two or more virtual events, and no
physical event masks the virtual events, one of the virtual event
bindings will be invoked, but which virtual event will be invoked is
indeterminate.

Example

```
# Write log of enter events
bind all <Enter> \
        [list puts "Entering widget %W @ %X,%Y"]
```

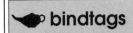 **bindtags**

The **bindtags** command manipulates the list of binding tags for a widget. (See also **bind**.) It takes the following forms:

> **bindtags** *widget*

> **bindtags** *widget tagList*

The arguments are as follows:

tagList
List of binding tags to associate with the widget.

widget
The path to the widget whose tags are to be manipulated.

bindtags *widget*

Retrieves the list of binding tags for *widget.*

RETURNS   A list of binding tags in the order they will be evaluated for *widget.*

ERROR   Raises an error if *widget* does not exist.

bindtags *widget tagList*

Sets or resets the list of binding tags to be evaluated for *widget.*

If *tagList* is {} (an empty list), the default binding tags are restored for *widget*; otherwise, *tagList* is set as the binding tags for *widget.*

ERROR   Raises an error if *widget* does not exist.

Example

```
# Create a button
button .b
# Get the default binding tags
set bindTags [bindtags .b]
# Add SpecialButton processing
set bindTags [linsert $bindTags 0 SpecialButton]
bindtags .b $bindTags
```

2

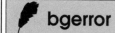

bgerror

The **bgerror** command is called by the interpreter to handle
background errors. (See also **error**; **errorCode**; **errorInfo**.) It takes
the following form:

bgerror *message*

The arguments are as follows:

message
String describing the error that occurred.

When a background error occurs (such as an **after** event trying to
call a nonexistent command), Tcl looks for a command named
bgerror and calls it with a single argument, a message describing
the error. More information can be found in the **errorInfo** and
errorCode global variables.

If multiple background errors occur, **bgerror** will be called once for
each error. This sequence can be interrupted by returning a **break**
exception.

If no **bgerror** command is found, Tcl handles the error by printing
the message to the **stderr** channel.

Example

```
proc bgerror { message } {
    global errorCode
    global errorInfo
```

```
# If there's a big problem, skip all other
# pending bgerror invocations. Otherwise,
# Handle the error.
if { [bigTrouble] } {
    return -code break
} else {
    puts stderr "Message: $message"
    puts stderr "Code: $errorCode"
    puts stderr "Info: $errorInfo"
}
}
```

Compatibility

Tk provides a default **bgerror** that displays the message in a
dialog box.

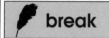
break

The **break** command skips the remaining iterations of a loop
created with commands such as **foreach** and **while**, or the
remaining scripts assigned to a Tk event with **bind**. (See also **bind**,
catch; **for**; **foreach**; **return**; **while**.) It takes the following form:

    break

The arguments are as follows:

None.

Example

```
while { 1 } {
    # Break out of loop if we are done processing
    if { [done] } {
        break
    }
    …do processing here
}
```

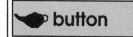

The **button** command creates and manipulates button widgets like the one shown here. (See also **checkbutton**; **radiobutton**.)

Button

Button Options

Button widgets recognize the following standard widget options. (See the Appendix for a complete list of standard widget options and their meanings.)

activebackground	cursor	highlightthickness	takefocus
activeforeground	disabledforeground	image	text
anchor	font	justify	textvariable
background	foreground	padx	underline
bitmap	highlightbackground	pady	wraplength
borderwidth	highlightcolor	relief	

In addition, button widgets recognize the following widget-specific options:

-command *script*
Specifies the script to associate with button invocation, typically bound to clicking the button with mouse button 1.

-default *state*
A button may be drawn with a ring around it, used to indicate when it is the default button for a dialog box. This option controls the appearance of the ring. Possible values for this option are the following:

- **normal** The button will be drawn with enough room around it for the default ring, but the ring will not be drawn.

- **active** The button will be drawn with the ring, indicating that it is the default button.

- **disabled**   The button will be drawn without allowing room around it for the default ring. This can lead to closer placement of widgets adjacent to the button.

-height *distance*
The desired height of the button, in screen units (when an image is specified) or lines of text (if button text is specified). If this option is omitted, Tk computes the correct height from the image or text dimensions.

-state *state*
Specifies the state of the button. Possible values for *state* are the following:

- **normal**   The button is drawn with the colors specified in *foreground* and *background*, and the button will respond to mouse clicks.

- **active**   The button is drawn with the colors specified in *activeForeground* and *activeBackground*. This setting corresponds to the button state when the mouse pointer is over the button, and is not usually set programmatically.

- **disabled**   The button is drawn with the colors specified in *disabledForeground* and *disabledBackground*, and the button will not respond to mouse clicks.

-width *distance*
The desired width of the button, in screen units (when an image is specified) or characters (if button text is specified). If this option is omitted, Tk computes the correct width from the image or text dimensions.

Button Commands

Button widgets respond to the **cget** and **configure** standard widget commands. (See the Appendix for details.) In addition, button widgets respond to the following widget-specific commands:

pathName flash
Redisplays the button several times, alternating between active and normal colors. This command is ignored if the button is disabled.

***pathName* invoke**

Invokes the script associated with the button, if one exists. This command is ignored if the button is disabled.

RETURNS   The value of the Tcl script, or an empty string if no script is associated with the button.

Default Bindings

2

Buttons are created with bindings that make them behave as expected consistent with the user interface conventions on each platform. Specifically:

- A button is active when the mouse pointer is over it.

NOTE: On Microsoft Windows, the button is only active if mouse button 1 has been pressed.

- The button is depressed when mouse button 1 is clicked over the button, and is released when mouse button 1 is released or the mouse pointer leaves the button.

- The button is invoked when mouse button 1 is clicked and released over the button, or when the button has input focus and SPACEBAR is pressed.

Example

```
button .exit -text Exit -command exit
```

Programmer's Tip: *Many of the default bindings on* **button** *widgets are provided through procs, including* **tkButtonDown,** **tkButtonEnter, tkButtonInvoke, tkButtonLeave,** *and* **tkButtonUp.** *These commands are not of general interest and thus are not documented in this reference. The* **bind, info args,** *and* **info body** *commands can be used to explore the use and implementation of these commands.*

Compatibility

On Macintosh systems with the Appearance Manager, the **-background** option for buttons is ignored.

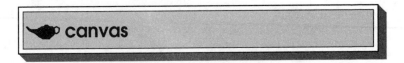

The **canvas** command creates and manipulates canvas widgets.

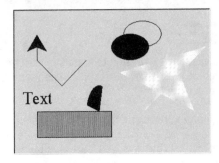

Canvas Overview

The canvas widget provides a general-purpose, object-oriented drawing region. The canvas logically consists of the following:

- **View** Determined by the canvas *width* (X size) and *height* (Y size). It controls the part of the canvas that can be seen without scrolling.

- **Scroll region** Extends the drawing area of the canvas beyond the view. Parts of the canvas outside the current view can be scrolled into view with the scroll bars attached to the canvas or with the **xview** and **yview** canvas commands.

The size of the canvas and the scroll region are specified in screen coordinates. The placement and coordinates of objects on the canvas are specified in window coordinates.

Figure 2-1 corresponds to the Solar Eclipse example at the end of this section.

Object Identification
Each object that is added to a canvas gets a unique serial number, called an *ID*. These numbers are not reused during the life of a canvas, even if objects are removed and others are added.

Objects may also have tags associated with them. Like binding tags for widgets, canvas object tags are freeform text strings (except that they cannot be a valid integer, such as "123"). A tag

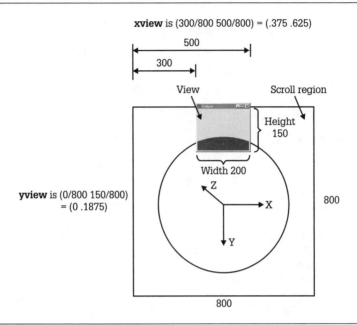

xview is (300/800 500/800) = (.375 .625)

500

300

View   Scroll region

Height
150

Width 200

yview is (0/800 150/800)
= (0 .1875)

800

800

Figure 2-1. Canvas components

may be placed on multiple objects on a canvas (logically grouping the objects), and an object on a canvas may have multiple tags (making it a member of multiple groups).

NOTE: The reserved tag **all** refers to all objects on a canvas. The reserved tag **current** refers to the object, if any, directly under the mouse pointer.

Object Manipulations

Objects may be manipulated individually (by ID) or in groups (by tag). The manipulations that may be performed on objects on a canvas are:

- Moving left, right, up, and down on the canvas (including dragging with a mouse)

- Reordering to control which objects obscure others (note that window objects always obscure all other objects in the region of the canvas they overlap)

- Resizing

- Reshaping

- Editing contents (for text objects)

- Changing colors, line width, fill pattern, etc. (depending on object type)

- Binding actions to events or event sequences

NOTE: The canvas does not support rotation.

Object Bindings
Actions may be bound to events and event sequences on the objects.

Mouse events are directed to the topmost object under the mouse pointer. Keyboard events are directed to the object with the keyboard focus.

Events may trigger more than one binding; this could happen, for example, if the same event had a binding on an object's ID and on one or more of its tags. In this case, all the bindings would be invoked in the following order:

1. Any binding associated with the tag **all**

2. The first matching binding on each of the object's tags, in order

3. A binding on the object's ID

If the event is also bound for the canvas widget itself, that binding is invoked after all object bindings have been invoked.

Canvas Objects
The objects that may be placed on a canvas are arcs, bitmaps, images, lines, ovals, polygons, rectangles, text strings, and other widgets.

NOTE: Support for additional object types may be added with C programming by using the **Tk_CreateItemType** function. Such additions are not covered here. Refer to the documentation that accompanies your Tk source distribution for information on using **Tk_CreateItemType** and other C-callable functions.

Canvas Options

Canvas widgets recognize the following standard widget options. (See the Appendix for a complete list of widget options and their meanings.)

background	insertbackground	selectbackground
borderwidth	insertborderwidth	selectborderwidth
cursor	insertofftime	selectforeground
highlightbackground	insertontime	takefocus
highlightcolor	insertwidth	xscrollcommand
highlightthickness	relief	yscrollcommand

In addition, canvas widgets recognize the following widget-specific options:

-closeenough *float*

Specifies a floating-point number indicating how close to an item the mouse pointer must be to be considered "inside" the item. If **-closeenough** is not specified, *float* defaults to 1.0.

-confine *boolean*

Specifies a boolean value indicating whether the canvas's view is restricted to the area specified in the *scrollregion* option. If *confine* is not specified, it defaults to true and the view is restricted to the scroll region.

-height *distance*

Specifies the desired height of the canvas, in screen units.

-scrollregion *screenCoordinates*

Specifies the data extents of the canvas as a list of four window coordinates, in this form:

    {*x1 y1 x2 y2* }

-width *distance*

Specifies the desired width of the canvas, in screen units.

-xscrollincrement *distance*

Specifies the increment to be used for horizontal scrolling, in screen units. If *xscrollincrement* is greater than zero, the horizontal view of the window is restricted so that the left edge of the view is always an integer multiple of *xscrollincrement* from the left edge of the canvas scroll region, and scrolling is in multiples of *xscrollincrement*. If *xscrollincrement* is less than or equal to zero, horizontal scrolling is unrestricted.

-yscrollincrement *distance*

Specifies the increment to be used for vertical scrolling, in screen units. If *yscrollincrement* is greater than zero, the vertical view of the window is restricted so that the top edge of the view is always

an integer multiple of *yscrollincrement* from the top edge of
the canvas scroll region, and scrolling occurs in multiples of
yscrollincrement. If *yscrollincrement* is less than or equal to zero,
vertical scrolling is unrestricted.

Canvas Commands

Canvas widgets respond to the **cget** and **configure** standard
widget commands. (See the Appendix for details.) In
addition, canvas widgets respond to the following widget-
specific commands:

> *pathName* **addtag** *tag searchSpec*
> *pathName* **dtag** *tagOrId ?tag?*
> *pathName* **bbox** *tagOrId ?tagOrId ... ?*
> *pathName* **bind** *tagOrId*
> *pathName* **bind** *tagOrId sequence*
> *pathName* **bind** *tagOrId sequence script*
> *pathName* **canvasx** *screenx ?gridspacing?*
> *pathName* **canvasy** *screeny ?gridspacing?*
> *pathName* **coords** *tagOrId ?x y ... ?*
> *pathName* **create** *type x y ?x y ... ? ?options?*
> *pathName* **delete** *tagOrId ?tagOrId ... ?*
> *pathName* **dchars** *tagOrId first ?last?*
> *pathName* **insert** *tagOrId beforeThis string*
> *pathName* **find** *searchSpec*
> *pathName* **focus** *?tagOrId?*
> *pathName* **gettags** *tagOrId*
> *pathName* **icursor** *tagOrId index*
> *pathName* **index** *tagOrId index*
> *pathName* **itemcget** *tagOrId option*
> *pathName* **itemconfigure** *tagOrId ?option?*
> *pathName* **itemconfigure** *tagOrId option value ?option value ... ?*
> *pathName* **lower** *tagOrId ?belowThis?*
> *pathName* **raise** *tagOrId ?aboveThis?*
> *pathName* **move** *tagOrId xAmount yAmount*
> *pathName* **postscript** *options*
> *pathName* **scale** *tagOrId xOrigin yOrigin xScale yScale*
> *pathName* **scan mark** *x y*
> *pathName* **scan dragto** *x y*
> *pathName* **select** *options*
> *pathName* **type** *tagOrId*
> *pathName* **xview**

> *pathName* **xview** *viewoptions*
> *pathName* **yview**
> *pathName* **yview** *viewoptions*

The arguments are as follows:

aboveThis
Tag or ID of object above which to raise *tagOrId*.

beforeThis
Text index of the character before which to insert *string*.

first
Text index of the first character to delete.

gridspacing
A distance in screen units.

index
A text index. (See the upcoming section, "Canvas Text Indices.")

last
Text index of the last character to delete.

option
A canvas object option name.

options
Options to use when creating the object or PostScript data.

screenx, screeny
A screen coordinate to convert.

script
A script to execute when the event sequence occurs as for the **bind** command.

searchSpec
An object search specification. (See the following section, "Searching the Canvas.")

sequence
An event sequence as for the **bind** command, except that the canvas object may respond only to keyboard and mouse events (such as **Enter**, **Leave**, etc.) and to virtual events.

string
Text to insert.

tag
A string to tag the object with. *tag* may be any sequence of characters that is not a valid integer.

tagOrId
A tag or a canvas object ID.

type
An object type; one of **arc**, **bitmap**, **image**, **line**, **oval**, **polygon**, **rectangle**, **text**, or **window**.

value
Value for the object option.

viewoptions
Options for setting the view. (See the following descriptions of **xview** and **yview** for details.)

x, y
Window coordinates to assign to the object.

xAmount, yAmount
Distance, in screen units, to move the object along the X or Y axis.

xOrigin, yOrigin
Window coordinates of point around which to scale objects.

xScale, yScale
Amount to scale objects in the X or Y direction.

Searching the Canvas
Many canvas widget commands take a search specification as an argument, to determine which objects to act upon. The search specification may take one of the following forms:

Search Specification	Resulting Selection
above *tagOrId*	The object above the one given by *tagOrId* in the Z order. If *tagOrId* matches more than one object, the one highest in the Z order (the last one drawn) is used. If no object is above *tagOrId*, this specification matches no objects.
all	All objects on the canvas.

Search Specification	Resulting Selection
below *tagOrId*	The object below the one given by *tagOrId* in the Z order. If *tagOrId* matches more than one object, the one lowest in the Z order (the first one drawn) is used. If no object is below *tagOrId*, this specification matches no objects.
closest *x y ?halo? ?start?*	The object closest to the point given by *(x,y)*. If more than one object matches (e.g., if two items overlap the point), the highest in the Z order is used. If *halo* is specified, any object within that distance of *(x,y)* is considered to overlap it. *halo* must be a non-negative canvas coordinate. If *start* is specified, it identifies an object below which the matching object must be in the Z order. *start* may be used to cycle through all the objects close to another object. If no object is below *start*, this specification matches *start*.
enclosed *x1 y1 x2 y2*	All objects *completely* within the rectangle from *(x1,y1)* and *(x2,y2)*. *x1* must be less than or equal to *x2*, and *y1* must be less than or equal to *y2*.
overlapping *x1 y1 x2 y2*	All objects that overlap with the rectangle from *(x1,y1)* and *(x2,y2)*. *x1* must be less than or equal to *x2*, and *y1* must be less than or equal to *y2*.
withtag *tagOrId*	All the items with the given tag or ID.

The following example illustrates the use of search specifications:

```
# Build a list of all objects within 1
# millimeter of x,y
set close {}
for {set id [.c find closest $x $y 1m]}
    {[lsearch $close $id] == -1}
    {set id [.c find closest $x $y 1m $id]} {
    lappend close $id
}
```

Canvas Text Indices

Several canvas widget commands take one or more text indices
as arguments. The text index may take one of the forms listed
in Table 2-7.

Programmer's Tip: *Text objects in a canvas are more like* **entry**
widgets than **text** *widgets. Compare the index forms in the*
preceding table with those for **entry** *widgets.*

pathName addtag *tag searchSpec*

Adds *tag* to each object in the canvas *pathName* that matches
searchSpec. If no objects match *searchSpec*, this command has
no effect.

pathName dtag *tagOrId ?tag?*

Deletes *tag* from each object that matches *tagOrId*. If *tag* is not
specified, it defaults to *tagOrId*.

pathName bbox *tagOrId ?tagOrId ... ?*

Retrieves the coordinates of a bounding box that includes all the
specified objects.

Text Index	Value
number	A character position within the text object: 0 refers to the first character, 1 refers to the second character, etc. *number* must be a decimal number. Any number less than 0 is treated as 0. Any number greater than the length of the text in the object is treated as the length of the text.
end	The character position just after the last character in the object.
insert	The character position just after the insertion cursor.
sel.first	The first character of the selected text, if any.[1]
sel.last	The last character of the selected text, if any.[1]
@x,y	The character at the point *(x,y)* relative to the upper-left corner of the canvas widget. If *(x,y)* lies outside the extents of the text object, this form refers to the first or last character in the line that is closest to *(x,y)*.

[1]This form raises an error if the specified text object does not have any selected text.

Table 2-7.   Canvas Text Indices

RETURNS   A list of four window coordinates: {x1 y1 x2 y2}, or {} (an empty list) if no object matches the given tags or IDs or if the objects have nothing to display.

NOTE: This is different from the result of the **bbox** command for widgets. The **bbox** command for entry, listbox, and text widgets returns a list in the form {x y w h}.

pathName bind tagOrId
Lists the sequences with bindings for the specified objects.

RETURNS   A list of all sequences with bindings for *tagOrId*.

ERROR   Raises an error if *tagOrId* is a numeric object identifier and the specified object does not exist.

pathName bind tagOrId sequence
Retrieves the script bound to *sequence* on the specified objects.

RETURNS   The script bound to *sequence* on *tagOrId*.

ERROR   Raises an error if *tagOrId* is a numeric object identifier and the specified object does not exist.

pathName bind tagOrId sequence script
Binds *script* to execute when *sequence* occurs on the specified object or objects.

NOTE: Only keyboard and mouse events, and virtual events based on keyboard and mouse events, may be bound on canvas objects.

If *script* starts with a plus sign (+), the rest of *script* is added to the existing binding for the object or objects and *sequence*; otherwise, *script* replaces the current binding. If *script* is {} (an empty list), the binding for *tagOrId* and *sequence* is destroyed.

script may include placeholders for fields that describe the event that occurred. (See Table 2-6 for a list of substitutions.)

If *script* invokes **continue**, the rest of the script is bypassed, but other bindings will be processed for the triggering event.

If *script* invokes **break**, the rest of the script is bypassed and no other bindings for the triggering event will be processed.

ERROR Raises an error if *tagOrId* is a numeric object identifier and the specified object does not exist.

pathName canvasx *screenx ?gridspacing?*
Converts *screenx* from screen units (for example, 1i) to pixels. *gridspacing* is in screen units.

RETURNS A floating-point number. If *gridspacing* is specified, the return value is rounded to the nearest multiple of *gridspacing*.

pathName canvasy *screeny ?gridspacing?*
Converts *screeny* from screen units (for example, 2.54c) to pixels. *gridspacing* is in screen units.

RETURNS A floating-point number. If *gridspacing* is specified, the return value is rounded to the nearest multiple of *gridspacing*.

pathName coords *tagOrId ?x y ... ?*
Retrieves or modifies the coordinates of an object. If no coordinates are specified, retrieves a list of coordinates for the specified object. If coordinates are specified, replaces the current coordinates of the object. If *tagOrId* refers to multiple objects, the lowest one is used.

pathName create *type x y ?x y ... ? ?options?*
Creates a new *type* object on the canvas. The first *x* and *y* are required and specify the placement of the object on the canvas. Additional coordinates and options are supplied based on *type*.

RETURNS A unique, numeric identifier for the new object.

pathName delete *tagOrId ?tagOrId ... ?*
Deletes each specified object from the canvas.

pathName dchars *tagOrId first ?last?*
Deletes the range of characters from *first* to *last* from each object that matches *tagOrId*. If *last* is not specified, it defaults to *first*+1, so one character is deleted. Any objects that do not support text operations are ignored.

pathName insert *tagOrId beforeThis string*
Inserts *string* before the index *beforeThis* in all objects that match *tagOrId*.

If multiple text objects match *tagOrId* and *index* is a symbolic index, such as **end,** the symbolic index is evaluated for each text. For example, if *beforeThis* were **end**, this command would append *string* to the contents of each object.

pathName find *searchSpec*
Searches the canvas for objects that match *searchSpec*.

RETURNS   A list of object identifiers, ordered from first to last (lowest to highest) in the Z order.

pathName focus *?tagOrId?*
Retrieves or sets the keyboard focus for the canvas.

If *tagOrId* is not specified, returns the object identifier for the object on the canvas that has the keyboard focus, or an empty string if no item has focus.

If *tagOrId* is specified as an empty string, resets the focus so that no object on the canvas has keyboard focus.

If *tagOrId* is specified, sets the keyboard focus to the first (lowest) object that matches *tagOrId* and may take focus.

Programmer's Tip: *This command is usually followed by a Tk focus command to give the canvas focus within the Tk widget hierarchy. Here is an example:*

```
# Create a canvas
canvas .c
# Put a text object on it
set textId [.c create text 10 10]
...
# Put focus within the canvas on the text
# object
.c focus $textId
# Put focus within the application on the
# canvas
focus .c
```

pathName gettags *tagOrId*
Retrieves a list of all tags for the specified object.

RETURNS   If *tagOrId* doesn't match any object, an empty list. If *tagOrId* matches one or more objects, a list of tags for the lowest object that matches.

pathName icursor *tagOrId index*
Positions the text insertion cursor in all objects matching *tagOrId* that support text insertion. The insertion cursor is shown only for

the object with keyboard focus, but it may be positioned even though it is not visible.

If multiple text objects match *tagOrId,* and *index* is a symbolic index, such as **end,** the symbolic index is evaluated for each text. For example, if one text object had three characters in it and another had five, **end** would set the insertion cursor to the fourth position in the first text object, and to the sixth position in the second text object.

pathName index *tagOrId index*
Normalizes *index* in the first (lowest) object that matches *tagOrId* and that supports indexing.

RETURNS   A decimal number corresponding to *index*. For example, if *index* were **end**, the length of the text in the matching text object would be returned.

pathName itemcget *tagOrId option*
Retrieves the value of *option* for the first (lowest) object that matches *tagOrId*. *option* may be any option valid for the object type. This is similar to the **cget** command for widgets, except that it operates on an object on the canvas, instead of a widget.

RETURNS   The value of the option.

pathName itemconfigure *tagOrId ?option?*
Retrieves the value for one or all options for the first (lowest) object that matches *tagOrId*. This is similar to the **configure** command for widgets, except that it operates on an object on the canvas, instead of a widget.

RETURNS   If *option* is specified, a list of values for the option, in this form:

    {optionName dbName dbClass defaultValue currentValue}

If *option* is not specified, a list of lists describing all options for *tagOrId*. (Each sublist is in the preceding form.)

pathName itemconfigure *tagOrId option* value *?option value...?*
Sets one or more options for all objects that match *tagOrId*. This is similar to the **configure** command for widgets, except that it operates on an object on the canvas, instead of a widget.

pathName lower *tagOrId ?belowThis?*
Moves all the objects matching *tagOrId* below the first (lowest) object that matches *belowThis*. The relative order of the objects that are moved is preserved.

NOTE: This canvas widget command has no effect on window objects. Use the Tk commands **raise** and **lower** to manipulate windows.

pathName raise *tagOrId ?aboveThis?*
Moves all the objects matching *tagOrId* above the last (highest) object that matches *aboveThis*. The relative order of the objects that are moved is preserved.

NOTE: This canvas widget command has no effect on window objects. Use the Tk commands **raise** and **lower** to manipulate windows.

pathName move *tagOrId xAmount yAmount*
Moves all objects that match *tagOrId* by *xAmount* relative to its X coordinate, and *yAmount* relative to its Y coordinate. *xAmount* and *yAmount* are in screen units.

pathName postscript *options*
Creates a string consisting of Encapsulated PostScript 3 code to draw all or part of the canvas. *options* may include the following:

Option	Purpose
-channel *channelId*	Specifies an open channel to write the PostScript to. *channelId* is a channel identifier, such as those returned by **open**.
-colormap *arrayName*	Specifies an array, each element of which contains PostScript code to set a particular color value (e.g., "1.0 1.0 0.0 setrgbcolor"). When outputting colors, Tk determines whether any element of the array has an index that matches the color name. If so, it uses the value of that element to set the color.
-colormode *mode*	Specifies how to output colors. *mode* is one of **color** (for full-color output), **gray** (for grayscale output), or **mono** (for black-and-white output).

Option	Purpose
-file *fileName*	Specifies the name of a file to write the PostScript output to.[1]
-fontmap *arrayName*	Specifies an array, each element of which contains a Tcl list with two elements in the form {fontName pointSize}. When outputting PostScript for a font, Tk determines whether any element in the array has an index that is the same as the font name. If so, it uses the value of that element when writing the PostScript for the font. Otherwise, Tk attempts to guess which font to use.
-height *size*	Specifies the height (in screen units) of the canvas area to output. If **-height** is not specified, *size* defaults to the height of the canvas widget.
-pageanchor *anchor*	Specifies which part of the output canvas area should appear over the position specified with **-pagex** and **-pagey**. *anchor* may be **n**, **ne**, **e**, **se**, **s**, **sw**, **w**, **nw**, or **center**. If **-pageanchor** is not specified, *anchor* defaults to **center**.
-pageheight *size*	Specifies that the output PostScript should be scaled in *x* and *y* so that the overall image is *size* high. *size* is a floating-point number with an optional unit specifier from the following list: **c** centimeters **i** inches **m** millimeters **p** points (1/72 inch) Unlike screen coordinates, if the unit specifier is omitted, points is used. If **-pageheight** is not specified, *size* defaults to the height of the canvas image.[2]
-pagewidth *size*	Specifies that the output PostScript should be scaled in *x* and *y* so that the overall image is *size* wide. *size* is a floating-point number with an optional unit specifier, as for **-pageheight**. If **-pagewidth** is not specified, *size* defaults to the width of the canvas image.[2]

Option	Purpose
-pagex *position*	Specifies the X position on the page of the point specified with **-pageanchor**. *position* is a floating-point number with an optional unit specifier, as for **-pageheight**. If **-pagex** is not specified, it defaults to the center of the page.
-pagey *position*	Specifies the Y position on the page of the point specified with **-pageanchor**. *position* is a floating-point number with an optional unit specifier, as for **-pageheight**. If **-pagey** is not specified, it defaults to the center of the page.
-rotate *boolean*	Specifies whether the output PostScript is rotated 90 degrees. Normal output is in portrait orientation. Rotated output is in landscape orientation. If **-rotate** is not specified, it defaults to false (nonrotated).
-width *size*	Specifies the width (in screen units) of the canvas area to output. If **-width** is not specified, *size* defaults to the width of the canvas widget.
-x *position*	Specifies the leftmost window coordinate of the canvas area to be output. If **-x** is not specified, *position* defaults to the left edge of the view.
-y *position*	Specifies the topmost window coordinate of the canvas area to be output. If **-y** is not specified, *position* defaults to the top edge of the view.

RETURNS   If the **-file** option is specified, the PostScript code is written to the specified file, and an empty string is returned. If the **-channel** option is specified, the PostScript code is written to the specified channel, and an empty string is returned. Otherwise, the command returns the PostScript code.

[1]This option is not valid in a safe interpreter.

[2]**-pageheight** is overridden by **-pagewidth** if both are specified. The height and width of the image can't be scaled by different amounts.

pathName scale *tagOrId xOrigin yOrigin xScale yScale*

Rescales all the objects matching *tagOrId*. Each coordinate of each object is modified so that its distance from (*xOrigin, yOrigin*) is scaled by *xScale* along the X axis and by *yScale* along the Y axis.

pathName scan mark *x y*

Records *x* and *y* and the coordinates of the current view for use by future **scan dragto** canvas widget commands. This is usually bound to a mouse-button press on the canvas.

pathName scan dragto *x y*

Adjusts the canvas view by ten times the difference between *x* and *y* and the coordinates of the last **scan mark** canvas widget command. This is usually bound to mouse motion events on the canvas and used to implement a high-speed scrolling of the scroll region within the view.

pathName select *options*

Manipulates the text selection for the canvas.

NOTE: At most, one object on the canvas that supports text selection may have a selection set at one time.

options may include the following:

Option	Purpose

adjust *tagOrId index*	Adjusts the text selection in the first (lowest) object that supports text selection, by moving the end of the selection nearest *index* to be at *index*. The other end of the selection is made the anchor for future **select to** widget commands. For example, if object 36 on canvas .c were a text object containing five characters, and its current selection included the second and third characters (index 1 to index 2), then
	    .c select adjust 36 4
	would change the selection to include the second to fifth characters, and
	    .c select adjust 36 3
	would further change the selection to include only the fourth and fifth characters, leaving the **select to** anchor at the end of the text.

Option	Purpose
	If the object specified by *tagOrId* does not currently have the selection, this command is the same as **select to**.
clear	Clears the text selection for the widget.
from *tagOrId index*	Sets the anchor for future **select to** widget commands to be just before *index* in the first (lowest) object that matches *tagOrId*. This does not change the current selection; it just changes the anchor for future **select to** commands.
item	Retrieves the ID of the object with the current text selection. If no object has the text selection (for example, after a **select clear** command), it returns an empty string.
to *tagOrId index*	Sets the text selection in the first (lowest) object that matches *tagOrId* and supports text selection to include characters from the selection anchor point (set with **select adjust** or **select from**) to *index*. If the specified object does not have an anchor set, the selection will include only the character at *index*. Otherwise, the selection will include the character at the anchor point only if *index* is at or after the anchor.

Programmer's Tip: *The canvas widget does not have an* **-exportselection** *option and does not export its selection; however, it is affected by selections in other widgets. If another widget with* **-exportselection** *enabled gets the selection, the current selection in a canvas text object will be lost.*

pathName type *tagOrId*
Retrieves the type for the first (lowest) object that matches *tagOrId*.

RETURNS   If no objects match *tagOrId*, an empty string. If *tagOrId* matches an object, the type, such as **rectangle**, **text**, etc.

pathName xview
Retrieves the current X view coordinate of the canvas.

RETURNS   A view coordinate list. These are the same values passed to scroll bars via the **-xscrollcommand** option.

pathName xview *viewoptions*

Sets the X coordinates of the canvas view. *options* may be any of the following:

Option	Purpose
moveto *fraction*	Adjusts the view so that *fraction* of the total width of the canvas is off the left of the view. *fraction* is a view coordinate.
scroll *number units*	Adjusts the view *number units*. *number* must be an integer. *units* is **units** or **pages**: **units** The view adjusts by *number* times the **xScrollIncrement** **pages** The view adjusts *number* times 9/10 of the view width Negative values of *number* adjust the view to the right (making objects off the left of the view visible) and vice versa for positive values.

pathName yview

Retrieves the current Y view coordinate of the canvas.

RETURNS   A view coordinate list. These are the same values passed to scroll bars via the **-yscrollcommand** option.

pathName yview *viewoptions*

Sets the Y coordinates of the canvas view. *options* may be the following:

Option	Purpose
moveto *fraction*	Adjusts the view so that *fraction* of the total height of the canvas is off the top of the view. *fraction* is a view coordinate.
scroll *number units*	Adjusts the view *number units*. *number* must be an integer. *units* is **units** or **pages**: **units** The view adjusts by *number* times the **yScrollIncrement** **pages** The view adjusts *number* times 9/10 of the view height Negative values of *number* adjust the view up (making objects off the top of the view visible) and vice versa for positive values.

Canvas Objects

The following sections describe creation and configuration of
canvas objects.

Arcs

Arc objects appear as pieces of an oval. They are created with a
command in this form:

> *pathName* **create arc** *x1 y1 x2 y2 ?option value ... ?*

The four coordinates define the bounding box of the oval. Here are
the options that may be used to specify the appearance of the arc:

Option	Purpose
-extent *angle*	Specifies the size of the arc. *angle* is in degrees, measured clockwise from the X axis. If *angle* is greater than 360 degrees, then *angle* modulo 360 is used.
-fill *color*	Specifies the fill color for the arc. If *color* is an empty string, the arc will not be filled. This is the default.
-outline *color*	Specifies the color for the outline of the arc. If **-outline** is not specified, *color* defaults to black. If *color* is an empty string, no outline is drawn for the arc.
-outlinestipple *bitmap*	Specifies the bitmap to use when drawing the outline of the arc. If *bitmap* is an empty string, a solid outline is used. This is the default.
-start *angle*	Specifies the start angle of the arc. *angle* is in degrees, measured clockwise from the X axis.
-stipple *bitmap*	Specifies the bitmap to use when filling the arc. If *bitmap* is an empty string, a solid fill is used. This is the default.

Option	Purpose
-style *type*	Specifies the style of the arc. *type* must be **arc**, **chord**, or **pieslice**: **arc** The arc is drawn using only the section of perimeter defined by **-start** and **-extent**. In this case, **-fill** is ignored. **chord** The arc is drawn by connecting the ends of the perimeter arc. **pieslice** The arc is drawn by connecting each end of the perimeter arc to the center of the oval. If **-style** is not specified, *type* defaults to **pieslice**.
-tags *tagList*	Specifies tags to apply to the arc. *tagList* replaces any existing tags on the arc. To remove all tags from an arc, set *tagList* to an empty list (⦃⦄).
-width *outlineWidth*	Specifies the width of the outline for the arc. *outlineWidth* is in screen units. If **-width** is not specified, *outlineWidth* defaults to 1.0.

Bitmaps

Bitmap objects appear as two-color images, like those created with the **image** command. They are created with a command in this form:

> *pathName* **create bitmap** *x y ?option value ... ?*

The two coordinates specify the anchor point for the bitmap. (See **-anchor** in the following table). The options listed here may be used to specify the appearance of the bitmap:

Option	Purpose
-anchor *anchorPos*	Specifies where on the bitmap (*x,y*) is located. *anchorPos* may be **n**, **ne**, **e**, **se**, **s**, **sw**, **w**, **nw**, or **center**. If **-anchor** is not specified, *anchorPos* defaults to **center**.
-background *color*	Specifies the color to be displayed where the bitmap pixels are 0. If *color* is an empty string, 0 pixels are transparent. This is the default.

Option	Purpose
-bitmap *bitmap*	Specifies the bitmap to be displayed. (See the description of the **-bitmap** option in the Appendix for valid values of *bitmap*.)
-foreground *color*	Specifies the color to be displayed where the bitmap pixels are 1. If **-foreground** is not specified, *color* defaults to black.
-tags *tagList*	Specifies tags to apply to the bitmap. *tagList* replaces any existing tags on the bitmap. To remove all tags from a bitmap, set *tagList* to an empty list ({}).

Images

Image objects display images created with the **image create** command. They are created with a command in this form:

> *pathName* **create image** *x y ?option value ... ?*

The two coordinates specify the anchor point for the image. The following options may be used to specify the appearance of the image:

Option	Purpose
-anchor *anchorPos*	Specifies where on the image (*x,y*) is located. *anchorPos* may be **n**, **ne**, **e**, **se**, **s**, **sw**, **w**, **nw**, or **center**. If **-anchor** is not specified, *anchorPos* defaults to **center**.
-image *name*	Specifies an image to be displayed. *name* is the name of an image created with the **image create** command.
-tags *tagList*	Specifies tags to apply to the image. *tagList* replaces any existing tags on the image. To remove all tags from an image, set *tagList* to an empty list ({}).

Lines

Line objects appear as one or more connected line segments or curves. They are created with a command in the form:

> *pathName* **create line** *x1 y1 x2 y2 ? ... xn yn? ?option value ... ?*

The coordinates specify the points to be connected. The following options may be used to specify the appearance of the line:

Option	Purpose
-arrow *where*	Specifies which ends, if any, should be drawn with an arrowhead. *where* is **none**, **first**, **last**, or **both**. If **-arrow** is not specified, *where* defaults to **none**.
-arrowshape *shape*	Specifies the shape of the arrowhead. *shape* is a list of three measurements in screen units. The first element is the length of the arrowhead along the line; the second is the distance along the line to the trailing points of the arrow; the third is the perpendicular distance from the line segment to the trailing tips of the arrowhead (one half the width of the arrowhead).
	If the first element of *shape* is less than the second, the arrowhead has a chevron shape. If they are equal, it is a triangle. If the second element is less than or equal to 0, the arrowhead is drawn backward and points back along the line segment.
	If **-arrowshape** is not specified, Tk picks a "reasonable" shape. If **-arrow** is not specified, this option is ignored.
-capstyle *style*	Specifies the style for the end points of the line. *style* may be **butt**, **projecting**, or **round**. If **-arrow** is specified, this option is ignored.[1]
-fill *color*	Specifies the color used to draw the line. If *color* is an empty string, the line is transparent. If **-fill** is not specified, *color* defaults to black.
-joinstyle *style*	Specifies the style for the points along the line. *style* may be **bevel**, **miter**, or **round**. If **-joinstyle** is not specified, *style* defaults to **miter**.[1]
-smooth *boolean*	Specifies whether the line should be drawn as a curve made of parabolic splines. A spline is drawn between each pair of points in the coordinate list.

[1]This option has no effect on Microsoft Windows systems.

Option	Purpose
-splinesteps *number*	Specifies the degree of smoothness desired for curves. Each curve will be approximated with *number* line segments. *number* must be an integer. If **-smooth** is not specified, this option is ignored.
-stipple *bitmap*	Specifies the bitmap to use when drawing the line. If *bitmap* is an empty string, a solid line is drawn. This is the default.
-tags *tagList*	Specifies tags to apply to the line. *tagList* replaces any existing tags on the line. To remove all tags from a line, set *tagList* to an empty list (())).
-width *outlineWidth*	Specifies the width of the line in screen units. If **-width** is not specified, *outlineWidth* defaults to 1.0.

Ovals

Ovals appear as circular or oval regions. They are created with a command in this form:

> *pathName* **create oval** *x1 y1 x2 y2 ?option value ... ?*

The four coordinates define the bounding box of the oval. The oval will intersect the left and top edges of the bounding box, but not the right and bottom edges. The following options may be used to specify the appearance of the oval:

Option	Purpose
-fill *color*	Specifies the fill color for the oval. If *color* is an empty string, the oval will not be filled. This is the default.
-outline *color*	Specifies the color for the outline of the oval. If **-outline** is not specified, *color* defaults to black. If *color* is an empty string, no outline is drawn for the oval.
-stipple *bitmap*	Specifies the bitmap to use when filling the oval. If *bitmap* is an empty string, a solid fill is used. This is the default.

Option	Purpose
-tags *tagList*	Specifies tags to apply to the oval. *tagList* replaces any existing tags on the oval. To remove all tags from an oval, set *tagList* to an empty list ({}).
-width *outlineWidth*	Specifies the width of the outline for the oval. *outlineWidth* is in screen units. If **-width** is not specified, *outlineWidth* defaults to 1.0.

Polygons

Polygon objects appear as closed, filled polygons or curves. They are created with a command in this form:

> *pathName* **create polygon** *x1 y1 x2 y2 x3 y3 ? ... xn yn?*
> *?option value ... ?*

The coordinates specify the points to be connected. At least three points must be specified. The first and last points need not be the same to close the polygon. The following options may be used to specify the appearance of the polygon:

Option	Purpose
-fill *color*	Specifies the color used to fill the polygon. If *color* is an empty string, the polygon is transparent. If **-fill** is not specified, *color* defaults to black.
-outline *color*	Specifies the color for the outline of the polygon. If *color* is an empty string, no outline will be drawn. This is the default.
-smooth *boolean*	Specifies whether the polygon should be drawn as a curve made of parabolic splines. A spline is drawn between each pair of points in the coordinate list.
-splinesteps *number*	Specifies the degree of smoothness desired for curves. Each curve will be approximated with *number* line segments. *number* must be an integer. If **-smooth** is not specified, this option is ignored.

Option	Purpose
-stipple *bitmap*	Specifies the bitmap to use when filling the polygon. If *bitmap* is an empty string, a solid polygon is drawn. This is the default.
-tags *tagList*	Specifies tags to apply to the polygon. *tagList* replaces any existing tags on the polygon. To remove all tags from a polygon, set *tagList* to an empty list ({}).
-width *outlineWidth*	Specifies the width of the polygon outline in screen units. If **-width** is not specified, *outlineWidth* defaults to 1.0.

Rectangles

Rectangles appear as square or rectangular regions. They are created with a command in this form:

> *pathName* **create rectangle** *x1 y1 x2 y2 ?option value ... ?*

The four coordinates define opposite corners of the rectangle. The rectangle will include the left and top edges of the box described by the coordinates, but not the right and bottom edges. The following options may be used to specify the appearance of the rectangle:

Option	Purpose
-fill *color*	Specifies the fill color for the rectangle. If *color* is an empty string, the rectangle will not be filled. This is the default.
-outline *color*	Specifies the color for the outline of the rectangle. If **-outline** is not specified, *color* defaults to black. If *color* is an empty string, no outline is drawn for the rectangle.
-stipple *bitmap*	Specifies the bitmap to use when filling the rectangle. If *bitmap* is an empty string, a solid fill is used. This is the default.
-tags *tagList*	Specifies tags to apply to the rectangle. *tagList* replaces any existing tags on the rectangle. To remove all tags from a rectangle, set *tagList* to an empty list ({}).
-width *outlineWidth*	Specifies the width of the outline for the rectangle. *outlineWidth* is in screen units. If **-width** is not specified, *outlineWidth* defaults to 1.0.

84 canvas

Text Strings

Text objects appear as one or more lines of characters. Text objects support indexing and selection via the following canvas object commands: **dchars**, **focus**, **icursor**, **index**, **insert**, and **select**. They are created with a command in this form:

pathName **create text** *x y ?option value ...?*

The two coordinates specify the anchor point for the text. The following options may be used to specify the appearance of the text.

Option	Purpose
-anchor *anchorPos*	Specifies where on the text (*x,y*) is located. *anchorPos* may be **n**, **ne**, **e**, **se**, **s**, **sw**, **w**, **nw**, or **center**. If **-anchor** is not specified, *anchorPos* defaults to **center**.
-fill *color*	Specifies the color for the characters in the text. If **-fill** is not specified, *color* defaults to black.
-font *fontName*	Specifies the font to use for the characters in the text. (See **font** for a description of font names.)
-justify *how*	Specifies how to justify characters in the text. *how* may be **left**, **right**, or **center**. This option only has an effect if the text object contains multiple lines. If **-justify** is not specified, *how* defaults to **left**.
-stipple *bitmap*	Specifies the bitmap to use when drawing the text. If *bitmap* is an empty string, a solid fill is used. This is the default.
-tags *tagList*	Specifies tags to apply to the text. *tagList* replaces any existing tags on the text. To remove all tags from a text, set *tagList* to an empty list ({}).
-text *string*	Specifies the characters to be displayed in the text object.

Option	Purpose
-width *lineLength*	Specifies the maximum line length for the text object. If *lineLength* is 0, text is broken only at new line characters. If *lineLength* is greater than 0, the text is word-wrapped to make all lines less than *lineLength* characters long. If **-width** is not specified, *lineLength* defaults to 0.

2

Windows

Window objects appear as a widget or widget hierarchy embedded in the canvas. They are created with a command in this form:

pathName **create window** *x y ?option value ... ?*

The two coordinates specify the anchor point for the window object. The following options may be used to specify the appearance of the window:

Option	Purpose
-anchor *anchorPos*	Specifies where on the window (*x,y*) is located. *anchorPos* may be **n**, **ne**, **e**, **se**, **s**, **sw**, **w**, **nw**, or **center**. If **-anchor** is not specified, *anchorPos* defaults to **center**.
-height *height*	Specifies the height of the window object. *height* is in screen units. If **-height** is not specified or if *height* is an empty string, the window object is the same height as *pathName*.
-tags *tagList*	Specifies tags to apply to the window. *tagList* replaces any existing tags on the window. To remove all tags from a window, set *tagList* to an empty list ({}).
-width *width*	Specifies the width of the window object. *width* is in screen units. If **-width** is not specified or if *width* is an empty string, the window object is the same width as *pathName*.
-window *pathName*	Specifies the path to the widget to embed in the canvas. *pathName* must be a child of the canvas, or in the same hierarchy as the canvas, and can't be a toplevel window.

Default Bindings

The canvas widget has no default bindings.

Example

This script draws a simple solar eclipse simulation:

```
proc getCirclePos { canvas tagOrId } {
    set coords [$canvas coords $tagOrId]
    set x [expr {([lindex $coords 2] + \
                  [lindex $coords 0])/2}]
    set y [expr {([lindex $coords 3] + \
                  [lindex $coords 1])/2}]
    return [list $x $y]
}

proc setCirclePos { canvas tagOrId center } {
    set currentPos [getCirclePos $canvas $tagOrId]
    set deltaX [expr {(-1 * \
                       [lindex $currentPos 0]) + \
                       [lindex $center 0]}]
    set deltaY [expr {(-1 * \
                       [lindex $currentPos 1]) + \
                       [lindex $center 1]}]
    $canvas move $tagOrId $deltaX $deltaY
}

proc distance { pt1 pt2 } {
    set x [expr {[lindex $pt2 0] - \
                 [lindex $pt1 0]}]
    set y [expr {[lindex $pt2 1] - \
                 [lindex $pt1 1]}]
    set d [expr {hypot($x,$y)}]
    return $d
}

# Create a canvas with a 200x150 view.
canvas .c -height 150 -width 200 \
       -background skyblue
pack .c

# Add a scrollregion so we can put (0,0) in a
# convenient place
```

```
.c configure -scrollregion {-400 -400 400 400}
# Scroll the region to move the origin where we
# want it.
.c yview moveto 0.0
set scrollregion [.c cget -scrollregion]
set viewWidth [.c cget -width]
set scrollWidth \
        [expr {[lindex $scrollregion 2] - \
               [lindex $scrollregion 0]}]
set offLeft [expr {($scrollWidth - $viewWidth)/2}]
.c xview moveto [expr {double($offLeft) / \
                       $scrollWidth}]

set earth [.c create oval 300 300 -300 -300 \
        -fill darkgreen -outline darkgreen \
        -tags earth]

set sun [.c create oval 10 10 -10 -10 \
        -fill yellow -outline gray -tags sun]
setCirclePos .c sun [list -200 -375]

set moon [.c create oval 10 10 -10 -10 \
        -fill gray -outline lightgray -tags moon]
setCirclePos .c moon [toCart [list 375 -1.5]]

proc animation { } {
    global stopAnimation
    set r 10
    set moonCoords [getCirclePos .c moon]
    set moonX [lindex $moonCoords 0]
    set moonY [lindex $moonCoords 1]
    .c configure -background skyblue

    set eclipse 0
    set theta1 [expr {int(-120 * 3.14152/2)}]
    set theta2 [expr {int( -60 * 3.14152/2)}]
    for {set theta $theta1} \
        { $theta < $theta2 } \
        {incr theta} {
        if {[info exists stopAnimation]} {
            unset stopAnimation
            return
        }
        setCirclePos .c sun \
            [toCart [list 375 \
```

```
                    [expr {double($theta)/100}]]]
        set close [.c find closest $moonX $moonY \
                    $r moon]
        if {[lsearch [.c gettags $close] sun] != \
                    -1} {
            set distance \
                [distance [getCirclePos .c sun] \
                        [getCirclePos .c moon]]
            set rgb [winfo rgb . skyblue]
            set overlap [expr {$distance / \
                            (2*$r)}]
            set R [expr {int([lindex $rgb 0] * \
                        $overlap)}]
            set G [expr {int([lindex $rgb 1] * \
                        $overlap)}]
            set B [expr {int([lindex $rgb 1] * \
                        $overlap)}]
            set color [format "#%3.3x%3.3x%3.3x" \
                        $R $G $B]
        } else {
            set color skyblue
        }
        .c configure -background $color
        update
        after 200
    }
}

.c bind moon <ButtonPress-1> animation
.c bind sun <ButtonPress-1> \
        [list set ::stopAnimation 1]
```

case

NOTE: **case** is deprecated. Use **switch**, which provides the same control function, with more flexible and powerful matching rules.

The **case** command executes one of several scripts based on a value. (See also **switch**; **string**.) It takes the following forms:

case *string ?in? patList body ?patList body ... ?*

case *string ?in?* { *patList body ?patList body ... ?* }

The arguments are as follows:

body
A script to evaluate if the corresponding *patList* matches *string*.

patList
A list of one or more patterns to test for a match. Matching is done the same as for **string match**. *patList* may be **default**, in which case the corresponding body is executed if no other pattern matches *string*.

string
The value to match against each *patList*.

case *string ?in?*
patList body ?patList body ... ?

Matches *string* against each *patList* in turn and, if a match is found, evaluates the corresponding *body*. Variable substitution is done on each *patList* and *body*.

RETURNS   The value, if any, returned by evaluating *body*, or an empty string if no *patList* matches *string*.

case *string ?in?*
{ *patList body ?patList body ... ?* }

Matches *string* against each *patList* in turn and, if a match is found, evaluates the corresponding *body*.

The braces around the list of *patList* and *body* pairs suppresses variable substitution but allows for flexible and readable formatting of the *patList* and *body*.

RETURNS   The value, if any, returned by evaluating *body*, or an empty string if no *patList* matches *string*.

catch

The **catch** command detects errors and allows controlled recovery. (See also **break**; **continue**; **error**; **return**.) It takes the following form:

> **catch** *script ?varName?*

The arguments are as follows:

script
Script to evaluate and check for errors.

varName
Name of variable to hold return value from script, or to hold the error message if an error is raised.

RETURNS   One of the following codes:

Code	Meaning
0	No error has occurred in *script*. The named variable contains the result of evaluating *script*.
1	*script* has generated an error. The named variable contains an error message.
2	*script* has invoked a return. The named variable contains the value returned by *script*.
3	*script* has invoked **break**. The named variable is set to an empty string.
4	*script* has invoked **continue**. The named variable is set to an empty string.
other	A user-defined error code (e.g., generated with **return -code 99**).

Example

```
if { [catch {open $inputFile r} fid] } {
    puts "Could not open $inputFile for\
          reading\n$fid"
} else {
    set contents [read $fid]
    close $fid
}
```

The **cd** command changes the current directory. (See also **pwd**.) It takes the following form:

   cd *?dirName?*

The arguments are as follows:

dirName
Directory to change to. If not specified, *dirName* defaults to the user's home directory (as specified in **env(HOME)**).

The **checkbutton** command creates and manipulates checkbutton widgets. (See also **button**; **radiobutton**.)

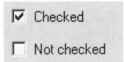

Checkbutton Options

Checkbutton widgets recognize the following standard widget options. (See the Appendix for a complete list of standard widget options and their meanings.)

activebackground	cursor	highlightthickness	text
activeforeground	disabledforeground	image	takefocus
anchor	font	justify	textvariable
background	foreground	padx	underline
bitmap	highlightbackground	pady	wraplength
borderwidth	highlightcolor	relief	

In addition, checkbutton widgets recognized the following widget-specific options:

-command *script*
Specifies a script to associate with checkbutton invocation, typically bound to clicking the checkbutton with mouse button 1. The checkbutton's global variable will be updated before the command is invoked.

-height *height*
The desired height of the checkbutton in either screen units (when an image is specified) or lines of text (if button text is specified). If this option is omitted, Tk computes the correct height from the image or text dimensions.

-indicatoron *boolean*
Specifies whether or not an indicator should be drawn for the checkbutton. If the value for this option is false, no indicator is drawn, the relief option is ignored, and the text of the checkbutton is sunken or raised to indicate the checkbutton's state.

-offvalue *value*
Specifies the value to be stored in the checkbutton's global variable when the checkbutton is off (deselected). The default value is 0.

-onvalue *value*
Specifies the value to be stored in the checkbutton's global variable when the checkbutton is on (selected). The default value is 1.

-selectcolor *color*
Specifies a background color to use when the checkbutton is on (selected). If **indicatoron** is true, this is the color used to fill the indicator. If **indicatoron** is false, this is the color used for the entire checkbutton background when the checkbutton is on (selected) and in place of **background** and **activebackground**. If the select color is an empty string, no special color is used to specify selection.

NOTE: On Microsoft Windows systems, this color is used as the background for the indicator regardless of state.

NOTE: On Macintosh systems, this option is ignored.

-selectimage *image*
If **-image** is specified, this option may be used to specify an image to be displayed when the checkbutton is on (selected).

-state *state*
Specifies the state of the checkbutton. Possible values for *state* are the following:

- **normal**   The checkbutton is drawn with the colors specified in *foreground* and *background*, and the checkbutton will respond to mouse clicks.

- **active**   The checkbutton is drawn with the colors specified in *activeForeground* and *activeBackground*. This setting corresponds to the checkbutton state when the mouse pointer is over the checkbutton, and is not usually set programmatically.

- **disabled**   The checkbutton is drawn with the colors specified in *disabledForeground* and *disabledBackground*, and the checkbutton will not respond to mouse clicks.

-variable *variable*
Specifies the name of the global variable to set to indicate the selection state of the checkbutton. If not specified, the variable defaults to the name of the checkbutton within its parent. For example, the checkbutton **.dialog.cb1** would set the global variable **cb1**.

-width *width*
The desired width of the checkbutton in either screen units (when an image is specified) or characters (if button text is specified). If this option is omitted, Tk computes the correct width from the image or text dimensions.

Checkbutton Commands

Checkbutton widgets respond to the **cget** and **configure** standard widget commands. (See the Appendix for details.) In addition, checkbutton widgets respond to the following widget-specific commands:

pathName deselect
Deselects (turns off) the checkbutton and sets its global variable to *offvalue*.

pathName flash
Redisplays the checkbutton several times, alternating between active and normal colors. This command is ignored if the checkbutton is disabled.

pathName invoke
Invokes the script associated with the checkbutton, if there is one. This command is ignored if the checkbutton is disabled.

RETURNS The value of the script associated with the checkbutton, or an empty string if there is no script associated with the checkbutton.

pathName select
Selects (turns on) the checkbutton and sets its global variable to *onvalue*.

pathName toggle
Toggles the selection state of the checkbutton and sets its global variable to reflect the new state.

Default Bindings

Checkbuttons are created with bindings that make them behave as expected, consistent with the user interface conventions on each platform. Specifically:

- A button is active when the mouse pointer is over it.

NOTE: On Microsoft Windows systems, the button is only active if mouse button 1 has been pressed.

- The checkbutton selection state toggles and its command is invoked when mouse button 1 is clicked and released over the button, or when the button has input focus and the SPACEBAR is pressed.
- The checkbutton is invoked when mouse button 1 is clicked and released over the checkbutton, or when the checkbutton has input focus and the SPACEBAR is pressed.

NOTE: On Microsoft Windows systems, when the checkbutton has input focus, + or = selects the button, and - deselects it.

Example

```
set cb [checkbutton .cb1 -text "Click me" \
        -variable click -onvalue tick
        -offvalue tock ]
```

Programmer's Tip: *Some of the default bindings on*
checkbutton *widgets are provided through procs. These
procs include* ***tkCheckRadioDown, tkCheckRadioEnter,*** *and*
tkCheckRadioInvoke. *These commands are not of general interest
and thus are not documented in this Reference. The* ***bind, info
args,*** *and* ***info body*** *commands can be used to explore the use and
implementation of these commands.*

2

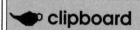

The **clipboard** command manipulates the Tk clipboard. (See also
selection.) It takes the following forms:

> **clipboard clear** *?-***displayof** *window?*

> **clipboard append** *?-***displayof** *window? ?-***format** *format?
> ?-***type** *type? ?--? data*

The arguments are as follows:

data
Data to add to append to the clipboard.

format
The format in which the data should be stored, such as **STRING**,
INTEGER, **ATOM**, or **PIXEL**. If **-format** is not specified, *format*
defaults to **STRING**.

NOTE: *format* is relevant only when putting data on the
clipboard, to be accessed by non-Tk applications. Tk converts all
data to strings when it is retrieved.

type
The type of data being placed on the clipboard, such as
FILENAME, **STRING**, or **TIMESTAMP**. In other words, how
data should be interpreted. If **-type** is not specified, *type* defaults
to **STRING**.

window
The Tk window whose display's clipboard should be accessed.

clipboard clear *?-displayof window?*

Claims ownership of the clipboard for *window*'s display and removes the current contents. *window* defaults to "." if **-displayof** is not specified.

clipboard append *?-displayof window? ?-format format? ?-type type? ?--? data*

Claims ownership of the clipboard for *window*'s display and appends *data* to it in the form given by *type* and with a representation given by *format*.

ERROR   Raises an error if *format* is different from that of the data appended to the clipboard since the last **clipboard clear**.

Example

```
# Clear the clipboard
clipboard clear
# Put some text on the clipboard
clipboard append -- \
        "This text can be pasted into\
         other applications."
```

Compatibility

For UNIX systems, values for *type* and *format* are documented at length in Section 2 of the *Inter-Client Communications Conventions Manual* (ICCCM).

clock

The **clock** command reads the system clock and manipulates time values. (See also **file**; **time**.) It takes the following forms:

clock clicks

clock format *clockValue* ?-**format** *formatString*? ?-**gmt** *gmt*?

clock scan *dateString* ?-**base** *clockValue*? ?-**gmt** *gmt*?

clock seconds

The arguments are as follows:

clockValue
An integer time value, such as that returned by **clock scan**, **clock seconds**, or the **file mtime**.

dateString
A string representing a date and/or time.

formatString
A string specifying how the *clockValue* should be formatted.

gmt
A boolean value indicating whether Greenwich Mean Time should be used in processing.

clock clicks

Retrieves a high-resolution value, which should be used only for relative measurement of elapsed time.

RETURNS   A system-dependent integer value.

clock format *clockValue* ?-format *formatString*? ?-gmt *gmt*?

Converts *clockValue* to a human-readable string according to *format. format* consists of text to be copied literally to the output and one or more time field specifiers. These fields consist of " % " (a percent sign) followed by a letter specifying what should be substituted in the field. (See the upcoming description of clock fields.) If -**format** is not specified, *format* defaults to "%a %b %d %H:%M:%S %Z %Y". If -**gmt** is not specified, *gmt* defaults to false.

If *gmt* is true, the time is formatted as the equivalent time in GMT. For example, using the format string "%T %Z", a *clockValue* that

formats as "19:27:07 Eastern Standard Time" with *gmt* would format
as "00:27:07 GMT" with *gmt* true.

RETURNS   A string containing *clockValue* formatted as requested.

Table 2-8 lists the format characters and their meanings:

Format Character	Substituted Value
%	A literal percent sign
a	Abbreviated weekday name (Mon, Tue, etc.)
A	Full weekday name (Monday, Tuesday, etc.)
b	Abbreviated month name (Jan, Feb, etc.)
B	Full month name
c	Locale-specific date and time
d	Day of month (01-31)
D	Date as %m/%d/%y (not available on all platforms)
e	Day of month without leading zeros (1-31) (not available on all platforms)
H	Hour in 24-hour format (00-23)
h	Abbreviated month name
I	Hour in 12-hour format (01-12)
j	Day of year (001-366)
m	Month number (01-12)
M	Minute (00-59)
n	A literal newline (not available on all platforms)
p	A.M./P.M. indicator
r	Time as %I:%M:%S %p (not available on all platforms)
R	Time as %H:%M (not available on all platforms)
S	Seconds (00-59)
t	A literal tab character (not available on all platforms)
T	Time as %H:%M:%S (not available on all platforms)
U	Week of year (01-52); Sunday is the first day of the week
w	Weekday number (Sunday=0)

Table 2-8.   Clock Format Characters

Format Character	Substituted Value
W	Week of year (01-52); Monday is the first day of the week[1]
x	Locale-specific date format
X	Locale-specific time format
y	Year without century (00-99)
Y	Year with century (e.g., 2001)
Z	Time zone name (e.g., Eastern Standard Time)

[1] %W is not quite an ISO 8601 week number. ISO week numbers can range from 01 to 53.

Table 2-8. Format Characters *(continued)*

clock scan *dateString* ?-base *clockValue*? ?-gmt *gmt*?

Converts *dateString* to an integer clock value, such as that returned by **clock seconds**. If *dateString* does not contain date information, the date portion of *clockValue* is added to the result of converting *dateString*. If **-base** is not specified, *clockValue* defaults to the current time. If **-gmt** is not specified, *gmt* defaults to false. If *gmt* is true, *dateString* is interpreted as a time in GMT, and the clock value returned is adjusted to local time after conversion.

dateString consists of one or more date, time, and relative time fields that are processed as follows:

1. Any absolute date or time (e.g., "13 February 2009" or "8:05") is converted. Midnight (00:00) is used if no time is specified. The current date is used if no date is specified.

2. Day-of-week specifications are added.

3. Relative-time specifications are applied.

4. A correction is applied for the possible change in daylight savings time between the current date and the converted date.

Date fields must include month and day and may optionally include a year. The following formats are recognized:

```
%m/%d
%m/%d/%y
%b %d
%b %d %y
%d %b
%d %b %y
%a %d %b %y
```

In addition, %A may be substituted for %a, %B for %b, and %Y for %y. Refer to Table 2-7 for the meanings of the field specifiers.

NOTE: The first two formats in the preceding list are American-format dates. **clock scan** assumes that 02/06 is February 6, not June 2. Also, month and day names are in English.

Time fields must include an hour and may include minutes and seconds. The following formats are recognized:

```
%I %p
%I:%M %p
%I:%M:%S %p
%H
%H:%M
%H:%M:%S
%I%M %P
%H%M
```

In addition, a time zone may be appended to all of the preceding formats. This time zone is not equivalent to the output of %Z; it's a three-letter abbreviation, such as EST, GMT, etc.

Relative time fields provide flexible, natural computation of time and date values in the format *number units* with modifiers. *units* is one of **year**, **fortnight**, **month**, **week**, **day**, **hour**, **minute**, **min**, **second**, or **sec**. Valid modifiers are **tomorrow**, **yesterday**, **today**, **now**, **last**, **this**, **next**, and **ago**.

Example

```
# How many seconds have elapsed since midnight?
puts [expr {[clock scan now] - \
            [clock scan 00:00]}]
# When is noon next Wednesday?
puts [clock scan "12:00 next Wednesday"]
```

clock seconds

Retrieves the current system time and date.

RETURNS A system-dependent integer number of seconds since an unspecified epoch. This value can be converted to human-readable form with **clock format** or used for relative time calculations.

close

The **close** command closes a channel opened with **open** or **socket**. (See also **open**; **socket**; **fconfigure**; **fileevent**; **interp**.) It takes the following form:

    close *channelId*

The arguments are as follows:

channelId
A channel identifier returned by a call to **open** or **socket**. Before closing, buffered output is flushed and buffered input is discarded. If the channel is blocking, **close** does not return until the buffered output has been flushed. If the channel is nonblocking, **close** returns immediately, and data is flushed and the channel closed in the background. If *channelId* is open for a command pipeline, close raises an error if the command pipeline wrote to stderr or had a nonzero status return. Any event handlers set with **fileevent** are removed from the channel.

Example

```
# Open a file, read it, and close the channel
set fid [open somefile.txt r]
set contents [read $fid]
close $fid
# Run a program, wait for it to complete and
# check its exit status
set fid [open "|someProg" r]
set output [read $fid]
```

```
if { [catch {close $fid} status] } {
    puts stderr \
        "someProg had a problem.\n\t$status"
}
```

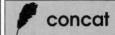

concat

The **concat** command concatenates two or more values lists to produce a new list. (See also **append**; **list**; **lappend**.) It takes the following form:

    concat *?arg arg ... ?*

The arguments are as follows:

arg
Value to include in resultant list. If *arg* is a string, leading and trailing spaces are removed before adding it to the list.

RETURNS   If no arguments are given, an empty string. Otherwise, a list made by concatenating all the arguments into a single list.

Example

```
concat foo [list bar baz] {{x y z}}
```

builds a four-element list:

```
foo bar baz {x y z}
```

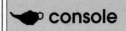

console

The **console** command controls the wish console window on Macintosh and Microsoft Windows systems. It takes the following forms:

    console eval *script*

    console show
    console hide

console title
console title *title*

The arguments are as follows:

script
Script to evaluate

title
The title for the console window.

console eval *script*

Evaluates *script* in the context of the console. This is an undocumented command of limited usefulness. However, one very useful application is to manipulate the console window, as in this example:

```
console eval {
    .console configure -font {-family courier}
}
```

The **.console** widget is a text widget. (See the **Text** entry or a list of configuration options for text widgets.)

console show

Displays the wish console. This is like **wm deiconify**, if the console were a normal Tk toplevel window.

console hide

Removes the wish console from the display. This is like **wm withdraw**, if the console were a normal Tk toplevel window.

console title

Retrieves the current console window title.

RETURNS   A string containing the console window title.

console title *title*

Sets the console window title to *title*.

Compatibility

The **console** command is available only on Macintosh and Microsoft Windows systems.

The **continue** command skips the remainder of the current iteration of a loop created with commands such as **foreach** and **while**, or the remainder of a script assigned to a Tk event with **bind**. (See also **bind**, **catch**; **for**; **foreach**; **return**; **while**.) It takes the following form:

    continue

The arguments are as follows:

None.

Example

```
# Total the positive numbers in a list
set sum 0
foreach n { 1 -2 3 -4 5 } {
    if { $n < 0 } {
        # Get the next number
        continue
    }
    incr sum $n
}
```

The **dde** command provides access to Microsoft Windows Dynamic Data Exchange (DDE). (See also **send**; **tk**; **winfo**.) It takes the following forms:

> **dde eval** *topic arg ?arg ... ?*
> *dde* **execute** *?-async? service topic data*
> **dde poke** *service topic data*
> **dde request** *service topic item*
> **dde servername** *?topic?*
> **dde services** *service topic*

NOTE: **dde poke** was added at version 8.2.

The arguments are as follows:

arg
Part of a script to evaluate.

data
Data for the server to act upon in the topic. For Tcl and many other applications, *data* is a script or macro to process.

item
Item to retrieve the value of.

service
The name of a DDE server, such as "TclEval", "NETSCAPE", or "WinWord".

topic
The name of the topic on the server. For file-oriented applications, this is usually a filename. For Tcl, this is an interpreter name as set with **dde servername**.

dde eval *topic arg ?arg ... ?*

Concatenates *args* and sends them to the Tcl interpreter specified by *topic* for evaluation.

RETURNS The result of evaluating the *args* in *topic*.

ERROR   Raises an error if evaluating *args* in *topic* raises an error.

Example
```
package require dde
dde eval wish81 {.b configure \
        -text "New button text"}
```

dde execute ?-async? *service topic data*

Sends *data* to *service* to be executed in *topic*.

ERROR   Raises an error if *service* or *topic* is invalid.

If **-async** is *not* specified, raises an error if *service* fails to
process *data*.

dde poke *service topic data*

Sends *data* to *service* for processing in *topic*.

ERROR   Raises an error if *service* or *topic* is invalid.

dde request *service topic item*

Requests the value of *item* in *topic* from *service*.

RETURNS   The value of *item*.

ERROR   Raises an error if *service*, *topic*, or *item* is invalid. This
could happen, for example, if you were to request the value of an
undefined variable from another Tcl interpreter.

Example
```
package require dde
# View a file in Netscape
dde request NETSCAPE WWW_ShowFile \
        "c:\\somepage.html"
# Get a value from another interpreter.
if {[catch {dde request TclEval wish81 someVar} \
        value]} {
    error "someVar is not defined in wish81"
}
```

dde servername

Retrieve the server name for the interpreter.

RETURNS   A server name.

dde servername *topic*

Set the server name to *topic*.

dde services *service topic*

Retrieves a list of services and topics currently available.

RETURNS   A list of lists. Each element is a two-element list consisting of a service and a topic. Here is an example:

```
{{TclEval Tk} {TclEval wish81}…}
```

If *service* and *topic* are both empty strings, the list includes all topics in all services. If *service* is an empty string and *topic* is not, the list includes all services with *topic*. If *service* is not an empty string and *topic* is, the list includes all topics for *service*. If no matches exist for the specified *service* and *topic*, the list may be empty.

Tcl Interpreters and DDE Services

DDE communication requires specification of a *service name* and a *topic*. Any Tcl interpreter that provides DDE services becomes part of the **TclEval** service and must provide its own topic. Here is an example:

```
package require dde
dde servername [tk appname]
```

A list of other Tcl interpreters which may process DDE commands can be retrieved with **dde services**:

```
proc tclServers { } {
    set servers {}
    foreach server [dde services TclEval {}] {
        set service [lindex $server 0]
```

```
        set topic [lindex $server 1]
        if {[string equal $service TclEval]} {
            lappend servers $topic
        }
    }
    return $servers
}
```

When Tcl processes a **dde eval** command, the args are concatenated and passed to the interpreter named by *topic* for evaluation.

When Tcl processes a **dde request** command, the value of the variable named by *data* in the interpreter named by *topic* is returned. The variable name **$TCLEVAL$EXECUTE$RESULT** is reserved, and requests for its value will give unpredictable results.

To run a script in another interpreter and get the script's result, save the value in a variable and retrieve its value with **dde request**, as in this example:

```
dde eval wish81 {set x 3}
set myX [dde request TclEval wish81 x]
```

Example

```
# View a web page with Netscape's browser,
# if possible. Try to start Netscape Communicator
# if it's not running
if {[llength [dde services NETSCAPE {}]] == 0} {
    set fullPath [auto_execok netscape.exe]
    if {[llength $fullPath] == 0} {
        error "Could not find a browser."
    }
    eval exec $fullPath &
}
dde request NETSCAPE WWW_OpenURL www.scriptics.com
```

Compatibility

The **dde** command is available only on Microsoft Windows systems.

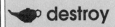 **destroy**

The **destroy** command destroys one or more widgets created with commands such as **button**, **text**, and **toplevel**. It takes the following form:

destroy *pathName ?pathName ... ?*

The arguments are as follows:

pathName
Path to a widget through the Tk widget hierarchy.

The widget specified by *pathName* and all widgets below it in the hierarchy are destroyed. The binding on the **<Destroy>** event, if any, is called for each widget. The binding is invoked <u>after</u> the widget is destroyed, so the widget and its contents are no longer available.

NOTE: In wish, destroying the default toplevel widget (.) exits the shell.

Example

```
# Create a new toplevel window for a message
toplevel .alert
# Put some content in it
label .alert.l \
      -text "Big Problem, click OK to continue"
button .alert.b -text "OK" \
       -command "destroy .alert"
pack .alert.l .alert.b
```

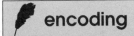 **encoding**

The **encoding** command manipulates encodings between Tcl's internal UTF8 Unicode characters and external representations, such as Shift-JIS. (See also **fconfigure**; **string**.) It takes the following forms:

> **encoding convertfrom** *?encoding? data*
> **encoding convertto** *?encoding? string*
> **encoding names**
> **encoding system** *?encoding?*

The arguments are as follows:

data
Data to convert from *encoding* format to internal, Unicode format.

encoding
The name of an encoding to use, such as **iso8859-2**, **shiftjis**, etc. Default encodings are found in the encoding subdirectory of the Tcl library directory (as returned by **[info library]**). If *encoding* is not loaded, Tcl looks for a file named *encoding*.**enc** in the encoding subdirectory of each directory listed in the **tcl_library** global variable.

string
Unicode string to convert to *encoding* format.

encoding convertfrom *?encoding? data*

Converts *data* from *encoding* to Unicode. If *encoding* is not specified, the current system encoding (as set with **encoding system**) is used.

RETURNS   The characters from *data*, converted to Unicode.

encoding convertto *?encoding? string*

Converts *string* from Unicode to *encoding*. If *encoding* is not specified, the current system encoding (as set with **encoding system**) is used.

RETURNS   The characters from *string*, converted to *encoding*.

encoding names

Retrieves a list of currently loaded encodings.

RETURNS   An unordered list of encoding names.

encoding system

Determines the current system encoding.

RETURNS   The name of the current system encoding.

encoding system *encoding*

Sets the system encoding to *encoding*.

Example

```
set jisString \
        [encoding convertto shifjis "foo bar baz"]
```

The **entry** command creates and manipulates entry widgets that may be used for a single line of editable text entry. (See also **text**.)

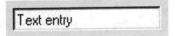

Entry Options

Entry widgets recognize the following standard widget options. (See the Appendix for a complete list of standard widget options and their meanings.)

background	highlightbackground	insertontime	selectforeground
borderwidth	highlightcolor	insertwidth	takefocus
cursor	highlightthickness	justify	textvariable
exportselection	insertbackground	relief	xscrollcommand
font	insertborderwidth	selectbackground	
foreground	insertofftime	selectborderwidth	

In addition, entry widgets recognize the following widget-specific options:

-show *string*

Specifies a character to show in place of the actual contents of the entry. This is useful for an entry that will contain a password or other secure information. If **-show** is specified, the first character of *string* is shown in place of the characters actually stored in the entry, and copying the value of the entry (for example, via the clipboard) copies the displayed characters, not the actual contents of the entry. If **-show** is not specified, characters are displayed as they are typed.

-state *state*

Specifies the state of the entry; either **normal** or **disabled**. If the state is **disabled**, no insertion cursor is displayed and the value may not be changed by user interaction or by script.

-width *characters*

Specifies an integer width for the entry, based on the average width of the characters in the font to be used in the entry. If *characters* is less than or equal to zero, the widget adjusts to hold its current contents only.

Entry Commands

Entry widgets respond to the **cget** and **configure** standard widget commands. (See the Appendix for details.) In addition, entry widgets respond to the following widget-specific commands:

> *pathName* **bbox** *index*
> *pathName* **delete** *first ?last?*
> *pathName* **get**
> *pathName* **icursor** *index*
> *pathName* **index** *index*
> *pathName* **insert** *index string*
> *pathName* **scan mark** *x*
> *pathName* **scan dragto** *x*
> *pathName* **selection adjust** *index*
> *pathName* **selection clear**
> *pathName* **selection from** *index*
> *pathName* **selection present**
> *pathName* **selection range** *first last*
> *pathName* **selection to** *index*

pathName **xview**
pathName **xview** *viewoptions*

The arguments are as follows:

first
Text index of the first character to process. (See Table 2-9 for a list of entry text indices.)

index
A text index. (See Table 2-9 for a list of entry text indices.)

last
Text index of the last character to process. (See Table 2-9 for a list of entry text indices.)

string
Text to insert into the entry.

viewoptions
Options for setting the view. (For detais, see the following section on the **view** command.)

x
Position relative to the left side of the entry.

Entry Text Indices
Many entry widget commands take one or more *text indices* as arguments. The text index may take one of the forms listed in Table 2-8.

Programmer's Tip: *entry widgets share many commands with text objects in a canvas. Compare the index forms in Table 2-9 with those for text objects on a canvas.*

pathName bbox index
Retrieves the coordinates of a bounding box that includes the character at the specified *index*. The coordinates may refer to an area outside the bounds of the entry if the specified character is scrolled out of view.

RETURNS   A list of four coordinates: {x y w h}.

pathName delete first ?last?
Deletes the range of characters from *first* to *last* from *pathName*. If *last* is not specified, it defaults to *first* +1, so a single character is deleted.

Text Index	Value
number	A character position within the entry. 0 refers to the first character, 1 refers to the second character, etc. *number* must be a decimal number. Any number less than 0 is treated as 0. Any number greater than the length of the text in the entry is treated as the length of the text.
anchor	The anchor point for the selection, as set with the **selection from** and **selection adjust** widget commands. The anchor point defaults to 0 until one of those commands is called.
end	The character position just after the last character in the object.
insert	The character position just after the insertion cursor.
sel.first	The first character of the selected text, if any.[1]
sel.last	The last character of the selected text, if any.[1]
@*number*	The character at the point x relative to the left side of the entry widget.

[1]This form raises an error if the entry does not have any selected text.

Table 2-9.   Entry Text Indices

pathName get
Retrieves the current contents of the entry.

RETURNS   A string containing the text of the entry.

pathName icursor *index*
Positions the text insertion cursor just before *index*.

pathName index *index*
Normalizes *index*. For example, if entry .e included 13 characters, then **[.e index end]** would return 13.

RETURNS   A decimal number corresponding to *index*.

pathName insert *index string*
Inserts *string* just before the specified *index*.

pathName scan mark *x*

Records *x* and the coordinates of the current view for use by future **scan dragto** entry widget commands. This is usually bound to a mouse button clicking the entry.

pathName scan dragto *x*

Adjusts the entry view by ten times the difference between *x* and the coordinate of the last **scan mark** entry widget command. This is usually bound to mouse motion events on the entry and is used to implement a high-speed scrolling of the text within the view.

pathName selection adjust *index*

Adjusts the text selection in the entry by moving the end of the selection nearest *index* to be at *index*. The other end of the selection is made the anchor for future **selection to** widget commands.

For example, if .e were an entry containing five characters, and its current selection included the second and third characters (index 1 to index 2), then [**.e selection adjust 4**] would change the selection to include the second to fifth characters, and [**.e selection adjust 3**] would further change the selection to include only the fourth and fifth characters, leaving the **selection to** anchor at the end of the text.

If the entry doesn't have the selection, this command is the same as **selection to**.

pathName selection clear

Clears the selection if it is currently in the entry. If the entry doesn't currently have the selection, this command has no effect.

pathName selection from *index*

Sets the anchor for future **selection to** widget commands to be just before *index*.

NOTE: This does not change the current selection; it just changes the anchor for future *selection to commands*.

pathName selection present

Determines whether the entry has the selection.

RETURNS   1 if the entry has the selection; 0 otherwise.

pathName selection range *first last*

Sets the text selection to include all characters from the index *first* to the index *last*. If *first* is at or before *last*, this command is the same as **selection clear**.

pathName selection to *index*

Sets the text selection in the entry to include characters from the selection anchor point (set with **selection adjust** or **selection from**) to *index*. If the entry does not have the selection, the most recent anchor point specified will be used.

pathName xview

Retrieves the view coordinates of the entry.

RETURNS   A view coordinate list. These are the same values passed to scroll bars via the **-xscrollcommand** option.

pathName xview *viewoptions*

Sets the *X* coordinates of the entry view. *options* may be any of the following:

Option	Purpose
index	Adjusts the view so that the character specified by *index* is displayed at the left edge of the entry.
moveto *fraction*	Adjusts the view so that *fraction* of the text in the entry is off the left of the view. *fraction* is a view coordinate.
scroll *number units*	Adjusts the view *number units*. *number* must be an integer. *units* is **units** or **pages**: **units** The view adjusts by *number* times the average width of characters in the entry. **pages** The view adjusts *number* pages. The size of a page is platform-dependent. On Microsoft Windows systems, it is half the entry width; on UNIX systems, it is 9/10 the entry width. Negative values of *number* adjust the view to the right (making characters off the left of the view visible) and vice versa for positive values.

Default Bindings

NOTE: If the entry is disabled, the view can be adjusted and text can be selected, but no insertion cursor is displayed and no modification (e.g., typing, cutting, or pasting) is allowed.

Entry widgets are created with bindings that make them behave as expected, consistent with the user interface conventions on each platform. Specifically:

Mouse Bindings

- Clicking mouse button 1 clears the selection and sets the insertion cursor just before the character under the mouse pointer.

- Double-clicking mouse button 1 selects the word under the mouse pointer and sets the insertion cursor to the beginning of that word.

- Dragging with mouse button 1 pressed selects from the insertion cursor to the current position of the mouse pointer. The selection is expanded by characters or words, depending on how the selection was started (as described in the preceding paragraphs). If the mouse pointer crosses the left or right side of the entry, the entry scrolls to reveal text, if any, out of view on that side of the entry.

- Dragging with mouse button 1 and the SHIFT key pressed expands the selection by characters or words, depending on how the selection was started (as described in the preceding paragraphs).

- Clicking mouse button 1 with the CTRL key pressed positions the insertion cursor without affecting the selection.

- Triple-clicking mouse button 1 selects all the text in the entry and sets the insertion cursor before the first character.

- Clicking mouse button 2 in the entry pastes the selection (from another widget or the clipboard) at the position of the mouse pointer.

- Dragging with mouse button 2 pressed scrolls the text in the entry.

Keyboard Bindings

- Typing printable characters inserts those characters in the entry at the insertion cursor.

The insertion cursor may be manipulated with the following keys:

- Pressing the LEFT ARROW or RIGHT ARROW key moves the insertion cursor left or right.

- Pressing the HOME key moves the insertion cursor to the beginning of the entry.

- Pressing the END key moves the insertion cursor to the end of the entry.

When moving the insertion cursor, the selection is affected as follows:

- If no modifier key is pressed, the selection is cleared and LEFT ARROW and RIGHT ARROW move the cursor by a single character.

- If the SHIFT key is pressed, the selection is expanded to follow the insertion cursor.

- If the CTRL key is pressed, LEFT ARROW and RIGHT ARROW move by words instead of characters.

  For example, SHIFT-CTRL-LEFT moves the cursor one word toward the beginning of the entry and expands the selection to include that word.

- Pressing SELECT or CTRL-SPACEBAR sets the selection anchor to the position of the insertion cursor.

- Pressing SHIFT-SELECT or SHIFT-CTRL-SPACEBAR adjusts the selection to the current position of the insertion cursor. If no selection was made, the text from the anchor to the insertion cursor is selected.

- Pressing CTRL-/ selects all text in the entry.

- Pressing CTRL-\ clears the selection in the entry.

- Pressing F16 (labeled COPY on some workstation keyboards) or CTRL-C copies the selection, if any, to the clipboard.

- Pressing F20 (labeled CUT on some workstation keyboards) or CTRL-X copies the selection, if any, to the clipboard and deletes it from the entry.

- Pressing F18 (labeled PASTE on some workstation keyboards) or CTRL-V inserts the contents of the clipboard at the position of the insertion cursor.

- Pressing DELETE deletes the selection, if any, or the character to the right of the insertion cursor if no selection was made.

- Pressing BACKSPACE deletes the selection, if any, or the character to the left of the insertion cursor if no selection was made.

NOTE: In addition to the preceding key bindings, entry widgets support most emacs key bindings. For example, CTRL-A is equivalent to Home, and Ctrl-t transposes the two characters to the right and left of the insertion cursor.

Example

```
# Create an entry that will show about 15
# characters
entry .e -width 15
# Put some text into it
.e insert end "This is a string that is longer\
               than the entry is wide"
# Make sure that the start of the string is
# visible.
.e xview 0
# Show the text starting in the middle of the
# string
.e xview moveto .5
# Select all the contents
.e selection range 0 end
```

Programmer's Tip: *Many of the default bindings on entry widgets are provided through procs. These procs include* **tkEntryAutoScan**, **tkEntryBackspace**, **tkEntryButton1**, **tkEntryClosestGap**, **tkEntryInsert**, **tkEntryKeySelect**, **tkEntryMouseSelect**, **tkEntryNextWord**, **tkEntryPaste**, **tkEntryPreviousWord**, **tkEntrySeeInsert**, **tkEntrySetCursor**, *and* **tkEntryTranspose**. *These commands are not of general interest and thus are not documented in this Reference. The* **bind**, **info args**, *and* **info body** *commands can be used to explore the use and implementation of these commands.*

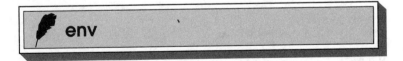

env

The **env** global variable is an array that provides read and write access to the script's environment. (See also **exec**.)

Macintosh

No system environment exists on the Macintosh, but Tcl creates an **env** array with the following entries:

APPLE_M_FOLDER
The path to the Apple Menu directory.

CP_FOLDER
The path to the control panels directory.

DESK_FOLDER
The path to the desktop directory.

EXT_FOLDER
That path to the system extensions directory.

LOGIN
The Chooser name of the Macintosh, as set in the File Sharing control panel.

PREF_FOLDER
The path to the preferences directory.

PRINT_MON_FOLDER
The path to the print monitor directory.

PWD
The path to the application's default directory.

SHARED_TRASH_FOLDER
The path to the network trash directory.

START_UP_FOLDER
The path to the startup directory.

SYS_FOLDER
The path to the system directory.

TRASH_FOLDER
The path to the trash directory.

USER
The Chooser name of the Macintosh. (This is the same as **LOGIN**.)

Additional variables can be added to **env** in two ways.
Environment entries may be added to a file named **Tcl Environment Variables** in the System Folder, or in a **STR#** resource

named **Tcl Environment Variables**. Each line of the file or resource is in the form:

```
VAR_NAME=var_data
```

Microsoft Windows

The system and user environments are copied into **env** as configured, except that **PATH** and **COMSPEC** always have uppercase array indices. That is, if the system configuration sets a variable named **pAtH**, this value will be found in **env(PATH)**.

Example
```
# Traverse the path
foreach dir [split $env(PATH) ";"] {
    processDir $dir
}
# Add the current directory to the path
append env(PATH) ";[pwd]"
```

 eof

The **eof** command tests for the end of data on a channel opened with **open** or **socket**. (See also **close**; **gets**; **open**; **read**; **socket**.) It takes the following form:

   eof *channelId*

The arguments are as follows:

channelId
A channel identifier returned by a call to **open** or **socket**.

RETURNS   1 if the end of the file has been reached; 0 otherwise.

ERRORS   Raises an error if *channelId* is not a valid channel.

Example

```
# Process a file line by line
set fid [open $dataFile r]
```

```
while { ! [eof $fid]} {
    processData [gets $fid]
}
close $fid
```

error

The **error** command raises an error that may be handled by **catch**. (See also **bgerror**; **catch**; **errorCode**; **errorInfo**; **return**.) It takes this form:

> **error** *message ?info? ?code?*

The arguments are as follows:

code
Value to be stored in the global variable **errorCode** for use by the caller. This can convey details of the error. Generally, this is a structured, machine-readable value that may be used in error handling code, whereas the *message* is intended to be human-readable. (See the following discussion of **errorCode** for details on how *code* should be formatted.) If no *code* is specified, it defaults to **NONE**.

info
Initial value for execution stack built by interpreter as error percolates up. When this **error** is caught, this information can be retrieved from the global variable **errorInfo**. If no *info* is specified, it defaults to an empty string.

message
Error message describing the problem

Description

When an error is raised, the Tcl interpreter moves up the call stack to the first **catch** command or to the top level of the call stack. As it goes, it appends information to the global variable **errorInfo**, which describes the context the error occurred in.

If no *info* is specified or if it is an empty string, **errorInfo** starts with

> *message*
>   while executing
> "error *message*"

with *message* filled in from the call to **error**. If *info* is supplied, it is used in place of these three lines.

As each level of the call stack is popped, the interpreter appends to **errorInfo** three lines, in this form:

> (procedure "*procname*" line *n*)
> invoked from within
> "sourceline"

procname, *n*, and *sourceline* are filled in from the context. Here is an example:

```
proc foo { {info ""} } {
    error "This is a foo error" $info
}
```

Invoking **foo** with no argument gives **errorInfo** the value:

```
This is a foo error
    while executing
"error "This is a foo error" $info"
    (procedure "foo" line 2)
    invoked from within
"foo "
```

Invoking **foo "This is some info"** gives **errorInfo** the following value:

```
This is some info
    (procedure "foo" line 1)
    invoked from within
"foo "This is some info""
```

This is most useful when attempting to handle errors in code, like the following:

```
if {[catch {someCommand} status]} {
    set holdInfo $errorInfo
    ...try to fix it
    error $status $holdInfo
}
```

Example

```
# Try to open a temporary file, raise an error if
# all the names are used up
foreach suffix { 0 1 2 3 4 5 6 7 8 9 } {
    if { ! [file exists temp$suffix]} {
        set fid [open temp$suffix w]
        break
    }
}
# If we couldn't open a file, raise an error
if { ! [info exists fid] } {
    error "Could not open temporary file in [cwd]"
}
```

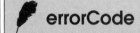

errorCode

The **errorCode** global variable is a list that contains formatted information about an error. (See also **bgerror**; **error**; **return**.)

When a core Tcl command generates an error, it sets **errorCode** to a value that is easily parsed to allow retrieval of information about the error event. The first element of **errorCode** is the class of error that occurred. The rest of the list can be processed based on the class. The following list shows **errorCode** formats for Tcl core commands. It is good practice to adopt a similar scheme for your application.

ARITH code msg

An arithmetic error occurred, such as an attempt to divide by zero in **expr**.

code
Specifies the precise error, with one of the following values:

- **DIVZERO**   Divide by zero
- **DOMAIN**   Domain error, such as acos(-3)
- **IOVERFLOW**   Integer overflow
- **OVERFLOW**   Floating-point overflow
- **UNKNOWN**   The cause of the error cannot be determined

msg
A human-readable description of the error.

CHILDKILLED pid sigName msg

A child process started with **exec** or **open** was killed because of a signal.

pid
The process's identifier (in decimal).

sigName
The symbolic name of the signal that caused the process to terminate; it will be one of the names from the include file signal.h, such as **SIGPIPE**.

msg
A human-readable message describing the signal, such as "Write on pipe with no readers" for **SIGPIPE**.

CHILDSTATUS pid code

A child process started with **exec** or **open** exited with a nonzero exit status.

pid
The process's identifier (in decimal).

code
The exit code returned by the process (in decimal).

CHILDSUSP pid sigName msg

A child process started with **exec** or **open** has been suspended because of a signal.

pid
The process's identifier (in decimal).

sigName
The symbolic name of the signal that caused the process to suspend; it will be one of the names from the include file signal.h, such as **SIGTTIN**.

msg
A human-readable message describing the signal, such as
"Background tty read" for **SIGTTIN**.

NONE

An error occurred and no additional information is available other
than the message returned with the error.

POSIX errName msg

An error occurred during a POSIX kernel call.

errName
The symbolic name of the error that occurred, such as **ENOENT**;
this will be one of the values defined in the include file errno.h.

msg
A human-readable message corresponding to *errName*, such as
"No such file or directory" for the **ENOENT**.

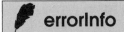
errorInfo

The **errorInfo** global variable is a string that contains a stack trace
built by the Tcl interpreter as an error is percolated up the call
stack. (See the preceding discussion of **error** for a detailed
discussion of how **errorInfo** is built and formatted; see also
bgerror; error; return.)

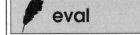
eval

The **eval** command concatenates its arguments and then evaluates
the result as a Tcl script. (See also **concat; uplevel; subst.**) It takes
the following form:

eval *arg ?arg ... ?*

The arguments are as follows:

arg
Part of the script to evaluate.

Tcl usually performs only one pass of substitution and evaluation on script source code, but forcing another level of evaluation sometimes is necessary, such as when building a list of arguments for another command, as shown in the following example.

2

RETURNS The value returned by the script.

ERROR Passes through any error raised by the script.

Example

```
# A basic proc
proc baseProc { a b c args } {
    ...
}
# Figures out a, b and c and manipulates args
# before calling baseProc
proc wrapperProc { args } {
    # The first wrong way to invoke baseProc.
    # This passes base proc four arguments
    # regardless of how long the args list is.
    baseProc aValue bValue cValue $args

    # The second wrong way to invoke baseProc
    # builds up the command as other results are
    # computed
    set cmd [list baseProc]
    # Compute the value of a to use
    set a "aValue"
    # Add the value of a to the command to invoke
    lappend cmd $a
    # Compute the values of b and c
    set b "bValue"
    set c "cValue"
    # Add the values of the fixed arguments to the
    # command
    lappend cmd $b $c
    # Process args
    ...
    # Now, evaluate the command
```

```
# This tries to invoke a command named
#     baseProc aValue bValue cValue
# and pass it a single argument, the value of
# args.
$cmd $args

# A third wrong way to invoke baseProc
# If wrapper was invoked with three arguments
# like:
#     wrapper arg1 arg2 arg3
# baseProc gets all of those arguments as one
# as if it were invoked directly with:
#     baseProc aValue bValue cValue \
#              {arg1 arg2 arg3}
# and baseProc will see args with a value
# like:
#     {{arg1 arg2 arg3}}
baseProc aValue bValue cValue $args

# The RIGHT way to invoke baseProc is to use
# eval to "flatten" the lists cmd and args.
# eval concatenates its arguments to make a
# string like:
#     baseProc aValue bValue cValue arg1 \
#              arg2 arg3
# Then calls the interpreter again. The
# interpreter parses "baseProc" as the command
# to invoke and passes it arguments aValue,
# bValue, cValue, etc. In baseProc,
# args will be the list {arg1 arg2 arg3}
eval $cmd $args
}
```

event

The **event** command manipulates and generates events. (See also **bind**.) It takes the following forms:

> **event add** *virtual sequence ?sequence ... ?*
> **event delete** *virtual ?sequence sequence ... ?*
> **event generate** *window event ?options?*
> **event info**
> **event info** *virtual*

The arguments are as follows:

event
An event specification as for the **bind** command.

options
Additional values to modify the event.

sequence
The sequence of events to associate with *virtual*. The events may be separated by white space, which is ignored. (See **bind** for more information.)

virtual
A virtual event specification, such as <<Paste>>. (See **bind** for more information.)

window
The path to a widget in the widget hierarchy or a window identifier, such as those returned by **winfo id**. This is the window that will receive the event.

event add *virtual sequence ?sequence ... ?*

Adds each *sequence* as a way to invoke the event *virtual*. Other existing *sequences* for *virtual* are not affected. *virtual* may be any string value surrounded by double angle brackets, as in <<**Copy**>>.

If a virtual event and a physical event (such as a key press) with the same sequence are bound to the same widget, the physical event takes precedence and the virtual event binding is not invoked.

ERROR   Raises an error if any *sequence* is invalid.

event delete *virtual ?sequence sequence ... ?*

Deletes each sequence as a way to invoke the event *virtual*. If no *sequence* is given, all sequences are removed. Any *sequence* not associated with *virtual* is ignored.

ERROR Raises an error if any *sequence* is invalid.

event generate *window event ?options?*

Generates *event* directed at *window*. *options* specifies additional data for the event. This data is substituted for % fields in the event bindings. Table 2-10 lists details of the event options.

ERROR Raises an error if *window* is invalid or an invalid option is specified.

Option	Field	Description
-above *window*	a	*window* is a widget path or a window ID. Valid for **Configure** events.
-borderwidth *size*	B	*size* is a screen distance. Valid for **Configure** events.
-button *number*	b	*number* is an integer. Valid for **ButtonPress** and **ButtonRelease** events.
-count *number*	c	*number* is an integer. Valid for **Expose** events.
-detail *detail*	d	*detail* is **NotifyAncestor**, **NotifyDetailNone**, **NotifyInferior**, **NotifyNonlinear**, **NotifyNonlinearVirtual**, **NotifyPointer**, **NotifyPointerRoot**, or **NotifyVirtual**. Valid for **Enter**, **Leave**, **FocusIn**, and **FocusOut** events.
-focus *boolean*	f	Valid for **Enter** and **Leave** events.
-height *size*	h	*size* is a screen distance. Valid for **Configure** events.
-keycode *number*	k	*number* is an integer. Valid for **KeyPress** and **KeyRelease** events.
-keysym *name*	K	*name* is a valid keysym name, such as **space** or **F1**. Valid for **KeyPress** and **KeyRelease** events.

Table 2-10. Event Generate Options

Option	Field	Description
-mode *notify*	m	*notify* is **NotifyNormal**, **NotifyGrab**, **NotifyUngrab**, or **NotifyWhileGrabbed**. Valid for **Enter**, **Leave**, **FocusIn**, and **FocusOut** events.
-override *boolean*	o	Valid for **Map**, **Reparent**, and **Configure** events.
-place *where*	p	*where* is **PlaceOnTop** or **PlaceOnBottom**. Valid for **Circulate** events.
-root *window*	R	*window* is a widget path or a window ID. Valid for **KeyPress**, **KeyRelease**, **ButtonPress**, **ButtonRelease**, **Enter**, **Leave**, and **Motion** events.
-rootx *coord*	X	*coord* is a screen distance. Valid for **KeyPress**, **KeyRelease**, **ButtonPress**, **ButtonRelease**, **Enter**, **Leave**, and **Motion** events.
-rooty *coord*	Y	*coord* is a screen distance. Valid for **KeyPress**, **KeyRelease**, **ButtonPress**, **ButtonRelease**, **Enter**, **Leave**, and **Motion** events.
-sendevent *boolean*	E	Valid for all events.
-serial *number*	#	*number* is an integer. Valid for all events.
-state *state*	s	*state* is an integer for **KeyPress**, **KeyRelease**, **ButtonPress**, **ButtonRelease**, **Enter**, **Leave**, and **Motion** events, and **VisibilityUnobstructed**, **VisibilityPartiallyObscured**, or **VisibilityFullyObscured** for **Visibility** events.
-subwindow *window*	S	*window* is a widget path or a window ID. Valid for **KeyPress**, **KeyRelease**, **ButtonPress**, **ButtonRelease**, **Enter**, **Leave**, and **Motion** events.

Table 2-10.   Event Generate Options *(continued)*

Option	Field	Description
-time *time*	t	*time* is an integer. Valid for **KeyPress, KeyRelease, ButtonPress, ButtonRelease, Enter, Leave, Motion,** and **Property** events.
-width *size*	w	*size* is a screen distance. Valid for **Configure** events.
-when *when*		*when* is **now, tail, head,** or **mark**: **now** The event is processed immediately. This is the default if **-when** is not specified. **tail** The event is placed at the end of Tcl's event queue. **head** The event is placed at the front of Tcl's event queue. **mark** The event is placed at the front of Tcl's event queue but behind other events added with **-when mark**. This can be used to put a series of events at the front of the queue without having to add them with **-when head** in reverse order.
-x *coord*	x	*coord* is a screen distance. Valid for **KeyPress, KeyRelease, ButtonPress, ButtonRelease, Motion, Enter, Leave, Expose, Configure, Gravity,** and **Reparent** events.
-y *coord*	y	*coord* is a screen distance. Valid for **KeyPress, KeyRelease, ButtonPress, ButtonRelease, Motion, Enter, Leave, Expose, Configure, Gravity,** and **Reparent** events.

Table 2-10. Event Generate Options *(continued)*

event info

Retrieves a list of all virtual events created with **event add**.

RETURNS A list of virtual event specifications, e.g., {<<Copy>>
<<Paste>> <<Cut>>}.

event info *virtual*

Retrieves a list of sequences bound to *virtual*.

RETURNS A list of event sequences, e.g., {<Control-Key-c>
<Control-Key-Insert>}.

Example

```
# A proc to respond to a virtual event only once
proc virtualBinding { virtualEvent } {
    # Print a message
    puts "Spring is here!"
    # Get rid of all associations for the virtual
    # event.
    event delete $virtualEvent
}
# An obscure mouse event
event add <<EasterEgg>> \
    <Control-Shift-Alt-Triple-ButtonPress-3>
# A keyboard alternative
event add <<EasterEgg>> <Alt-Triple-KeyPress-F1>
# What to do when either sequence occurs
bind . <<EasterEgg>> \
        [list virtualBinding <<EasterEgg>>]
```

 exec

NOTE: **exec** is not supported on the Macintosh. The **AppleScript**
command provides a means to run other applications on
the Macintosh.

The **exec** command combines its arguments into a process pipeline
and executes the result as a subprocess. (See also **open**.) It takes
this form:

  exec *?options? arg ?arg ... ?*

The arguments are as follows:

arg
A part of the process pipeline.

Options

-keepnewline
Retains the last newline in the output of the child program or programs. If not specified, the last newline is removed.

--
The last option. The argument following this will be treated as *arg* even if it starts with a - (a dash).

exec is used to execute one or more external programs in a process pipeline, much like commands entered at a system command prompt in a UNIX shell, or MS-DOS or Microsoft Windows Command Interpreter. Input and output for the processes can be redirected in most conventional ways plus some additional ways that provide better integration with the Tcl interpreter. (See the following section, "Input/Output Redirection," for details.)

NOTE: Unlike many UNIX shells, such as sh, csh, etc., Tcl's **exec** command does not replace the current process; it runs the pipeline as a subprocess and then returns to executing the script at the next line.

RETURNS   If the last *arg* is **&**, then the pipeline is executed in the background, and **exec** returns a list of process identifiers for the processes in the pipeline. **stdout** and **stderr** of the pipeline are directed to the script's **stdout** and **stderr**, unless they are redirected.

If the last *arg* is not **&**, and the output of the pipeline is not redirected, **exec** returns the output of the last process in the pipeline. The -**keepnewline** option controls whether or not this return value has a trailing newline character.

ERROR   Raises an error if any of the processes in the pipeline either:

- Exit abnormally, or are killed or suspended
- Write to **stderr**, and **stderr** is not redirected

The error message will include the pipeline's output, followed by error messages (if any) describing the abnormal termination, followed by the data (if any) written to stderr. The **errorCode** global variable will have more information about the abnormal termination.

Input/Output Redirection

Table 2-11 details the input/output redirection options for pipelines processed by **exec**. Generally, white space between an operator (for example, < or >>&) and the operand (a filename, channel, etc.) can be omitted.

Option	Purpose
I	Directs stdout from the preceding process to stdin of the following process.
I &	Directs stdout and stderr from the preceding process to stdin of the following process.
< *filename*	Opens the named file and uses it as stdin of the first process in the pipeline.
<@ *handle*	Directs the data read from *handle* to stdin of the first process in the pipeline. *handle* is an open channel, such as **stdin**, or a handle returned by **open** or **socket**.
<< *value*	Passes *value* as the stdin for the first process in the pipeline.
> *filename*	Opens the named file for writing and directs the stdout of the pipeline to the file. The previous contents of the file, if any, are lost.
2> *filename*	Opens the named file for writing and directs the stderr from all processes in the pipeline to the file. The previous contents of the file, if any, are lost.
>& *filename*	Opens the named file for writing and directs stdout of the pipeline and stderr of all processes in the pipeline to that file. The previous contents of the file, if any, are lost.
>> *filename*	Opens the named file for appending and directs stdout of the pipeline to that file, appending to existing contents.

Table 2-11. Input/Output Redirection Options

Option	Purpose
2>> *filename*	Opens the named file for appending and directs stderr from <u>all</u> processes in the pipeline to that file, appending to existing contents.
>>& *filename*	Opens the named file for appending and directs stdout of the pipeline and stderr of all processes in the pipeline to that file, appending to existing contents.
>@ *handle*	Directs stdout of the pipeline to *handle*. *handle* is an open channel, such as **stdout**, or a handle returned by **open** or **socket**.
2>@ *handle*	Directs stderr from all processes in the pipeline to *handle*. *handle* is a channel opened for writing, such as **stdout**, or a handle returned by **open** or **socket**.
>&@ *handle*	Directs stdout of the pipeline and stderr of all processes in the pipeline to *handle*. *handle* is a channel opened for writing, such as **stdout**, or a handle returned by **open** or **socket**.

Table 2-11.   Input/Output Redirection Options *(continued)*

Example

```
# Pass in-line data to prog1,
# Route prog1's stdout to prog2's stdin
# Route prog2's stdout to the open channel $fid.
exec prog1 | prog2 >@$fid << {
    This is input to prog1
    prog1 reads this text as if
    it was read from a file redirected to
    prog1's stdin.
}
```

Compatibility

Using **exec** on Microsoft Windows includes several restrictions:

- Reading from or writing to a socket with @< or @> does not work.

- The console in the wish shell does not provide stdin, stdout, or stderr to the process pipeline. Reading from stdin always results in an end-of-file condition. Data written to stdout and stderr is discarded.

- The path to an application used in a pipeline may be specified with forward or backward slashes, but arguments to applications in the pipeline will not be converted and should be specified as expected by the application.

- Long filenames are not recognized by 16-bit DOS or Microsoft Windows 3.x applications. Arguments to such program should be in 8.3 format.

- Two or more forward or backward slashes in a row in a path refer to a network path. For example, c://windows/system refers to the system directory on the machine named windows, not to the c:\windows\system directory. Use the **file join** command to combine parts of filenames and avoid this problem.

Programmer's Tip: *To execute Microsoft Windows Command Interpreter commands from Tcl, prepend $env(COMPSEC) /c to the list of args to **exec**.*

In Microsoft Windows NT, if a directory is not part of the program specification, **exec** looks for programs in the following directories, in order:

1. The directory from which the Tcl executable was loaded

2. The current directory

3. The Windows NT 32-bit system directory

4. The Windows NT 16-bit system directory

5. The Windows NT home directory

6. The directories listed on the path

If the program name as specified is not found, the search repeats, adding **.com**, **.exe**, and **.bat** to the name on each pass until a match is found or all possibilities have been exhausted.
On Microsoft Windows 95 and 98, if a directory is not part of the program specification, **exec** looks for programs in the following directories, in order:

1. The directory from which the Tcl executable was loaded

2. The current directory

3. The Windows 95 or 98 system directory

4. The Window 95 or 98 home directory

5. The directories listed on the path

If the program name as specified is not found, the search repeats, adding **.com**, **.exe**, and **.bat** to the name on each pass until a match is found or all possibilities have been exhausted.

exit

The **exit** command ends script execution. It takes the following form:

   exit *?returnCode?*

The arguments are as follows:

returnCode
Integer value to return as the interpreter's exit status. If no *returnCode* is specified, it defaults to 0.

expr

The **expr** command evaluates mathematical and logical expressions. (See also **if**; **while**.) It takes the following form:

   expr *arg ?arg arg ... ?*

The arguments are as follows:

arg
An expression or subexpression to evaluate.

NOTE: **expr** can be used for some string expressions, but it is inefficient and error-prone for string operations. Use the **string** command instead.

expr concatenates all of its **arg**s with spaces between them (similar to **concat**) and then evaluates the resulting expression.

RETURNS   The result of evaluating the expression. The type of the return value (integer, floating-point number, boolean, etc.) depends on the type of the operands and the operators used.

ERROR   Raises an error if any of the calculations or function calls result in an error, such as a division by zero or an invalid argument.

Expressions

An expression is a combination of operands, operators, and parentheses for grouping. A subset of C operators is supported and all operators have the same meaning and precedence as in C.

Operands
Operands may include the following:

- Decimal integer constants (such as 5432)
- Octal integer constants (noted with a leading 0, such as 0177)
- Hexadecimal integer constants (noted with a leading 0x, such as 0xfe)
- Floating-point constants (including scientific notation, such as 6.02e+23)
- Tcl variable references (such as $x)
- Tcl command invocations (such as [llength $s])
- Strings
- Calls to mathematical functions. (See Table 2-12 for a list of supported functions)

Programmer's Tip: *Octal notation can be problematic, especially in date processing. When processing a month field that has leading zeros to preserve sorting order, 01, 02, etc. are valid, but 08 and 09 are not, because the leading 0 forces octal interpretation, and 8 and 9 are not valid octal digits. This often leads to a message like the following:*

```
expected integer but got "08"
```

One workaround for this is to preprocess such strings to remove the leading 0:

```
set month [string trimleft $month 0]
```

However, this turns a string of all zeros into an empty string.

Operators

The valid operators are listed in Table 2-12, in decreasing order of precedence. Parentheses may be used for grouping and to force lower precedence operators to be evaluated before higher ones. For example, the value of **3 + 1 * 5** is 8, but the value of **(3 + 1) * 5** is 20. Operators at the same level of precedence group from left to right. For example, the value of **3 / 4 * 5** is 3.75, the same as **(3 / 4) * 5**.

Logical operators (&&, | |, ?:) have McCarthy ("lazy") evaluation. That is, only as much of the expression is evaluated as is necessary to determine the outcome. For example, if **a** were logically false, then **{$a && $b}** would not evaluate **b**, because the overall expression would be recognized as false as soon as **a** was evaluated. Similarly, if **a** were logically true, then **{$a | | $b}** would not evaluate **b**, because the overall expression would be recognized as true as soon as **a** was evaluated.

NOTE: Tcl allows the strings **true**, **yes**, **on**, **false**, **no**, and **off** as logical constants (for example, when specifying Tk options), but these cannot be combined with logical operators. **[expr on]** results in a logically true value, but **[expr on | | 1]** results in an error, because | | does not accept string operands.

Functions

Table 2-13 lists mathematical functions supported by **expr**. Many of the functions can cause **expr** to raise an error if their arguments are invalid. For example, **asin(3)** raises an error, because sine must be in the range -1 to 1, inclusive.

NOTE: Support for additional functions may be added with C programming by using the **Tcl_CreateMathFunc** function. Such additions are not covered here. Refer to the documentation that accompanies your Tcl source distribution for information on using **Tcl_CreateMathFunc** and other C-callable functions.

Operators	Description
- + ~ !	Unary minus (-), unary plus (+), bitwise negation (~), and logical negation (!). Valid for all types of operands except strings. Result is the same type as the operand. ~ is valid only for integer operands.
* / %	Multiply (*), divide (/), and remainder (%). Valid for all types of operands except strings. Result is a number. % is valid only for integers. The result of % will have the same sign as the divisor and an absolute value smaller than the divisor. For example, **12 % 5** is 2, **-12 % 5** is 3, and **12 % -5** is -3.
+ -	Add and subtract. Valid for any numeric operand. Result is the same type as the operands.
<< >>	Arithmetic left shift (<<) and right shift (>>). Valid only for integer operands. Result is an integer. Right shift always propagates the sign bit. For example, **-7 >> 2** is **-2**.
< > <= >=	Less than (<), greater than (>), less than or equal to (<=), and greater than or equal to (>=). Valid for all types of operands, but **string** should be used to compare strings. Result is a boolean (0 or 1).
== !=	Equal (==) and not equal (!=). Valid for all types of operands, but **string** should be used to compare strings. Result is a boolean (0 or 1).
&	Bitwise AND. Valid only for integer operands. Result is an integer.
^	Bitwise exclusive OR. Valid only for integer operands. Result is an integer.
		Bitwise OR. Valid only for integer operands. Result is an integer.
&&	Logical AND. Valid for boolean, integer, and floating-point operands. Result is a boolean (0 or 1).
||	Logical OR. Valid for boolean, integer, and floating-point operands. Result is a boolean (0 or 1).
a?b:c	if-then-else. If a evaluates to true, the result is the result of evaluating b; otherwise, it is the result of evaluating c. a must have a numeric result.

Table 2-12. Tcl Expression Operators

Function	Value Returned
abs(arg**)**	The absolute value of arg. arg may be an integer or a floating-point value. The return value is the same type as arg.
acos(arg**)**	The angle whose cosine is arg. The return value is a floating-point number in radians between 0 and π, inclusive.
asin(arg**)**	The angle whose sine is arg. The return value is a floating-point number in radians between -π/2 and π/2, inclusive.
atan(arg**)**	The angle whose tangent is arg. The return value is a floating-point number in radians between -π/2 and π/2, inclusive.
atan2(y,x**)**	The angle whose tangent is y/x. The return value is a floating-point number in radians between -π and π, inclusive.
ceil(arg**)**	The first integer not less than arg, as a floating-point number. For example, **ceil(-1.4)** is -1.0 and **ceil(1.4)** is 2.0.
cos(arg**)**	The cosine of arg. arg is in radians.
cosh(arg**)**	The hyperbolic cosine of arg.
double(arg**)**	A floating-point value corresponding to arg. For example, **double(4)** is 4.0.
exp(arg**)**	The exponential of arg (e raised to the power of arg).
floor(arg**)**	The largest integer not more than arg, expressed as a floating-point number. For example, floor(1.3) would return 1.0.
fmod(x,y**)**	The remainder of x/y, expressed as a floating-point number. For example, fmod(344,23) is 22.0
hypot(x,y**)**	sqrt(x*x+y*y), the Euclidean distance from (0,0) to (x,y).
int(arg**)**	The integer part of arg. For example, **int(2.71828)** would return 2.
log(arg**)**	The natural (base e) logarithm of arg.
log10(arg**)**	The base 10 logarithm of arg.

Table 2-13.   Tcl Expression Mathematical Functions

Function	Value Returned
pow(*x*,*y*)	*x* to the power of *y*. For example, **pow(2,10)** is 1024.0.
rand()	A floating-point number greater than or equal to 0 and less than 1. The seed for the random-number generator comes from the system's internal clock but can be set with the **srand()** function.
round(*arg*)	The closest integer to *arg*.
sin(*arg*)	The sine of *arg*. *arg* is in radians.
sinh(*arg*)	The hyperbolic sine of *arg*.
sqrt(*arg*)	The square-root of *arg*.
srand(*arg*)	Seeds the random-number generator with *arg*. *arg* must be an integer. Returns the first random number using the new seed.
tan(*arg*)	The tangent *arg*. *arg* is in radians.
tanh(*arg*)	The hyperbolic tangent of *arg*.

Table 2-13.   Tcl Expression Mathematical Functions *(continued)*

Example

```
# Convert Cartesian coordinates to polar.
proc toPolar { xyList } {
    # Break down the list
    set x [lindex $xyList 0]
    set y [lindex $xyList 1]
    # Radius is the distance from (0,0) to (x,y)
    set r [expr {hypot($x,$y)}]
    # sin(t) = y / r; t in radians
    set t [expr {asin($y / $r)}]
    # Return the list of polar coordinates
    return [list $r $t]
}
# Convert polar coordinates to Cartesian
proc toCart { rtList } {
    # Break down the list
    set r [lindex $rtList 0]
    set t [lindex $rtList 1]
```

```
# Compute raw x and y
set x [expr {$r * cos($t)}]
set y [expr {$r * sin($t)}]
# Return the list of Cartesian coordinates
return [list $x $y]
}
```

Programmer's Tip: *To take advantage of McCarthy evaluation, arguments to* **expr** *must be surrounded by braces ({}). For example, in* **[expr $a | | [someProc $b]]**, *the Tcl parser would evaluate* **$a** <u>and</u> **[someProc $b]**, *and then pass the results on to* **expr**. *To allow* **expr** *to optimize evaluation of subexpressions, the code should instead be written as* **[expr {$a | | [someProc $b]}]**. *In this case, the Tcl parser would pass one argument to* **expr**, *which would then invoke* **someProc** *only if needed.*

fblocked

The **fblocked** command tests to see whether input on a channel is blocked because no data is available. (See also **gets**; **read**.) It takes the following form:

> **fblocked** *channelId*

The arguments are as follows:

channelId
A channelId such as those returned by **open** or **socket**.

RETURNS 1 if the last input operation on *channelId* returns less data than requested; 0 otherwise.

Example

```
# Try to read a line
set line [gets $fid]
# Handle the empty string case
if {[string length $line] == 0} {
    if {[fblocked $fid]} {
        puts "no newline in input.\
            Try again later."
```

```
} elseif {[eof $fid]} {
    puts "end-of-file. We're done."
} else {
    puts "Empty string in input"
}
}
```

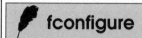

fconfigure

The **fconfigure** command gets and sets channel configuration options. (See also **close**; **flush**; **gets**; **puts**; **read**; **socket**.) It takes the following forms:

fconfigure *channelId*

fconfigure *channelId name*

fconfigure *channelId name value ?name value ... ?*

The arguments are as follows:

channelId
The ID of the channel to process.

name
A channel option name.

value
Value for the option.

fconfigure *channelId*

Retrieves all configuration options for *channelId*.

RETURNS   A list with an even number of elements, including all channel options and their values. Here is an example:

```
{-blocking 1 -buffering none -buffersize 4096
-encoding utf-8 -eofchar {} -translation lf}
```

ERROR   Raises an error if *channelId* is not a valid channel.

fconfigure *channelId name*

Retrieves the value of option *name* for *channelId*.

RETURNS   The current value of the named option.

ERROR   Raises an error if *channelId* is not valid or if *name* is not a valid option name.

fconfigure *channelId name value ?name value ... ?*

Sets one or more option values.

ERROR   Raises an error if *channelId* is not valid, if any *name* is not a valid option name, or if any value is invalid for the corresponding option.

The valid **fconfigure** options are listed in Table 2-14.

Option	Purpose
-blocking *boolean*	Specifies whether the I/O operations on the channel block until completed. Channels are created in blocking mode. For nonblocking mode to work properly, the script must enter an event loop.
-buffering *value*	Specifies the buffering to be used on the channel. *value* must be **full**, **line**, or **none**: **full** All output is buffered until the output buffer is full or **flush** is called on the channel. This is the default state for all channels that are not directed to a terminal, console, etc. **line** Output is flushed whenever a newline character is encountered. This is the default state for all channels that are directed to a terminal, console, etc. **none** No buffering is performed; data is flushed after every output.

Table 2-14.   fconfigure Options

2

Option	Purpose
-buffersize *size*	Specifies the size of the input and output buffers for *channelId*. *size* must be an integer between 10 and 1,000,000, inclusive.
-encoding *name*	Specifies the character encoding used for *channelId*. Tcl converts between this encoding and Unicode, as needed, when doing I/O. The **encoding names** command returns a list of available encoding names.
-eofchar *value*	Specifies the end-of-file character (for MS-DOS file systems that use CTRL-Z as an-end-of file marker). If *value* is an empty string, no special end-of-file character is used. If *channelId* is a read-only or write-only channel, *value* is the character recognized as the EOF on input, or written to the channel when the file is closed. If *channelId* is a read/write channel, *value* may be a single value to use for input and output or a two-element list: {inChar outChar}. When retrieving the **eofchar** for a read/write channel, a two-element list will always be returned.
-translation *mode*	Specifies how translation of end-of-line sequences will be done. Tcl always uses a single newline (\n) character internally, but input commands (**gets**, **read**) and output commands (**puts**) can translate to different conventions, as appropriate for different platforms or channels. If *channelId* is a read-only or write-only channel, *mode* is a single translation mode. If *channelId* is a read/write channel, *mode* may be a single value to use for input and output or a two-element list: {inMode outMode}. When retrieving the **translation** for a read/write channel, a two-element list will always be returned. The following are the translation modes: **auto** On input, carriage return (**cr**), line feed (**lf**), or carriage return followed by line feed (**crlf**) is translated to a newline. (This may vary from line to line within a file.) On output, the end-of-line sequence depends on the channel type and the

Table 2-14.   fconfigure Options *(continued)*

Option	Purpose
	platform. On all platforms, the end-of-line sequence for network sockets is **crlf**. For nonsocket channels, the UNIX end-of-line sequence is **lf**, the Macintosh end-of-line sequence is **cr**, and the Microsoft Windows sequence is **crlf**. This is the default translation mode.
	binary No end-of-line sequence translation is performed on input or output. This is nearly the same as **lf**, except that setting **binary** as the **translation** mode also sets the **eofchar** to an empty string, and sets the encoding to **binary** (which disables encoding).
	cr On input, each carriage return (**cr**) is converted to a newline. On output, each newline is converted to a carriage return (**cr**). This is the usual mode for Macintosh systems.
	crlf On input, each carriage return/line feed pair (**crlf**) is converted to a newline. On output, each newline is converted to a **crlf**. This is the usual mode for Microsoft Windows platforms and for network connections.
	lf This mode is consistent with Tcl's internal representation, so no translation is done on input or output. This is the usual mode for UNIX systems.

Table 2-14.   fconfigure Options *(continued)*

Programmer's Tip: *Text files can be converted to native newline conventions by reading and writing them with translation set to* **auto***. Here is an example:*

```
fconfigure $in -translation auto
fconfigure $out -translation auto
fcopy $in $out
```

fcopy

The **fcopy** command copies data from one channel to another efficiently. (See also **eof**; **fblocked**; **fconfigure**; **vwait**.) It takes the following form:

> **fcopy** *in out ?-size size? ?-command callback?*

The arguments are as follows:

callback
Command to invoke when the copy is complete. **fcopy** appends one or two arguments to *callback* when it is invoked:

- The number of bytes written to *out*
- An error string (only if an error occurred)

in
Open channel to copy from.

out
Open channel to copy to.

size
Number of bytes to copy. Defaults to all data up to end-of-file.

The **fcopy** command is an efficient way to copy bulk data from one channel to another by using Tcl's internal buffering. Additionally, if *callback* is specified, the copy occurs via an asynchronous event while the script proceeds.

NOTE: Event handling requires that the script enter an event loop. Tk-based scripts always have an event loop. Tcl-based scripts should use **vwait**.

When using **fcopy** for background copying, no other part of the script should access *in* or *out*. Event handlers set up with **fileevent** should be disabled.

RETURNS   If *callback* is specified, an empty string is returned immediately. If *callback* is not specified, **fcopy** returns an integer number of bytes written after the copy is complete.

NOTE: If the -**translation** modes of *in* and *out* are different, the number of bytes read from *in* may be different from the number of bytes written to *out*. **fcopy** reports the number of bytes written to *out*. For more information on -**translation**, see the **fconfigure** entry.

ERROR Raises an error if *in* isn't open for reading or if *out* isn't open for writing.

Example

```
# Copy from in to out in background while keeping
# the user informed of progress.
proc bgCopy {
    in out size notifyCmd errorName
            {written 0} {error ""}
} {
    uplevel \#0 $notifyCmd $written
    # errorName is prefixed by a global namespace
    # qualifier (::) rather than using the
    # [global] command so that it may be an array
    # element.
    if {[string length $error] != 0 } {
        set ::$errorName $error
    } elseif { [eof $in] } {
        set ::$errorName ""
    } else {
        fcopy $in $out -size $size \
            -command \
                [namespace code \
                        [list bgCopy $in $out \
                                $size $notifyCmd \
                                $errorName]]
    }
}


# A notifyCmd for bgCopy. fid is supplied by the
# main script, written is appended by bgCopy each
# time progress is invoked.
# In a Tk application, progress might take the
# path to a scale widget and a total size as fixed
# arguments so it could show progress graphically
proc progress { fid written } {
    puts -nonewline $fid "."
    flush $fid
}
```

```
# Copy from fid1 to fid2 in background
bgCopy $fid1 $fid2 1024 \
        [list progress stdout] done
vwait done
```

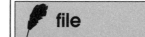
file

2

The **file** command manipulates filenames and attributes. It takes
the following forms:

file atime *name*
file mtime *filename*

file attributes *name ?attribute?*
file attributes *name ?attribute value attribute value ... ?*

file copy *?-force? ?--? source target*
file copy *?-force? ?--? source ?source source ... ? targetDir*

file delete *?-force? ?--? pathname ?pathname ... ?*

file dirname *name*
file extension *name*
file rootname *name*
file tail *name*

file executable *name*

file exists *name*

file isdirectory *name*
file isfile *name*

file join *name ?name ... ?*
file split *name*

file lstat *name varName*
file stat *name varName*

file mkdir *dirname ?dirname ... ?*

file nativename *name*

file owned *name*

file pathtype *name*

file readable *name*
file writable *name*

file readlink *name*

file rename *?-force? ?--? source target*
file rename *?-force? ?--? source ?source ... ? targetDir*

file size *name*

file type *name*

file volume

The arguments are as follows:

attribute
Name of file attribute.

name
Name of the file or directory to act on.

source
Source file or directory.

target
Target file or directory.

value
Value of file attribute.

varName
Name of variable to hold value.

file atime *name*

Retrieves the file access time.

RETURNS   A decimal string representing the number of seconds from a base time (epoch) to the last time the file was accessed.

ERROR   Raises an error if *name* doesn't exist or if its access time can't be queried.

file mtime *filename*

Retrieves the file modification time.

RETURNS   A decimal string representing the number of seconds from a base time (epoch) to the last time the file was modified.

ERROR   Raises an error if *name* doesn't exist or if its modification time can't be queried.

file attributes *name ?attribute?*

Retrieves one or more attributes for *name*.

RETURNS   If no *attribute* is specified, a list of all attributes for the file, in the following form:

```
{-archive 0 -hidden 0 … }
```

If *attribute* is specified, only the value for that attribute is returned. (See Tables 2-15, 2-16, and 2-17 to see the valid attributes.)

file attributes *name*
?attribute value attribute value ... ?

Sets the value for one or more attributes of *name*. Attributes vary from platform to platform. Tables 2-15, 2-16, and 2-17 list valid attributes for the three standard platforms.

Attribute	Value
-group	The file owner's group. The group may be set by ID, but is always retrieved as a name.
-owner	The file's owner. The owner may be set by ID, but is always retrieved as a name.
-permissions	The file access permissions, in octal (for example, 0777 for unlimited access). Symbolic attributes such as **r** and **w** are not supported.

Table 2-15.   UNIX File Attributes

file copy *?-force? ?--? source target*

Copies a file or directory to a new location. If *source* is a directory, the whole directory tree starting there is copied. If *target* is an existing directory, *source* is copied into it. Otherwise, a new file or directory named *target* is created. Existing files will not be overwritten unless -**force** is specified.

ERROR   Raises an error either if *source* is a directory and *target* is an existing nonempty directory or if *source* is a directory and *target* is an existing file.

Attribute	Value
-archive	A 0 or 1 representing the archive bit for the file.
-hidden	A 0 or 1 representing the hidden bit for the file.
-longname	The long name of the file. This attribute cannot be set.
-readonly	A 0 or 1 representing the read-only bit for the file.
-shortname	The name of the file in 8.3 format. This attribute cannot be set.
-system	A 0 or 1 representing the system bit for the file.

Table 2-16.   Microsoft Windows File Attributes

Attribute	Value
-creator	The Finder creator type of the file.
-hidden	The hidden attribute of the file.
-readonly	The read-only attribute of the file.
-type	The Finder file type of the file.

Table 2-17.   Macintosh File Attributes

file copy *?-force? ?--?*
source ?source source ... ? targetDir

Copies one or more files or directories to a new location. If *source* is a directory, the whole directory tree starting there is copied. *targetDir* must be a directory and is created if it doesn't exist. Existing files will not be overwritten unless **-force** is specified.

ERROR   Raises an error either if *source* is a directory and *target* is an existing nonempty directory or if *source* is a directory and *target* is an existing file.

file delete *?-force? ?--?*
pathname ?pathname ... ?

Deletes one or more files or directories. Read-only files will be deleted if file access permissions allow. *pathName* need not exist; that is, it is not an error to try to delete a file or directory that does not exist.

file dirname *name*

Determines what directory *name* is in, substituting for tilde (~) if necessary.

RETURNS   *name*, without the last path component. If *name* is a relative name and contains only one element, either "." (on UNIX and Microsoft Windows systems) or ":" is returned (on Macintosh systems).

file extension *name*

Retrieves the extension part of a filename.

RETURNS   The last dot-delimited component of *name*. If *name* contains no dots, the empty string is returned.

NOTE: Prior to version 8.1, dots at the end of the filename were included in the extension. Thus, *[file dirname foo..bar]* would have returned *"..bar". Starting with version 8.1, this would return ".bar".*

file rootname *name*

Retrieves all of *name* except the extension.

RETURNS   All of *name* up to the last dot (.). If no dot exists in *name*, returns *name*.

file tail *name*

Retrieves the part of *name* after the last path separator. If *name* refers to a directory, this is the last subdirectory on the path. If *name* refers to a file, **file tail** returns the name of the file within its directory.

RETURNS   All of *name* after the last path separator. If *name* contains no path separators, *name* is returned.

file executable *name*

Determines whether the user has execute permission for *name*.

RETURNS   1 if the user can execute *name*; 0 otherwise.

file exists *name*

Determines whether *name* exists and is visible to the user.

RETURNS   1 if the user can see *name*; 0 otherwise.

file isdirectory *name*

Determines whether *name* is a directory.

RETURNS   1 if *name* is a directory; 0 otherwise.

file isfile *name*

Determines whether *name* is a file.

RETURNS   1 if *name* is a file; 0 otherwise.

file join *name ?name ... ?*

Combines path components in a platform-appropriate way. For example, on UNIX and Microsoft Windows systems, **[file join foo bar]** would return "foo/bar", but on Macintosh systems, it would return "foo:bar".

RETURNS   A string consisting of all the *names* joined by the correct path separator for the platform.

Programmer's Tip: *file join discards all names before an absolute path, so it can be used to include a default directory. For example, to designate that a file be found in the user's home directory, unless fileName contains an absolute path, you would use this form:*

    set fullPath [file join [file dirname ~] $fileName]

file split *name*

Splits *name* into components of its path.

RETURNS   A list containing the component elements of *name*.

file lstat *name varName*

On systems that support symbolic links, this returns the same information as **stat** (see the following section), except that it refers to the link rather than to the file the link points to. On systems that do not support symbolic links, this command is identical to the **stat** command.

file stat *name varName*

Retrieves file statistics for *name* into the array *varName*. The array will have the elements listed in Table 2-18.

file mkdir *dirname ?dirname ... ?*

Creates one or more directories and all parent directories, as needed. If *dirname* exists, it is not an error.

Index	Contents
atime	The last access time for the file. Same as the value returned by **file atime**.
ctime	The creation time for the file. The value is a decimal string representing seconds since a base time, which is the same as for **atime**.
dev	ID of the device the file is on. On Microsoft Windows systems, this is 0 for the A drive, 1 for the B drive, etc.
gid	The group ID number for the file owner's group. On Microsoft Windows and Macintosh systems, this element is meaningless and is set to 0.
ino	An I-node number. On Microsoft Windows and Macintosh systems, this element is meaningless and is set to 0.
mode	File type, attributes, and access control summary.
mtime	The last modification time for the file. Same as the value returned by **file mtime**.
nlink	Number of links to this file.
size	The size of the file in bytes.
type	The file type. Same as the value returned by **file type**.
uid	The user ID number of the file's owner. On Microsoft Windows and Macintosh systems, this element is meaningless and is set to 0.

Table 2-18.   file stat Array Elements

ERROR   Raises an error if *dirname* refers to an existing file.

file nativename *name*

Converts a filename to native form.

RETURNS   *name* converted to native format. For example, in Microsoft Windows, **[file join foo bar baz]** would returns "foo/bar/baz", but **file nativename** could be used to convert the result to "foo\bar\baz".

file owned *name*

Determines whether the user owns *name*.

RETURNS   1 if the user owns *name*; 0 otherwise.

file pathtype *name*

Determines *name*'s path type.

RETURNS   One of the following:

- **absolute**   *name* refers to a specific file on a particular volume. For example, in Microsoft Windows, c:\somedir\somefile.ext would be an absolute path.
- **relative**   *name* refers to a file or path relative to the current directory, such as ".."
- **volumerelative**   *name* refers to a file or path relative to the current directory on a volume, or to a specific file on the current volume. For example, in Microsoft Windows, d:somefile.ext would be relative to the current directory on volume D, and \somedir\somefile.ext would refer to a specific path on the current volume.

file readable *name*

Determines whether *name* is readable by the user.

RETURNS   1 if the user can read *name*; 0 otherwise.

file writable *name*

Determines whether the user can write to *name*.

RETURNS   1 if the user can write to *name*, 0 otherwise,.

file readlink *name*

Determines what file a symbolic link points to.

RETURNS   The name of the file pointed to by *name*.

ERROR   Raises an error if *name* isn't a symbolic link or can't be read.

NOTE: On systems that do not support symbolic links, this command exists, but its results are undefined.

file rename *?-force?* *?--?* *source target*

Moves a file or directory to a new location. If *source* is a directory, the whole directory tree starting there is moved. If *target* is an existing directory, *source* is moved into it. Otherwise, a new file or directory named *target* is created. Existing files will not be overwritten unless **-force** is specified.

file rename *?-force? ?--? source ?source ... ? targetDir*

Moves one or more files or directories to a new location. If *source* is a directory, the whole directory tree starting there is moved. *targetDir* must be a directory and is created if it doesn't exist. Existing files will not be overwritten unless **-force** is specified.

ERROR   Raises an error if *source* is a directory and *target* is an existing nonempty directory, or if *source* is a directory and *target* is an existing file.

file size *name*

Retrieves the size of *name*.

RETURNS   A decimal string indicating the size of *name* in bytes.

ERROR   Raises an error if *name* doesn't exist or can't be queried.

file type *name*

Retrieves the file type for *name*.

RETURNS   One of either **file**, **directory**, **characterSpecial**, **blockSpecial**, **fifo**, **link**, or **socket**. Not all types are supported on all platforms.

file volume

Retrieves a list of mounted volumes.

RETURNS   A list of volumes. On UNIX systems, this is always /, because separate volumes don't exist. On Microsoft Windows systems, this is a list, such as {a:/ c:/}, including mapped network drives. On Macintosh systems, this includes all mounted local and network drives.

NOTE: On Macintosh systems, this list may include multiple drives by the same name, but no way currently exists to access any but the first drive with a specified name.

Example

```
# Experiment with various filename parsing
# routines
set path [file join /foo bar baz somefile.ext]
foreach subcommand {dirname ext nativename
                    rootname tail} {
    puts "$subcommand returns\
        [file $subcommand $path]"
}
```

On Microsoft Windows, this script has the following output:

```
dirname returns /foo/bar/baz
ext returns .ext
nativename returns \foo\bar\baz\somefile.ext
rootname returns /foo/bar/baz/somefile
tail returns somefile.ext
```

Compatibility

On UNIX systems, the **file** command always operates with the real
user and group identifiers, not the effective ones.

Tcl Filename Handling

Tcl originated on UNIX systems, but the **file** command
and some assumptions that Tcl makes about filenames
makes manipulating file and directory names easy on other
platforms. This section discusses Tcl's filename handling on
different platforms.

UNIX
On UNIX systems, all files are organized in a single hierarchy
of directories and files rooted at the special directory named /.
Even drives on other systems mounted over the network are
part of this hierarchy. All files and directories can be named
uniquely by specifying a path through the hierarchy to the file
or directory. The parts of the path are separated by forward
slashes (/). An *absolute path* starts at the root directory (/) and
ends with a file or directory name. For example, /foo/bar/baz
would be located in the bar subdirectory of the foo
subdirectory of root.

A user or program can set a *current working directory* to be
some position within the hierarchy and specify a *relative path*
to a file or subdirectory from that current working directory.
Special, shorthand notations are provided for referring to a
directory (.) and its parent (..). If the current working directory
is /foo/bar, the file from the prior example could be referenced
with the relative path ./baz, and a file in /foo could be
referenced with ../somefile. A leading ./ may be omitted, so
./baz and baz are equivalent. Also, /foo/bar/../baz is the same
as /foo/baz if /foo/bar is not a symbolic link.

Each user on a UNIX system has a *home* directory assigned to them. The symbol ~ refers to the current user's home directory (which is also stored in **env(HOME)**). Other users' home directories can be referenced with ~*username*. For example, ~joeuser/somefile would refer to somefile in joeuser's home directory.

Special characters in filenames require special handling. For example, to refer to a file named ~bar in the current directory, you would need to specify it as ./~bar; otherwise, Tcl would look for the home directory of a user named "bar".

Microsoft Windows

The file system on Microsoft Windows systems is hierarchical like that on UNIX systems, but traditionally lacks a single root. Instead, a Microsoft Windows system may have several *volumes* of files on different disk drives. Each volume is specified with a drive letter followed by a colon (e.g., C:), and a user or program may maintain a separate current working directory on each volume. Path components are separated by backslashes (\), and a backslash after the volume specifier indicates the root directory of that volume. For example, C:\foo\bar\baz would be an absolute path to a file on volume C.

Because Tcl uses backslashes to specify special characters on input, the string **C:\thisDir** would be interpreted as C: followed by a tab, followed by hisDir. To enter this in native format, it would have to be typed as **C:\\thisDir**. For convenience, Tcl allows paths to be specified with forward slashes, so **C:\\thisDir** and **C:/thisDir** are equivalent.

Whereas Tcl handles \ and / interchangeably, other programs on Microsoft Windows treat / as an option specifier. Care must be taken when passing filenames built in Tcl to external programs. Consider the following:

```
# auto_exec returns a UNIX-style name with /'s
set progPath [auto_execok $applName]
# file join returns a UNIX-style name
dataPath [file join [pwd] $dataFile]
# exec accepts UNIX-style names, the
# application does not so this fails
exec $progPath $dataPath
# Need to convert the path to the data to
```

```
# native format
exec $progPath [file nativename $dataPath]
```

A user or program can set a current working directory on
each volume that leads to a third type of path: *volume relative.*
The path C:foo/bar/baz is relative to the current working
directory on C, and /foo/bar/baz is relative to the root of the
current volume.

The shorthand notations . (a directory), .. (the parent of a
directory), and ~ (the user's home directory) are supported, but
referring to another user's home directory with *~username*
isn't possible.

Modern Microsoft Windows systems support a version of a
unified hierarchy of files via Uniform Naming Convention
(UNC) names. A path starting with two backslashes is a fully
qualified path to a file on some server on the network. The
form of a UNC name is

   *servername**sharename**path**file*

A path may include . and .. notation.

Macintosh

The Macintosh file system is hierarchical, like that used with
Microsoft Windows, but the Mac file system uses names for
disks rather than volume labels. Also, the only path separator
is the colon character (:).

An absolute path starts with a disk name, in MyDisk:MyFile
(the file MyFile in the root folder of the disk named MyDisk). A
relative path starts with a colon, as in :MyFolder:MyFile,
which indicates the file MyFile in the folder MyFolder within
the current folder.

Whereas UNIX and Microsoft Windows use only . and .. for
specifying relative paths, any sequence of two or more colons
in a Macintosh path may be used to traverse the tree upward;
each colon moves the reference one level up the hierarchy.
Thus, :::MyFile refers to MyFile in a folder two levels up from
the current folder.

The shorthand notations . (a directory), .. (the parent of a directory), and ~ (the user's home directory) are supported. Tcl also supports a limited subset of UNIX-style names on Macintosh systems. /MyDisk/MyFile is equivalent to MyDisk:MyFile, and ../MyFile is equivalent to ::MyFile. Referring to another user's home directory with ~*username* isn't possible.

The name "Tcl/Tk" presents a special problem for Macintosh file specifications. The command **cd "Tcl/Tk Folder"** is interpreted as **cd "Tcl:Tk Folder"**, because Tcl tries to convert UNIX-style paths to native format. In this case, the path could be specified as **:Tcl/Tk Folder** (a relative path) or **Tcl/Tk Folder:** (an absolute path), and the presence of the colon suppresses the conversion from UNIX-style to native format.

In general, you should use **file join** to build paths with special characters (such as /) in them. The paths MyDisk:MyFile and ../MyFile are both equivalent to ::MyFile. Referring to another user's home directory with ~*username* isn't possible.

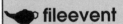

fileevent

The **fileevent** command associates scripts with a channel for asynchronous execution when the channel becomes readable or writable. (See also **bgerror**; **close**; **fconfigure**; **gets**; **puts**; **read**.) It takes the following forms:

> **fileevent** *channelId* **readable** *?script?*

> **fileevent** *channelId* **writable** *?script?*

The arguments are as follows:

channelId
A channel identifier returned by **open**, **socket**, etc. The channel should be configured for nonblocking mode using **fconfigure**.

script
A script to be executed when the event occurs. *script* is evaluated in the background at global scope. Errors in the use of *script* invoke **bgerror**.

fileevent *channelId* readable

Retrieves the current handler for readable events on *channelId*.

RETURNS   The currently assigned handler for readable events on *channelId*, or an empty string if no handler is assigned.

fileevent *channelId* readable *script*

Sets the handler for readable events on *channelId*. If *script* is an empty string or list (for example, {}), the current handler is deleted. Otherwise, *script* is assigned to handle the readable event for *channelId*, replacing any existing handler.

A channel is *readable* if any of the following conditions exists:

- Unread data exists on the underlying device.
- Unread data exists in the input buffer and the data is complete for the buffering mode. (For example, a newline is in the buffer for a line buffered channel.)
- End-of-file has been reached on the channel.
- An error has occurred on the channel.

NOTE: *script* must check for end-of-file and errors on the channel, or an infinite loop will result.

If *script* returns an error, it is deleted as the event handler for *channelId*.

fileevent *channelId* writable

Retrieves the current handler for writable events on *channelId*.

RETURNS   The currently assigned handler for writable events on *channelId*, or an empty string if no handler is assigned.

fileevent *channelId* writable *?script?*

Sets the handler for writable events on *channelId*. If *script* is an
empty string or list (for example, {}), the current handler is deleted.
Otherwise, *script* is assigned to handle the writable event for
channelId, replacing any existing handler.

A channel is *writable* if:

- At least 1 byte of data can be written to the underlying device
  or file

- An error has occurred on the channel

If *script* returns an error, it is deleted as the event handler
for *channelId*.

Example

```
# A proc to handle readable events
proc readChannel { channel } {
    # First check for end-of-file
    # If not EOF, read and process.
    if {[eof $channel]} {
        close $channel
    } else {
        set line [gets $channel]
        processChannel $fid $line
    }
}
...
# Set readChannel to handle channels
fileevent $fid1 readable [list readChannel $fid1]
fileevent $fid2 readable [list readChannel $fid2]
```

flush

The **flush** command flushes buffered output for a channel. (See also
fconfigure; open; socket.) It takes the following form:

flush *channelId*

The arguments are as follows:

channelId
A channel identifier, such as those returned by **open** or **socket**. *channelId* must be open for writing. Flushes any output data that has been buffered for *channelId*. If *channelId* is in blocking mode, **flush** does not return until all buffered data has been flushed. If *channelId* is not in blocking mode, **flush** may return before all data is flushed, and the remaining data will be flushed in the background as quickly as the underlying device allows.

ERROR   Raises an error if *channelId* is invalid or isn't open for writing.

Example

```
# Prompt for data and leave the cursor at the end
# of the prompt
puts -nonewline "Enter something: "
# Flush is needed because stdout is line buffered.
flush stdout
set input [gets stdin]
```

 focus

The **focus** command sets and queries the input focus for a Tk application. (See also **tk_focusFollowsMouse**; **tk_focusNext**; **tk_focusPrev**; **wm**.) It takes the following forms:

   focus *?-force? window*

   focus *?-displayof window?*

   focus *-lastfor window*

The arguments are as follows:

window
Path to a Tk widget.

focus *?*-force*? window*

Sets the input focus for the application to *window*. If **-force** is not specified, the setting is recorded, but has immediate effect only if the application has focus. If **-force** is specified, the application takes focus from another application if necessary to have the setting take immediate effect.

NOTE: **-force** should be used sparingly. Under normal circumstances, an application should allow the user or window manager to control focus. One possible use of **-force** is to regain focus after another, cooperating process has interacted with the user.

focus *?*-displayof *window?*

Retrieves the path to the Tk widget that has focus on *window*'s display. If **-displayof** is not specified, *window* defaults to the application's main window.

NOTE: **-displayof** should always be specified to handle systems with multiple displays properly.

RETURNS   If the application has the focus on *window*'s display, the path to the widget in the application that has the focus. If the application does not have the focus on *window*'s display, an empty string is returned.

focus -lastfor *window*

Retrieves the path to the widget that will get focus the next time the application has focus.

RETURNS   A widget path.

Example

```
# Take an action depending on whether the
# application has focus or not
if {[string length [focus -displayof $w]] == 0} {
    # We don't have focus
}
```

font

The **font** command manipulates Tk fonts and queries the system for font properties. It takes the following forms:

> **font actual** *fontdesc* *?-**displayof** window? ?option?*
>
> **font configure** *fontname ?option?*
>
> **font configure** *fontname option value ?option value ... ?*
>
> **font create** *?fontname? ?option value ... ?*
>
> **font delete** *fontname ?fontname ... ?*
>
> **font families** *?-**displayof** window?*
>
> **font measure** *fontdesc ?-**displayof** window? text*
>
> **font metrics** *fontdesc ?-**displayof** window? ?metric?*
>
> **font names**

The arguments are as follows:

fontdesc
A font description. See the following section, "Font Options," for details of the forms that a font description may take.

fontname
The name of a font created with **font create**.

metric
A measure of the font.

option
A font option name. (See Table 2-19 for valid options.)

text
The text string to measure.

value
A font option value. (See Table 2-19 for valid options and their values.)

window
The window whose display should be queried for font information.

Font Options

Table 2-19 lists the options that can be used when creating a named font or building a font description.

Font Descriptions

A font description can take several different forms for the **font** command, as well as for situations in which a -**font** option is supplied to Tk widget commands. Tk attempts to match a font description to each of the following patterns, in order. To match a Tk or system font name, the match must be exact. When matching the other forms, a "closest match" is used if no exact match is found. In some circumstances, a well-formed font description doesn't match any available font, so a system-dependent default font is used. If the font description doesn't match any of the patterns, an error is generated.

1. **Tk font name**   A value returned by the **font create** command. Using a named font is the most general and reliable method of specifying fonts.

2. **System font name**   A system-dependent font name recognized by the display server. For UNIX systems, this includes all valid X font names, including those listed by the **xlsfonts** utility. For Microsoft Windows systems, this includes **system**, **systemfixed**, **ansi**, **ansifixed**, **device**, and **oemfixed**. For Macintosh systems, this includes **system** and **application**.

3. Family, size, and styles   A list containing a font family, followed by optional size and style information, in this form:

{*family size style style ...*}

Here is an example:

```
{courier 12 bold overstrike}
```

The family and size elements in the list follow the same rules as the **-family** and **-size** font options described in the preceding section. Possible styles are **normal**, **bold**, **underline**, **roman**, **italic**, and **overstrike**.

4. **X-font names (XLFD)**   An X Window System font name in the form *-foundry-family-weight-slant-setwidth-addstyle-pixel-point-resx-resy-spacing-width-charset-encoding*.

5. **Font options**   A list containing font option names and values, such as {-family courier -size 12 -slant italic -overstrike true}. Option names and values are described in the preceding section.

font actual *fontdesc* ?-displayof *window*? ?*option*?

Retrieves the value for one or all options of *fontdesc* as it will actually be drawn on *window*'s display. If **-displayof** is not specified, *window* defaults to the application's main window.

RETURNS   If an *option* is specified, just the value of that option. For example, **[font actual {-family Times} -family]** might return "Times New Roman" on a Microsoft Windows system.

If no *option* is specified, a list of all options for the font and their values. For example, **[font actual system]** might return {-family System -size 10 -weight bold -slant roman -underline 0 -overstrike 0}.

font configure *fontname* ?*option*?

Retrieves the value of one or all options for a named font.

RETURNS   If an *option* is specified, just the value of that option. If no *option* is specified, **font** returns a list of all options for the font and their values. (See **font actual** for detailed examples.)

font configure *fontname* option value ?option value ... ?

Sets the value for one or more options of a named font.

Option	Purpose
-family *name*	Specifies the desired font family. *name* is the name of a font family. Tk always provides three families: **Courier** (a fixed-width "typewriter" font), **Times** (a serifed, proportional-spaced font), and **Helvetica** (a sans-serif proportional-spaced font). Other font families depend on the platform. If the family is unspecified or unrecognized, a platform-dependent default is used.*name* is compared to internal font names in a case-insensitive fashion, so **Courier**, **COURIER**, and **CoUrIeR** are all equivalent.
-size *size*	Specifies the desired size of the font. If *size* is positive, it is in points (1/72"). If *size* is negative, its absolute value specifies the font size in pixels. If an exact match can't be found, a nearby size is used. If the size is unspecified or 0, a platform-dependent default is used.*size* generally should be specified in points, for portability, but pixels may be used instead (for example, to match text height to a bitmap or image).
-weight *weight*	Specifies the relative thickness of characters in the font. *weight* is **normal** or **bold**. If **-weight** is not specified, *weight* defaults to **normal**.
-slant *slant*	Specifies the slant for characters in the font. *slant* is **roman** (vertical) or **italic**. If **-slant** is not specified, *slant* defaults to **roman**.
-underline *boolean*	Specifies whether characters in the font are underlined. If **-underline** is not specified, *flag* defaults to false.
-overstrike *boolean*	Specifies whether a horizontal line should be drawn through the middle of characters. If **-overstrike** is not specified, *boolean* defaults to false.

Table 2-19. Font Options

NOTE: When the font configuration is changed, all widgets that use the named font will immediately be redrawn with the new font attributes.

font create *?fontname? ?option value ... ?*

Creates a new, named Tk font with the specified attributes. If *fontname* is not specified, Tk assigns a unique name in the form **font**n, where *n* is an integer.

RETURNS   The name of the font.

Example

```
set bigFont [font create -family courier -size 24]
label .banner -font $bigFont
```

font delete *fontname ?fontname ... ?*

Deletes one or more Tk fonts. If *fontname* is being used by a widget, it will not actually be deleted until the widget is destroyed or a new font is assigned to it. If a font that is in use is re-created with **font create** before the widget using it is destroyed, the widget will be redrawn with the new font.

ERROR   Raises an error if *fontname* is not a valid font name (for example, if it does not exist).

font families *?-displayof window?*

Retrieves a list of all font families available for *window*'s display. If **-displayof** is not specified, *window* defaults to the application's main window.

RETURNS   An unordered list of font families, as in this example:

```
{fixed charter lucidatypewriter {open look glyph}
        prestige ... }
```

font measure *fontdesc*
?-displayof window? text

Determines the width, in pixels, of *text* if drawn on *window*'s
display using *fontdesc*. If **-displayof** is not specified, *window*
defaults to dot (.), the default toplevel window. **font metrics** can be
used to estimate the height of *text*.

RETURNS   The width, in pixels, of *text*, expressed as an integer.

NOTE: The measured width may not include all pixels from
exaggerated or extreme characters in unusual or decorative
fonts. Also, newlines and tabs are not considered when
computing the width.

font metrics *fontdesc*
?-displayof window? ?metric?

Retrieves information about *fontdesc* when drawn on *window*'s
display. (See Figure 2-2.) If **-displayof** is not specified, *window*
defaults to the application's main window.

metric may be one of the following:

Option	Value
-ascent	The integer number of pixels by which the tallest letter extends above the baseline, plus any extra blank space added by the designer of the font.
-descent	The integer number of pixels by which the lowest decender in the font extends below the baseline, plus any blank space added by the designer of the font.
-linespace	The integer number of pixels between lines of text in the font. This generally is the sum of the ascent and descent.
-fixed	A boolean value indicating whether the font is fixed-space (1) or proportional (0).

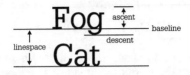

Figure 2-2. Font metrics

RETURNS If a *metric* is specified, just the value of that metric. For example, **[font metrics system -linespace]** might return 16. If *metric* is not specified, **font metrics** returns a list of all metrics for the font, and their values. **[font metrics courier]**, then, might return {-ascent 14 -descent 4 -linespace 18 -fixed 1}.

Programmer's Tip: *font metrics is inefficient on UNIX because it has to query the X server. If you need to use the metrics of a font repeatedly, query it once and store it in a variable for later use.*

font names

Retrieves the names of all existing fonts.

RETURNS An unordered list of Tk font names.

Example

```
# Create a family of fonts that are easy to
# maintain. Changing the properties on the first
# line changes all the fonts the next time the
# code is evaluated.
# Create a base font
font create basic -family courier -size 18
# Create italic and bold fonts from it
# Eval is important to "flatten" the list from
# [font actual]
eval font create italic [font actual basic] \
        -slant italic
eval font create bold [font actual basic] \
        -weight bold
```

for

The **for** command provides a general looping control structure.
(See also **break**; **continue**; **expr**; **foreach**; **while**.) It takes the
following form:

2

    for *start test next body*

The arguments are as follows:

body
A script to execute as the loop body.

next
A script to evaluate at the end of each loop.

start
A script to evaluate before any loops.

test
A test to indicate loop completion; evaluated before the start of
each loop. Must be a valid **expr** expression that returns a
boolean value.

for evaluates *start* and then checks to see whether *test* evaluates
to true. If it is true, *body* and *next* are evaluated, *test* is evaluated
again, etc. until *test* evaluates to false.

If **continue** is invoked within *body*, the remaining commands in the
body are skipped for that loop, and **for** continues with the next loop
by evaluating *next* and *test*.

If **break** is invoked within *body* or *next*, all remaining loops are
skipped and **for** returns.

Example

```
# Do something 10 times
for {set x 0} {$x < 10} {incr x} {
    something $x
}
```

Programmer's Tip: *for is a command, just like **puts** and **button**. It takes four arguments and operates on them. Braces ({}) around the arguments are important to ensure that they are evaluated by **for**, and not by the Tcl parser.*

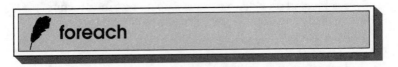

foreach

The **foreach** command provides for looping controlled by the contents of a list or lists. (See also **break**; **continue**; **for**; **while**.) It takes this form:

foreach *varList valueList ?varList valueList ... ? body*

The arguments are as follows:

body
A script to execute for each iteration of the loop.

valueList
A list of values to assign to corresponding variables from *varList* on each iteration of the loop.

varList
A list of one or more variables to assign from *valueList*.

foreach provides a looping control structure that is driven by the contents of one or more lists.

Programmer's Tip: *The lists are usually the result of invoking a command, as shown in the example at the end of this section.*

In the simplest form, with one variable and one list of values, **foreach** assigns the value of each element in *valueList* to the variable and evaluates *body*. Thus,

```
foreach e $someList {
    someCommand $e
}
```

is equivalent to, but more compact and efficient than

```
for {set i 0} \
    { $i < [llength $someList] } \
    {incr i} {
```

```
    set e [lindex $someList $i]
    someCommand $e
}
```

If *varList* contains more than one variable name, the variables are
assigned in groups from *valueList* until all elements of *valueList*
are used. If the length of *valueList* is not an integer multiple of the
length of *varList*, variables from *varList* that do not have
corresponding elements in *valueList* will be assigned an empty
string on the last iteration. Here is an example:

```
foreach {a b} {1 2 3 4 5} {
    puts "$a $b"
}
```

loops three times. On the last iteration, *b* has a value of " ".

Programmer's Tip: *The values of the variables in varList persist
after* **foreach** *returns. This leads to an efficient idiom for multiple
assignments from a list:*

```
foreach {a b c} {val1 val2 val3} {}
```

This assigns **a** *the value "val1", * **b** *the value "val2", and* **c** *the value
"val3", and then evaluates the empty body and returns. This is
equivalent to, but more compact and efficient than the following:*

```
set a val1
set b val2
set c val3
```

*Finally, if there is more than one pair of varList and valueList, each
pair is processed independently, but in synchronization with the
other pairs. The following example loops four times (until the
second valueList is exhausted), but on the last two loops,* **num** *is
assigned to " ".*

```
foreach num {1 2} \
        {name char} \
            {bang ! at @ hash # percent %} {
    puts "$num : $name : $char"
}
```

The output looks like this:

```
1 : bang : !
2 : at : @
```

```
: hash : #
: percent : %
```

Example

```
# A variation on parray
foreach {index value} [array get someArray] {
    puts "someArray($index) is $value"
}
# A better variation that allows sorting indices
foreach index [lsort [array names someArray]] {
    puts "someArray($index) is $someArray($index)"
}
```

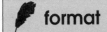

format

The **format** command formats values into a string. (See also
binary; **scan**; **subst**.) It takes this form:

format *formatString ?arg arg ... ?*

The arguments are as follows:

arg
A value to be represented in the result according to the
specification in *formatString*.

formatString
A string containing literal text and field specifiers indicating how
each *arg* should be represented in the result.

format copies text from *formatString* to its return string from left
to right. When it encounters a percent sign (%), it processes the
following characters as a *field specifier* that describes how to
format an *arg* in the return string. (See the following section, "Field
Specifiers," for details.)

RETURNS   A formatted string.

ERROR   Raises an error if not enough *arg* values exist for the
field specifiers in *formatString* or if *formatString* contains an invalid
field specifier.

Programmer's Tip: *format works just like the ANSI C function* **sprintf**, *with a few exceptions noted in the upcoming "Compatibility" section.*

Field Specifiers

A field specifier consists of several parts, in the following order:

1. An XPG3 position specifier

2. A set of flags

3. Minimum field width

4. Precision

5. Length modifier

6. Conversion character

All parts but the conversion character are optional.

XPG3 Position Specifier

The XPG3 format specifier consists of a decimal integer followed by a dollar sign ($). The *arg* counter is reset to the integer before the field is processed. *args* are numbered starting with 1.

Programmer's Tip: *Because the dollar sign ($) is a special character to Tcl, formatStrings containing XPG3 position specifiers should be quoted with braces ({}) when specified in source code. However, such format strings typically come from external repositories, such as message catalogs. (See the discussion of* **msgcat** *for more information on message catalogs.)*

Without the optional XPG3 position specifier, **format** matches *arg*'s with field specifiers from left to right, in order. XPG3 format specifiers allow the *formatString* to override that order with a goal of providing better localization support. For example, an English message might be formatted with code such as the following,

```
set msg [format "The %s %s." $adjective $noun]
```

producing something such as "The red hat." Translating to Italian the literal text in the format string, the adjectives and nouns used by the program might lead to a message such as "La rosa capella." However, the expected word order in Italian is noun and then adjective, so this sounds as strange to an Italian speaker as "The hat red." sounds to an English speaker. The XPG3 position specifier gets around this by allowing the *arg* values to be inserted in the correct order. Thus, the English format string might be "The %s %s." but the Italian might be "La %2$s %1$s.", which substitutes the second *arg* (the noun) first and the first *arg* (the adjective) second.

NOTE: An XPG3 position specifier must be present in all field specifiers in *formatString* or in none of them.

Flags

The flags part of the field specifier may contain any of the following characters in any order:

Character	Purpose
-	Left-justifies the formatted value of *arg* in the space allotted to it.
+	Includes a leading sign, even for positive numbers. (Usually, negative numbers have a leading - sign and positive numbers have no sign.)
space	Includes a blank space before numbers if no sign is present. (Without +, this character causes positive numbers to be formatted with a leading space.)
0	Pads numbers with leading zeros. (The default is to pad with spaces.)
#	Use alternate output form based on the conversion character: **o and O** Always output a leading 0 **x and X** Output 0x or 0X, respectively, before any nonzero number **e, E, f** Always include a decimal point **g and G** Always include a decimal point, and don't remove trailing zeros

Minimum Field Width

The minimum field width specifies the fewest spaces that the formatted value will occupy. This is useful in formatting tabular data. Usually, the minimum width is achieved by adding blanks on the left of the value, but the - and 0 flags described in the preceding section can affect padding and alignment.

The width may be specified as an integer or an asterisk (*). If an asterisk is specified, the width is taken from the next *arg*, which must be a numeric string.

If XPG3 positional specifications are used, the "next" *arg* is the one specified in the XPG3 positional specification. For example, **[format {/%2$*s/%1$3s/} a 5 b]** would set the *arg* counter to 2, and then find **5** as the minimum field width. After the minimum field width was processed, the *arg* counter would be incremented, and the **s** conversion character would be satisfied with the arg **b**.

Precision

The precision consists of a period (.) followed by an integer or an asterisk (*). If an asterisk is specified, the width is taken from the next *arg*, which must be a numeric string. If XPG3 positional specifications are used, the "next" *arg* is the one before the one being formatted.

The precision is interpreted differently for the different conversion characters:

- **e, E, f**   The precision specifies the number of digits to appear after the decimal point in the converted value.

- **g, G**   The precision specifies the total number of digits to appear on both sides of the decimal point. Note that trailing zeros are removed unless the # flag is specified.

- **d, u, i, o, x, X**   The precision is the minimum number of digits to print. Leading zeros are added as needed.

- **s**   The precision is the maximum number of characters to print. Trailing characters are trimmed as needed.

Length Modifier

The length modifier may be **l** or **h**. A length modifier of **h** causes the numeric value of *arg* to be truncated to a 16-bit value before formatting. A length modifier of **l** is ignored. This option is rarely used.

Conversion Character

The conversion character is the only required part of the field specifier. Table 2-20 lists valid conversion characters and their effects.

Example

```
# Format a string exactly 10 characters wide,
# regardless of its length
format "%10.10s" "abcdefghijklmop"
# Format 255 as 0xff
format "0x%2x" 255
```

```
# Format 255 as 0xFF
format "0x%2X" 255
# One more variation. Produces "0xff" using
# "alternate output" flag
format "%#x" 255
```

Conversion Character	Purpose
%	No conversion; just puts a % in the output.
c	Converts an integer to the 8-bit character it represents.
d	Converts an integer to a signed decimal string.
e	Converts a floating-point number to scientific notation in the form x.yyyyyye± zz, where the number of y's is determined by precision. If precision is 0, no decimal point is used unless the # flag is specified. If precision is not specified, it defaults to 6.
E	Converts a floating-point number to scientific notation, in the form x.yyyyyyE± zz, where the number of y's is determined by precision. If precision is 0, no decimal point is used unless the # flag is specified. If precision is not specified, it defaults to 6.
f	Converts a floating-point number to signed decimal string, in the form xx.yyy, where the number of y's is determined by the precision. If precision is 0, no decimal point is used unless the # flag is specified. If precision is not specified, it defaults to 6.
g	If the exponent is less than -4 or greater than or equal to the precision, converts the floating-point number the same as for **e**. Otherwise, converts the same as for **%f**. Trailing zeros and a decimal point are omitted unless the # flag is specified.
G	Converts a floating-point number the same as for **g**, but uses a capital E if scientific notation is used.

Table 2-20. Format Conversion Characters

Conversion Character	Purpose
i	Converts an integer string to a decimal string. *arg* may be an octal string (with a leading 0) or a hexadecimal string (with a leading 0x or 0X).
o	Converts an integer to an unsigned octal string.
s	No conversion; just inserts the string (with padding and alignment as specified in other parts of the field specifier).
u	Converts an integer to an unsigned decimal string. For example, **[format %u -1]** would return 4294967295 on Intel Pentium systems.
x	Converts an integer to an unsigned hexadecimal string, using lowercase hexadecimal digits. For example, **[format %x 254]** would return fe.
X	Converts integer to an unsigned hexadecimal string, using uppercase hexadecimal digits. For example, **[format %x 254]** would return FE.

Table 2-20. Format Conversion Characters *(continued)*

Compatibility

format differs from the ANSI C **sprintf** function in the following ways:

- %p and %n conversions are not supported.
- %c conversions require a decimal string for *arg*.
- The l modifier is ignored. Integer values are always converted as if no modifier exists, and floating-point values are always converted as if the l modifier were specified.
- If the **h** modifier is specified, integer values are truncated to **short** before conversion.

frame

The **frame** command creates and manipulates frame widgets to group or space other widgets. (See also **toplevel**.)

Frame Options

Frame widgets recognize the following standard widget options. (See the Appendix for a complete list of standard widget options and their meanings.)

borderwidth	highlightthickness
cursor	relief
highlightbackground	takefocus
highlightcolor	visual

In addition, frame widgets recognize the following widget-specific options:

-background *color*
The background color for the frame, which is the same as for the standard **background** option for other widgets except that the color may be specified as an empty string to cause the frame to be drawn with no background and no border.

-class *string*
Specify the class for the frame. The class is used when querying the option database for other options.

NOTE: The *class* option may be set only when the frame is created, and cannot be changed with the **configure** widget command.

-colormap *colormap*
Specify a color map to use for the frame. *colormap* may be **new** or the path to another widget. If **new**, a new color map is created for this frame and any widgets that it contains. If a widget path is

supplied, the frame uses the color map of the specified widget. The widget must be on the same display as the frame. If **colormap** is not specified, the frame gets its color map from the parent widget.

NOTE: The colormap option may be set only when the frame is created, and cannot be changed with the **configure** widget command.

-container *boolean*
Specify whether this frame is a container for another toplevel Tk window or another application. If true, no widgets should be created in this frame.

NOTE: The container option may be set only when the frame is created, and cannot be changed with the **configure** widget command.

-height *distance*
Specify the height of the frame as a screen distance. The height may be less than or equal to zero, in which case the frame does not request any size from the window manager.

-width *distance*
Specify the width of the frame as a screen distance. The width may be less than or equal to zero, in which case the frame does not request any size from the window manager.

Frame Commands

Frame widgets respond to the **cget** and **configure** standard widget commands. (See the Appendix for details.) The frame widget does not have any widget-specific commands.

Default Bindings

Frame widgets have no default bindings.

Example

```
# A frame to hold a few widgets
frame .f
pack .f
# The outer frame holds a text widget and a frame
text .f.text -width 40 -height 10
```

```
pack .f.text -side top
frame .f.buttons -relief groove -borderwidth 2
pack .f.buttons -side top -expand 1 -fill x \
        -padx 1m -pady 1m
# The inner frame hold two buttons
button .f.buttons.ok -width 8 -text OK
button .f.buttons.cancel -width 8 -text Cancel
pack .f.buttons.ok .f.buttons.cancel -side left \
        -expand 1 -pady 2m
```

gets

The **gets** command reads a line from a channel. (See also **eof**; **fblocked**; **fconfigure**; **puts**) It takes this form:

> **gets** *channelId ?varName?*

The arguments are as follows:

channelId
Handle to a channel, such as those returned by **open** or **socket**. *channelId* must be open for reading.

varName
Name of variable to be assigned the line read from *channelId*.

Reads the next line from *channelId* and discards the newline at the end of the line. If end-of-file occurs while reading *channelId*, the available data is retrieved. If *channelId* is nonblocking and no newline is in the input buffer, no data is retrieved.

RETURNS   If no *varName* is specified, the line read from *channelId*. This may be an empty string if

- An empty line exists in the input.
- Less than a line of input is available in nonblocking mode (**fblocked** will be true for *channelId*).
- End-of-file is reached (**eof** will be true for *channelId*).

If *varName* is specified, **gets** returns the number of characters transferred to *varName*, or -1 if no data can be transferred. If -1 is returned, use **eof** and **fblocked** to determine why no data has been transferred.

ERROR   Raises an error if *channelId* isn't open for reading or does not exist.

Example

2

```
# Try to read a line
set line [gets $fid]
# Handle the empty string case
if {[string length $line] == 0} {
    if {[fblocked $fid]} {
        puts "no newline in input.\
            Try again later."
    } elseif {[eof $fid]} {
        puts "end-of-file. We're done."
    } else {
        puts "Empty string in input"
    }
}
```

glob

The **glob** command finds files that match a pattern. (See also **file**.) It takes this form:

glob *?options? pattern ?pattern ... ?*

The arguments are as follows:

pattern
A filename pattern to match filenames against. The options are as follows:

-nocomplain
Do not complain if no files match *pattern*.

--

The last option. The argument following this is treated as *pattern* even if it starts with a dash.

glob allows processing of files in groups based on patterns in their names. For example, you might wish to group all files ending with ".tmp" or with a ".tcl" extension. This is a common feature of command interpreters, including MS-DOS's command.com and UNIX shells. The rules and characters used by **glob** are more like those in UNIX shells than the more-restrictive rules and characters in command.com. **glob** recognizes the following special characters:

Characters	Match
?	Any single character.
*	Zero or more characters. Note that MS-DOS command interpreters treat "foo*bar" and "foo*" the same, because the first * extends to the end of the filename. **glob** processes these patterns differently. For **glob**, "foo*bar" doesn't match "foo123". In command.com, it does match.
[*chars*]	Any one of the characters in *chars*. *chars* may include a range of characters, such as *a-z*, which matches any character from *a* to *z*.
x	*x*. For example, "\ ?" matches only a question mark; the \ overrides the special meaning of *?* in **glob** patterns.
{*str1,str2,...*}	Any of the strings *str1*, *str2*, etc. — "*.{dll,exe}" for example—matches any file with an extension of "dll" or "exe".

If *pattern* starts with a ~ (tilde), then it represents a user's home directory. If the tilde is followed by /, it is the current user's home directory. Otherwise, all characters from the ~ to the first / are assumed to be the user's name. (See the **file** command entry for more information.)

RETURNS An unordered, possibly empty, list of files matching any of the *pattern* arguments. The names in the list are in UNIX format, with forward slashes (/) between path elements.

ERROR Raises an error if no files match any *pattern* and **-nocomplain** was not specified.

Example

```
# Process all temporary files in the user's home
# directory
foreach file [glob -nocomplain ~/*.tmp] {
    doSomething $file
}
```

2

Compatibility

On Macintosh and Microsoft Windows systems, **glob** patterns match files without regard to case. For example, "*.HTML" would match foo.html.

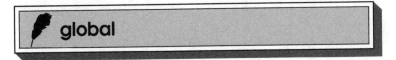

global

The **global** command indicates that a variable is global rather than local to a proc. (See also **namespace**; **variable**.) It takes this form:

    global *varName ?varName ... ?*

The arguments are as follows:

varName
Name of a variable to access from the global scope.

By default, variables referenced inside the body of a proc are local to that proc. Procs may share global variables, but each proc that uses the variable must declare it global.

ERROR   Raises an error if *varName* already exists in the local scope.

Example

```
# This line has no effect because it's outside
# of any proc
global x
```

```
# proc1 sets a global variable
proc proc1 { } {
    global x
    set x 1
}
# proc2 fails because it doesn't declare x global
# so there is no variable named x to increment.
proc proc2 { } {
    incr x
}
# proc3 creates a local first so global raises an
# error
proc  proc3 { } {
    set x "one two three"
    ...
    global x
    set x 2
}
# proc4 creates a button which increments the
# global variable buttonVar, not the local
# variable buttonVar
proc proc4 { } {
    set buttonVar 1
    button .b -text "Increment" \
        -command {incr buttonVar}
}
```

Programmer's Tip: *Three ways exist to access a global variable. The* **global** *command may be used to declare the variable global;* **upvar #0** *may be used to specify that the variable is in the topmost stack frame; and the :: global namespace qualifier may be used before the variable's name. Of the subtle differences that exist between these three methods, one of the most important is that a single array element cannot be made global with the* **global** *command. The following example fails when invoked like* **foo a(1)***:*

```
proc foo {varName} {
    global $varName
    set $varName foo
}
```

However, the next example works even if varName is an array element or namespace variable:

```
proc bar {varName} {
    set ::$varName bar
}
```

*Grouping all **global** commands at the start of the proc body is good practice. Also, a global array can be used to group a set of global variables and reduce the maintenance necessary to add new global variables to each proc they are used in.*

grab

The **grab** command restricts mouse and keyboard events to a widget and its children. (See also **focus**.) It takes the following forms:

grab *?***set***? ?-***global***? window*

grab current *?window?*

grab release *window*

grab status *window*

The arguments are as follows:

window
Path to a widget to have exclusive use of the mouse and keyboard.

grab *?set? ?-global? window*

Restricts mouse and keyboard input to *window*. If **-global** is specified, the grab is global (across all windows on *window*'s display); otherwise, it is local (only within *window*'s application's windows).

If the application already has a grab set, it is automatically released.

NOTE: **-global** has no effect on Microsoft Windows systems.

grab current *?window?*

Retrieves a list of windows with grabs set.

RETURNS If *window* is specified, the name of the window on *window*'s display with a grab set, or an empty string if no grab is set.

If *window* is not specified, **grab current** returns a list of all the windows on all displays with a grab set, or an empty string if no grab is set.

grab release *window*

Releases the grab on *window*, if there is one.

ERROR Does <u>not</u> raise an error, even if *window* does not exist.

grab status *window*

Retrieves the type of grab on *window*.

RETURNS Either **none**, **local**, or **global**, indicating the type of grab, if any, on *window*.

Example

```
# Create two toplevel windows
toplevel .t1
toplevel .t2
# Set up a button in .t1 to release the grab
button .t1.b -text Release \
        -command {grab release .t1}
# Lock the keyboard and mouse focus on .t1.
# .t2 is insensitive
# On UNIX, other applications on .t1's display are
# insensitive, too. On Microsoft Windows, other
# applications are usable
grab -global .t1
```

grid

The **grid** command provides a geometry manager that arranges widgets in a flexible grid of rows and columns. (See also **pack**; **place**.) It takes the following forms:

> **grid bbox** *master ?column row? ?column row?*

> **grid columnconfigure** *master index ?rcoption?*
> **grid columnconfigure** *master indices ?rcoptions?*
> **grid rowconfigure** *master index ?rcoption?*
> **grid rowconfigure** *master indices ?rcoptions?*

> **grid ?configure?** *slave ?slave ... ? ?gridoptions?*
> **grid forget** *slave ?slave ... ?*
> **grid remove** *slave ?slave ... ?*

> **grid info** *slave*

> **grid location** *master x y*

> **grid propagate** *master ?flag?*

> **grid size** *master*

> **grid slaves** *master ?which index?*

The arguments are as follows:

column
An integer column number. The first column in the grid is column 0.

flag
A boolean value.

gridoptions
One or more pairs of option names and values to control how *slave* is gridded into *master*. (See the discussion of **grid columnfigure** for a list of valid options and values.)

index
A column or row number.

indices
A list of one or more row or column numbers.

master
The widget to contain the grid. Usually a frame or a toplevel window.

rcoption
A row or column option name.

rcoptions
One or more pairs of option names and values to control the appearance of an entire row or column in the grid.

row
An integer row number. The first row in the grid is row 0.

slave
A widget to grid into *master* or one of the special placeholders, - (dash), x, or ^ (caret). (See the discussion of **grid configure** for details about these placeholders.) *slave* must be a child of *master* in the widget hierarchy.

which
-row or **-column**.

x, y
Window coordinates.

grid bbox *master* ?*column row*? ?*column row*?

Retrieves the bounding box of the whole grid, a single slave, or a rectangular region within the grid.

RETURNS   A list of four window coordinates, expressed in pixels, in this form:

{*x y w h*}

If no *column* or *row* is specified, **grid bbox** returns the bounding box of the entire grid. If one *column* and *row* are specified, it returns the bounding box of the slave at that location in the grid. If two *columns* and *rows* are specified, it returns the bounding box of all the slaves included in that range of columns and rows.

grid columnconfigure
master index ?rcoption?

Retrieves the properties of column *index*. (Valid options are listed in the upcoming discussion of **grid columnconfigure**.)

RETURNS   If no *rcoption* is specified, a list of options and values, in this form:

    {-minsize 0 -pad 0 -weight 0}

If *rcoption* is specified, only the value of the specified option is returned.

grid columnconfigure
master indices ?rcoptions?

Sets the properties of one or more columns in the grid. Valid options are the following:

Option	Purpose
-minsize *size*	Specifies the minimum column width for the columns. *size* is in screen coordinates.
-weight *weight*	Specifies the relative weight of the column when allotting space as the grid is resized. *weight* is an integer. A column with a *weight* of 2 grows twice as fast as a column with a *weight* of 1. A *weight* of 0 causes the column to be fixed-width.
-pad *gutter*	Specifies the additional space to put on both sides of the widest slave in the column. *gutter* is in screen coordinates.

grid rowconfigure *master index ?rcoption?*

Retrieves the properties of row *index*. (Valid options are listed in Table 2-21.)

RETURNS   If no *rcoption* is specified, a list of options and values in this form:

    {-minsize 0 -pad 0 -weight 0}

If *rcoption* is specified, only the value of the specified option is returned.

grid rowconfigure *master indices ?rcoptions?*

Sets the properties of one or more rows in the grid. Valid options are as follows:

Option	Purpose
-minsize *size*	Specifies the minimum row height for the columns. *size* is in screen coordinates.
-pad *space*	Specifies the additional space to put above and below the tallest slave in the row. *space* is in screen coordinates.
-weight *weight*	Specifies the relative weight of the row when allotting space as the grid is resized. *weight* is an integer. A row with a *weight* of 2 grows twice as fast as a row with a *weight* of 1. A *weight* of 0 causes the row to be fixed-height.

grid *?configure?* *slave ?slave ... ? ?gridoptions?*

Puts one or more *slaves* into a grid. All *slaves* must have a common parent, the *master*. Each **grid configure** command appends a new row to the grid unless the **-row** grid option is specified. The new row contains all the listed *slaves*, one per·column starting at column 0, unless the **-column** grid option is specified. Table 2-21 provides a full list of grid options

2

Option	Purpose
-column *index*	Specifies the column in which to put all *slaves* for this **grid configure** command. If **-column** is not specified, the first *slave* goes in column 0, the second in column 1, etc.
-columnspan *n*	Specifies the number of columns taken by all *slaves* for this **grid configure** command. If **-columnspan** is not specified, *n* defaults to 1.
-in *master*	Specifies an alternate *master* for the grid. If **-in** is not specified, *master* defaults to the parent of the first *slave*. *master* must be a descendent of *slave*'s parent.
-ipadx *amount*	Specifies the amount of horizontal internal padding for the *slaves*. Internal padding is between the *slave*'s border and its contents (child widgets, text, etc.). *amount* is a screen distance.
-ipady *amount*	Specifies the amount of vertical internal padding for the *slaves*. Internal padding is between the *slave*'s border and its contents (child widgets, text, etc.). *amount* is a screen distance.
-padx *amount*	Specifies the amount of horizontal external padding for the *slaves*. External padding is between *slaves*. *amount* is a screen distance.
-pady *amount*	Specifies the amount of vertical external padding for the *slaves*. External padding is between *slaves*. *amount* is a screen distance.
-row *n*	Specifies the row in which to put all *slaves* for this **grid configure** command. If **-row** is not specified, the *slaves* go in a new row after that last occupied row in the grid.

Table 2-21.   Grid Options

Option	Purpose
-rowspan *n*	Specifies the number of rows taken by <u>all</u> slaves for this **grid configure** command. If **-rowspan** is not specified, *n* defaults to 1.
-sticky *side*	Specifies the sides of the grid cell that *slave* will stick to. This is somewhat like a combination of the -**anchor** and -**fill** options for the **pack** geometry manager. *side* is a string or list of anchor points, commas, and spaces. Spaces and commas are ignored. If **n** and **s** are specified, *slave* expands to fill the full height of its row. Similarly, specifying **e** and **w** causes *slave* to fill the full column width. If a side is specified without its opposite, *slave* retains its size, but is attached to the specified side of the cell. For example, specifying just **n** would cause *slave* to be stuck to the middle of the top of its cell, but would not cause *slave* to resize to fill the cell. If -**sticky** is not specified, it defaults to an empty list (⦃⦄) and *slave* is centered in its cell.

Table 2-21.   Grid Options *(continued)*

The following special values for *slave* affect the placement of other *slaves* in the list:

Value	Effect
-	Continues the slave in the column to the left into this column
x	Leaves an empty column in the grid
^	Continues the slave in the row above into this row

Example

```
# Create six buttons in a frame
foreach b { 1 2 3 4 5 6 } {
```

```
      button .f.b$b -text $b
}
# Arrange them in a spiral…
grid  .f.b1  -       .f.b2 -sticky news
grid  .f.b3  .f.b4   ^      -sticky news
grid  ^      .f.b5   -      -sticky news
# …with a tail
grid x .f.b6
```

2

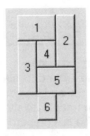

grid forget *slave ?slave ... ?*

Removes one or more *slaves* from *master* and forgets all configurations for *slaves*. (See also **grid remove**.)

grid remove *slave ?slave ... ?*

Removes *slaves* from *master* so that they aren't visible, but remembers their grid options. (See also **grid forget**.)

grid info *slave*

Retrieves the current grid configuration for *slave*.

RETURNS   A list of options and values, such as the following:

```
{-in .f -column 0 -row 12 -columnspan 1 ...}
```

grid location *master x y*

Retrieves the column and row index of the cell (*x,y*) from the upper-left corner of *master*. *x* and *y* are window coordinates.

RETURNS   -1 if (*x,y*) is above or to the left of *master*. If (*x,y*) is within *master*, a list is returned in the form {*column row*}, indicating the cell at the specified position. If (*x,y*) is to the right or below *master*, a list is returned in the form {*column, rows*}, indicating the
cell nearest the specified position. For example, **[grid location .f 0 100000000]** would refer to the last cell in the first column of the grid in **.f**.

grid propagate *master ?flag?*

Specifies whether geometry propagation is enabled. If *flag* is true, **grid** "shrink-wraps" *master* around its slaves when it is displayed, by propagating up their width and height requirements so that *master* is just large enough to hold its slaves. If *flag* is false, *master* retains its configured size, regardless of the size or number of slaves.

If **grid propagate** is not called for *master*, geometry propagation is enabled by default.

RETURNS   0 or 1 if *flag* is not specified, to indicate the current state of geometry propagation. If *flag* is specified, **grid propagate** sets the state of geometry propagation.

NOTE: More than one geometry manager may be used to manage slaves of a single *master*. However, only one geometry manager may have geometry propagation enabled; otherwise, an infinite loop occurs, with each manager trying to adjust after each propagation by the other. Because both **grid** and **pack** default to having geometry propagation turned on, you must take great care when mixing geometry managers in a single *master*. The **place** geometry manager doesn't do geometry propagation, so it may be used with **grid** or **pack** without concern.

grid size *master*

Retrieves the size of *master* in rows and columns.

RETURNS   A list in the form {*columns rows*}.

grid slaves *master ?which index?*

Retrieves a list of slaves in *master*. *which* may be **-row** or **-column**, to limit the list to a single row or column. *index* is the row or column number to access.

RETURNS   A list of slave widget paths. The last slave added is first in the list. If *index* is larger than the dimensions of the grid, the list is empty.

2

Programmer's Tip: *Jeff Hobbs has created a spreadsheet-like widget called TkTable. It acts somewhat like a grid of entry widgets with lots of features added. Look for it at* **www.purl.org/net/hobbs/tcl/capp**.

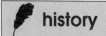

history

The **history** command implements a command history facility for interactive shells. It takes the following forms:

> **history** *?info count?*

> **history add** *script ?exec?*

> **history change** *script ?eventId?*

> **history clear**

> **history event** *?eventId?*

> **history keep** *?count?*

> **history nextid**

> **history redo** *eventId*

The arguments are as follows:

count
Number of history events.

eventId
A history event identifier.

script
A script to put in the history list.

History Events

The command history list is made up of *events* that consist of executable Tcl scripts. Events are numbered, starting at 1, when the shell is started. Event numbering is reset by **history clear**.

A history *event identifier* can take one of four forms:

- **A positive integer**   Refers to an event by the number it was assigned when it was put in the history.

- **A negative integer**   Refers to an event relative to the current event. -1 refers to the previous event, etc.

- **A string prefix**   Refers to the most recent event that starts with the prefix.

- **A glob-style pattern**   Refers to the most recent event that matches the pattern (this uses the same rules as **string match**).

history ?info *count*?

Retrieves the last *count* events from the history. If *count* is not specified, it defaults to 20 or the total number of events in the history, whichever is smaller.

RETURNS   A multiline string formatted to be human-readable. Each line contains an event number, followed by the script for the event.

history add *script* ?exec?

Appends *script* to the history and, optionally, evaluates it.

RETURNS   If *exec* is not specified, an empty string. If *exec* is specified, the result of evaluating *script* is returned.

history change *script ?eventId?*

Changes the script for *eventId* to *script*. If *eventId* is not specified, it defaults to 0 (the current event). This may be used to implement new forms of history substitution.

history clear

Removes all events from the history and starts numbering again at 1.

history event *?eventId?*

Retrieves the script for *eventId*. If *eventId* is not specified, it defaults to -1.

RETURNS   The script for *eventId*.

history keep

Retrieves the size of the history list.

RETURNS   The size of the history list, expressed as an integer.

history keep *count*

Sets the size of the history list.

RETURNS   The new size of the history list, expressed as an integer.

history nextid

Retrieves the number of the next event to be recorded in the history list. May be used in command-line prompts (much like ! in csh prompts on UNIX).

RETURNS   An event identifier, expressed as an integer.

history redo *eventId*

Reevaluates the script for *eventId*. If *eventId* is not specified, it defaults to -1.

RETURNS   The result of evaluating the script.

Example

```
# Clear the list, restart numbering
history clear
# do some stuff
puts "foo"
puts "bar"
puts "baz"
puts "blat"
# See what we've done
history info
# Print "bar" again
history redo 2
```

Compatibility

Before version 8.0, the **history** command had a more complex history-revision mechanism and additional commands (**substitute** and **words**).

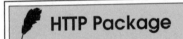

HTTP Package

The **http** package provides client-side support for version 1 of the Hypertext Transfer Protocol. (See also **Safe Package**; **socket**.) It takes the following forms:

   ::**http::config** ?*option*?

   ::**http::config** *option value* ?*option value*?

   ::**http::geturl** *url* ?*options*?

   ::**http::formatQuery** *query*

   ::**http::reset** *token* ?*why*?

   ::**http::wait** *token*

::**http::status** *token*

::**http::size** *token*

::**http::code** *token*

::**http::data** *token*

The arguments are as follows:

options
Command-specific options.

query
One or more pairs of key and value.

token
A token returned by ::**http::geturl**.

url
Universal Resource Locator to retrieve data from.

why
Reason for the reset.

HTTP State Array

Each call to **geturl** creates a new global array to hold the state of
the HTTP transaction. **geturl** returns the name of this array. This
name may be used either as a *token* when calling other ::**http::**
routines, or to access the state array directly. Here is an example:

```
set token [::http::geturl $url]
uplevel #0 $token httpState
puts "The transaction status was\
     $httpState(status)"
```

When the data from the transaction has been processed, the array
should be unset to free memory. Here is an example:

```
unset $token
```

Table 2-22 lists the elements of the HTTP state array.

Element	Content
body	The contents of the URL. This is an empty string if -**channel** was specified.
currentsize	The number of bytes transferred so far.
error	If the HTTP transaction aborted, this is the error string.
http	The HTTP status of the reply in the form "code string". Code is a three-digit status code as defined in the HTTP standard. A code of 200 means "OK". Codes starting with 4 or 5 are errors. A code beginning with 3 is a redirection error, in which case the **Location** part of the **meta** element specifies a new URL that contains the requested information.
meta	A list of metadata keys and values returned by the HTTP server. This may be used with an **array set** command to initialize an array of metadata. Common keys are **Content-Type**, **Content-Length**, and **Location**.
status	The completion status of the transaction; either **ok**, **reset**, or **error**. If the transaction hasn't completed, this is an empty string.
totalsize	A copy of the **Content-Length** metadata.
type	A copy of the **Content-Type** metadata.
url	The requested URL.

Table 2-22.   HTTP state array elements

::http::config *?option?*

Retrieves the current HTTP settings. *option* is an HTTP option, as described in the following section.

RETURNS   If *option* is specified, only the value of the specified option. If no *option* is specified, a list is returned of all options and their values, in this form:

{*optionName optionValue optionName optionValue ...*}

::http::config *option value ?option value?*

Sets the value of one or more HTTP options. The following table lists valid options:

Option	Meaning
-accept *mimetypes*	Specifies the Accept header to be used in requests. *mimetypes* is a string containing mime type patterns separated by commas, such as "text/*, image/jpeg, application/tcl". If -**accept** is not specified, *mimetypes* defaults to "*/*" and all types of documents are accepted.
-proxyhost *hostname*	Specifies the name of the proxy host. If -**proxyhost** is not specified, *hostname* defaults to an empty string. If *hostname* is an empty string, the URL host is contacted directly.
-proxyport *number*	Specifies the port number to contact on *hostname*. If -**proxyport** is not specified, *number* defaults to an empty string. This option is meaningful only if -**proxyhost** is specified.
-proxyfilter *command*	Specifies a command to invoke to determine whether a proxy is required for a host. When invoked, *command* has the hostname appended to it. If a proxy is needed to contact that host, *command* should return a two-element list, in the form {*proxyServer proxyPort*}. Otherwise, *command* should return an empty list ({}). If -**proxyfilter** is not specified, the default filter returns the values set with -**proxyhost** and -**proxyport**, if they aren't empty.
-useragent *string*	Specifies a string to be used in the User-Agent header of HTTP requests. If -**useragent** is not specified, *string* defaults to "Tcl http client package 2.0".

2

::http::geturl *url ?options?*

Retrieves data from *url*. **geturl** waits for the data, unless
-**command** is specified. To use -**command,** the application must
enter an event loop. Tk-based applications always have an event
loop. Tcl-based applications must call **vwait** or ::**http::wait.** The
HTTP operation performed depends on *options*:

- If -**query** is specified, a POST operation is done
- If -**validate** is specified, a HEAD operation is done
- Otherwise, a GET operation is done

RETURNS   A token that may be used with **reset, wait, status,** etc.

The following table lists **geturl** options and their effects:

Option	Purpose
-**blocksize** *size*	Specifies the maximum block size for the transfer. *size* is an integer. After each block, the -**progress** command is invoked.
-**channel** *name*	Specifies a channel to copy the data to. If -**channel** is not specified, the data is stored in **state(body)**.
-**command** *command*	Specifies a callback to be invoked when the HTTP transaction completes. When invoked, *command* has the token for the transaction appended to it. If -**command** is not specified, **geturl** waits for the transaction to complete. If -**command** is specified, **geturl** returns immediately.
-**handler** *command*	Specifies a callback to be invoked when HTTP data is available for the transaction. When invoked, *command* has two arguments appended to it: the socket from which the HTTP data may be read, and the token for the transaction. *command* should return the number of bytes read from the socket. If -**handler** is specified, nothing else is done with the data. If -**handler** is not specified, the default handler puts the data in **state(body)** or writes it to *name,* as described for -**channel**.

Option	Purpose
-headers *list*	Specifies extra headers to add to the HTTP request. *list* must have an even number of elements. The first, third, etc. elements are keys. The second, fourth, etc. elements are the corresponding values. For example, if *list* were {Pragma no-cache}, the header "Pragma: no-cache" would be added to the request. Newlines are removed from the values.
-progress *command*	Specifies a callback to invoke after each block of data is transferred. When invoked, *command* has three arguments appended to it: the token for the transaction, the expected total size of the transfer (or 0 if the total size is unknown), and the number of bytes transferred so far.
-query *query*	Specifies the query to be used for a POST request. *query* must be a properly formatted x-url-encoding query, such as those returned by **formatQuery**.
-timeout *ms*	Specifies the timeout for the request. If *ms* is 0, no timeout occurs. If *ms* is nonzero, it is a number of milliseconds to wait for data before invoking **reset** and the **-command** callback. After a timeout, **status** returns "timeout".
-validate *boolean*	Specifies that a HEAD request should be done. The meta information from the head is put in **state(meta)**.

::http::formatQuery *query*

Performs x-url-encoding on *query*. *query* must be a list with an even number of elements. The first, third, etc. elements are query keys. The second, fourth, etc. elements are query values.

RETURNS   A properly encoded query string that may be used with the **-query** option of **geturl**.

Example

The following request

```
::http::formatQuery \
    "key 1" "~user/file" foo bar "key 3" "value 3"
```

returns this string:

```
key+1=%7euser%2ffile&foo=bar&key+3=value+3
```

::http::reset *token* *?why?*

Resets the transaction for *token*, sets **state(status)** to *why*, and invokes the **-command** callback command. If *why* is not specified, it defaults to **reset**.

::http::wait *token*

Waits for the transaction for *token* to complete.

NOTE: This uses **vwait** and works only in trusted code.

::http::status *token*

Retrieves the completion status from the transaction for *token*.

RETURNS The value of **state(status)**.

::http::size *token*

Retrieves the number of bytes transferred for the transaction for *token*.

RETURNS The value of **state(currentsize)**.

::http::code *token*

Retrieves the HTTP status reply from the server.

RETURNS The value of **state(http)**.

::http::data *token*

Retrieves the data from the transaction for *token*.

RETURNS   The value of **state(body)**.

Example

```
# Callback invoked when transfer is complete.
proc httpCommand { label button token } {
    upvar #0 $token state
    $button configure -state disabled
    $label configure \
        -text "Done. Status=$state(status)"
}
# Callback invoked after each packet
proc httpProgress {
    label token expected received
} {
    if {$expected != 0} {
        set percent [expr {100.0 * $received / \
                           $expected}]
        $label configure \
                -text [format "%2.2f%%" $percent]
    } else {
        $label configure \
                -text "$received received"
    }
}
# Some widgets to implement a simple interface
label .progress -width 25
pack .progress
frame .buttons
pack .buttons -expand 1 -fill x
button .buttons.cancel -text "Cancel" -width 8
button .buttons.exit   -text "Exit"   -width 8 \
         -command exit
pack .buttons.cancel .buttons.exit -expand 1
# Make sure we have access to HTTP commands
package require http 2.0
# Start transaction to get data
set token [http::geturl "www.scriptics.com" \
    -command [list httpCommand .progress \
                      .buttons.cancel] \
```

```
        -progress [list httpProgress .progress]]
# Reconfigure cancel button to cancel this
# transaction.
.buttons.cancel configure \
    -command [list http::reset $token "Canceled"]
```

The **if** command performs conditional execution of one or more scripts. (See also **while**; **expr**.) It takes the following form:

> **if** *expr* ?**then**? *body* ?**elseif** *expr* ?**then**? *body* **elseif** *expr* ... ? ?**else**? ?*body*?

Programmer's Tip: *The keywords* **then** *and* **else** *may be omitted. Generally accepted Tcl style includes* **else** *and omits* **then**.

The arguments are as follows:

body
A script to execute when the corresponding *expr* evaluates to a true value.

expr
An expression to evaluate. The expression is evaluated as with **expr** and must result in a boolean value. Because **if** uses **expr** to evaluate expressions, you can use parentheses for grouping, to perform arithmetic, etc. in the *expr* without explicitly calling **expr**.

Programmer's Tip: *Include braces around* expr *and* body. *This improves performance in version 8.0 and beyond and causes no problems in earlier versions.*

Example

```
# Check the value of a number
set x 1
if { $x+1 == 2 } {
   puts "x = 1!"
}
# Compare two strings
```

```
set s1 "this is a string"
set s2 "this is another string"
if { ! [string compare $s1 $s2] } {
    puts "s1 equals s2"
} elseif { [someProc] || [anotherProc] } {
    doSomethingElse
} else {
    doDefaultStuff
}
```

2

Programmer's Tip: *When testing strings, always use* **string**, *and do not rely on* **expr***'s == and != operators.* **string compare** *and* **string equal** *are safer for strings that may look like numbers, and twice as fast as using ==.*

The **image** command creates and manipulates images. It takes the following forms:

> **image create** *type ?name? ?options?*
> **image delete** *?name name ... ?*
>
> **image height** *name*
> **image width** *name*
>
> **image names**
> **image types**
>
> **image type** *name*

Programmer's Tip: *Jan Nijtmans's Img extension adds BMP, XBM, XPM, GIF (with transparency), PNG, JPEG, TIFF, and PostScript. Look for it at* **home.wxs.nl/~nijtmans/img.html***.*

The arguments are as follows:

name
A name for the image.

options

One or more combinations of an option name and a value. Each *type* has its own options. **bitmap** and **photo** options are described in the following sections.

type

An image type; **bitmap**, **photo**, or a type defined by an image extension.

NOTE: The standard Tk distribution supports bitmap and photo images, but extensions may add other types.

image create *type ?name? ?options?*

Creates a new *type* image and an image command to access it. If *name* is not specified, Tk assigns a unique name in the form **image***n*, where *n* is an integer. If *name* already exists, it is replaced with the new image and any instances of that image are redisplayed with the new contents.

RETURNS   The name of the image.

Just as widget creation commands such as **button** return the name of a new command that can be used to manipulate the newly created widget, **image create** creates a new command that can be used to manipulate the image. Here is an example:

```
# Load a bitmap from a file.
set bm [image create bitmap mybitmap \
        -file mybitmap.xbm]
# Change its colors.
$bm configure -foreground red -background blue
```

image delete *?name name ... ?*

Deletes one or more images. If any instances of *name* are being displayed, the image won't be deleted until all instances are released. The instances retain their size but are redisplayed as empty areas. If *name* is reused while the instances still exist, the instances are redisplayed with the new image.

image height *name*

Retrieves the height of image *name*.

RETURNS　　The height of *name*, expressed in pixels.

image width *name*

Retrieves the width of image *name*.

RETURNS　　The width of *name*, expressed in pixels.

image names

Retrieves the names of all existing images.

RETURNS　　An unordered list of image names.

image types

Retrieves the names of all supported types.

RETURNS　　A list of type names, such as {photo bitmap}, including any extension-defined types.

image type *name*

Retrieves the type of image *name*.

RETURNS　　**bitmap**, **photo**, or an extension-defined type name.

Bitmap Images

A bitmap image is a two-color image that may allow underlying graphics to show through transparent areas. It is specified with two colors and two bitmaps:

- **Source mask**　Controls which color to display for the bitmap: 1 for foreground, 0 for background.

- **Transparency mask**　Controls whether the bitmap data is displayed (as determined by *source*) or is transparent, showing the underlying data: 1 shows the source data, 0 is transparent.

If no transparency mask is supplied, the bitmap defaults to all 1's to show all source data, with no transparent bits.

Each bitmap is a rectangular array of bits, and the dimensions of the two bitmaps must match. The bitmap may be specified as a string in the script source, or read from a file. In either event, the format of the bitmap is the same as that used for X Window System bitmaps.

The bitmap data consists of three parts:

- A width
- A height
- A list of bytes containing the bits of the mask

Each byte of the bit mask represents 8 bits of the mask. Bit 0 is the leftmost bit in the mask. For example, a bitmap with the first, third, fifth, etc. pixels set would start at with 0x55.

The following example defines a bitmap 7 pixels wide and 9 pixels high. The top and bottom rows are blank, and the remaining 7-pixel by 7-pixel area has an *X* drawn through it.

```
#define simple_width 7
#define simple_height 9
static unsigned char simple_bits[] = {
    0x00,0x41,0x22,0x14,0x08,0x14,0x22,0x41,0x00};
```

Bitmap Image Options

Table 2-23 lists the options that may be used for creating **bitmap** images.

Bitmap Image Commands

Bitmap images respond to the following standard widget commands: **cget** and **configure**. (See the Appendix for details.)

Photo Images

A *photo image* is a full-color image whose pixels can be any color or transparent. Photo images are stored internally in 24 bits per pixel and may be dithered for display, as needed. The standard Tk distribution supports GIF and PPM/PGM formats. Additional formats can be added by extensions.

Option	Purpose
-background *color*	Specifies the background color for the image (displayed where *source* is 0 and *mask* is 1).
-data *string*	Specifies the source mask for the bitmap. *string* must be in X Window System bitmap format.[1]
-file *name*	Specifies the file where the source mask for the bitmap is stored. The contents of *name* must be in X Window System bitmap format.[1]
-foreground *color*	Specifies the foreground color for the image (displayed where *source* and *mask* are both 1).
-maskdata *string*	Specifies the transparency mask for the bitmap. *string* must be in X Window System bitmap format.[1]
-maskfile *name*	Specifies the file where the transparency mask for the bitmap is stored. The contents of *name* must be in X Window System bitmap format.[1]

2

[1] If a bitmap is specified in both a *string* and file, the string takes precedence and the file is ignored.

Table 2-23.   Bitmap Image Options

Installable format handlers handle different formats (or different variations of formats). Each handler has a name associated with it. For example, suppose that standard support of GIF format data were provided by handlers named GIF87 and GIF89. When trying to read data, Tk would ask each handler in turn whether it recognized the data. The first one that could read the data would do so.

Programmer's Tip: *The list of handlers to try can be restricted by specifying a format name; only handlers whose name starts with the specified format name will then be tried.*

Photo Image Options

Table 2-24 describes options that may be used for creating **photo** images

Option	Purpose
-data *string*	Specifies the contents of the image as a string. The format of *string* must match an installed file format.[1]
-format *format-name*	Specifies the name of the format for the data in *string* or the contents of *name*.
-file *name*	Specifies the file that contains the image data. The format of the file must match an installed file format.[1]
-gamma *value*	Specifies the gamma correction factor for the data. *value* is a real number and must be greater than 0. Generally, values greater than 1 make the image lighter, and values less than 1 make it darker. If **-gamma** is not specified, *value* defaults to 1.
-height *height*	Specifies the height of the image in pixels. If **-height** is not specified, *height* defaults to 0 and the image sizes to fit the data.
-palette *palette-spec*	Specifies the number of colors to be used to display the image. *palette-spec* may be a single integer specifying the number of shades of gray to use, or three integers separated by slashes (/) specifying the number of shades of red, green, and blue (respectively) to use.
-width *width*	Specifies the width of the image in pixels. If **-width** is not specified, *width* defaults to 0 and the image sizes to fit the data.

[1]If a photo is specified in both a string and file, the file takes precedence and the string is ignored.

Table 2-24.   Photo Image Options

Photo Image Commands

Photo images respond to the following standard widget commands: **cget** and **configure**. (See the Appendix for details.) In addition, the following commands are supported:

imageName **blank**

imageName **copy** *sourceImage ?cmdoptions?*

imageName **get** *x y*
imageName **put** *data ?cmdoptions?*

imageName **read** *filename ?cmdoptions?*
imageName **write** *filename ?cmdoptions?*

imageName **redither**

Photo image commands take the following arguments:

cmdoptions
Options specific to each photo image command.

data
Photo data to copy into *imageName*. (For formatting details, see following description of the **put** photo image command.)

filename
Name of the file to access.

sourceImage
Name of photo image to copy data from.

x, y
X or Y image coordinate for pixel to access.

Photo Image Regions
Many photo image commands take four coordinates to specify a region to manipulate, in the form: *x1 y1 x2 y2*. Each coordinate is an integer pixel count from the upper-left corner of the image, (0,0). Together, the four coordinates specify a rectangular region from (*x1,y1*) to (*x2,y2*). The region includes the top and left edges but *not* the right and bottom edges. For example, 0 0 10 10 would indicate a square, 100-pixel region.

imageName blank
Clears the contents of the image, so that it is displayed as transparent.

imageName copy sourceImage ?cmdoptions?
Copies a rectangular region of *sourceImage* into *imageName*. *sourceImage* must be a photo image. The data from *sourceImage*

may be zoomed or subsampled to match the target region. If no *cmdoptions* are specified, all of *sourceImage* is copied to *imageName* at (0,0).

cmdoptions may include any of the following:

Option	Purpose
-from *x1 y1 x2 y2*	Specifies the region to copy from *sourceImage*. If **-from** is not specified, the region to copy defaults to the entire source image.
-shrink	Specifies that the size of *imageName* should be reduced, if necessary, so that the copied data just fits into it. This does not affect the height or width of *imageName* if **-height** or **-width** (respectively) were specified when it was created.
-subsample *x? y?*	Specifies that only the upper-left pixel of each *x* by *y* rectangle in *sourceImage* should be copied to *imageName*. *x* and *y* are signed integers. Negative values cause *sourceImage* to be flipped around the *X* or *Y* axis, respectively. If *y* is omitted, it defaults to the same value as *x*.
-to *x1 y1 x2 y2*	Specifies the region to overwrite in *imageName*. If **-to** is not specified, *x1* and *y1* default to (0,0), and *x2* and *y2* default to the width and height of the source region.
-zoom *x? y?*	Specifies that each pixel from *sourceImage* should be expanded to fill an *x* by *y* rectangle in *imageName*. *x* and *y* must both be integers greater than 0. If *y* is omitted, it defaults to the same value as *x*.

imageName get *x y*
Retrieves the color of the pixel at (*x,y*) in *imageName*.

RETURNS   A list of three integers between 0 and 255, in the form {*red green blue*}.

imageName put *data* ?-to *x1 y1 x2 y2*?
Sets pixels in *imageName* to colors specified in *data*. *data* is a list of lists. Each element in *data* is a list of colors for one row of the

target region. Each color is a color name (such as blue) or a hexadecimal RGB specification (such as #ff5522). For example, the following would set 4 pixels in each of two rows:

```
set data {
    {red pink brown white}
    {blue #ff0000 #00ff00 #0000ff}
}
$img put $data
```

If all four coordinates are specified, *data* is replicated as needed to fill the region. If *x2* and *y2* are not specified, the length of *data* determines how many rows are set, and the length of the elements of *data* determine how many columns are set. If **-to** is not specified, the target region starts at (0,0).

imageName read *filename ?cmdoptions?*

Reads data from *filename* into *imageName*. *cmdoptions* may include any of the following:

Option	Purpose
-format *format-name*	Specifies the format of the data in *filename*. Only format handlers whose names begin with *format-name* will be checked to see whether they can handle the file. For example, if *format-name* were **gif**, the GIF87 and GIF89 handlers would be tried, but a JPEG handler, if present, would not. *format-name* is case-insensitive.
-from *x1 y1 ?x2 y2?*	Specifies the region in *filename* to copy to *imageName*. If *x2* and *y2* are omitted, all data from (*x1,y1*) to the bottom-right corner of the image is copied. If **-from** is not specified, the entire contents of the file is copied into *imageName*.
-shrink	Specifies that the size of *imageName* should be reduced, if necessary, so that the copied data just fits into it. This does not affect the height or width of *imageName* if **-height** or **-width** (respectively) were specified when it was created.

Option	Purpose
-to *x1 y1*	Specifies the location in *imageName* where the contents of *filename* should be put. If **-to** is not specified, *x1* and *y1* default to 0.

imageName write *filename* ?cmd*options*?

Writes data from *imageName* into *filename*.

cmdoptions may include any of the following:

Option	Purpose
-format *format-name*	Specifies the format of the data in *filename*. If **-format** is not specified, the first handler that can write image data is used.
-from *x1 y1 ?x2 y2?*	Specifies the region in *imageName* to copy to *fileName*. If *x2* and *y2* are omitted, all data from (*x1,y1*) to the bottom-right corner of the image is copied. If **-from** is not specified, the entire image is written.

imageName redither

Dithers the image again in each window where it is displayed, to account for errors from images assembled from pieces with **copy**.

Example

```
canvas .c -height 200 -width 300
set image [image create photo]
.c create image 100 150 -image $imag
foreach file [glob *.gif] {
    $image read $file -shrink
    tk_messageBox -message \
            "Click OK to view next image"
}
```

incr

The **incr** command increments a variable. (See also **expr**; **set**.) It takes the following form:

> **incr** *varName ?increment?*

The arguments are as follows:

increment
How much to add to *varName*. Defaults to 1.

varName
Name of the variable to add to.

RETURNS   The new value of *varName*.

ERROR   Raises an error if *varName* does not exist or does not have an integer value.

Example

```
# Print some even numbers
for {set x 0} {$x < 11} {incr x 2} {
    puts $x
}
```

info

The **info** command returns information about the Tcl interpreter, such as what commands and variables are defined. (See also **winfo**.) It takes the following forms:

> **info args** *procName*
> **info body** *procName*
> **info default** *procName arg varName*

info cmdcount

info commands *?pattern?*
info globals *?pattern?*
info locals *?pattern?*
info procs *?pattern?*
info vars *?pattern?*

info complete *script*

info exists *varName*

info hostname

info level *?level?*

info library

info loaded *?interp?*

info nameofexecutable
info script

info patchlevel
info tclversion

info sharedlibextension

The arguments are as follows:

arg
Argument name.

interp
Interpreter name.

number
Integer number of stack levels.

pattern
glob-style pattern to limit matches.

procName
Name of proc to access.

script
Script to test.

varName
Variable name.

info args *procName*

Retrieves a list of arguments for *procName*.

RETURNS   An ordered list of the names of the arguments to *procName*.

info body *procName*

Retrieves the body of *procName*.

RETURNS   A string containing the body of *procName*.

info default *procName* arg *varName*

Retrieves the default value, if any, for the *arg* argument to *procName*.

RETURNS   1 If *arg* has a default value; in this case, *varName* is set to the default value. 0 otherwise.

info cmdcount

Retrieves a count of the commands invoked in this interpreter.

RETURNS   A number of commands, expressed as an integer.

info commands *?pattern?*

Retrieves a list of all commands matching *pattern*. If *pattern* is not specified, it defaults to "*". This is a superset of the list returned by **info procs**, and includes commands implemented in C or another compiled language and linked or loaded into the interpreter. It does not include commands that may be available via auto-loading but that have not yet been loaded.

RETURNS   An unordered list of commands. If *pattern* includes namespace qualifiers, the elements of the returned list will also include namespace qualifiers.

info globals *?pattern?*

Retrieves a list of all global variables matching *pattern*. If *pattern* is not specified, it defaults to "*".

Programmer's Tip: *The* **global** *command does not cause a variable to exist; it just establishes its scope when it is created.* pattern *is the list of global variables that exists; they may not be visible in the current context if* **global** *has not been called to make them visible.*

RETURNS   An unordered list of global variables.

info locals *?pattern?*

Retrieves a list of all local variables that match *pattern*. If *pattern* is not specified, it defaults to "*". This list includes arguments to the current proc.

RETURNS   An unordered list of local variable and argument names.

info procs *?pattern?*

Retrieves a list of all procs whose names match *pattern*. If *pattern* is not specified, it defaults to "*". This list is a subset of that returned by **info commands**; it include only the commands implemented in Tcl.

RETURNS   An unordered list of proc names.

info vars *?pattern?*

Retrieves a list of all currently visible variables, including local variables, proc arguments, and globals that have been brought in scope with the **global** command.

RETURNS   An unordered list of variable names. If *pattern* includes namespace qualifiers, the elements of the returned list will also include namespace qualifiers.

info complete *script*

Tests whether *script* is complete. For example,

```
[info complete "{a "]
```

would be false, because the *script* value has an open brace but no close brace. This is useful to test for completeness of data or commands read from a file or channel. Here is an example:

```
set command ""
set prompt "#"
while { ! [eof $stdin] } {
    puts -nonewline $prompt
    flush stdout
    set line [gets $stdin]
    append command "\n$line"
    if { ! [info complete $command]} {
        set prompt ">"
    } else {
        eval $command
        set command ""
        set prompt "#"
    }
}
```

RETURNS   1 if *script* is complete; 0 otherwise.

info exists *varName*

Determines whether *varName* exists.

RETURNS   1 if *varName* exists; 0 otherwise.

info hostname

Retrieves the name of the computer on which the script is running.

NOTE: This requires networking support to be installed.

RETURNS   The name of the host.

info level *?level?*

Retrieves either the call stack depth of the current procedure or the call stack frame number *level*. (See also **uplevel**.)

level may be either of the following:

- **A positive integer**   Specifies a stack frame starting at the top level (outside any procs). The first proc called is at level 1, the second proc called is at level 2.
- **A negative integer**   Specifies a stack frame relative to the current proc. The current proc is 0, the caller is -1.

RETURNS   If *level* is not specified, an integer indicating the current call stack level. If *level* is specified, a list is returned containing the name and actual arguments of the proc at *level* on the call stack. For example, **[info level 0]** would return the invocation of the current proc.

info library

Retrieves the name of the Tcl library directory.

RETURNS   The value of the global variable **tcl_library**.

info loaded *?interp?*

Retrieves a list of all the packages loaded into *interp* with the **load** command. If *interp* is not specified, the list contains all packages loaded in all interpreters in the application. If *interp* is {}, the list contains only the packages loaded into the current interpreter.

This is different from **package names**, because **info loaded** doesn't report the Tcl package or packages implemented only in Tcl code that was sourced in.

RETURNS   A list of lists. Each element in the list represents a loaded package, and takes the form {*filename packageName*}. For packages linked into the interpreter, the filename is {}.

info nameofexecutable

Retrieves the name of the binary file that contains the interpreter.

NOTE: Compare this with the **argv0** global variable and **info script**.

RETURNS   The fully qualified name of the executable, or an empty string if the name cannot be determined.

info script

Retrieves the name of the script, if any, being evaluated (e.g., with the **source** command).

NOTE: Compare this with the *argv0 global variable and info nameofexecuteable.*

RETURNS   The name of the script, or an empty string if no file is being evaluated.

info patchlevel

Retrieves the patch level of the interpreter.

RETURNS   The value of the **tcl_patchLevel** global variable.

info tclversion

Retrieves the version of the interpreter.

RETURNS   The value of the **tcl_version** global variable.

info sharedlibextension

Retrieves the platform-dependent extension for shared library files, such as .dll for Microsoft Windows and .so for Solaris.

RETURNS   The extension, including the leading dot.

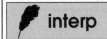

interp

The **interp** command creates and manipulates Tcl interpreters. (See also **dde**; **Safe Package**; **send**.)

Interpreter Overview

A Tcl or Tk application or shell is created with a single interpreter. Additional interpreters can be created with the **interp** command to execute scripts in a restricted or augmented environment. Interpreters created with **interp** are Tcl interpreters; they do not have access to Tk commands for widget creation and manipulation, interacting with the windowing system, and so forth.

Any interpreter with access to the **interp** command can create one or more child interpreters, which, in turn, can create more interpreters, creating a hierarchy of interpreters. An interpreter is said to be the *master* of the *slave* interpreters it creates. A master has control over what commands are visible to its slaves and how the slaves share resources with the master and with each other.

Each slave has a name that must be unique to its master. This name is used not only to identify the interpreter in the hierarchy, but also as the name of a *slave command* in the master. The slave command may be used in an object-oriented fashion to access the slave, much like Tk widget commands access and manipulate widgets.

A master may uniquely identify its slaves, its slave's slaves, and so on, by specifying the path from the master to the desired interpreter. The path is a list of interpreter names. For example, if interpreter A had slaves 1, 2, and 3, and {A 2} had slaves a, b, and c, then A would refer to c as {2 c}. A's master, if it had one, would refer to c as {A 2 c}. An interpreter may refer to itself as {} (an empty list).

NOTE: No well-known top-level interpreter exists, and interpreters can't determine their level in the overall hierarchy. In the previous example, it is impossible for {A 2} to tell that it is not the primary and only interpreter in the application.

An interpreter may be *trusted* or *safe*. Trusted interpreters have unrestricted access to all Tcl commands and resources. Safe interpreters have restricted access to certain commands and resources, and typically are used to evaluate untrusted scripts while protecting the host application and system. For example, safe interpreters cannot create files or subprocesses (as in via **exec**) or interact with other programs (as in via **dde** or **send**).

Each interpreter has its own namespace for commands and variables. A master may provide additional or modified commands to its slaves via *aliases*. An alias may make a command created in the master or a slave visible in another slave. For example, a trusted master might provide controlled access to dangerous commands to a safe slave via an alias to a command in the master that enforces certain constraints.

Each interpreter also has its own set of *channel identifiers*. Channels such as open files or sockets opened in one interpreter aren't visible to other interpreters. A master may allow a channel to be shared or transferred between itself and a slave or between its slaves. Once transferred, a channel is no longer visible in the interpreter that opened it. When an interpreter is destroyed, all the channels it owns (those not shared with another interpreter) are closed and file events on those channels in that interpreter are canceled.

Safe Interpreters
Safe interpreters are created with the following subset of Tcl commands exposed:

after	format	read
append	gets	regexp
array	global	regsub
binary	if	rename
break	incr	return
case	info	scan
catch	interp	seek
clock	join	set
close	lappend	split
concat	lindex	string
continue	linsert	subst
encoding	list	switch
eof	llength	tell

error	lrange	time
eval	lreplace	trace
expr	lsearch	unset
fblocked	lsort	update
fcopy	namespace	uplevel
fileevent	package	upvar
flush	pid	variable
for	proc	vwait
foreach	puts	while

These commands can be hidden to further limit the capabilities of the slave interpreter, or aliased to alter their behavior.

Safe interpreters are created with the following Tcl commands hidden:

cd	file	pwd
exec	glob	socket
exit	load	source
fconfigure	open	

These commands can be exposed or aliased to provide more functionality to the safe interpreter. The **safe** package provides one way to do this.

Safe interpreters also lack an **env** global variable.

Alias Invocation

Alias invocation is somewhat different from normal command invocation, because it has to make sure no code from an untrusted slave is evaluated in a trusted master. For example, the following code would create a slave and an alias in that slave:

```
interp create -safe s
interp alias s foo {} bar a
```

If **s** invokes **foo x [baz $y] $z**, the following steps will be performed:

1. **foo** is parsed from its argument list.

2. **$y** and **$z** are evaluated in **s** (for example, to the values 1 and 2).

3. **baz** is invoked in **s** (for example, resulting in the value 3).

4. foo is looked up and found to be an alias and replaced by **bar a**.

5. bar a x 3 2 is evaluated in the parent of **s** without further evaluation of **bar**'s arguments.

If **baz** returns a string that looks like a command, such as

```
[eval [file delete -force [glob -nocomplain *.*]]]
```

2

bar would see that as a value, and the dangerous command would <u>not</u> be evaluated in the master, which might be a trusted interpreter.

Syntax

> **interp alias** *srcPath srcCmd*
> **interp alias** *srcPath srcCmd* {}
> **interp alias** *srcPath srcCmd targetPath targetCmd ?arg arg ... ?*
> **interp aliases** *?path?*
>
> **interp create** *?-safe? ?--? ?path?*
> **interp delete** *?path ... ?*
>
> **interp eval** *path arg ?arg ... ?*
>
> **interp exists** *?path?*
>
> **interp expose** *path hiddenCmdName ?exposedCmdName?*
> **interp hidden** *path*
> **interp hide** *path exposedCmdName ?hiddenCmdName?*
> **interp invokehidden** *path ?-global? hiddenCmdName ?arg ... ?*
>
> **interp issafe** *?path?*
> **interp marktrusted** *path*
>
> **interp share** *srcPath channelId targetPath*
> **interp transfer** *srcPath channelId targetPath*
>
> **interp slaves** *?path?*
>
> **interp target** *path alias*

The arguments are as follows:

alias
Command alias to access.

arg
Additional arguments to command.

channelId
Channel to share or transfer between interpreters.

exposedCmdName
Name of the exposed command.

hiddenCmdName
Name of the hidden command.

path
Path to an interpreter.

srcCmd
Command name in *srcPath*.

srcPath
Path to interpreter to use as the source.

targetCmd
Command name in *targetPath*.

targetPath
Path to interpreter to use as the target.

interp alias *srcPath srcCmd*

Retrieves information about the target of *srcCmd* when invoked in *srcPath*.

NOTE: *srcCmd* is the name that was used when the alias was created. The command may have since been renamed in *srcPath*.

RETURNS A list containing *targetCmd* and *args* to be used when *srcCmd* is invoked in *srcPath*. If *srcCmd* is not aliased in *srcPath*, an empty string is returned.

ERROR Raises an error if *srcPath* is {} (an empty list, referring to the invoking interpreter) or does not exist.

interp alias *srcPath srcCmd* {}

Deletes the alias for *srcCmd* from *srcPath*. If *srcCmd* has been renamed in *srcPath*, the renamed command is deleted.

ERROR   Raises an error if *srcCmd* was not aliased in *srcPath*.

interp alias *srcPath srcCmd targetPath targetCmd ?arg arg ... ?*

Creates or replaces an alias in *srcPath* named *srcCmd*, which invokes *targetCmd* in *targetPath* with additional arguments. *targetCmd* does not have to exist in *targetPath* until the alias is invoked.

When *srcPath* invokes *srcCmd*, the *args* will be inserted at the start of the argument list.

RETURNS   The *srcCmd* argument.

ERROR   Raises an error if *srcPath* or *targetPath* does not exist.

Example

```
# Create a slave
set i [interp create A]
# A proc to log a string
proc slaveLog { slave string } {
    puts "$slave says <<$string>>"
}
# Alias log in the slave.  Specify the slave
# argument in the alias. A will invoke this like
# [log "Some string"] but it will get
# executed as [slaveLog A "Some string"].
interp alias $i log {} slaveLog $i
# Try it out
interp eval $i log "This is a test"
```

This produces the following output:

```
A says <<This is a test>>
```

interp aliases *?path?*

Retrieves a list of aliases in *path*. If *path* isn't specified, it defaults to {}.

RETURNS   An unordered list of aliases.

ERROR   Raises an error if *path* does not exist.

interp create *?-safe? ?--? ?path?*

Creates a new slave interpreter named *path*. If **-safe** is specified or the master of *path* is a safe interpreter, *path* will be a safe interpreter with a restricted set of commands and resources. If *path* may begin with a - (dash), -- must be specified to mark the end of options. If *path* is not specified, Tcl assigns a unique name in the form **interp***n*, where *n* is an integer.

NOTE: If a command named *path* already exists, it is replaced without warning.

RETURNS   The *path* argument.

ERROR   Raises an error if *path* already exists.

interp delete *?path ... ?*

Deletes one or more slave interpreters. File events in *path* are removed. Channels owned by *path* are closed. Channels shared with other slaves have their usage counts decremented so that they are closed when the last slave using them is deleted.

ERROR   Raises an error if *path* does not exist. If more than one *path* is specified, they are only processed up to the first one that raises an error.

interp eval path *arg ?arg ... ?*

Evaluates a command in *path*. All *arg*'s are combined as if passed to **concat** and the resulting script is evaluated in *path*.

RETURNS   The result of evaluating the script.

ERROR   Raises an error if an error occurs while evaluating the
script. The invoking interpreter's **errorInfo** and **errorCode** are
also set.

interp exists *?path?*

Tests whether *path* is an existing interpreter. If *path* is not
specified, it defaults to {} (an empty list representing the invoking
interpreter).

RETURNS   1 if *path* exists; 0 otherwise.

interp expose *path*
hiddenCmdName ?exposedCmdName?

Makes *hiddenCmdName* visible to *path* as *exposedCmdName*. (See
the earlier section, "Interpreter Overview," for a discussion of
hidden commands.) *exposedCmdName* cannot include any
namespace qualifier, including :: for the global namespace. If
exposedCmdName is not specified, it defaults to *hiddenCmdName*.
(See also **interp hidden**; **interp hide**.)

ERROR   Raises an error if *path* doesn't exist, if *hiddenCmdName*
doesn't exist in *path* or isn't hidden, or if *exposedCmdName*
already exists in *path*.

interp hidden *path*

Retrieves a list of hidden commands in *path*. (See also **interp
expose**; **interp hide**.)

RETURNS   An unordered list of command names.

ERROR   Raises an error if *path* doesn't exist.

interp hide path
exposedCmdName ?hiddenCmdName?

Hides *exposedCmdName* from *path*. The hidden command will be
reported by **interp hidden** as *hiddenCmdName*. If
hiddenCmdName isn't specified, it defaults to *exposedCmdName*.

ERROR   Raises an error if *path* doesn't exist, if *exposedCmdName* doesn't exist or is already hidden in *path*, or if *hiddenCmdName* already exists in *path*.

interp invokehidden *path* ?-*global*? *hiddenCmdName* ?*arg* ... ?

Invokes *hiddenCmdName* in *path* with specified additional *args*. If **-global** is specified, *hiddenCmdName* is invoked in the global scope of *path*. Otherwise, *hiddenCmdName* is invoked in the current context and can access local variables directly and use **upvar**, **uplevel**, and so forth to access the call stack.

NOTE: hiddenCmdName and args are interpreted by the parser as the **invokehidden** command is parsed, and then passed to the hidden command without further interpretation by the parser.

RETURNS   The result of invoking *hiddenCmdName*.

ERROR   Raises an error if *hiddenCmdName* does not exist.

Example
```
# Provide a restricted [open] command to a safe
# interpreter
proc safeOpen {slave fileName access} {
    if { ! [someSafetyTest $fileName $access] } {
        error "Can't safely open $fileName with\
            $access access"
    }
    return [interp invokehidden $slave open \
            $fileName $access]
}
# Create a safe slave
interp create -safe safe1
# Give it access to open
interp alias safe1 open {} safeOpen safe1
```

interp issafe ?*path*?

Determines whether *path* is a safe interpreter. If *path* is not specified, it defaults to {}, the invoking interpreter.

RETURNS   1 if *path* is a safe interpreter; 0 otherwise.

ERROR   Raises an error if *path* does not exist.

interp marktrusted *path*

Makes *path* a trusted interpreter. This can be invoked only from a
trusted interpreter.

NOTE: Hidden commands remain hidden and must be explicitly
exposed.

NOTE: No **marksafe** command exists. After a safe interpreter is
marked trusted, it is trusted until it is deleted.

ERROR   Raises an error if *path* does not exist.

interp share *srcPath channelId targetPath*

Lets *srcPath* and *targetPath* share *channelId*. *channelId* must be
open in *srcPath*. *targetPath* will have the same permissions on
channelId as *srcPath*. Additional calls to **interp share** allow
channelId to be shared by more than two interpreters. The
underlying channel is not closed until all interpreters with access
to it close it or are deleted.

ERROR   Raises an error if *srcPath* or *targetPath* doesn't exist or if
channelId isn't open in *srcPath*.

Programmer's Tip: *Conflicts in* **fileevent** *handlers in multiple
interpreters can lead to application lockups. Only one interpreter
should have a* **fileevent** *active on a channel, no matter how many
may share it.*

interp transfer *srcPath channelId targetPath*

Transfers control of *channelId* from *srcPath* to *targetPath*.
channelId will no longer be accessible in *srcPath*, just as if it
were closed.

ERROR   Raises an error if *srcPath* or *targetPath* doesn't exist or if
channelId isn't open in *srcPath*.

interp slaves *?path?*

Reports slave interpreters of *path*. If *path* isn't specified, it defaults to {}, the invoking interpreter.

RETURNS   An unordered list of slaves of *path*.

ERROR   Raises an error if *path* does not exist.

interp target *path alias*

Determines the interpreter in which processing will occur if *path* invokes *alias*.

RETURNS   An interpreter path. If the target is the invoking interpreter, {} is returned.

ERROR   Raises an error if *path* is {} (an empty list, referring to the invoking interpreter) or does not exist.

Interp Slave Commands

When a slave interpreter is created, a new *slave command* is created simultaneously that can be used to more conveniently access many features of the slave interpreter. For example, after executing

```
set s [interp create mySlave]
```

the following commands are all equivalent:

```
$s eval someCommand someArg
mySlave eval someCommand someArg
interp eval mySlave someCommand someArg
```

The following "Syntax" section lists the features available via the slave command. All arguments, return values, and errors are the same as for the corresponding **interp** commands described in the preceding sections. For each command,

   interp *command slave arg ?arg ...?*

is equivalent to

   slave command arg ?arg ...?

Syntax

slave **alias** *srcCmd*

slave **alias** *srcCmd* {}

slave **alias** *srcCmd targetCmd* ?*arg* ... ?

slave **aliases**

slave **eval** *arg* ?*arg* ... ?

slave **expose** *hiddenCmdName* ?*exposedCmdName*?

slave **hide** *exposedCmdName* ?*hiddenCmdName*

slave **hidden**

slave **invokehidden** ?**-global**? *hiddenCmdName* ?*arg* ... ?

slave **issafe**

slave **marktrusted**

join

The **join** command combines list elements into a string. (See also **append**; **concat**; **lappend**; **split**.) It takes this form:

> **join** *list* ?*joinString*?

The arguments are as follows:

joinString
String to put between each two elements of *list*. If *joinString* is not specified, it defaults to a single blank space.

list
Lists whose elements are to be joined.

RETURNS A string resulting from combining all elements of *list* with *joinString* between each pair.

Example

```
set l [list a b c [list d e f]]
set s [join $l ","]
```

s has the value:

```
a,b,c,d e f
```

The **label** command creates and manipulates widgets that are usually used to hold short, static, or script-controlled text. (See also **entry**; **message**; **text**.)

Label:

Label Options

Label widgets recognize the following standard widget options. (See the Appendix for a complete list of standard widget options and their meanings.)

anchor	font	image	takefocus
background	foreground	justify	text
bitmap	highlightbackground	padx	textvariable
borderwidth	highlightcolor	pady	underline
cursor	highlightthickness	relief	wraplength

In addition, label widgets recognize the following widget-specific options:

-height *distance*
The desired height of the label in either screen units (when an image is specified) or lines of text (if label text is specified). If this option is omitted, Tk computes the correct height from the image or text dimensions.

-width *distance*

The desired width of the label in either screen units (when an image is specified) or characters (if label text is specified). If this option is omitted, Tk computes the correct width from the image or text dimensions.

Label Commands

Label widgets respond to the **cget** and **configure** standard widget commands. (See the Appendix for details.) Labels have no widget-specific commands.

Default Bindings

There are no default bindings on label widgets. They are not intended to be interactive.

Example

```
label .label -justify left -text "Filename:"
entry .entry -textvariable filename
grid .label .entry
```

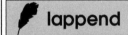

lappend

The **lappend** command appends elements to a list. (See also **append**; **concat**; **join**.) It takes this form:

> **lappend** *varName ?value value value ... ?*

The arguments are as follows:

value
The value to append to variable. *value* may be a string (e.g., "foo"), a number (e.g., 2.4), a list (e.g., {a b c}), or the binary data, such as that returned by **binary format**.

varName
Name of a list variable to append to. This variable is created if it
doesn't exist.

NOTE: Most Tcl commands operate on the value of their
arguments directly. **lappend** is different in that it takes the name of
a variable and modifies the variable.

Description

lappend is an efficient way to build lists. **lappend a $b** is more
efficient than **set a [concat $a [list $b]]**.

RETURNS The new value of the variable named by *varName*.

Example

```
# Process all elements in listIn
foreach v $listIn {
    lappend listOut [someProc $v]
}
```

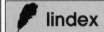

lindex

The **lindex** command retrieves an element from a list using a
numeric index. (See also **lreplace**.) It takes this form:

   lindex *list index*

The arguments are as follows:

index
Index into *list*. The first element is 0. The special value **end** may be
used to get the last element of *list*.

list
List to access.

RETURNS   If *index* is between 0 and the length of *list*, the
requested element. If *index* is negative, or greater than the length
of *list*, an empty string is returned.

Example

```
set list {"first" "second" "third"}
puts "The first item in the list is:\
     [lindex $list 0]"
puts "The second item in the list is:\
     [lindex $list 1]"
```

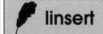

linsert

The **linsert** command inserts new elements in a list. (See also
lappend; **lreplace**.) It takes this form:

   linsert *list index element ?element ... ?*

The arguments are as follows:

element
Value to insert into *list*.

index
Location in *list* before which to insert new elements. The special
value **end** may be used to insert at the end of the list.

list
List to insert into.

RETURNS   *list* with new elements inserted.

Example

```
# Two ways to append
set l [linsert $l end a b c]
lappend m a b c
# Insert at the beginning ("prepend")
set n [linsert $n 0 a b c]
```

list

The **list** command builds lists from elements, grouping elements with braces ({}), as needed, so that the list is properly formatted and will be properly parsed by **lindex** and other list-processing commands. (See also **concat**.) It takes this form:

    list ?arg arg ... ?

The argument is as follows:

arg
An element to use in building the list.

Description

Tcl lists and strings are often interchangeable, but are not quite identical. Here is an example:

```
set first "foo bar"
set second baz
set string "$first $second"
set list [list $first $second]
```

The string has three words in it: "foo bar baz". The list has two elements: "foo bar" and "baz". The **list** command preserves the structure of *first* when adding it as a list element. **list** is also different than **concat** in that **concat** strips one level of grouping. For example,

```
list a {b c} {d {e f}}
```

would produce a list of three elements

```
{a {b c} {d {e f}}}
```

whereas

```
concat a {b c} {d {e f}}
```

produces a list of five elements:

```
{a b c d {e f}}
```

RETURNS   A new list made up of the *args*.

listbox

The **listbox** command creates and manipulates widgets that display lists of choices.

Programmer's Tip: *Bryan Oakley has developed two excellent listbox derivatives—a combobox and a multicolumn listbox. Look for them at **www.purl.org/net/oakley/tcl**.*

Listbox Options

Listbox widgets recognize the following standard widget options. (See the Appendix for a complete list of standard widget options and their meanings.)

background	highlightbackground	selectforeground
borderwidth	highlightcolor	setgrid
cursor	highlightthickness	takefocus
exportselection	relief	xscrollcommand
font	selectbackground	yscrollcommand
foreground	selectborderwidth	

Programmer's Tip: *All elements of a listbox are displayed in the same colors and with the same font. Fancier listboxes can be simulated with **text** widgets and complex bindings.*

*Having multiple listboxes in a single application is common. The default behavior of the listbox widgets is such that when a selection is made in one listbox (or any other widget in the application), the selection is lost in the others. To maintain the selection in the listbox widgets, set -**exportselection** to false.*

The listbox widgets recognizes the following widget-specific options:

-height *distance*
Specifies the desired height for the listbox in lines of text. If *height* is 0 or less, the listbox is displayed just high enough to hold all of its elements.

-selectmode *mode*
Specifies the mode for selections. *mode* may be any string, but the default bindings expect one of the following:

* **single**   At most, one element may be selected.

* **browse**   At most, one element may be selected. The selection may be moved by dragging with mouse button 1 pressed.

* **multiple**   Any number of elements may be selected. Clicking an element with mouse button 1 toggles the selection of that element.

* **extended**   Any number of elements may be selected. Clicking an element selects it and deselects all other elements. The selection may be extended by dragging with mouse button 1 pressed.

mode is usually **browse** or **extended**; the others are special-purpose modes.

NOTE: These modes are implemented in the default bindings for the listbox widget user interactions and are not inherent in the widget. For example, it is possible for a script to select more than one entry in **browse** mode.

-width *distance*
Specifies the desired width of the listbox, in characters. If the font used for the listbox is not fixed-width, the width of the character "0" is used. If *width* is 0 or less, the listbox is displayed just wide enough to hold the widest element.

Listbox Commands

Listbox widgets respond to the **cget** and **configure** standard widget commands. (See the Appendix for details.) In addition, listbox widgets respond to the following widget-specific commands:

pathName **activate** *index*

pathName **bbox** *index*

pathName **curselection**
pathName **selection** *options*

pathName **delete** *first ?last?*
pathName **insert** *index ?element element ... ?*

pathName **get** *first ?last?*

pathName **index** *index*

pathName **nearest** *y*

pathName **scan mark** *x y*
pathName **scan dragto** *x y*

pathName **see** *index*

pathName **size**

pathName **xview**
pathName **xview** *viewoptions*
pathName **yview**
pathName **yview** *viewoptions*

The arguments for listbox widget commands are as follows:

element
Item to add to the listbox.

first
The listbox index of the first element to process.

index
A listbox index.

last
The listbox index of the last element to process.

viewoptions
Options for setting the view.

x, y
Window coordinates to process.

Listbox Indices

Many listbox widget commands take one or more *indices* as
arguments. The index may take one of the following forms:

Index	Value
number	A position within the list. 0 refers to the first element, 1 refers to the second element, etc. *number* must be a decimal number. Any number less than 0 is treated as 0. Any number greater than the length of the list is treated as **end**.
active	The entry under the mouse pointer. If the listbox has keyboard focus, this entry is displayed with an underline.
anchor	The anchor point for the selection as set with the **selection anchor** widget command. The anchor point defaults to **end** until that command is called.
end	The end of the list. For most commands, this is the last element. For **insert** and **index**, it is the position just after the last element in the list.
insert	The character position just after the insertion cursor.
@*x,y*	The element nearest (*x,y*). *x* and *y* are in pixels relative to the upper-left corner of the listbox.

pathName activate *index*
Sets the active element to the one nearest *index*. The active
element is drawn with an underline and may be accessed with the
index **active**.

pathName bbox *index*
Retrieves the coordinates of a bounding box that includes the
element at the specified *index*.

RETURNS   And empty list if *index* does not exist or is not visible.
If *index* is visible, a list of four window coordinates is returned,
expressed in pixels in the form {*x y w h*}.

pathName curselection
Retrieves the current selection.

RETURNS   A list of numeric indices of all the elements currently
selected. If no elements are selected, the list is empty.

pathName selection *options*
Manipulates the selection in the listbox. *options* may be any of
the following:

Option	Purpose
anchor *index*	Sets the selection anchor to *index*. If *index* does not exist, the closest element is used.
clear *first ?last?*	Deselects any elements between *first* and *last*. If *last* is not specified, it defaults to *first*. Other elements are not affected.
includes *index*	Determines whether *index* is currently selected. Returns 1 if it is, and 0 otherwise.
set *first ?last?*	Selects all elements between *first* and *last*. If *last* is not specified, it defaults to *first*. Other elements are not affected.

pathName delete *first ?last?*
Deletes one or more elements from the list. If *last* is not specified, it defaults to *first*, and just one element is deleted.

pathName insert *index ?element element ... ?*
Inserts *elements* before *index* in the list.

pathName get *first ?last?*
Retrieves elements from the listbox. If specified, *last* must be greater than *first*.

RETURNS If *last* is not specified, the element at *first*. If *first* doesn't exist in the listbox, an empty string is returned. If *last* is specified, a list is returned of listbox elements from *first* to *last*.

pathName index *index*
Converts *index* to a numeric index.

RETURNS If *index* is **end**, the number of elements in the listbox. Otherwise, the numeric index corresponding to *index* is returned.

pathName nearest *y*
Determines which element is nearest *y*. *y* is a window coordinate, in pixels.

RETURNS The index of the nearest visible listbox element to *y*.

pathName scan mark *x y*
Records *x* and *y* and the coordinates of the current view for use by future **scan dragto** listbox widget commands. This is usually bound to a mouse button press on the listbox.

***pathName* scan dragto** *x y*
Adjusts the listbox view by ten times the difference between *x* and
y and the coordinates of the last **scan mark** listbox widget
command. This is usually bound to mouse motion events on the
listbox and used to implement a high-speed scrolling of the list
within the view.

***pathName* see** *index*
Makes *index* visible.

***pathName* size**
Determines the number of elements in the list.

RETURNS   An integer.

***pathName* xview**
Determines the current view coordinates.

RETURNS   A view coordinate list. This list includes the same
values passed to scroll bars via the **-xscrollcommand** option.

***pathName* xview** *viewoptions*
Sets the X coordinates of the listbox view. *options* may be any of
the following:

Option	Purpose
index	Adjusts the view so that the character specified by *index* is displayed at the left edge of the listbox.
moveto *fraction*	Adjusts the view so that *fraction* of the total width of the listbox is off the left of the view. *fraction* is a view coordinate.
scroll *number units*	Adjusts the view *number units. number* must be an integer. *units* is either of the following:
	units View adjusts by *number* times the **xScrollIncrement.**
	pages View adjusts *number* times 9/10 of the view width.
	Negative values of *number* adjust the view upward (making characters off of the top of the listbox visible). Positive values adjust the view downward.

***pathName* yview**
Determines the current view coordinates.

RETURNS   A view coordinate list. These are the same values passed to scroll bars via the **-yscrollcommand** option.

pathName* yview *viewoptions

Sets the Y coordinates of the listbox view. *options* may be any of the following:

Option	Purpose
index	Adjusts the view so that the element specified by *index* is displayed at the top edge of the listbox.
moveto *fraction*	Adjusts the view so that the element *fraction* down the list is at the top of the listbox. *fraction* is a view coordinate. For example, if *fraction* is .33, the element that is one-third down the list will be displayed at the top. If *fraction* is large, the desired element may not move to the top of the window. Generally, a listbox will not scroll up far enough to leave more than one blank line at the bottom of the window.
scroll *number units*	Adjusts the view *number units*. *number* must be an integer. *units* is either of the following: **units** View adjusts by *number* times the **yScrollIncrement** **pages** View adjusts *number* times half the number of visible elements Negative values of *number* adjust the view upward (making characters off of the top of the listbox visible). Positive values adjust the view downward.

Default Bindings

Listbox widgets are created with default bindings that are grouped into four classes of behavior based on **selectmode**.

Mouse Bindings

- Dragging out of the listbox with mouse button 1 pressed scrolls the listbox away from the mouse pointer until the mouse reenters the listbox, mouse button 1 is released, or the data has scrolled as far as it can.

- Dragging within the listbox with mouse button 2 pressed scrolls the listbox.

- Clicking an item with mouse button 1 in **single** or **browse** select mode selects it and deselects all others.

- Dragging with mouse button 1 pressed in **browse** select mode moves the selection to follow the mouse pointer.

- Clicking an item with mouse button 1 in **multiple** select mode toggles its selection state and leaves other items unaffected.

- Clicking an item with mouse button 1 in **extended** select mode selects it, deselects all others, and sets the anchor for extending the selection.

- Clicking an item with mouse button 1 while pressing SHIFT in **extended** select mode extends the selection from the anchor point to the item under the mouse pointer.

- Clicking an item with mouse button 1 while pressing CTRL in **extended** select mode toggles its selection state and leaves other items unaffected.

- Dragging with mouse button 1 pressed while pressing CTRL in **extended** select mode sets the selection state of all items between the anchor point and the mouse pointer to match the anchor item, and leaves other items unaffected.

- Dragging with mouse button 1 pressed in **extended** select mode extends the selection from the anchor point to the item under the mouse pointer.

Keyboard Bindings

- Pressing the UP ARROW and DOWN ARROW keys moves the active element up or down one item.

- Pressing the UP ARROW and DOWN ARROW keys in **browse** select mode selects the active element and deselects all others.

- Pressing the UP ARROW and DOWN ARROW keys in **extended** select mode selects the active element, deselects all others, and sets the anchor point to the active element.

- Pressing the LEFT ARROW and RIGHT ARROW keys scrolls the listbox left or right by one character (the width of 0).

- Pressing CTRL-LEFT ARROW, CTRL-PRIOR, CTRL-RIGHT ARROW, or CTRL-NEXT scrolls the listbox left or right by the width of the listbox.

- Pressing HOME and END scroll the listbox horizontally to show the left edge or right edge of the listbox.

- Pressing PRIOR and NEXT pages the listbox up or down by the height of the listbox.

- Pressing CTRL-HOME sets the location cursor to the first item in the listbox, selects that item, and deselects all others.

- Pressing CTRL-END sets the location cursor to the last item in the listbox, selects that item, and deselects all others.

- In **extended** select mode, pressing SHIFT with UP or DOWN ARROW key, HOME, or END extends the selection from the anchor point to the new active item.

- In **multiple** select mode, pressing SHIFT with HOME or END makes the active item the first or last, respectively.

- Pressing SELECT or the SPACEBAR selects the active item.

- Pressing SHIFT-SELECT or the SPACEBAR while pressing CTRL and SHIFT in **extended** select mode extends the selection to the active item.

- Pressing ESC in **extended** select mode cancels the most recent selection.

- Pressing CTRL-/ in **browse** or **single** select mode selects the active item.

- Pressing CTRL-/ in **extended** or **multiple** select mode selects all items in the listbox.

- Pressing CTRL-\ in all modes but **browse** deselects all items in the listbox.

- Pressing F16 (labeled COPY on some keyboards) or invoking the <<**Copy**>> virtual event copies the selection to the clipboard.

Example

```
# Create a short listbox
set l [listbox .listbox -height 10 -width 0 \
            -selectmode extended]
pack $l
# Put a lot of data in it
eval $l insert end [array names env]
# Make sure the first element is visible
$l see 0
# Make the last element visible
```

```
$1 see end
# Make the middle element visible
$1 yview moveto 0.5
# Select the first and last elements
$1 selection set 0
$1 selection set end
# Print out the selected elements
foreach index [$1 curselection] {
    puts [$1 get $index]
}
```

Programmer's Tip: *Many of the default bindings on listbox widgets are provided through procs. These procs include* **tkListboxAutoScan, tkListboxBeginExtend, tkListboxBeginSelect, tkListboxBeginToggle, tkListbox Cancel, tkListboxDataExtend, tkListboxExtendUpDown, tkListboxMotion, tkListboxSelectAll,** *and* **tkListboxUpDown.** *These commands are not of general interest and are not documented in this reference. The* **bind, info args,** *and* **info body** *commands can be used to explore the use and implementation of these commands.*

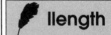

llength

The **llength** command returns the number of elements in a list. It takes this form:

> **llength** *list*

The arguments are as follows:

list
The list value to process.

RETURNS   The number of elements in *list*, expressed as an integer.

Example

```
puts "[llength $argv] arguments were passed in."
```

load

The **load** command loads binary code, such as a shared library, into the shell or application. Generally, this adds commands implemented in a compiled language, such as C, to a Tcl interpreter. (See also **info sharedlibextension**; **package**; **pkg_mkIndex**; **Safe Package**.) It takes this form:

> **load** *fileName ?packageName? ?interp?*

The arguments are as follows:

fileName
The file to load, such as mypackage.so or somepackage.dll. *fileName* may be an empty string if *packageName* refers to a statically loaded package or a dynamically loaded package that has already been loaded.

interp
Interpreter to load *packageName* into. If *interp* isn't specified, it defaults to the current interpreter.

packageName
Name of the package to load. If *packageName* is an empty string or is not specified, Tcl tries to guess the package name. The heuristics for guessing vary by platform. On most UNIX systems, the tail of *fileName* is stripped of the prefix "lib" (if present) and then the leading alphabetic and underscore characters are used as the package name. For example, **load libdir/libmy_pkg0.9.so** would load **my_pkg**.

packageName also controls the entry point in *fileName* used to initialize the package.

Description

The first time **load** is called for a file, the file is loaded into the shell or application. The exact mechanism for performing this load depends on the platform's support of dynamic or shared libraries. It is not possible to unload or reload a package. Each time **load** is called, it calls an initialization entry point for the package. The name of that entry point depends on the name of the package and whether *interp* is a safe or trusted interpreter.

The prefix of the entry point is built from *packageName* by making the first letter uppercase, making all other letters lowercase, and adding an underscore. For example, if *packageName* were **MYPKG**, **mypkg**, or **MyPkg**, the prefix would be **Mypkg_**.

If *interp* is trusted, the suffix for the entry point is **Init**. If *interp* is safe, the suffix for the entry point is **SafeInit**.

If *fileName* is an empty string, *packageName* must be specified, and Tcl tries to find a statically linked package or previously loaded dynamically linked package by that name. If more than one version of a package have been dynamically loaded, the first loaded is used.

RETURNS   The result of executing the initialization entry point.

ERROR   Raises an error if *fileName* does not exist, no appropriate initialization entry point can be found, or the initialization entry point returns an error.

Example

```
load Tktable.dll Tktable
```

The **lower** command changes a window's position in the Z order. (See also **raise**.) It takes this form:

    lower *window ?belowThis?*

The arguments are as follows:

belowThis
The window below which *window* should be moved. If *belowThis* is not specified, it defaults to the lowest sibling of *window*.

window
The path through the widget hierarchy to the window to move.

Example

```
label .riddle \
        -text "Why did the chicken cross the road"
grid .riddle -row 1 -column 1
label .answer -text "To get to the other side"
grid .answer -row 2 -column 1
button .answerCover \
        -text "Click here for answer" \
        -command {lower .answerCover}
grid .answerCover -row 2 -column 1
```

2

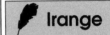

The **lrange** command extracts a sublist from a list. (See also **lindex**.) It takes this form:

> **lrange** *list first last*

The arguments are as follows:

first
The numeric index, starting at 0, of the first element of *list* to retrieve, or **end** to retrieve the last element. If *first* is less than 0, it is treated as if it were 0.

last
The numeric index, starting at 0, of the last element of *list* to retrieve, or **end** to retrieve the last element. If *last* is greater than the number of elements in *list*, it is treated as if it were **end**.

list
The list value to extract from.

Description

lrange returns a list, even if *first* and *last* are the same. Thus, **lrange $l $i $i** is not the same as **lindex $l $i**.

RETURNS   If *last* is greater than or equal to *first*, the specified elements of *list*. If *last* is less than *first*, an empty list is returned.

Example

```
# Make a list
set l1 [list a b c d]
# Extract {b c}
set l2 [lrange $l1 1 2]
```

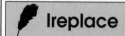 **lreplace**

The **lreplace** command makes a new list from another list by
replacing or deleting elements. It takes this form:

> lreplace *list first last ?element element ... ?*

The arguments are as follows:

element
Element to put in new list. If *element* isn't specified, the new list
has *first* to *last* deleted from it.

first
The numeric index, starting at 0, of the first element of *list* to
replace or delete, or **end** to retrieve the last element. If *first* is less
than 0, it is treated as if it were 0.

last
The numeric index, starting at 0, of the last element of *list* to
replace or delete, or **end** to retrieve the last element. If *last* is
greater than the number of elements in *list*, it is treated as if it
were **end**.

list
The list value to process.

RETURNS   If *last* is greater than or equal to *first*, a new list with
elements *first* to *last* deleted, and *elements*, if any, inserted in their
place. If *last* is less than *first*, a new list is returned with *elements*
inserted before *first*. Thus, **lreplace $l $i -1 foo** is the same as
linsert $l $i foo.

Example

```
# If $toFind is present in $1, remove it.
set index [lsearch $1 $toFind]
if {$index != -1} {
    set 1 [lreplace $1 $index $index]
}
```

lsearch

The **lsearch** command searches a list for a value. It takes this form:

lsearch *?mode? list pattern*

The arguments are as follows:

list
The list value to search.

mode
The mode for the search. *mode* may be one of the following:

Option	Purpose
-exact	*pattern* is a string that must match an element of *list* exactly.
-glob	*pattern* is a **glob**-style pattern as for **string match**. This is the default if *mode* is not specified.
-regexp	*pattern* is a regular expression as for **regexp**.

pattern
A mode-dependent pattern.

RETURNS   If *pattern* matches an element of *list*, the numeric index of the element. If *pattern* does not match an element of *list*, -1 is returned.

Example

```
# Find the element of the list after -foo
set index [lsearch $list -foo]
if {[$index != -1]} {
    set fooValue [lindex $list [incr $index]]
}
```

lsort

The **lsort** command sorts a list and returns a new list with the
elements in sorted order. It takes the following form:

> **list** *?options?* *list*

The following is its only argument:

list
The list value to sort.

The options are as follows:

Options specify what part of each element to compare, how to
compare it, and whether the resulting list is in ascending or
descending order. By default, each element in its entirety is used
for comparisons. This may be overridden with the **-index** option:

-index *index*   Treats each element of *list* as a list and uses the
                    index element of that sublist for comparison. *index*
                    may be **end**, to use the last element of each sublist.

By default, items are compared as ASCII strings. The following
options control how comparisons are done:

-ascii	Compares items as ASCII strings. This is the default.
-dictionary	Compares items as dictionary entries. This is the same as **-ascii**, except that case is ignored, and embedded digit strings are compared as integers, not characters. For example, **I18n** would sort between **i17n** and **i19n**.
-integer	Compares items as integers. For example, **20** would sort before **100**.
-real	Compares items as floating-point numbers.
-command *command*	Compares items by invoking *command*. For each two elements, e1 and e2, **lsort** invokes **eval** *command* **e1 e2**. *command* should return an integer less than 0 if **e1** is less than **e2**, an integer greater than 0 if **e1** is greater than **e2**, or 0 if **e1** is equal to **e2**.

The order of the sorted list may be controlled with the following options:

-increasing	Each element of the list is less than or equal to the next. This is the default.
-decreasing	Each element of the list is greater than or equal to the next.

RETURNS   The sorted list.

Example

```
# Dump an array in alphabetical order
foreach e [lsort [array names a]] {
    puts "$e:$a($e)"
}
```

menu

The **menu** command creates and manipulates widgets that display
choices in drop-down and cascaded menus. (See also **menubutton**;
tk_optionMenu; **tk_popup**; **toplevel**.)

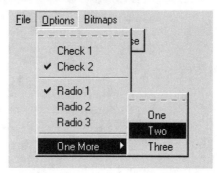

Menu Overview

Menu widgets provide a means to organize a hierarchical set of
choices, such as those for invoking application commands. Menus
can be displayed in several ways. A menu can be either attached to
a toplevel window as a menu bar (see discussion of the **-menu**
option under the **toplevel**), displayed "torn off" and free floating,
popped up over part of the application, or invoked by a
menubutton.

However a menu is invoked, its *postcommand* is invoked before it
is displayed. The postcommand can be used to rebuild the menu or
to enable and disable elements based on application state.

A menu is made up of entries of various sorts:

- **command** Invokes a script to perform some action
- **tear-off** Detaches the menu from its parent and leaves it
  displayed for more convenient use
- **cascade** Ties one menu to an entry in another menu
- **checkbutton** Displays on/off choices
- **radiobutton** Displays one-of-many choices
- **separator** Separates other entries into groups

Menus can be *cloned* and used in more than one context; for example, a single menu might be used both as a tear-off and on a menu bar. Changes to the original menu affect its clones.

Menu entries may contain text labels, bitmaps, or images (created with **image create**), and may be arranged in multiple columns, making it possible to display a palette or table of choices as a menu.

2

Each entry has up to three fields. The first field is valid only for checkbutton and radiobutton entries and is used to display the state of the entry. The second field displays the label, bitmap, or image. The third field displays the accelerator text for the entry.

Menus may be traversed either with the keyboard (using mnemonics and cursor keys) or with the mouse. Clicking a menu entry with the mouse invokes the entry. This has a different effect for each type of entry. Menu entries may be disabled, in which case they cannot be invoked. As a menu is traversed, each time the active entry is changed, a <<**MenuSelect**>> virtual event is generated. Binding to this event can allow, for example, context-sensitive hints based on the active entry of the menu.

Menu bars

A menu may be set as the menu bar for a toplevel window via the -**menu** option when the top level window is created or reconfigured. On UNIX and Microsoft Windows systems, the entries in the menu are displayed below the title bar of the toplevel window, and the first menu in the menu bar may be invoked by pressing F10. On Macintosh systems, the menu bar is displayed across the top of the main monitor whenever the toplevel window is in front.

Certain submenus of a menu bar are treated specially, depending on the operating system:

- **UNIX**   A submenu named .**help** is moved to the end of the menu bar and is right-justified.

- **Microsoft Windows**   A submenu named .**help** is moved to the end of the menu bar and is right-justified, as appropriate to the Microsoft Windows version. Also, entries in a submenu named .**system** are appended to the window's system menu (displayed by clicking the icon on the left end of the title bar). Font attributes, images, bitmaps, colors, and tear-off entries are not displayed in the system menu.

- **Macintosh** Items in an submenu named **.apple** are displayed at the top of the Apple menu, followed by a separator, and items in a submenu named **.help** are displayed at the bottom of the Help menu whenever the toplevel window is in front. Font attributes, images, bitmaps, and colors are not displayed in these Macintosh menus.

NOTE: On Macintosh systems, **.apple** and **.help** submenus should always be created with the -tearoff option disabled (false).

Command Entries

A command entry works much like a button widget. Each time a command entry is invoked, the script, if any, specified with **-command** is evaluated.

Separator Entries

Separator entries are displayed as horizontal lines between other entries. A separator may not be activated or invoked.

Checkbutton Entries

A checkbutton entry works much like a checkbutton widget. Each time a checkbutton entry is invoked, the value of the variable specified with **-variable** is toggled between the values specified with **-onvalue** and **-offvalue**. If a script was specified with **-command**, it is evaluated after the new value for the checkbutton is set.

Radiobutton Entries

A radiobutton entry works much like a radiobutton widget. Each time a radiobutton entry is invoked, the variable specified with **-variable** gets the value specified for the entry with **-value**, and other radiobutton entries that share that variable are deselected. If a script was specified with **-command**, it is evaluated after the new value for the radiobutton is set.

Cascade Entries

A cascade entry has a cascaded menu associated with it. Each time a cascade entry is invoked, the menu specified with **-menu** is *posted* (displayed) and other cascaded menus are *unposted* (removed from the display). If a script was specified with **-command**, it is evaluated whenever the menu entry is invoked.

NOTE: Commands for cascade menu entries are not supported on Microsoft Windows systems.

The **postcascade** menu command may be used to display cascaded menus.

Tear-off Entries

A tear-off entry appears at the top of the menu as a dashed line. When invoked, the menu and all of its submenus are cloned and displayed in a new toplevel window. A tear-off entry appears if **-tearoff** was set to True when the menu was created or reconfigured. Tear-off entries cannot be created with **add**, deleted with **delete**, or disabled with **configure**.

Menu Options

Menu widgets recognize the following standard widget options. (See the Appendix for a complete list of standard widget options and their meanings.)

activebackground	borderwidth	foreground
activeborderwidth	cursor	relief
activeforeground	disabledforeground	takefocus
background	font	

In addition, menu widgets recognize the following widget-specific options:

-postcommand *script*

Specifies a script to evaluate each time the menu is posted; for example, to enable and disable entries based on the state of the application.

NOTE: On Windows and Macintosh systems, all postcommand scripts are invoked only when the highest-level menu is posted.

-selectcolor *color*

Specifies the background color for the indicator for checkbutton and radiobutton entries when those entries are selected.

NOTE: The option database class for menu selection color is **Background**.

-tearoff *boolean*

Specifies whether this menu should include a tear-off entry. If **-tearoff** is not specified, *boolean* defaults to True.

-tearoffcommand *command*
Specifies a script to be evaluated whenever the menu is torn off.
When *command* is invoked, it will have two arguments appended
to it: the original name of the menu, and the name of the torn-off
clone. For example, if a menu were created as follows,

```
menu .mb.palette ... -tearoffcommand newTearOff
```

and .mb.palette were later torn off, newTearOff would be invoked
something like this:

```
newTearOff .mb.palette .mb.tearoff1
```

-title *string*
Specifies the title to be used when the menu is torn off. If the *string*
is an empty string (the default), the title of the tear-off menu
window is taken from the label of the cascade entry or menubutton
that displayed the menu.

-type *menutype*
Specifies the type of the menu. *menutype* must be **menubar**,
normal, or **tearoff**. The **-type** option is set automatically when a
menu is created and is used internally when menus are cloned.

Menu Commands

Menu widgets respond to the **cget** and **configure** standard widget
commands. (See the Appendix for details.) In addition, menu
widgets respond to the following widget-specific commands:

> *pathName* **activate** *index*
>
> *pathName* **add** *type ?option value ... ?*
> *pathName* **delete** *first ?last?*
> *pathName* **insert** *index type ?option value ... ?*
>
> *pathName* **clone** *newPathName ?cloneType?*
>
> *pathName* **entrycget** *index option*
> *pathName* **entryconfigure** *index ?option value ... ?*
>
> *pathName* **index** *index*
>
> *pathName* **invoke** *index*

> *pathName* **post** *x y*
> *pathName* **postcascade** *index*
> *pathName* **unpost**
>
> *pathName* **type** *index*
>
> *pathName* **yposition** *index*

Menu command arguments are as follows:

cloneType
The type of clone to create. Valid values are **menubar**, **normal**, and **tearoff**.

first
Entry index of the first menu entry to process.

index
A menu entry index. (See the following section, "Menu Indices," for details on the valid formats.)

last
Entry index of the last menu entry to process.

newPathName
Path name to give the cloned menu.

option
A menu entry option name. (See the following discussion of the **add** menu command for details.)

type
The menu entry type. Valid values are **cascade**, **checkbutton**, **command**, **radiobutton**, and **separator**.

value
A menu option value. (See the following discussion of the **add** command for details.)

x, y
Screen coordinates (in pixels) where the menu should be posted.

Menu Indices
Many **menu** widget commands take an *entry index* to specify which entry to act on. The menu index can take one of the following forms:

Index	Value
number	A menu entry by number. The first entry in a menu is 0, the second is 1, etc.
active	The currently active entry. If no entry is active, this is the same as **none**.
end	The last entry in the menu.
last	The last entry in the menu.
none	No entries. This is used most often with the **activate** menu command to deactivate all entries.
@y	The entry closest to position *y* from the top of the menu. *y* is a window coordinate.
pattern	The first menu entry whose label matches *pattern*. *pattern* is a **glob**-style pattern like those used by **string match**.

pathName activate *index*

Activates entry *index* and deactivates all others. If *index* is **none**, all entries are deactivated.

pathName add *type ?option value ... ?*

Creates a new *type* menu entry in *pathName* with the specified options. Valid options are the following:

Option	Purpose
-activebackground *color*	Specifies the background color to use when the entry is active. Not valid for separator or tear-off entries. If **-activebackground** isn't specified or *color* is an empty string, *color* defaults to the background color for the entry (the default). If **tk_strictMotif** is true, this option is ignored.
-activeforeground *color*	Specifies the foreground color to use when the entry is active. Not valid for separator and tear-off entries. If **-activeforeground** isn't specified or *color* is an empty string, *color* defaults to the foreground color for the entry (the default). If **tk_strictMotif** is true, this option is ignored.

Option	Purpose
-accelerator *string*	Specifies a string to be displayed on the right side of the entry. Usually, this is a shortcut key sequence, such as "Ctrl-s". Not valid for separator and tear-off entries.
-background *color*	Specifies the background color to use when the entry is in the normal state (not disabled and not active). Not valid for separator or tear-off entries. If **-background** isn't specified or *color* is an empty string, the background color for the menu is used (the default).
-bitmap *bitmap*	Specifies the bitmap to be displayed in the entry in place of a text label. Not valid for separator or tear-off entries. (See the description of the **-bitmap** option in the Appendix for valid values of *bitmap*.)[1]
-columnbreak *boolean*	Specifies that the entry should start a new column. If *boolean* is true, the entry starts a new column. If *boboolean* is false, the entry is displayed under the previous entry (the default).
-command *script*	Specifies a script to be evaluated when the entry is invoked. Not valid for separator or tear-off entries. Not valid for cascade entries on Microsoft Windows systems.
-font *font*	Specifies the font to use when drawing the label and/or accelerator for the entry. Not valid for separator or tear-off entries. If **-font** isn't specified or *font* is an empty string, the font for the menu is used.
-foreground *color*	Specifies the foreground color to use when the entry is in the normal state (not disabled and not active). Not valid for separator or tear-off entries. If **-foreground** isn't specified or *color* is an empty string, the foreground color for the menu is used (the default).

2

[1]**-image** has the highest precedence, then **-bitmap**, then **-label**. That is, if an image is specified, it overrides any bitmap or label, and if no image is specified, a bitmap overrides a label.

Option	Purpose
-hidemargin *boolean*	Specifies whether the standard margins should be drawn around the menu entry. If **-hidemargin** isn't specified, *bboolean* defaults to false (margin is drawn).
-image *image*	Specifies an image to be displayed in the menu entry. *image* is the name of an image created with the **image create** command. Not valid for separator or tear-off entries.[1]
-indicatoron *boolean*	Specifies whether an indicator should be displayed at left of entry. Valid only for checkbutton and radiobutton entries.
-label *string*	Specifies a string to be displayed in the entry. Not valid for separator and tear-off entries.[1]
-menu *menuPath*	Specifies the path name of a menu to be displayed when the entry is invoked. Valid only for cascade entries. *menuPath* must be a child of *pathName*. So **.mb add cascade Foo -menu .mb.foo** is a valid example; **.mb add cascade Foo -menu .foo** is not.
-offvalue *value*	Specifies a value to assign to the entry's variable when it is deselected. Valid only for checkbutton entries. If **-offvalue** isn't specified, *value* defaults to 0.
-onvalue *value*	Specifies a value to assign to the entry's variable when it is selected. Valid only for checkbutton entries. If **-onvalue** isn't specified, *value* defaults to 1.
-selectcolor *color*	Specifies a color to be displayed in the indicator when the entry is selected. Valid only for checkbutton and radiobutton entries. If **-selectcolor** isn't specified or *color* is an empty string, the select color for the menu is used (the default).

Option	Purpose
-selectimage *image*	Specifies an image to be displayed in the entry when it is selected. Valid only for checkbutton and radiobutton entries. *image* is the name of an image created with the **image create** command. This option is ignored unless **-image** is also specified.
-state *state*	Specifies the state of the entry. Not valid for separator or tear-off entries. *state* must be one of the following: **normal** Entry is displayed using the values from the **foreground** and **background** options. **active** Entry is displayed using the values from the **activeforeground** and **activebackground** options. This state is usually associated with the mouse pointer being over the entry. **disabled** Entry is displayed using the values from the **disabledforeground** of the menu and the **background** of the entry. Disabled entries cannot be activated or invoked by the user.
-underline *n*	Specifies which character in the label should be underlined and used as a mnemonic when navigating menus with the keyboard. Not valid for separator or tear-off entries. *n* is 0 for the first character in the label, 1 for the second, etc. This option is ignored if a bitmap or image is displayed in the entry.
-value *value*	Specifies a value to be assigned to the entry's variable when the entry is selected. Valid only for radiobutton entries. If **-value** isn't specified, or if *value* is an empty string, the entry's label string is used (the default).

2

Option	Purpose
-variable *value*	Specifies the name of the global variable to set when the entry is invoked. Valid only for checkbutton and radiobutton entries. If **-variable** isn't specified or *value* is an empty string, the entry's label string is used (the default).

pathName delete *first ?last?*

Deletes entries *first* to *last* from *pathName*. If *last* isn't specified, it defaults to *first* and only one entry is deleted. Attempting to delete the tear-off menu item is harmless but ineffective; use the **-tearoff** configuration option instead.

pathName insert *index type ?option value ... ?*

Inserts a new *type* entry before *index* with the specified options. Options are the same as for the **add** menu command.

NOTE: Attempting to insert before 0 if pathName *has tear-off enabled will insert before 1, after the tearoff.*

pathName clone *newPathName ?cloneType?*

Creates a *cloneType* clone of *pathName* named *newPathName*. *cloneType* may be **normal**, **menubar**, or **tearoff**. If *cloneType* isn't specified, it defaults to **normal**. Future changes to *pathName* are reflected in *newPathName*, and vice versa.

NOTE: This command usually is used only by the Tk library.

pathName entrycget *index option*

Retrieves the value of *option* for entry *index*. *option* may be any entry option supported by the **add** menu command.

RETURNS   The value of *option*.

pathName entryconfigure *index ?option?*

Retrieves the value for one or all options for the specified menu entry. Similar to the **configure** command for widgets (as described in the Appendix) except that it operates on an entry in the menu rather than on a widget.

RETURNS   If *option* is specified, a list of values for the option, in this form:

{*optionName dbName dbClass defaultValue currentValue*}

If *option* isn't specified, a list of lists is returned describing all the options for *index*. Each sublist is in the preceding form.

pathName entryconfigure *index option value* ?*option value ...* ?
Sets one or more options for entry index. Similar to the **configure** command for widgets except that it operates on a menu entry rather than on a widget.

pathName index *index*
Converts *index* to a numeric index.

RETURNS   A numeric index, or **none** if *index* is **none**.

pathName invoke *index*
Invokes entry *index* if it is not disabled.

RETURNS   If a *script* is specified for the entry with the -**command** option, the result of evaluating *script*. Otherwise, an empty string is returned.

pathName post *x y*
Displays *pathName* at screen coordinates (*x,y*). *x* and *y* are in pixels.

pathName postcascade *index*
Posts the cascade menu for *index* and unposts any other cascade menu currently posted. If *pathName* isn't posted or *index* isn't a **cascade** entry, just unposts any currently posted cascade menus.

pathName unpost
Removes *pathName* and any posted cascades from the display.

NOTE: This doesn't work on Microsoft Windows or Macintosh systems.

pathName type *index*
Retrieves the entry type for *index*.

RETURNS   **cascade, checkbutton, command, radiobutton,** or **separator**

pathName yposition *index*
Determines vertical window coordinates of the top of the bounding box for *index*.

RETURNS The number of pixels, expressed as an integer.

Default Bindings

Menu widgets are created with default bindings that are grouped into three classes of behavior:

- **Pull-down menus** This is the most common behavior. First-level menu entries are arranged in a menu bar, and cascaded menus are "pulled down" by invoking the first-level entries. The first-level entries may be either **cascade** entries in a menu set as the application's menu bar, with the **-menu** option of a **toplevel** widget, or **menubutton** widgets in a frame.

- **Pop-up menus** Displayed via a mouse click or keystroke bound to **tk_popup**.

- **Torn-off menus** Created by invoking the tear-off entry in a menu, and displayed as a free-floating menu that remains posted until dismissed by the user.

Mouse Bindings

- Dragging the mouse pointer into a menu activates the entry under the mouse pointer.

- Dragging the mouse pointer out of a menu deactivates all entries in the menu unless the mouse pointer is moving from a **cascade** entry to its cascaded menu.

- Releasing mouse button 1 over a menu invokes the active entry and, if the menu is not torn off, unposts the menu.

Keyboard Bindings

- Pressing SPACEBAR or ENTER invokes the active entry and, if the menu if not torn off, unposts the menu.

- Pressing the underlined letter for an entry in the menu (in upper- or lowercase) invokes that entry and, if the menu isn't torn off, unposts the menu.

- Pressing ESC in a non-torn-off menu deactivates all the entries in the menu and unposts the menu.

- Pressing the UP and DOWN ARROW keys activates the previous and next entry in the menu, respectively. Moving down from the last entry wraps to the first entry, and moving up from the first entry wraps to the last entry.

- Pressing the LEFT ARROW key in a cascaded menu unposts the cascaded menu and makes the cascaded entry in the parent active.

- Pressing the RIGHT ARROW key on a cascaded entry posts the cascaded menu and activates the first entry.

- Pressing the LEFT ARROW key in a pull-down menu unposts the pull-down menu and posts the pull-down menu for the previous entry in the menu bar.

- Pressing the RIGHT ARROW key in a pull-down menu unposts the pull-down menu and posts the pull-down menu for the next entry in the menu bar.

Example

```
# Create a menu
menu .mb
# Make it the menu bar for the main Tk window
. configure -menu .mb

# Create a basic File menu: Open, Close, Save,
# Exit. The post command disables Close if there's
# no file open
menu .mb.file -tearoff 0 \
        -postcommand \
            [list UpdateFileMenu .mb.file]

# Add the Open command to the file menu
.mb.file add command \
    -label Open -underline 0 \
    -accelerator "Ctrl-o" \
    -command FileOpen
# Make the accelerator work
bind . <Control-o> {.mb.file invoke Open}

# Add the Close command to the file menu, no
# accelerator
```

```
.mb.file add command \
    -label Close -underline 0 \
    -command FileClose

# Add the Save command to the file menu
.mb.file add command \
    -label Save -underline 0  \
    -accelerator "Ctrl-s" \
    -command FileSave
# Make the save accelerator work
bind . <Control-s> {.mb.file invoke Save}

# Add a separator above Exit
.mb.file add separator

# Add the Exit command and accelerator
.mb.file add command \
    -label Exit -underline 1 \
    -accelerator "Ctrl-x" \
    -command exit
bind . <Control-x> {.mb.file invoke Exit}

.mb add cascade -label File -underline 0 \
        -menu .mb.file


# Add some special options
menu .mb.options -title ""

.mb.options add checkbutton -label "Check 1" \
        -variable check1
.mb.options add checkbutton -label "Check 2" \
        -variable check2
.mb.options add separator
.mb.options add radiobutton -label "Radio 1" \
        -variable radio -value 0
.mb.options add radiobutton -label "Radio 2" \
        -variable radio -value 1
.mb.options add radiobutton -label "Radio 3" \
        -variable radio -value 2

.mb add cascade -label Options -underline 0 \
        -menu .mb.options

# A menu with bitmaps instead of labels
```

```
menu .mb.bitmaps -tearoff 0
.mb.bitmaps add command -bitmap error \
    -command {puts "Error"}
.mb.bitmaps add command -bitmap info \
    -command {puts "Info"}
.mb.bitmaps add command -bitmap question \
    -command {puts "Question"}

.mb add cascade -label Bitmaps -menu .mb.bitmaps

# Add to the System menu.
menu .mb.system
.mb.system add command \
    -label "Surprise" -underline 0 \
    -command {puts "Boo!"}


# Called each time the file menu is displayed to
# update the Close option
proc UpdateFileMenu { m } {
    if {[isOpen]} {
        $m entryconfigure Close -state normal
    } else {
        $m entryconfigure Close -state disabled
    }
}

# Invoked by the Open option of the File menu
proc FileOpen { } {
    set file [tk_getOpenFile]
    if {[string length $file] != 0} {
        puts "User wants to open $file"
    } else {
        puts "Open canceled"
    }
}

proc FileSave { } {
    set file [tk_getSaveFile]
    if {[string length $file] != 0} {
        puts "User wants to save to $file"
    } else {
        puts "Save canceled"
    }
}
```

2

```
proc isOpen { } {
    global flag
    if { ! [info exists flag]} {
        set flag 1
    }
    set flag [expr {! $flag}]
    return $flag
}

bind . <Button-3> \
    [list tk_popup .mb.options %X %Y]
```

Programmer's Tip: *Many of the default bindings on*
menu *widgets are provided through procs, which include*
tkMenuDownArrow, tkMenuEscape, tkMenuFind,
tkMenuFindName, tkMenuFirstEntry, tkMenuInvoke,
tkMenuLeave, tkMenuLeftArrow, tkMenuMotion,
tkMenuNextEntry, tkMenuNextMenu, tkMenuRightArrow,
tkMenuUnpost, tkMenuUpArrow *and* ***tkTraverseWithinMenu.***
These commands aren't of general interest and thus aren't
documented in this reference. The ***bind,*** **info args,** *and* ***info***
body *commands can be used to explore the use and*
implementation of these commands.

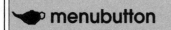 **menubutton**

The **menubutton** command creates and manipulates button
widgets that display menus. Menu buttons are typically arranged
into a menu bar at the top of an application window. (See also
listbox; menu; tk_optionMenu.)

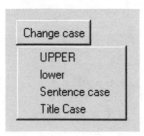

Menubutton Options

Menubutton widgets recognize the following standard widget
options. (See the Appendix for a complete list of standard widget
options and their meanings.)

activebackground	cursor	highlightthickness	takefocus
activeforeground	disabledforeground	image	text
anchor	font	justify	textvariable
background	foreground	padx	underline
bitmap	highlightbackground	pady	wraplength
borderwidth	highlightcolor	relief	

In addition, menubutton widgets recognize the following
widget-specific options:

-direction *direction*
Specifies where the menu is to be popped up. *direction* may be one
of the following:

- **above**   Tries to pop up the menu above the button
- **below**   Tries to pop up the menu below the button
- **left**   Tries to pop up the menu to the left of the button
- **right**   Tries to pop up the menu to the right of the button
- **flush**   Pops up the menu in front of the button

-height *distance*
Specifies the desired height of the menubutton in either screen
units (if an image is specified) or in lines of text (if button text is
specified). If this option is omitted, Tk computes the correct height
from the image or text dimensions.

-indicatoron *boolean*
Specifies whether or not an indicator should be drawn for the
menubutton. If *boolean* is false, no indicator is drawn. If *boolean* is
true, an indicator rectangle is drawn on the right of the
menubutton, and the default menu bindings treat the menubutton
as an option menu. If **-indicatoron** isn't specified, *boolean* defaults
to false.

-menu *menu*
Specifies the menu to be displayed when the menubutton is
invoked. *menu* must be a child of the menubutton in the widget
hierarchy.

-state *state*
Specifies the state of the entry. *state* must be one of the following:

- **normal**   The menubutton is displayed using the values from
  the **foreground** and **background** options.

- **active**   The menubutton is displayed using the values from
  the **activeforeground** and **activebackground** options. This
  state is usually associated with the mouse pointer being over
  the menubutton.

- **disabled**   The menubutton is displayed using the values from
  the **disabledforeground** and the **background** of the
  menubutton. Disabled menubuttons cannot be activated or
  invoked by the user.

-width *distance*
The desired width of the menubutton in either screen units (when
an image is specified) or in characters (if button text is specified).
If this option is omitted, Tk computes the correct width from the
image or text dimensions.

Menubutton Commands

Menubutton widgets respond to the **cget** and **configure** standard
widget commands. (See the Appendix for details.) Menubuttons
have no widget-specific commands.

Default Bindings

Menubuttons are created with bindings that make them behave as
expected consistent with the user interface conventions on each
platform. Specifically:

Mouse Bindings

- Dragging the mouse pointer into a menubutton activates it.

- Dragging the mouse pointer out of a menubutton deactivates it.

- Pressing mouse button 1 over the menubutton posts the associated menu and allows an entry to be selected by dragging into the menu.

- Releasing mouse button 1 in the menu invokes the active entry.

- Releasing mouse button 1 outside the menubutton and its menu unposts the menu.

- Clicking mouse button 1 over the menubutton posts the associated menu and leaves it posted until another event unposts it.

2

Keyboard Bindings

- Pressing SPACEBAR or ENTER while the menubutton has input focus posts the associated menu.

Example

```
menubutton .case -text "Change case" \
        -direction above -takefocus 1 \
        -relief raised -borderwidth 2

menu .case.choices -tearoff 0
.case.choices add command -label UPPER
.case.choices add command -label lower
.case.choices add command -label "Sentence case"
.case.choices add command -label "Title Case"

.case configure -menu .case.choices
```

Programmer's Tip: *Many of the default bindings on*
menubutton *widgets are provided through procs, which include*
tkMbButtonUp, tkMbEnter, tkMbLeave, tkMbMotion, tkMbPost,
and ***tkMenuButtonDown***. *These commands aren't of general
interest and thus aren't documented in this reference. The* ***bind***,
info args, *and* ***info body*** *commands can be used to explore the use
and implementation of these commands.*

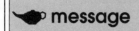

The **message** command creates and manipulates widgets that contain read-only formatted text. (See also **entry**; **label**; **text**; **tk_messageBox**.)

> This is line 1
> This is line 2

Message Overview

A message widget differs from a label widget in several important ways:

- The text in the message is broken over several lines, as needed, to preserve the specified aspect ratio
- The text in the message may be left-, right-, or center-justified
- Tabs are replaced with enough blank space to line up with the next eight-character boundary (this works best with left-justified text)
- Newlines cause line breaks
- Other control characters and characters not defined in the font used for the message are expanded to hexadecimal escape sequences in the form \x*hh*, where *hh* is the two-digit hexadecimal number representing the character

Message Options

Message widgets recognize the following standard widget options. (See the Appendix for a complete list of standard widget options and their meanings.)

anchor	foreground	pady
background	highlightbackground	relief
borderwidth	highlightcolor	takefocus
cursor	highlightthickness	text
font	padx	textvariable

In addition, message widgets recognize the following widget-specific options:

-aspect *integer*
Specifies the desired aspect ratio for the message widget. *integer* must be a nonnegative integer representing: 100 * width/height. For example, 200 means that the text will be twice as wide as it is tall. If **-aspect** isn't specified, *integer* defaults to 150. **-aspect** is ignored if **-width** is specified with a value greater than 0.

-justify *justification*
Specifies either **left**, **center**, or **right** to control the justification of all lines in the message.

-width *distance*
Specifies the width of the message in screen units. If *distance* is greater than 0, **-aspect** is ignored. If *distance* is less than or equal to 0, it is ignored and **-aspect** determines the width of the message.

Message Commands

Message widgets respond to the **cget** and **configure** standard widget commands. (See the Appendix for details.) Messages have no widget-specific commands.

Default Bindings

There are no default bindings on label widgets. They aren't intended to be interactive.

Example

```
message .msg \
        -text "This is line 1\nThis is line 2"
```

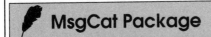

MsgCat Package

The **msgcat** package provides commands to manipulate message catalogs, to support internationalized applications. (See also **format**; **namespace**; **package**; **scan**.)

Message Catalog Overview

Message catalogs provide a means to "localize" or "internationalize" applications, without making source code changes, by storing strings that will be shown to the user separate from the source code. (In addition, the **format** command may be used to reorder words to account for differences in languages.) For example, whereas someone in the U.S. would tell you about the color of his truck, someone in Britain would specify the colour of a lorry. The following would display a dialog box comfortable and familiar to users in either of these locations:

```
mcset en_US truck
mcset en_US color
mcset en_UK truck lorry
mcset en_UK color colour
tk_chooseColor -title "What [mc color]\ [mc truck]?"
```

Locale Specifications
Each supported language or dialect is represented by a *locale*. In the previous example, **en_US** and **en_UK** are the locales for U.S. English and British English. A locale specification is made up of one to three fields, separated by underscores:

- **ISO-639 language code**   For example, **en** for English. This is the only required field.

- **ISO-3166 country code**   For example, **US** for the United States; **UK** for the United Kingdom (Great Britain). This field is optional, but must be specified to include the system-specific code.

- **system-specific code**   A field to specify an application- or system-specific level of detail in translations. This might be used to distinguish between user levels or products.

Each locale has its own *message catalog*. Message catalogs are searched from the most specific to the least specific. For example, if the current locale is **en_US_friendly**, **mc** would search **en_US_friendly**, and then **en_US**, and then **en**. The locale defaults to the contents of **$env(LANG)**, if it exists, and to "**C**" if it does not.

Message Files
A message catalog may be stored in a *message file* containing **mcset** commands registering messages for that locale. The name of

the message file must be the name of the locale followed by a **.msg** extension. In the previous example, the first two lines might be put in the file en_US.msg, the second two might be put in en_UK.msg, and then **mcload** would load the correct message file.

Message files may be stored in any directory, but all message files for a package must be in the same directory. It is recommended that this be a directory named **msgs** under the package directory. This allows the package initialization to load packages with a simple command, like:

```
::msgcat::mcload [file join \
                    [file dirname [info script]] \
                    msgs]
```

Messages and Namespaces
Strings in a message catalog are stored with an indication of which namespace they were stored from. In this way, a package may store short strings without fear of collisions with other packages. For example, the following code:

```
mcset en prompt "I'm ::. What's your name?"
namespace eval ns {
    mcset en prompt "I'm ns. What's your name?"
}
puts [mc prompt]
namespace eval ns {
    puts [mc prompt]
}
```

produces the following output:

```
I'm ::. What's your name?
I'm ns. What's your name?
```

Syntax

::msgcat::mc *src-string*

::msgcat::mclocale
::msgcat::mclocale *locale*

::msgcat::mcpreferences

::**msgcat::mcload** *dirname*

::**msgcat::mcset** *locale src-string ?translate-string?*

::**msgcat::mcunknown** *locale src-string*

The arguments are as follows:

dirname
The directory to search for message files.

locale
A locale specification. (See the preceding section for details.)

src-string
The string to translate.

translate-string
The translation of *src-string*.

::msgcat::mc *src-string*

Translates *src-string* to the current locale.

RETURNS   The translation for *src-string*, if it is found. If no
translation if found, **mcunknown** is called and its result is returned.

::msgcat::mclocale

Determines the current locale.

RETURNS   The name of the current locale.

::msgcat::mclocale *locale*

Sets the current locale to *locale*.

RETURNS   The new locale name, *locale*.

::msgcat::mcpreferences

Retrieves a list of the locales preferred by the user.

RETURNS   A list of locales, in the order in which they will be searched for translation strings.

::msgcat::mcload *dirname*

Searches *dirname* for files with a **.msg** extension and matching the list returned by **mcpreferences**, and sources each one that is found.

2

RETURNS   The number of files found and loaded.

::msgcat::mcset *locale src-string ?translate-string?*

Sets the translation of *src-string* in *locale* to be *translate-string*. If *translate-string* isn't specified, it defaults to *src-string*.

::msgcat::mcunknown *locale src-string*

Handles strings not found in any message catalog. **mc** calls **mcunknown** when a string has no translation in the current locale. The default behavior is to return *src-string*. Applications may redefine **mcunknown** to, for example, log an error message.

NOTE: mcunknown is called via **uplevel** so that it is at the same call level as the original call to **mc**.

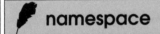 namespace

The **namespace** command creates and manipulates scopes for commands and variables. (See also **global**; **variable**.)

Programmer's Tip: *William H. Duquette has written a useful and practical guide to namespaces and packages. Look for Will's guides at **www.cogent.net/~duquette/tcl/namespaces.html**.*

Namespace Overview

A Tcl namespace provides a means to protect libraries from one another by segregating variable and command names into named spaces or scopes, like a C module or a C++ class or namespace.

A namespace may contain commands, variables, and other namespaces. By creating namespaces within namespaces, a hierarchy much like the Tk widget hierarchy or **interp** hierarchy results. The root of the namespace hierarchy has the empty string as its name. The parts of the path through a namespace hierarchy are separated by the scoping operator, ::. Just as Tk widget names cannot contain . (dot), namespace names cannot contain ::.

The *qualified* name of any command, variable, or namespace includes its name and the name of the namespace it is in, such as **foo::bar**. A *fully qualified* name starts at the top-level namespace and specifies all namespaces down to the item of interest. Because the name of the top-level namespace is an empty string, a fully qualified name always starts with ::. A *relative* name specifies a path to the item of interest relative to the current namespace. Relative names do not include the leading ::. An *unqualified* name includes no namespace information.

Namespace variables may be shared between commands in the namespace (like static variables in a C module), but may also be accessed from outside the namespace by using a qualified name.

Namespace commands may be used without qualification within a namespace, and may be exported for ease of use by other namespaces. Exported commands may be imported by another namespace, after which they may be used with an unqualified name. However, commands that aren't exported may still be accessed from outside the namespace by using a qualified name.

When trying to resolve a relative or unqualified variable or command name, Tcl looks first in the current namespace, and then in the global (top-level) namespace. For example, the following script:

```
set ::x 1
namespace eval ::foo {
    variable y
    set y 2
}
proc ::foo::printxy { } {
    variable x
    variable y
    puts "x:$x y:$y"
}
::foo::printxy
```

produces the following output:

```
x:1 y:2
```

because y is found as a variable in the current namespace and x is found in the top-level namespace (global scope).

When trying to resolve a relative or unqualified namespace name, Tcl looks only in the current namespace. If a qualified command or variable name ends in ::, the name of the command or variable is assumed to be {} (and empty list). If a qualified namespace name ends in ::, the :: is ignored.

Syntax

namespace children *?namespace? ?pattern?*
namespace parent *?namespace?*

namespace code *script*

namespace current

namespace delete *?namespace namespace ... ?*

namespace eval *namespace script*

namespace export
namespace export *?-**clear**? ?pattern pattern ... ?*

namespace forget *?pattern pattern ... ?*
namespace import *?-**force**? ?pattern pattern ... ?*

namespace inscope *namespace arg ?arg ... ?*

namespace origin *command*

namespace qualifiers *?string?*

namespace tail *?string?*

namespace which *?-**command**? ?-**variable**? name*

The arguments are as follows:

arg
An argument to evaluate.

command
An imported command name.

name
A relative name to resolve.

namespace
The namespace name.

pattern
A **glob**-style pattern to specify what will be operated on.

script
A Tcl script.

string
A qualified name to parse.

namespace children ?namespace? ?pattern?

Retrieves a list of namespaces in *namespace* that match *pattern*.
If *namespace* isn't specified, it defaults to the current namespace.
If *pattern* doesn't start with ::, the fully qualified name of
namespace is prepended to it.

RETURNS   An unordered list of fully qualified namespace names.

namespace parent ?namespace?

Retrieves the parent namespace for *namespace*. If *namespace* isn't
specified, it defaults to the current namespace.

RETURNS   The fully qualified name of the parent namespace.

namespace code *script*

Encapsulates *script* so that when it is evaluated later, it is done in
the current namespace. One important use of this is for widget

bindings and commands that are evaluated in the global scope, as in this example:

```
button .b -command [namespace code \
                    [list namespaceCmd arg1 arg2]]
```

NOTE: The encapsulation is done in such a way that if the resulting script has additional arguments appended when it is invoked, the arguments are handled correctly.

RETURNS   The encapsulated script.

namespace current

Retrieves the fully qualified name of the current namespace.

RETURNS   :: for the top-level namespace; for all others, the fully qualified namespace name.

namespace delete ?namespace namespace ... ?

Deletes one or more namespaces and all the variables, commands, and namespaces they contain.

ERROR   Raises an error if *namespace* doesn't exist.

namespace eval *namespace script*

Evaluates *script* in *namespace*. If *namespace* doesn't exist, it is created. Thus, **namespace eval *namespace* {}** creates a new namespace. If *namespace* contains multiple levels of namespaces, all required levels are created.

RETURNS   The result of evaluating *script*.

namespace export

Retrieves a list of commands exported by the current namespace.

RETURNS   A list of unqualified command names.

namespace export ?-clear? ?pattern pattern ... ?

Adds *pattern* to the list of command name patterns to export. *pattern* must specify unqualified names. If **-clear** is specified, the current list of command name patterns is cleared first.

namespace forget ?pattern pattern ... ?

Removes imported commands from the current namespace. *pattern* may specify qualified names, but the **glob** characters may only appear in the command name.

namespace import ?-force? ?pattern pattern ... ?

Imports the commands currently matching *pattern* to the current namespace. *pattern* specifies qualified names, but the **glob** characters may only appear in the command name. The commands must be exported by the namespace they are imported from and may have been created in or imported into it.

ERROR   Raises an error if a command by the same name already exists, unless **-force** is specified.

namespace inscope namespace arg ?arg ... ?

Evaluates *args* in *namespace*. This is used by **namespace code** and isn't expected to be used directly in scripts. It is like **namespace eval**, but handles its arguments slightly different so that callbacks and bindings work as expected.

RETURNS   The result of evaluating the combined *args*.

namespace origin command

Retrieves the fully qualified name of *command*. Typically, *command* is an imported command, and **namespace origin** returns the path command from which it was imported.

RETURNS   The fully qualified name of the source command.

namespace qualifiers *?string?*

Retrieves the namespace part of the qualified name *string*. *string* need not refer to an existing namespace. (This is like **file directory**, except that it parses namespace names rather than filenames.)

RETURNS   The part of *string* up to, but not including, the last ::.

namespace tail *?string?*

Retrieves the last part of the qualified name *string*. *string* need not refer to an existing namespace. (This is like **file tail**, except that it parses namespace names rather than filenames.)

RETURNS   The part of *string* after the last ::.

namespace which *?-command?* *?-variable? name*

Resolves *name* as a command or variable. If neither **-command** nor **-variable** is specified, **-command** is the default.

RETURNS   If *name* exists in the current or top-level namespace, the fully qualified name of *name*. If *name* doesn't exist, an empty string is returned.

Example

```
namespace eval stack {
    namespace export \
            init \
            push \
            pop \
            done

    variable Stack
}

proc stack::init { } {
    variable Stack
```

```
    if {[info exists Stack(count)] } {
        incr Stack(count)
    } else {
        set Stack(count) 0
    }
    set Stack($Stack(count)) {}
    return $Stack(count)
}

proc stack::done { s } {
    variable Stack
    catch {unset Stack($s)}
}

proc stack::push { s item } {
    variable Stack
    lappend Stack($s) $item
}

proc stack::pop { s } {
    variable Stack
    set item [lindex $Stack($s) end]
    set Stack($s) [lreplace $Stack($s) end end]
    return $item
}
```

open

The **open** command creates a channel to perform I/O on a file,
command pipeline, or serial port. (See also **close**; **exec**; **file**; **gets**;
read; **puts**; **socket**.) It takes the following forms:

open *name ?access? ?permissions?*

The arguments are as follows:

access
How the resulting channel will be accessed. (See the following
section, "Access," for details.)

name
A string specifying the name of a file or serial port to open, or the commands to execute.

permissions
File system permissions for *name*. Valid only if *name* is a file.

RETURNS   A handle for the newly opened channel.

Access

The *access* argument may take one of two forms: a one- or two-character short specification, or a list of POSIX flag words. Valid access characters are the following:

Character	Purpose
r	Opens an existing file for reading. This is the default if *access* isn't specified.
r+	Opens an existing file for reading and writing.
w	Opens a new file for writing; overwrites an existing file by the same name, if one exists.
w+	Opens a new file for reading and writing; overwrites an existing file by the same name, if one exists.
a	Opens an existing file for writing at the end of the file. Valid only for files.
a+	Opens an existing file for reading and writing at the end of the file. Valid only for files.

POSIX flags specify the I/O usage of the file and other modifiers. The list of flags must include one of the three following I/O flags:

Flag	Purpose
RDONLY	Opens the file for reading only
WRONLY	Opens the file for writing only
RDWR	Opens the file for reading and writing

The following are the modifier flags:

Flag	Purpose
APPEND	Sets the file pointer to the end of file before each write.

Flag	Purpose
CREAT	Creates the file if it doesn't exist. If **CREAT** isn't specified, an error is raised if the file doesn't exist.
EXCL	If **CREAT** is specified, raises an error if the file already exists.
NOCTTY	If *name* is a terminal device (e.g., stdin), doesn't let it be the controlling terminal for this process.
NONBLOCK	Uses nonblocking I/O. Note, this flag shouldn't be used. Use **fconfigure** to set blocking mode.
TRUNC	Truncates the file if it exists.

Opening Files

If *name* isn't recognized as a serial port name and doesn't start with | (a vertical bar), it is assumed to be the name of a disk file to open. (See the **file** entry for the valid filename formats.) If this results in creating a new file, *permissions* specifies the file system permissions for the file as an integer. If *permissions* isn't specified, it defaults to 0666.

permissions is a UNIX-style integer "mode." A file mode is usually presented in octal (thus the leading 0 in the default, 0666). Each octal digit represents a different class of user: the first digit is for the file's owner, the second digit is for the owner's user group, and the third digit is for all others. Each of the three bits for the octal digit represents a different type of access: the first digit is for read access, the second is for write access, and the third is for execute access.

On UNIX systems, *permissions* accurately describes the file mode given to the newly created file. On Microsoft Windows systems, the second bit of the first octal digit controls the read-only attribute. *permissions* may be 0*nxx*, where *x* is any octal digit (0-7) that is ignored. The file is read-only if *n* is 0, 1, 4, or 5, and is read/write if *n* is 2, 3, 6, or 7. Other file system permissions for a file may be set for existing files with **file attributes**.

On Macintosh systems, *permissions* is ignored.

Example

```
set infile [open "input.txt" "r"]
set outfile \
        [open "output.txt" "CREAT | WRONLY" 0666]
```

```
while { ! [eof $infile]} {
    set len [gets $infile line]
    set modified [modify_line $line]
    puts $outfile $modified
}
```

Opening Serial Ports

On UNIX systems, serial port names are generally in the form
/dev/ttyX, where *X* is **a** or **b**, but any pseudofile that maps to a
serial port may be opened for serial I/O. On Microsoft Windows
systems, serial port names are generally in the form *comX:*, where
X is an integer, generally from 1 to 4. Trying to open a serial port
that doesn't exist raises an error. On Macintosh systems, accessing
serial ports requires an extension such Sean Wood's **Odie** available
at **www.wdsdsgn.com/odie**.

Once a serial port is open, **fconfigure** can be used to set its options.
The general form is as follows:

fconfigure *$port* **-mode** *mode*

mode is a string of four, comma-separated values specifying
the following:

- **Baud rate**   An integer
- **Parity**   **n** (none), **o** (odd), **e** (even), **m** (mark), or **s** (space)
- **Number of data bits**   An integer from 5 to 8
- **Number of stop bits**   1 or 2

For example,

```
set port [open /dev/ttya w]
fconfigure $port -mode 9600,n,8,1
```

opens /dev/ttya and sets it to 9600 baud, no parity, 8 data bits, and
1 stop bit.

Starting a Command Pipeline

If the first character of *name* is a vertical bar (|), then the rest of
name is treated as a command pipeline to execute the same as

exec. The channel handle returned by **open** may be used to write to the pipeline's stdin or read from its stdout (depending on *access*). Opening a command pipeline in an interactive, console-based shell (such as tclsh) can lead to conflicts accessing stdin and stdout.

On Macintosh systems, **open** cannot be used to run applications.

Example

```
# Handle data on channel, set doneName on eof,
# use callback to handle each line of output
proc handleOutput { channel doneName callback } {
    set line [gets $channel]
    if {[eof $channel]} {
        close $channel
        set ::$doneName 1
    }
    eval $callback $line
}
# Start the pipeline
set fid [open "|someProg | someFilter" r]
# Set up to handle its output in background
fileevent $fid readable \
        [list handleOutput $fid done puts]
# Wait until done
vwait done
```

 **option**

The **option** command manipulates the option database.

Option Overview

The Tk option database is based on the method of specifying options in the X Window System, but it differs from the X Window System facilities in important ways. One of the most important distinctions is that X Window option patterns are processed in such a way that if two or more patterns match a request, the most specific is used. In Tk, the last defined is used. This means that the order of specifying options (with **option add** or in option files) is important. Generally, if the options are added or specified from most general to most specific, the desired effect will be achieved.

One unfortunate effect of **option**'s X Window System heritage is that, unlike most of Tcl and Tk, it has no introspection features. It is impossible to request a list of defined values or to distinguish between a blank value stored in the database and a value that isn't present.

2

Syntax

> **option add** *pattern value ?priority?*
>
> **option clear**
>
> **option get** *window name class*
>
> **option readfile** *fileName ?priority?*

The arguments are as follows:

class
A database option or widget class.

filename
The name of the file to read from.

name
A database option name. (The Appendix describes using the **configure** widget command to determine database option classes.)

pattern
A string of option names and/or classes describing the option. (See the following discussion of **option add** for details.)

priority
The priority to assign a new database entry. When two database entries conflict, the one with a higher priority number is used. *priority* may be an integer from 0 to 100, or one of the following symbolic priorities. Use of numeric priorities is discouraged. If *priority* isn't specified, it defaults to **interactive**.

Priority Symbol	Meaning
widgetDefault	Equivalent to priority 20. Used for default values hard-coded in Tk widgets.
startupFile	Equivalent to priority 40. Used for options in application startup files (e.g., those read with **option readfile**).
userDefault	Equivalent to priority 60. Used for options in user startup files (e.g., .Xdefaults on UNIX).
interactive	Equivalent to priority 80. Used for options set interactively in the application (e.g., with **option add**). This is the default.

value
The value to store in the database.

window
A path through the widget hierarchy. *window* must exist.

option add *pattern value ?priority?*

Adds *value* to the option database for *pattern* at *priority*. If *priority* isn't specified, it defaults to **interactive**. *value* may be a value of any type: string, list, integer, floating-point number, and so on. *pattern* is a list of database option names, widget names, and class names separated by dots (.). This is much like a widget path except that one or more nodes in the path may be replaced by an asterisk (*) to match all intermediate levels, much like a **glob**-style pattern match.

Option database entries are primarily used for two purposes: to establish widget defaults for an application and to pass configuration or other data between parts of an application. A complete pattern starts with an application class, includes a full widget path, and ends with an option name. For example,

```
Appl.mainwindow.text.font
```

sets the font for a widget named **.mainwindow.text** in an application whose class is **App1**. To set all fonts in the application, the pattern would be **App1*font**. To set fonts for all applications, regardless of class, use ***font**.

Classes may appear within the pattern, as well. For example, to set the font only for buttons, use the pattern ***Button.font**. To set the background only for buttons in frames of class **Toolbar**, use pattern **Toolbar*Button.background**.

Once widget default values are stored in the database, they are used automatically as new widgets that match the patterns are created. Note that options specified explicitly when a widget is created always override any value in the option database.

When using the option database to pass configuration data, the last part of the pattern isn't a standard option name, but rather is an arbitrary, user-specified string (which cannot contain dots or asterisks). Because there is no introspection of the option database, this value must be agreed upon; otherwise, the intended recipient of the data cannot retrieve it. Here is an example:

```
option add *Myclass.somename "a b c"
...
frame .f -class Myclass
option get .f somename {}
```

option clear

Removes all entries from the option database.

NOTE: On UNIX systems, default options from the RESOURCE_MANAGER or .Xdefaults will be loaded the next time any other **option** command is called.

option get *window name class*

Retrieves the value of an option for *window. name* or *class* may be {} (an empty list).

RETURNS   The highest priority value from the database. If no patterns match *name* and *class*, an empty string is returned.

Programmer's Tip: *Because standard widget options from the database are automatically used when creating a widget, and because a window must already exist to call* **option get***, this is most useful to retrieve arbitrary data stored in the option database by another part of the application. (See the* **option add** *example.)*

option readfile *fileName ?priority?*

Reads option settings from *fileName* and stores them in the database at *priority*. If *priority* isn't specified, it defaults to **interactive**. Each line of *fileName* includes a pattern, as described for **option add**, and a value, separated by a colon and a space. Here is an example:

```
*background: white
*font: Courier
```

Example

```
# Font size for normal dialog boxes
option add *Normal*font {-size 12}
# Make stuff bigger in Big dialog boxes
option add *Big*borderWidth 5
option add *Big*font {-size 18}
# Shows multiple classes
option add *Big*Small*font {-size 9}
# Create two toplevel windows that differ only in
# class. The option database makes them appear
# very different.
foreach tl {.tl1 .tl2} class { Normal Big } {
    toplevel $tl -class $class

    button $tl.b -text "$class button"
    label $tl.l  -text "$class label"
    frame $tl.f -width 100 -height 50 -class Small
    pack $tl.b $tl.l $tl.f

    label $tl.f.l -text "Small"
    pack $tl.f.l
}
```

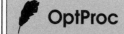 **OptProc**

The **OptProc** command creates a new Tcl procedure with flexible option processing. (See also **proc**.) It takes this form:

> ::**tcl**::**OptProc** *name arguments body*

The arguments are as follows:

arguments

A list of arguments to *name*. If *name* takes no arguments, the list is empty (⦃⦄). Each element of *arguments* is a list of one to four fields which specifies one argument to *name* in the following form:

> *argumentName ?argumentType? ?defaultValue? ?helpText?*

The fields are described below.

body

The script to evaluate when *name* is invoked. *body* is evaluated in the context of its namespace. Each argument listed in *arguments* is created as a local variable to *name* and assigned a value from the invocation of *name*. Additional local variables may be created by assignment (for example, with **set**). All local variables are deleted when the script terminates.

Global variables may be brought in scope with the **global** and **variable** commands, namespace variables may be brought in scope with the **variable** command, and variables in other call stack frames may be accessed with **upvar**.

body may include a **return** statement to return a value when *name* is invoked. If *body* doesn't include a **return** statement, the value of the last command in *body* is returned.

name

The name to give the new procedure. If *name* is an unqualified name (doesn't include any namespace qualifiers), the procedure is created in the current namespace; otherwise, it is created in the specified namespace.

Argument Names

Arguments may be *flags*, *options*, or *positional arguments*.

If *argumentName* starts with a dash (-), it is treated as a flag or option. When *name* is invoked, a local variable will be created corresponding to the flag or option. The name of the local variable is *argumentName* with the leading dash removed.

Flags default to off (false) and are turned on (true) when specified. The following flags are predefined:

- **-help**   Displays a list of arguments, types, defaults, and help text from the OptProc header.

- **--**   Marks the end of flags. Arguments following this one will not be treated as flags even if they start with a -.

Options are specified with the usual option value syntax when *name* is invoked. When invoking *name*, flags and options may be specified in any order.

Arguments not starting with a dash are positional. Positional arguments may be freely mixed with flags and options when *name* is invoked but must be specified in the correct order. Default values for positional arguments are not meaningful (except for the optional arguments discussed just ahead). As for **proc**, the last argument may be the keyword **args** to permit a variable number of arguments.

If *argumentName* is surrounded by question marks (?), it is treated as an *optional* argument. Optional argments default to type **any** with an empty value (" "). A default value may be supplied to force another type. For example, a default value of " " forces type **string** without changing the actual default. Optional arguments cannot be used with the **args** keyword.

Argument Types

The *argumentType* maybe omitted and **OptProc** will attempt to infer the type from other fields. For example, if the default value is " ", the type will be **string**. Valid argument types are:

- **-any**   An untyped argument.

- **-boolean**   A boolean option (true/false, 1/0, on/off, yes/no). Option value must be specified when name is invoked.

- **-boolflag**   A boolean flag (switch). Value cannot specified when *name* is invoked. Default value overridden by presence of flag. If no *defaultValue* is specified, the default is false.

- **-choice**   An option restricted to one entry from a list of valid values. *defaultValue* lists value choices. The first element of the list is the default.

- **-float**   An floating point option.

- **-int**   An integer option.

- **-string**   A string option.

NOTE: OptProc infers types for default values and supplements the help text with type information. Thus, "1" (a string) is different from 1 (a number).

Example

```
package require opt
::tcl::OptProc foo {
    {a1    -any      "a"        \
           "First required argument"}
    {a2    -int                 \
           "Second req. argument, an integer"}
    {?a3?             3.14159    \
           "An optional argument.  Defaults to pi"}
    {-f1                         \
           "A flag which defaults to FALSE"}
    {-f2   -boolflag true        \
           "A flag which defaults to TRUE"}
    {-o1              true       \
           "A boolean option.  Defaults to TRUE"}
    {-o2   -choice   {up down}   \
           "A choice switch.  Defaults to up"}
    {-o3              1          \
           "An integer option"}
} {
    puts "a1:$a1"
    puts "a2:$a2"
    puts "a3:$a3"
    puts "f1:$f1"
    puts "f2:$f2"
    puts "o1:$o1"
    puts "o2:$o2"
    puts "o3:$o3"
}
```

pack

The **pack** command provides a geometry manager that arranges widgets along the inside edges of another widget. (See also **grid**; **place**.)

Pack Overview

pack arranges one or more *slave* widgets within a *master* widget (usually a frame or toplevel widget). The empty space inside the *master* (that not already occupied by other slaves) is called the *cavity*.

As each slave is packed, it is given a rectangular *parcel* that takes up an entire side of the cavity. The parcel is sized in one direction to fill the side of the cavity, and in the other direction to allow room for the slave and any external padding that may be supplied. A parcel will always *expand* to fill its side of the cavity. It may also be configured to expand in the other direction, to take up space as other slaves are packed and forgotten, or as the master is resized.

A slave is anchored to one of the nine anchor points in its parcel and will always remain attached to that anchor point. A slave may be configured to *fill*, its parcel in one or both directions. If a slave is configured to not fill and its parcel is configured to expand, the slave will remain the same size as its parcel expands and shrinks around it. If a slave is configured to fill, it will change size as needed to fill its parcel as it expands and shrinks.

Syntax

pack *?***configure***? slave ?slave ... ? ?packoptions*

pack forget *slave ?slave ... ?*

pack info *slave*

pack propagate *master ?flag?*

pack slaves *master*

The arguments are as follows:

flag
A Boolean value.

master
The widget to contain the *slave*; usually a frame.

packoptions
One or more pairs of option names and values to control how *slave* is packed into *master*. (See Table 2-25 for a list of valid options and values.)

slave
A widget to pack into *master*, which must be *slave*'s parent or a descendent of *slave*'s parent in the widget hierarchy.

pack *?configure? slave ?slave ... ? ?packoptions?*

Sets the options for managing *slave*'s packing in *master*. If *slave* hasn't previously been packed (or has been packed and then forgotten), it is inserted in the packing list for *master* according to *packoptions*. Table 2-25 lists the pack options.

NOTE: If *master* isn't *slave's* parent, it should be lower than slave in the Z order. This may be accomplished by creating master before slave or by using **raise** and **lower**.

pack forget *slave ?slave ... ?*

Removes one or more *slaves* from their master's packing list and from the display.

pack info *slave*

Retrieves the current pack configuration state of *slave*.

RETURNS   A list, with an even number of elements, specifying the pack options and their values for *slave*.

pack propagate *master ?flag?*

Specifies whether geometry propagation is enabled. If *flag* is true, **pack** will "shrink-wrap" *master* around its slaves when it is displayed, by propagating their width and height requirements up so that *master* is just large enough to hold its slaves. If *flag* is false, *master* will retain its configured size, regardless of the size or number of slaves.

If **pack propagate** isn't called for *master*, geometry propagation is enabled by default.

RETURNS   0 or 1 if *flag* isn't specified, to indicate the current state of geometry propagation. If *flag* is specified, **pack propagate** sets the state of geometry propagation.

NOTE: It is possible to use more than one geometry manager to manage slaves of a single *master*. However, only one of the geometry managers may have geometry propagation enabled; otherwise, an infinite loop occurs, with each manager trying to adjust after each propagation by the other. Since both **grid** and **pack** default to having geometry propagation enabled, great care must be taken when mixing geometry managers in a single *master*. The **place** geometry manager doesn't do geometry propagation, so it may be used with **grid** or **pack** without concern.

Option	Purpose
-after *other*	Specifies that all *slaves* should be inserted after *other* in its master's packing list.[1]
-anchor *anchor*	Specifies where to anchor *slave* in its parcel. *anchor* is an anchor point.
-before *other*	Specifies that all *slaves* should be inserted before *other* in its master's packing list.[1]
-expand *boolean*	Specifies whether *slave*'s parcel should expand to fill extra space in its master. If **-expand** isn't specified, *boolean* defaults to 0.
-fill *style*	Specifies how *slave* should expand to fill extra space in its parcel. *style* is one of the following: **none** Doesn't expand *slave*, except to add internal padding as specified with **-ipadx** and **-ipady**. **x** Expands *slave* to use the full width of its parcel, except external padding specified with **-padx**. **y** Expands *slave* to use the full height of its parcel, except external padding specified with **-pady**. **both** Expands *slave* to fill the full width and height of its parcel, except external padding specified with **-padx** and **-pady**. If **-fill** isn't specified, *style* defaults to **none**.

Table 2-25.   Pack Options

Option	Purpose
-in *master*	Specifies the widget to pack *slave* into.[1]
-ipadx *amount*	Specifies the amount of horizontal padding to add between *slave*'s contents and its left and right edges. If **-ipadx** isn't specified, *amount* defaults to 0.
-ipady *amount*	Specifies the amount of vertical padding to add between *slave*'s contents and its top and bottom edges. If **-ipady** isn't specified, *amount* defaults to 0.
-padx *amount*	Specifies the amount of horizontal padding to add outside *slave*. If **-padx** isn't specified, *amount* defaults to 0.
-pady *amount*	Specifies the amount of vertical padding to add outside *slave*. If **-pady** isn't specified, *amount* defaults to 0.
-side *side*	Specifies the side of *master*'s cavity that *slave*'s parcel will be attached to. *side* is **left**, **right**, **top**, or **bottom**. If **-side** isn't specified, *side* defaults to **top**.

[1]At most, one of **-after**, **-before**, or **-in** may be specified. If none is specified when a slave is first packed, the default is to pack it into its parent at the end of the packing list.

Table 2-25.   Pack Options *(continued)*

pack slaves *master*

Retrieves a list of the widgets packed into *master*.

RETURNS   A list of slave widgets, in packing order.

Example

```
# Two ways to achieve the same effect - grid and
# pack.
# In this simple case, pack is more compact.
# In general, grid is more flexible and powerful.
#
# f1 will resize only in x
# f2 will resize in x and y

set t [toplevel .tl1]
wm title $t "Packed"
frame $t.f1 -background green -height 50 \
        -width 100
frame $t.f2 -background red    -height 50 \
        -width 100
pack $t.f1 -side top -fill x
pack $t.f2 -side top -fill both -expand 1

set t [toplevel .tl2]
wm title $t "Gridded"
frame $t.f1 -background green -height 50 \
        -width 100
frame $t.f2 -background red    -height 50 \
        -width 100
grid $t.f1 -sticky ew
grid rowconfigure $t 0 -weight 0
grid $t.f2 -sticky news
grid rowconfigure $t 1 -weight 1
grid columnconfigure $t 0 -weight 1
```

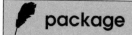

package

The **package** command manages loadable packages. (See also
auto_mkindex; **load**; **pkg_mkIndex**.)

Package Overview

Tcl's package mechanism provides a means to manage different
versions of sets of commands that are implemented in Tcl scripts

and/or binary modules (such as Microsoft Windows DLLs and UNIX shared libraries).

Packages must be installed in a directory listed in **tcl_pkgPath** or **auto_path**, or in a subdirectory of a directory listed in those variables. Each package has a package index file named **pkgIndex.tcl** in its directory. Package index files are usually created with the **pkg_mkIndex** command.

The first time a script executes a **package require** command, Tcl searches **tcl_pkgPath** and **auto_path** and all of their subdirectories and loads all the package index files that it finds. The first time a command from a package is invoked, the commands from the package index are evaluated to load the package into memory.

NOTE: Immediately after a **package require** command, the commands in the package may not be shown in the results of **info commands**. However, the commands will be auto-loaded the first time they are used.

Syntax

package forget *package*

package ifneeded *package version ?script?*

package names

package provide *package ?version?*
package require *?-exact? package ?version?*

package unknown *?command?*

package vcompare *version1 version2*
package vsatisfies *version1 version2*

package versions *package*

The arguments are as follows:

command
Prefix of command to evaluate if package cannot be found.

package
A package name.

script
Script to evaluate to load *package*.

version
A package version number. A sequence of integers and dots, such as 1.2 or 2.5.4.

version1, version2
Package version numbers to operate on.

package forget *package*

Removes all information about *package* from the interpreter.

package ifneeded
package version ?script?

Specifies the script to evaluate to create *package version* if it is needed. This is typically found in configuration files that describe a package installation, such as the **pkgIndex.tcl** files created by **pkg_mkIndex**.

RETURNS   The current script if *script* is not specified. If *script* is specified, **package ifneeded** sets the script to create *package version*.

package names

Retrieves a list of packages for which a **package provide** or **package ifneeded** command has been executed.

RETURNS   An unordered list of package names.

package provide *package ?version?*

Indicates that *version* of *package* is available in the interpreter. This is usually found at the top of a script that implements a package.

RETURNS   If *version* isn't specified, the currently available version of *package*. If *version* is specified, **package provide** sets the currently available version of *package*.

package require
?-exact? package ?version?

Indicates that *version* of *package* is needed. If *version* isn't specified, any version will be accepted. If *version* is specified and -**exact** isn't, any version of *package* with the same major version number will be accepted; for example, if *version* is 2.1, then 2.0 or 2.3 would be accepted. If *version* and -**exact** are both specified, only *version* will be accepted.

RETURNS   The version of *package* that is found.

ERROR   Raises an error if no acceptable version of *package* was found.

package unknown *?command?*

Sets or queries the command to be invoked if a package cannot be found. When *command* is invoked, it has two additional arguments appended to it: the name and version of the package sought. For example, if *command* were **findPackage**, a failed attempt to require version 3.14 of **somePackage** would end with a call to **findPackage somePackage 3.14**.

Tcl provides a default **package unknown** command that sources all pkgIndex.tcl files in all directories listed in **tcl_pkgPath** and **auto_path**. pkgIndex.tcl files are typically created with **pkg_mkIndex**.

RETURNS   If *command* isn't specified, the current **package unknown** command. If *command* is specified, the **package unknown** command is set. (If *command* is an empty string, the **package unknown** command is removed.)

package vcompare *version1 version2*

Compares *version1* and *version2*.

RETURNS   -1 if *version1* is less than *version2*; 0 if *version1* equals *version2*; 1 if *version1* is greater than *version2*.

package vsatisfies *version1 version2*

Determines whether *version2* of a package will satisfy scripts expecting *version1*. Specifically, *version1* must be greater than or equal to *version2* and they must share the same major version number.

RETURNS   1 if *version2* satisfies *version1*; otherwise 0.

package versions *package*

Determines which versions of *package* are available.

RETURNS   An unordered list of version numbers for *package*.

Example

```
set version [package require opt 0.1]
```

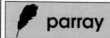

parray

The **parray** command prints all the elements of an array. (See also **array**.) It takes this form:

parray *arrayName*

The following is the argument:

arrayName
The name of the array to print.

Example

```
parray env
```

The **pid** command retrieves the process ID of the current process or the processes in a command pipeline. (See also **open**.) It takes this form:

pid *?fileId?*

The following is the argument:

fileId
The handle returned by **open** when a command pipeline was created.

RETURNS   If *fileId* isn't specified, the process ID of the current process. If *fileId* is specified, a list of process IDs is returned for the processes in the command pipeline. (If *fileId* doesn't refer to a command pipeline, the list is empty.)

Example

```
set tmpName [file join $env(TEMP) \
                  [file tail [info script]].[pid]]
```

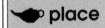

The **place** command provides a geometry manager that positions widgets at specific absolute or relative locations within another widget. (See also **grid**; **pack**.) It takes the following forms:

place *?configure?* *slave placeoptions*

place forget *slave*

place info *slave*

place slaves *master*

The arguments are as follows:

master
The widget relative to which *slave* will be placed.

placeoptions
One or more pairs of option names and values to control how *slave*
is placed into *master*. (See Table 2-26 for a list of valid options and
values.)

slave
A widget to place relative to *master*.

place ?configure? *slave placeoptions*

Sets the options for managing *slave*'s place in *master*. If *slave*
hasn't previously been placed (or has been placed but then
forgotten), it is inserted in the placing list for *master* according to
placeoptions. Table 2-25 lists all the place options.

place forget *slave*

Removes *slave* from its master's placing list and from the display.

NOTE: The **forget** commands for the **grid** and **pack** geometry
managers will remove more than one slave at a time. The
forget command for the **place** geometry manager removes only
a single slave.

place info *slave*

Retrieves the current place configuration state of *slave*.

RETURNS   A list, with an even number of elements, specifying the
place options and their values for *slave*.

place slaves *master*

Retrieves a list of the widgets placed in *master*.

RETURNS   A list of slave widgets. The last widget placed is first
in the list.

Option	Purpose
-anchor *anchor*	Specifies the anchor point on *slave* to be placed in the position specified by **-relx, -x, -rely,** and **-y**. If **-anchor** isn't specified, *anchor* defaults to **nw**.
-bordermode *mode*	Specifies how the width of *master's* borders affect the placement of *slave*. Valid values are the following: **inside** *slave's* placement will be relative to the inside of *master's* border. For example, if *master* is a frame with a 2-pixel raised border, the area available for slaves is 4 pixels narrower and shorter than the width and height of *master*. **outside** *slave's* placement will be relative to the outside of *master's* border. This is most useful when placing slaves outside *master*. **ignore** *slave's* placement will be relative to the true size of *master* in the window system (e.g., X Windows). This option isn't generally useful. If **-bordermode** isn't specified, *mode* defaults to **inside**.
-height *height*	Specifies the height of *slave* in addition to *relHeight*. *height* is in screen coordinates.[2] If **-height** isn't specified, *height* defaults to an empty string.
-in *master*	Specifies the widget to pack *slave* into. If **-in** isn't specified, *master* defaults to *slave's* parent.
-relheight *relHeight*	Specifies the base height of *slave* relative to *master's* height. *relHeight* is a floating-point number used to multiply *master's* height.[2] If **-relheight** isn't specified, *relHeight* defaults to 0.0.
-relwidth *relWidth*	Specifies the base width of *slave* relative to *master's* width. *relWidth* is a floating-point number used to multiply *master's* width. For example, if *relWidth* is 0.5, *slave* will be half the width of *master* (plus *width*).[2] If **-relwidth** isn't specified, *relWidth* defaults to 0.0.

Table 2-26. Place Options

Option	Purpose
-relx *relX*	Specifies the base X coordinate of *slave*'s anchor point in *master* relative to *master*'s left and right side. *relX* is a view coordinate (0.0 is the left edge of *master* and 1.0 is the right edge).[1] If **-relx** isn't specified, *relX* defaults to 0.0, the left side of *master*.
-rely *relY*	Specifies the base Y coordinate of *slave*'s anchor point in *master* relative to *master*'s top and bottom. *relY* is a view coordinate (0.0 is the top of *master* and 1.0 is the bottom).[1] If **-rely** isn't specified, *relY* defaults to 0.0, the top of *master*.
-width *width*	Specifies the width of *slave* in addition to *relWidth*. *width* is in screen coordinates.[2] If **-width** isn't specified, *width* defaults to an empty string.
-x *x*	Specifies the offset of the X coordinate of *slave*'s anchor point in *master* from *relX*. *x* is in screen coordinates.[1] If **-x** isn't specified, *x* defaults to 0.
-y *y*	Specifies the offset of the Y coordinate of *slave*'s anchor point in *master* from *relY*. *y* is in screen coordinates.[1] If **-y** isn't specified, *y* defaults to 0.

[1]The base and offset specifications interact so that *slave* will be placed at ((*relX* * *masterWidth*) + *x*, (*relY* * *masterHeight*) + *y*). The resulting coordinate need not be within *master*. That is, *slave* may be placed outside *master*. Unlike canvas objects placed outside the canvas view, *slave*s placed outside *master* will be visible if no other widget obscures them.

[2]The base and additional specifications for width and height interact:

- If **-width** and **-relwidth** both are specified, *slave* is sized to be ((*relWidth* * *masterWidth*) + *width*).

- If only **-relwidth** is specified, *slave* is sized to be (*relWidth* * *masterWidth*).

- If only **-width** is specified, the width of *slave* will be *width*.

- If neither is specified, *slave*'s width is used.

The same logic is true for *slave*'s height using *relHeight* and *height*.

Table 2-26.   Place Options *(continued)*

Example

```
# Arrange four buttons around the center of the
# window
set t [toplevel .tl1]
foreach b { 1 2 3 4 } {
    button $t.b$b -text B$b
}
place $t.b1 -relx 0.5 -x -2 -rely 0.5 -y -2 \
        -anchor se
place $t.b2 -relx 0.5 -x +2 -rely 0.5 -y -2 \
        -anchor sw
place $t.b3 -relx 0.5 -x -2 -rely 0.5 -y +2 \
        -anchor ne
place $t.b4 -relx 0.5 -x +2 -rely 0.5 -y +2 \
        -anchor nw

# Arrange four buttons cascaded from the upper
# left of the window
set t [toplevel .tl2]
set offset 0
foreach b { 1 2 3 4 } {
    button $t.b$b -text B$b
    place $t.b$b -x $offset -y $offset
    incr offset 8
}

# Reverse stack
proc reverse { t } {
    foreach b { 4 3 2 1} {
        raise $t.b$b
    }
}
$t.b4 configure -command [list reverse $t]

# Link two frames
set t [toplevel .tl3]
frame $t.f1 -background red  -width 100 -height 50
frame $t.f2 -background blue -width 100 -height 50
pack propagate $t false
# Put frame 1 at the top-left corner of the window
pack $t.f1 -anchor e
```

2

```
# Attach frame 2 to its bottom edge
place $t.f2 -in $t.f1 -relx 0.5 -rely 1.0 \
        -anchor n -bordermode outside

# A proc to demonstrate f2 follows f1
proc cycleAnchor { w } {
    array set info [pack info $w]
    set anchors { nw center ne nw }
    set index [lsearch $anchors $info(-anchor)]
    set anchor [lindex $anchors [incr index]]
    pack configure $w -anchor $anchor
}
bind $t.f1 <Button-1> [list cycleAnchor $t.f1]
```

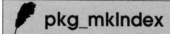

pkg_mkIndex

The **pkg_mkIndex** command creates package index files used for automatically loading packages. (See also **auto_load**; **auto_mkIndex**; **package**.) It takes the following form:

> **pkg_mkIndex** *?-direct? ?-load pkgPattern? ?-verbose? dir ?pattern ... ?*

The arguments are as follows:

dir
The directory to search for script and shared library files making up the package and in which to store the resulting pkgIndex.tcl file.

pattern
A **glob**-style pattern specifying the files to **source** or **load** when building the package index. If no patterns are specified, the default is to use the patterns ***.tcl** and ***.[info sharedlibextension]**.

NOTE: The files matching *pattern* may provide more than one package. The resulting pkgIndex.tcl file will have entries for each package encountered.

If a package consists of scripts and shared library files, the script files should generally precede shared libraries in the list of patterns, and the **-load** option should be avoided. If more than one package is being indexed and one package depends on another being indexed, specify the files for the independent package earlier in the list of patterns.

pkgPattern
A **glob**-style pattern specifying packages that may be required when loading the files specified by *pattern*. The options are as follows:

-direct
The pkgIndex.tcl file will load the package immediately when a **package require** command is invoked, instead of loading it when the first command from the package is used. This is helpful if the package uses namespaces and/or requires special initialization.

-load
Preloads packages matching *pkgPattern* into the slave interpreter used to generate the index.

-verbose
Writes progress messages with **tclLog**. (By default, these messages are written to stderr.)

--
The last option. The argument following this will be treated as *dir* even if it starts with a - (a dash).

ERROR   Raises an error if *dir* doesn't exist or can't be made the current directory, or if no files match the specified *patterns*.

Example

```
# Make a package index in the current directory
# using myPkg1.tcl, myPkg2.tcl, etc.
pkg_mkIndex -direct -verbose . myPkg*.tcl
```

proc

The **proc** command creates or replaces a Tcl procedure. (See also **namespace**; **OptProc**.) It takes this form:

> **proc** *name arguments body*

The arguments are as follows:

arguments
A list of arguments to *name*. If *name* takes no arguments, the list is empty ({}). Each element of *arguments* specifies one argument to *name* and may take one of the following forms:

- A simple value specifying the name of the argument; for example, foo.

- A two-element list specifying the name of the argument and its default value; for example, {foo 1}. Arguments with default values must be grouped at the end of *arguments*.

- The keyword **args** indicating a variable-length list of additional arguments. This must be the last element of *arguments*.

body
The script to evaluate when *name* is invoked. *body* is evaluated in the context of its namespace. Each argument listed in *arguments* is created as a local variable to *name* and assigned a value from the invocation of *name*. Additional local variables may be created by assignment (for example, with **set**). All local variables are deleted when the script terminates.

Global variables may be brought in scope with the **global** and **variable** commands, namespace variables may be brought in scope with the **variable** command, and variables in other call stack frames may be accessed with **upvar**.

body may include a **return** statement to return a value when *name* is invoked. If *body* doesn't include a **return** statement, the value of the last command in *body* is returned.

name
The name to give the new procedure. If *name* is an unqualified name (doesn't include any namespace qualifiers), the procedure is created in the current namespace; otherwise, it is created in the specified namespace.

Example

```
set ::g foo
namespace eval ns {
    variable v
    set v bar
```

```
}
proc ns::p { a1 {a2 baz} args } {
    global g
    variable v
    puts "g:$g v:$v"
    puts "a1:$a1, a2:$a2"
    puts "[llength $args] args given:"
    set i 0
    foreach arg $args {
        puts "    $i:$arg"
        incr i
    }
}
# ns::p
```

With these definitions in place, the following output is produced:

Invocation	Output
ns::p a	g:foo v:bar a1:a, a2:baz 0 args given:
ns::p a b	g:foo v:bar a:a, a2:b 0 args given:
ns::p a b c	g:foo v:bar a:a, a2:b 1 args given: 0:c

ns::p a b c d	g:foo v:bar
	a1:a, a2:b
	2 args given:
	    0:c
	    1:d

puts

The **puts** command writes to a channel. (See also **fconfigure**; **gets**.)
It takes this form:

puts *?-nonewline? ?channelId? string*

The arguments are as follows:

channelId
Handle to a channel, such as those returned by **open** or **socket**. *channelId* must be open for writing. If *channelId* isn't specified, it defaults to **stdout**.

string
Value to be written to *channelId*. *string* will be processed as needed by *channelId*'s translation and encoding, as set with **fconfigure**. *string* may not be immediately written to *channelId*, depending on the buffering set with **fconfigure**. Use **flush** to send buffered data immediately. The options are as follows:

-nonewline
Suppresses the newline at the end of the output. If **-nonewline** isn't specified, the default is to follow *string* with a newline.

Example

```
puts -nonewline stdout "Enter something: "
flush stdout
gets stdin response
```

pwd

The **pwd** command returns the current working directory. (See also **cd**.) It takes this form:

pwd

RETURNS   The current working directory.

Example

```
# If filename is unqualified, look for it in the
# current directory
set filename [file join [pwd] $filename]
```

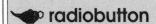

The **radiobutton** command creates and manipulates widgets that can be grouped together to indicate mutually exclusive options. (See also **button**; **checkbutton**.)

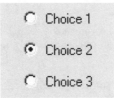

Radiobutton Options

Radiobutton widgets recognize the following standard widget options. (See the Appendix for a complete list of standard widget options and their meanings.)

activebackground	cursor	highlightthickness	takefocus
activeforeground	disabledforeground	image	text
anchor	font	justify	textvariable
background	foreground	padx	underline
bitmap	highlightbackground	pady	wraplength
borderwidth	highlightcolor	relief	

In addition, radiobutton widgets recognize the following widget-specific options:

-command *script*
Specifies the script to associate with radiobutton invocation, typically bound to clicking the radiobutton with mouse button 1. The radiobutton's global variable will be updated before the command is invoked.

-height *distance*
The desired height of the radiobutton in either screen units (when an image is specified) or lines of text (if button text is specified). If this option is omitted, Tk computes the correct height from the image or text dimensions.

-indicatoron *boolean*
Specifies whether or not an indicator should be drawn for the
radiobutton. If *boolean* is false, no indicator is drawn, the relief
option is ignored, and the text of the radiobutton is sunken or
raised to indicate the radiobutton's state.

-offvalue *value*
Specifies the value to be stored in the radiobutton's global variable
when the radiobutton is off (deselected). The default value is 0.

-onvalue *value*
Specifies the value to be stored in the radiobutton's global variable
when the radiobutton is on (selected). The default value is 1.

-selectcolor *color*
Specifies a background color to use when the radiobutton is on
(selected). If **indicatoron** is true, this is the color used to fill the
indicator. If **indicatoron** is false, this is the color used for the entire
radiobutton background when the radiobutton is on (selected), in
place of **background** and **activebackground**. If *color* is an empty
string, no special color is used to specify selection.

-selectimage *image*
If **-image** is specified, this option may be used to specify an image
to be displayed when the radiobutton is on (selected).

-state *state*
Specifies the state of the radiobutton. The following are the
possible values for *state*:

- **normal** The radiobutton is drawn with the colors specified in
  foreground and *background*, and will respond to mouse clicks.

- **active** The radiobutton is drawn with the colors specified in
  activeForeground and *activeBackground*. This setting
  corresponds to the radiobutton state when the mouse pointer
  is over the radiobutton, and isn't usually set programmatically.

- **disabled** The radiobutton is drawn with the colors specified
  in *disabledForeground* and *disabledBackground*, and will not
  respond to mouse clicks.

-value *value*
Specifies the value to store in the radiobutton's global variable
when the radiobutton is selected.

Programmer's Tip: *The mutual exclusion of a set of radiobuttons is accomplished by specifying the same variable but different values for each radiobutton in the group. When one button is selected, it sets the shared variable to its value, and the other radiobuttons detect the change and set their state to deselected.*

-variable *varName*
Specifies the name of the global variable to set when the radiobutton is selected. If **-variable** is not specified, *varName* defaults to **selectedButton**.

-width *distance*
The desired width of the radiobutton in either screen units (when an image is specified) or characters (if button text is specified). If this option is omitted, Tk computes the correct width from the image or text dimensions.

Radiobutton Commands

Radiobutton widgets respond to the **cget** and **configure** standard widget commands. (See the Appendix for details.) In addition, radiobutton widgets respond to the following widget-specific commands:

pathName **deselect**
Deselects (turns off) the radiobutton and sets its global variable to an empty string.

pathName **flash**
Redisplays the radiobutton several times, alternating between active and normal colors. This command is ignored if the radiobutton is disabled.

pathName **invoke**
Invokes the Tcl command associated with the radiobutton, if there is one.

RETURNS The value of the Tcl command, or an empty string if no command is associated with the radiobutton. Note that this command is ignored if the radiobutton is disabled.

select
Selects (turns on) the radiobutton and sets its global variable to the on value.

Default Bindings

Radiobuttons are created with bindings that make them behave as expected consistent with the user interface conventions on each platform. Specifically:

- A button is active when the mouse pointer is over it.

NOTE: In Microsoft Windows, the button is only active if mouse button 1 has been clicked.

- The radiobutton is selected and its command is invoked when mouse button 1 is pressed and released over the button, or when the button has input focus and SPACEBAR is pressed.

Example

```
set rb1 [radiobutton .rb1 -text "Option 1" \
        -variable rb -value 1]
set rb2 [radiobutton .rb2 -text "Option 2" \
        -variable rb -value 2]
```

Programmer's Tip: *Some of the default bindings on* **radiobutton** *widgets are provided through procs, including* **tkCheckRadioDown**, **tkCheckRadioEnter**, *and* **tkCheckRadioInvoke**.

(These commands aren't of general interest and thus aren't documented in this reference. The **bind**, **info args**, *and* **info body** *commands can be used to explore the use and implementation of these commands.)*

raise

The **raise** command changes a window's position in the Z order. (See also **lower**.) It takes the following forms:

    raise *window ?aboveThis?*

The arguments are as follows:

aboveThis
The window above which *window* should be moved. If *aboveThis* isn't specified, it defaults to the highest sibling of *window*.

window
The path through the widget hierarchy to the window to move.

2

Example

```
# Create two buttons
button .b1 -text 1
button .b2 -text 2
# Put them in the same place on the screen,
# b2 on top
place .b1 0 0
place .b2 0 0
# Put b2 below b1
raise .b1
```

 read

The **read** command reads data from a channel. (See also **eof**; **fblocked**; **fconfigure**; **gets**.) It takes the following forms:

>**read** *?*-**nonewline***?* channelId

>**read** channelId numBytes

The arguments are as follows:

channelId
Handle to a channel, such as those returned by **open** or **socket**. *channelId* must be open for reading.

numBytes
Number of bytes to read from *channelId*.

The options are as follows:

-nonewline
Removes the newline at the end of the input. If **-nonewline** isn't
specified, the default is to include the trailing newline, if any.

read ?-nonewline? *channelId*

Reads all available data from *channelId* up to the end of file.

RETURNS   The data read from *channelId*, processed to translate
newlines and encode data as specified with the **-translation** and
-encoding options of **fconfigure**. If *channelId* is blocking, all data
from *channelId* is returned. If *channelId* is nonblocking, all
available data from *channelId* is returned. In this case, **-nonewline**
is ignored.

Programmer's Tip: *For moderate-sized files,* **read** *is faster than*
gets. *The following two examples are functionally equivalent. The
first is slower but uses less memory:*

```
# Memory-efficient way to process a file
while { ! [eof $fid] } {
    set line [gets $fid]
    processLine $line
}
```

*The second example is faster, but reads the whole input file into
memory, which can be a problem with large files.*

```
# Time-efficient way to process a file
foreach line [split [read $fid] \n] {
    processLine $line
}
```

read *channelId numBytes*

Read *numBytes* from *channelId*.

RETURNS   The data read from *channelId*, processed to translate
newlines and encode data as specified with the **-translation** and
-encoding options of **fconfigure**. If fewer than *numBytes* of data is

available from *channelId*, the remaining data is returned; otherwise, *numBytes* of data is returned.

regexp

2

The **regexp** command matches a string against a regular expression and optionally parses the string by storing the matched expressions in variables. (See also **lsearch**; **regsub**; **switch**; **text**.)

Regular Expression Overview

Regular expressions provide a means of matching strings against patterns of characters that is much more powerful than the simple **glob**-style patterns. The POSIX 1003.2 specification defines "standard" regular expressions, and many languages (such as Perl) and applications and tools (such as grep, awk, and emacs) have enhanced regular expression features based on or derived from the POSIX standard. Tcl 8.1 includes a completely revamped regular expression processor, which includes many features previously available only in Perl, as well as full support of Unicode and binary data.

Entire books have been written on the nuances of regular expressions. The following sections describe the basics and provide a few examples that should serve many needs. For a more detailed treatment, consult a more exhaustive regular expression reference, such as the regular expression documentation that accompanies the Tcl distribution.

NOTE: Regular expressions use several special characters that also have special meaning in Tcl syntax, such as bracket ([]) and dollar signs. Generally, regular expressions should be enclosed in braces ({}) to suppress Tcl interpretation of these characters. When some Tcl evaluation is needed when building a regular expression, and braces cannot be used around the whole expression, backslashes may be used to quote individual characters.

Type of Regular Expression
Tcl's regular expression support is based on Henry Spencer's implementation. It is based on the POSIX 1003.2 specification and

includes many, but not all, Perl 5 extensions. Tcl regular expressions come in three forms:

- **BRE** POSIX *basic* regular expressions
- **ERE** POSIX *extended* regular expressions
- **ARE** *Advanced* regular expressions, generally a superset of EREs, with a few incompatibilities

Tcl interprets regular expressions as AREs by default. BRE and ERE interpretation may be selected with embedded options.

Regular Expression Syntax

A regular expression (RE) is made up of *atoms* that match characters in a string, and *constraints* that limit where those matches occur. The simplest atom is a single character to be matched literally. For example, the regular expression **a** consists of one atom that matches the start of "abc" or "apple", the middle of "bat", or the end of "comma".

Any single character can be matched with "." (dot). For example the RE **a.c** matches any three-character substring starting with *a* and ending with *c* anywhere within a string.

One of several specific characters can be matched with a *class*. A class consists of square brackets surrounding a string of characters, collating elements, equivalence classes, or named character classes to match. Characters, collating elements, equivalence classes, and named classes may be freely mixed in a class, except that equivalence classes and named character classes may not be used as the end of a range.

If the first character of a class is ^ (caret), the class is *negated* and matches any character not in the class. For example, [^0-9] matches any nondigit. A caret after the first character of a class has no special meaning.

Characters may be listed explicitly (for example, **[0123456789]**) or may be described with an implicit range of characters, by specifying the first and last character in the range, separated by a dash (for example, **[0-9]**).

A Unicode *collating element* is a character or multi-character string that sorts as a single character, such as "ae" for æ. A collating element is represented by the multi-character string or the collating element's name surrounded by [. and .] such as [.ae.].

A Unicode *equivalence class* is a set of characters that sort to the same position, such as o, ò, ó, ô, õ, ö. An equivalence class is represented by a member of the class surrounded by [= and =], such as [=o=] for the preceding list of o variants. For example, if π and p were members of an equivalence class, [[=p=]], [[=π=]], and [pπ] all match either character.

NOTE: Character ranges, collating elements, and equivalence classes are highly locale-dependent, not portable, and not generally useful in regular expressions. Their support in **regexp** is a side effect of Tcl's general support of Unicode encoding.

A *named character class* is specified with a class name between [: and :] and stands for all characters (not all the collating elements) belonging to that class. A named character class may not be used as the endpoint of a range. The POSIX.1 standard class names are listed in the following table. A locale may define others.

Class Name	Description
alnum	Alphanumeric characters
alpha	Alphabetic characters
blank	A blank character
cntrl	Control characters (e.g., ASCII characters less than 32, and 127)
digit	Decimal digits
graph	All printable characters except blank
lower	Lowercase alphabetic characters
print	Printable characters
punct	Punctuation
space	White space
upper	Uppercase alphabetic characters
xdigit	Hexadecimal digits

For example, {[[:alpha:]]+[[:digit:]]+} matches "abcd1234".

Two other named classes act as constraints that may aid parsing:

<	The start of a word
>	The end of a word

A *word* is defined as a sequence of word characters preceded and followed by nonword characters. Word characters are letters, digits, and underscores. The < and > classes match the empty string between the word and nonword characters. For the C locale, [^0-9a-zA-Z_][0-9a-zA-Z_]*[^0-9a-zA-Z_] is roughly equivalent to [[:<:]].*[[:>:]].

NOTE: The < and > character class names are deprecated and the equivalent ARE escapes should be used when possible.

An atom can be *quantified* with one of several suffixes:

Suffix	Frequency of Matches
*	0 or more times in the string
+	At least once, but may be repeated more times
?	0 or 1 times

NOTE: The + and ? quantifiers are not supported by BREs.

Thus, .* matches any string, including an empty string, **a+b** matches one or more a's followed by a *b*, and **a[bc]?d** matches "ad", "abc", and "acd", but not "abcd".

In Tcl 8.1, you can also explicitly specify *bounds* on the instances of an atom match:

Boundary	Number of Matches
{m}	Exactly m times
{m,}	m or more times
{m,n}	m to n times (inclusive). m must be less than or equal to n.

m and n may be in the range 0 to 255, inclusive.

NOTE: In basic regular expressions, the braces ({}) must be preceded by backslashes, like \{m,n\}.

Regular expressions may be constrained to only match at certain places in a string. For basic regular expressions, there are two constraints, also called *anchors*:

Anchor	Location of Matches
^	Only at the start of a line
$	Only at the end of a line

Thus, ^a*$ matches only lines made up of all a's.

These anchor constraints, and others, also apply to EREs and AREs.

Regular expressions are built up by catenating quantified atoms and constraints. The REs in the preceding paragraphs are simple examples. The regular expression **a?b** consists of the atoms **a?** and **b**, and the regular expression **[ab]?c** consists of the atoms **[ab]?** and **c**.

NOTE: In theory, regular expressions may be arbitrarily long, to match complex patterns; in practice, POSIX allows implementations to impose a limit of 256 characters on the total length of a regular expression.

The match to a part of a regular expression can be *captured*, or tagged, for later reference. To capture the match of a subexpression, enclose it in parentheses. The parentheses must occur between atoms and are otherwise ignored for matching purposes. For example, **([ab]?)c** is the same as **[ab]?c**, except that whatever matches the class will be captured. Thus, **([ab]?)c** matches **bc** and captures **b**.

NOTE: In basic regular expressions, the parentheses must be preceded by backslashes, like \([ab?\)c.

By default, regular expressions are *greedy*; that is, they match as much of a string as possible. The pattern **(a*)(a?)b** matches "aaaaaaab" but the second capture is an empty string, because **a*** matches all the a's.

In Tcl 8.1, a quantifier may be followed with a question mark (?), to make it not greedy. Thus, **(a*?)(a?)b** matches "aaaaaaab" and processes the first capture while leaving an a for the second capture.

Capture indicators may be nested to capture sub-subexpressions. For example, **(([abc])([abc]))** matches any pair of letters that includes **a**, **b**, and **c**, such as **ab** or **ca**, and captures each of the letters separately. It also captures the entire match. The order of the captures is determined by the order of the opening capture indicators. If the previous pattern is applied to **ca**, the resulting captures are, in order, **ca**, **c**, and **a**.

In EREs and AREs, atoms and constraints may be grouped into *branches* separated by | (a vertical bar). A regular expression matches anything that matches any one of its branches. For example, ^**foo | bar$** matches a string starting with "foo" or ending in "bar".

Advanced Regular Expressions
Advanced regular expressions allow options that control matching to be embedded in regular expressions, and provide numerous shorthand *escapes* for constraints, special characters, and character classes.

In addition to ERE atoms, AREs may include **(?:***re***)** to specify that *re* is to be matched but not captured. *re* may be an empty string and may *not* contain back references, and all parentheses in *re* are noncapturing. AREs also provide *lookahead* constraints:

Constraint	Description
(?=*re***)**	A positive lookahead. This matches *string* at any point where a substring matching *re* begins.
(?!*re***)**	A negative lookahead. This matches *string* at any point where no substring matching *re* begins.

ARE escapes are formed with a leading backslash followed by one or more characters specifying the escape. They come in several types: back references, character escapes, class shorthand escapes, and constraint escapes.

NOTE: This is the one incompatibility between EREs and AREs. In EREs, a backslash (\) inside a character class is a normal character; in an ARE, it must begin a valid escape. ARE is the default interpretation.

A *back reference* represents a string captured by a match earlier in the overall regular expression. It has the form \n, where n is an integer (which can't have leading zeros). For example, **([abc])([def])\1** matches any three-character string beginning with **a**, **b**, or **c**, with **d**, **e**, or **f** in the middle, and ending with the same character it started with. It matches "ada", "bfb", and "afa", but not "adc".

Character escapes provide a convenient means of entering special and nonprinting characters into regular expressions. Character escapes are always treated as normal characters. For example, \135 is] in ASCII, but \135 does not close a class. The following table lists valid character escapes:

Escape	Meaning
\a	Alert
\b	Backspace
\B	A backslash; useful to reduce doubling of backslashes in contexts where the regular expression is evaluated multiple times
\c*X*	A character whose low-order 5 bits are the same as *X* and whose other bits are all 0
\e	The character whose collating sequence name is ESC or, if none exists, the character with the decimal value 27
\f	Formfeed
\n	Newline
\r	Carriage return
\t	Horizontal tab
\u*hhhh*	The Unicode character U+*hhhh*; *h* is a hexadecimal digit
\U*hhhhhhhh*	Reserved for future 32-bit Unicode characters
\v	Vertical tab
\x*hhh*	The character whose hexadecimal value is 0x*hhh*; *h* is a hexadecimal digit
\0	A NUL character
\oo \ooo	The character whose octal value is 0*oo* or 0*ooo*, unless *oo* (or *ooo*) is a valid back reference; *o* is an octal digit (0-7)

Class shorthand escapes make it easier to enter character classes in regular expressions. The following table lists class shorthand escapes and their equivalents:

Escape	Class	Meaning
\d	[[:digit:]]	Any digit
\D	[^[:digit:]]	A nondigit

Escape	Class	Meaning
\s	[[:space:]]	Any whitespace character (such as a blank, tab, or newline)
\S	[^[:space:]]	Any nonwhitespace character
\w	[[:alnum:]_]	Any alphanumeric or underscore character
\W	[^[:alnum:]_]	Any character, excluding letters, digits, and the underscore

When used in a character class, \d, \s, and \w behave as if the outer [] were not present. The escapes \D, \S, and \W may not be used in character classes.

Constraint escapes provide an alternative way to specify anchors, and specify other types of constraints only available in AREs. Constraint escapes may not be used in character classes, so [\Aabc\Z] is illegal, but \A[abc]\Z is allowed. The following table lists valid constraint escapes:

Constraint	Match
\A	Only at the beginning of the string. This differs from the ^ anchor, depending on whether newline-sensitive matching is being used.
\m	Only at the beginning of a word. This is preferred over the ERE named character class <.
\M	Only at the end of a word. This is preferred over the ERE named character class >.
\y	Only at the beginning or end of a word.
\Y	Only at points not at the beginning or end of a word.
\Z	Only at the end of the string. This differs from the $ anchor, depending on whether newline-sensitive matching is being used.

Embedded Options
Embedded options may be specified at the start of an ARE in the form **(?***options***)**, where *options* is any sequence of option letters from the following table. If conflicting options are specified (such as **b** and **e**), the last specified is used.

Option	Purpose
b	Treats the regular expression as a basic regular expression.
e	Treats the regular expression as an extended regular expression.
c	Use case-sensitive matching. This is the default.
i	Use case-insensitive matching. This is the same as specifying the **-nocase** option to the **regexp** command.
m	Newline-sensitive matching. (Same as **n**.)
n	Newline-sensitive matching. (Same as **m**.) This is the same as specifying the **-line** option to the **regexp** command.
p	Partial newline-sensitive matching. This is the same as specifying the **-linestop** option to the **regexp** command.
q	Treat the regular expression as a quoted (literal) string.
s	Non-newline-sensitive matching. This is the default.
w	Inverse, partial newline-sensitive matching. This is the same as specifying the **-lineanchor** option to the **regexp** command.
t	Tight syntax. This is the default.
x	Expanded syntax. This is the same as specifying the **-expanded** option to the **regexp** command.

Programmer's Tip: *Embedded options are important to access the full power of the regular expression processor with commands such as **lsearch** and **switch**, which take a **-regexp** option but have no command options to specify; for example, case-insensitive matching.*

Syntax

regexp *?options? exp string ?matchVar? ?subMatchVar ... ?*

The arguments are as follows:

exp
Regular expression to match. *regexp* may not end in a backslash (\).

matchVar
Name of a variable to hold the part of *string* that matches *exp*.

string
String to match against *exp*.

subMatchVar
Name of variable to hold the part of *string* that matches a captured subexpression. The first captured string is put in the first *subMatchVar*, the second in the second, and so forth. If no match occurs for the corresponding captured subexpression, *subMatchVar* is set to an empty string (or to {-1 -1} if **-indices** is specified).

The options are as follows:

-nocase
Performs case-insensitive matching.

-indices
Stores the indices in *string* of the substring matching the expression in the *subMatchVar* instead of the matched substring. In this case, each *subMatchVar* will be assigned a two-element list containing the indices of the start and end of the matched substring.

-expanded
Uses expanded syntax that ignores whitespace and comments. The default *tight* syntax evaluates all characters in *exp* as regular expression characters. With *expanded* syntax, whitespace characters and characters between a number sign (#) and the following newline are ignored. This allows long regular expressions to be formatted and commented for easier comprehension. Whitespace and number signs can be included in regular expressions by quoting them with a backslash (for example, \#). Also note that whitespace and number signs are processed normally in character classes and are illegal within multicharacter symbols like **(?:** and **\(**.

-line
Enables newline-sensitive matching. This is the same as specifying both the **-linestop** and **-lineanchor** options.

-linestop
Does not include newlines when processing dot (.) atoms and negated character classes. For example, without **-linestop**, [^0-9] and .* will match strings including newlines. With **-linestop** specified, they both stop at the first newline they encounter.

-lineanchor

Matches ^ and $ anchors at the end of lines, not only at the end of *string*. For example, without -**lineanchor**, ^**d.*$** doesn't match "abc\ndef" because the string doesn't start with d. With -**lineanchor**, it does match, because the ^ may match at the beginning of each line (at the beginning of *string* and after each new line).

-about

Returns a list containing information about *exp* instead of trying to match it against *string*. This is provided primarily for debugging.

--

The last option. The argument following this is treated as *exp* even if it starts with a dash.

RETURNS   If -**about** isn't specified, an integer count of the number of expressions matched. If -**about** is specified, a two-element list describing *exp* is returned. The first element is the number of subexpressions found, and the second element is a list of property names that describe attributes of *exp*.

Example

```
# Find a list element that starts with at least
# three x's and/or X's (that is, starts "xxx"
# without regard to case)
set index [lsearch -regexp $list {(?i)x{3,}}]

# Find a string in a text widget's contents for a
# word that begins and ends with a vowel in upper-
# or lowercase
set vowels "aeiou"
.t search \
     -regexp "(?i)\\m\[$vowels\]\\w\[$vowels\]\\M" \
     1.0

# Parse data from a file. Each "field" is a line
# that starts with a field name followed by a
# colon. The field name determines what to do with
# the data.
set fields {Name Birthdate Notes}
# ...
# Build an expanded regular expression with embedded
# comments.
```

```tcl
# Note, backslashes have to be escaped for Tcl
# parser. This is equivalent to
#    "(?ix)^([join $fields |]):\\s*(.*)\\s*$"
# or
#    {(?ix)^(Name|Birthdate|Notes):\s*(.*)\s*$}
set re "(?ix)              # Ignore case (i)
                          #   expanded syntax (x)
        ^                 # Start at the start of
                          #   the string
        ([join $fields |]) # Match and capture any
                          #   field names
        :                 # followed by a colon
        \\s*              # Optional whitespace
                          #   after the colon
        (.*)              # Capture the rest of
                          #   the line
        \\s*              # excluding trailing
                          #   whitespace
        $                 # Use the whole line
        "                ;# Can't comment after
                          # the " without a ;
                          # to terminate the set
                          # command
# Open the input file
set fid [open redata.txt r]
# While not done, read and process the next line
while {! [eof $fid] } {
    set len [gets $fid line]
    switch -- $len {
        0 {
            # Skip blank lines
            continue
        }
        -1 {
            # EOF
            break
        }
    }
    # See if we can parse this line
    if {![regexp $re $line whole field value] } {
        puts stderr "No field found in <<$line>>"
        continue
    }
```

```
# Use case-insensitive regexp to match fields
# We could do
#    "set field [string toupper $field]"
switch -regexp -- $field {
    (?i)NAME {
        set name $value
        lappend a(names) $name
    }
    (?i)BIRTHDATE {
        set a($name,dob) [clock scan $value]
    }
    (?i)NOTES {
        set a($name,notes) $value
    }
  }
}
close $fid
```

Compatibility

Regular expression handling changed significantly with Tcl version 8.1. Many ERE and ARE features are not available in version 8.0 and earlier.

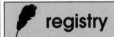 **registry**

The **registry** command provides access to the Microsoft Windows Registry. It takes the following forms:

registry delete *keyName ?valueName?*

registry get *keyName valueName*

registry keys *keyName ?pattern?*

registry set *keyName ?valueName data ?type??*

registry type *keyName valueName*

registry values *keyName ?pattern?*

The arguments are as follows:

data
Data to assign to the key and value.

keyName
A Registry key in one of the following forms:
*hostName**rootName**keyPath*, *rootName**keyPath*, or *rootName*.
hostName may refer to any host that has exported its Registry.
rootName is one of the following:

- **HKEY_LOCAL_MACHINE**
- **HKEY_USERS**
- **HKEY_CLASSES_ROOT**
- **HKEY_CURRENT_USER**
- **HKEY_CURRENT_CONFIG**
- **HKEY_PERFORMANCE_DATA**
- **HKEY_DYN_DATA**

keyPath is one or more Registry key names separated by
backslashes.

pattern
A **glob**-style pattern of keys or values to match. *pattern* is
interpreted as for **string match**.

type
The type of data in the Registry. The following table lists
predefined types. Other types are converted to a 32-bit integer
corresponding to the type code returned by the system.

Type	Registry Value
binary	Binary data. The data isn't converted when stored or retrieved.
none	Binary data. The data isn't converted when stored or retrieved.
sz	A null-terminated string. The data is converted to and from Tcl strings, as needed.
expand_sz	A null-terminated string including unexpanded references to environment variables (e.g., **%windir%**). The data is converted to and from Tcl strings, as needed.

Type	Registry Value
dword	A 32-bit integer in little-endian format. The data is converted to and from a Tcl decimal string, as needed.
dword_big_endian	A 32-bit integer in big-endian format. The data is converted to and from a Tcl decimal string, as needed.
link	A symbolic link. The data isn't converted when stored or retrieved.
multi_sz	An array of null-terminated strings. The data is converted to and from a Tcl list of strings, as needed.
resource_list	A device-driver resource list. The data isn't converted when stored or retrieved.

2

valueName
The name of a value for *keyName*.

registry delete *keyName* *?valueName?*

Removes a value or key from the Registry. If *valueName* is specified, it is deleted from the Registry. If *valueName* isn't specified, *keyName* and all of its values and subkeys are deleted from the Registry.

ERROR   Raises an error if the key or value could not be deleted.

NOTE: Use this command with caution. Deleting required Registry entries can cause your system to be unusable.

registry get *keyName* *valueName*

Retrieves the data from *valueName* for *keyName*.

RETURNS   The requested data. (See the table above.)

ERROR   Raises an error if *keyName* or *valueName* doesn't exist.

registry keys *keyName* *?pattern?*

Retrieves a list of subkeys for *keyName* that match *pattern*. If *pattern* isn't specified, it defaults to *, which matches all subkeys.

RETURNS   A list of subkeys.

ERROR   Raises an error if *keyName* doesn't exist.

registry set *keyName* ?*valueName data* ?*type*??

Creates a key or sets a value for a key. If *keyName* doesn't exist, it is created. If *valueName* and *data* are specified, sets the value of *valueName* for *keyName* to *data* using type *type*. If *type* isn't specified, it defaults to **sz**.

registry type *keyName valueName*

Retrieves the type of data in *valueName* for *keyName*.

RETURNS   A type from the preceding table of Registry entry types.

ERROR   Raises an error if *keyName* or *valueName* does not exist.

registry values *keyName* ?*pattern*?

Retrieves a list of values for *keyName* that match *pattern*. If *pattern* isn't specified, it defaults to *, which matches all values.

RETURNS   A list of value names.

ERROR   Raises an error if *keyName* does not exist.

Example

```
package require registry
proc showHtml { htmlFile } {
    # Look for the application under
    # HKEY_CLASSES_ROOT
    set root HKEY_CLASSES_ROOT
    # Get the application key for HTML files
    set appKey [registry get $root\\.html ""]
    # Get the command for opening HTML files
    set appCmd [registry get \
        $root\\$appKey\\shell\\open\\command ""]
    # Substitute the HTML filename into the
```

```
    # command for %1
    set appCmd [perSub $appCmd %1 $htmlFile]
    # Double up the backslashes for eval (below)
    regsub -all {\\} $appCmd  {\\\\} appCmd
    # Invoke the command
    eval exec $appCmd &
}
showHtml C:/foobar.html
```

2

Compatibility

The **registry** command is available only on Microsoft
Windows systems.

The **regsub** command substitutes substrings that match regular
expressions. (See also **regexp**.) It takes the following form:

> **regsub** *?options? exp string subSpec varName*

The arguments are as follows:

exp
Regular expression to look for in *string*.

string
String to look for *exp* in.

subSpec
Substitution specification for matches of *exp* in *string*. *subSpec*
may contain markers to indicate where captured subexpressions in
exp are to be inserted in the replacement string. The markers **&**
and **\0** represent the entire match (like the *matchVar* argument to
regexp). The markers **\1** to **\9** may be used to insert the
corresponding captured subexpression.

Programmer's Tip: *Because this use of backslashes conflicts
with the Tcl parser, it is a good practice to enclose subSpec in
braces ({}).*

varName
Variable to put result in.

The options are as follows:

-all
Replaces each match of *exp* in *string* with *subSpec*. If **-all** isn't specified, the default is to replace only the first match.

-nocase
Treats uppercase characters in *string* and *exp* as lowercase for matching purposes.

--
The last option. The argument following this is treated as *exp* even if it starts with a -dash.

Description

regsub copies *string* to *varName* while testing for matches against *exp*. When a match is found, *subSpec* is copied in place of the matching substring.

RETURNS   The number of substitutions performed.

Example

```
# Substitute for % "variables" (like %W, etc. in
# event bindings)
# Based on [percent_subst] from Effective Tcl/Tk
# Programming by Mark Harrison and Michael
# McLennan
# Example:
#    tclsh>perSub "%1 %2 %3" %1 one %3 three %2 two
#    one two three
::tcl::OptProc perSub {
    {string  -string "" "String to work on"}
    {pattern -string ""
             "What to substitute for, e.g., %v"}
    {subst   -string ""
             "What to put in for $pattern"}
    {args    -list   {}
             "More pattern/subst pairs"}
```

```
} {
    # Add the required instances to the optional
    # list
    set args [linsert $args 0 $pattern $subst]
    # Process the list
    foreach {pattern subst} $args {
        # Validate pattern
        if { ! [string match %* $pattern]} {
            error "Bad pattern <<$pattern>>:\
                Should be %something"
        }
        # Escape dangerous characters
        # ('\' and '&') in substitution string
        regsub -all {\\|&} $subst {\\\0} subst
        # Do substitutions on string
        regsub -all $pattern $string $subst string
    }
    return $string
}
```

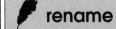

rename

The **rename** command renames or deletes a command. (See also
namespace.) It takes the following forms:

> **rename** *oldName newName*

The arguments are as follows:

newName

The new name for the proc or an empty string ("") to delete the
proc. *newName* may include namespace qualifiers. If *oldName* and
newName have different namespace qualifiers, the effect is to
move the proc from one namespace to another.

oldName

The name of the proc to rename or delete. *oldName* may include
namespace qualifiers.

Example

```
namespace eval atexit {
    variable count

    # Implement a new exit command that calls the
    # handlers in turn
    proc newexit { {code 0} } {
        set count $atexit::count
        while {$count > 0} {
            ::atexit::atexit$count
            incr count -1
        }
        ::atexit::baseexit $code
    }
}

proc atexit { script } {
    # If we've been here before, just increment
    # the count. Otherwise, initialize things
    if {[info exists atexit::count]} {
        incr atexit::count
    } else {
        # Initialize the exit handler count
        set atexit::count 1
        # Rename the base exit command down into
        # the namespace for later use
        rename ::exit ::atexit::baseexit
        # Rename the replacement exit to the
        # global scope
        rename ::atexit::newexit ::exit
    }

    # Create a new exit handler with the given
    # script
    proc atexit::atexit$atexit::count {} $script
}
```

resource

The **resource** command manipulates Macintosh resources.
(See also **AppleScript**.) It takes the following forms:

> **resource close** *resourceRef*
> **resource open** *fileName ?access?*
>
> **resource delete** *?options? resourceType*
>
> **resource files** *?resourceRef?*
>
> **resource list** *resourceType ?resourceRef?*
>
> **resource read** *resourceType resourceId ?resourceRef?*
> **resource write** *?options? resourceType data*
>
> **resource types** *?resourceRef?*

The arguments are as follows:

access
File access permissions as for **open**.

fileName
Name of the file whose resources are to be read.

resourceId
A Macintosh resource name or number.

resourceRef
A handle to a resource returned by **resource open**.

resourceType
A four-character Macintosh resource type, such as **TEXT** or **STR#**.

The options are follows:

-id *resourceNum*
Specifies the number of the resource.

-name *resourceName*
Specifies the name of the resource.

-file *resourceRef*
Specifies the file to manipulate resources in.

-force
Overwrites existing resources. Valid for **resource write** only.

resource close *resourceRef*

Closes *resourceRef* (opened by **resource open**).

resource open *fileName* *?access?*

Opens the resource fork of *fileName*.

RETURNS   A handle to an open resource that can be used with
resource list, and so forth.

resource delete *?options?* *resourceType*

Deletes the specified resource. If both **-name** and **-id** are specified,
the resource to be deleted must match both. If only **-id** is specified,
the resource will be deleted regardless of its name. If **-file** is
specified, the resource will be deleted from *resourceRef*; otherwise,
the first matching resource on the resource file path is deleted.

resource files *?resourceRef?*

Retrieves information about open resources.

RETURNS   If *resourceRef* is specified, the path to the file whose
resource fork is pointed to by *resourceRef*. If *resourceRef* isn't
specified, a list of resource references for all open files is returned,
in Macintosh resource search order.

resource list *resourceType ?resourceRef?*

Retrieves a list of all resources for *resourceType* resources in
resourceRef.

RETURNS   A list of resources. For each named resource, the name
is listed. Otherwise, the number is listed. If *resourceRef* is
specified, only resources in that file are listed. If *resourceRef* isn't
specified, all matching resources in all open files are listed.

resource read
resourceType resourceId ?resourceRef?

Retrieves the resource matching *resourceType* and *resourceId*. If
resourceRef is specified, it will be read from that file. Otherwise,
Tcl searches all open resources.

RETURNS   The value of the resource.

NOTE: This is usually binary data that may contain embedded
NULs and other unprintable characters.

resource write
?options? resourceType data

Writes *data* to the resource fork of a file, as specified by *options*.
If **-file** isn't specified, *resourceRef* defaults to the most recently
opened resource. If **-name** isn't specified, *resourceName* defaults to
an empty string.

ERROR   Returns an error if the specified resource already exists
and **-force** isn't specified.

resource types *?resourceRef?*

Retrieves a list of resource types. If *resourceRef* is specified,
only resources in that file are listed. If *resourceRef* isn't specified,
all resources in all open files are listed.

RETURNS   A list of resource types.

Example

The following example is adapted from the Macintosh FAQ
(available at **www.scriptics.com**) by Jim Ingham:

```
# Read the STR# resource in resource specified in
# args, which contains a resource specification
# (name or id) and optionally a resource file
# token.
#
# Result:
#     A list of the strings found
#----------------------------------------------------
proc readStrList {args} {
    if {[llength $args] == 1} {
        set strList [resource read "STR#" \
                                    [lindex $args 0]]
    } elseif {[llength $args] == 2} {
        set strList [resource read "STR#" \
                    [lindex $args 0] [lindex $args 1]]
    } else {
        error "Wrong # of args, should be\
                \"resource ?resourceFile?\""
    }
    binary scan $strList S numStrs
    if {$numStrs == 0} {
        return
    }

    set pointer 2

    for {set i 0} {$i < $numStrs} {incr i} {
        binary scan $strList x${pointer}c numChars
        set $numChars [expr ( $numChars + 0x100 )\
                            % 0x100]
        incr pointer
        binary scan $strList \
                x${pointer}a$numChars string
        lappend result $string
        incr pointer $numChars
    }
    return $result

}
```

Compatibility

The **resource** command is available only on Macintosh systems.

return

The **return** command returns from a proc. (See also **break**; **continue**; **error**; **errorCode**; **errorInfo**.) It takes the following form:

return *?-***code** *code? ?-***errorinfo** *errorinfo? ?-***errorcode**
errorcode? ?value?

The arguments are as follows:

code
Specifies the type of return. Valid values are the following, or an integer value:

- **ok**   A normal return is performed. This is the default.

- **error**   An error is raised, similar to using the **error** command.

- **return**   The proc will return with a completion code of TCL_RETURN that will cause the caller to return also.

- **break**   The proc will return with a completion code of TCL_BREAK that will break out of the innermost loop in the caller.

- **continue**   The proc will return with a completion code of TCL_CONTINUE that will stop the current iteration of the innermost loop in the caller.

When an integer value is specified, it will be returned as the completion code of the proc.

Programmer's Tip: *The -***code** *option (and the -***errorinfo** *and -***errorcode** *options that depend on it) is rarely used. It exists primarily to implement new control structures like* **if** *and* **while**.

errorcode
Specifies a value to store in the global **errorCode** variable. Typically, this is retrieved by a proc up the call stack after **catch** has been used to detect an error. Defaults to NONE. This option is ignored unless **code** is **error**.

errorinfo

Specifies a call stack to store in the global **errorInfo** variable. Typically, this is retrieved by a proc up the call stack after **catch** has been used to detect an error. Defaults to a call stack including the current proc, but not the context within the current proc. (See the **error** command entry for more information.) This option is ignored unless **code** is **error**.

value

Specifies the value to return for the proc. *value* may have any type except array.

Example

```
# A proc to return the square of a number
proc square { x } {
    return [expr $x * $x]
}
# A new control structure:
#    repeat script ?until? condition
# For example:
#    set x 1
#    repeat {
#        incr x
#    } until { $x == 5 }
#
proc repeat { args } {
    global errorCode
    global errorInfo
    foreach {body keyword cond} $args {break}
    if {[string length $cond] == 0} {
        set cond $keyword
        set keyword until
    }
    if {[string compare $keyword until] != 0} {
        error "invalid format. \
                Should be \"repeat script ?until?\
                cond\""
    }

    set done 0
    while {! $done} {
        set code [catch {uplevel $body} result]
        switch -- $code {
```

```
        0 {
            # NO OP
        }
        1 {
            return -code error \
                    -errorcode $errorCode \
                    -errorinfo $errorInfo \
                    $result
        }
        3 {
            # break
            return
        }
        4 {
            # continue
        }
        2 -
        default {
            return -code $code $result
        }
    }
    if {[catch [list uplevel expr $cond] \
                                done]} {
        return -code error \
                -errorcode $errorCode \
                -errorinfo $errorInfo $done
    }
    }
}
```

Safe Package

The **safe** package provides a means of creating and controlling safe slave interpreters. (See also **interp**.)

Safe Overview

The **safe** package provides a convenient, higher level means of creating and manipulating safe slave interpreters than the **interp** command. It secures your system and other parts of the application from integrity and privacy attacks. The **safe** package makes no attempt to prevent annoyance or denial of service attacks, such as by displaying a toplevel window on top of all other windows or by using all available CPU time.

Interpreters managed by the **safe** package have several aliases that make them more capable than those created by **interp create -safe**. These aliases provide safe alternatives to **source** and **load** and a subset of **file**. An alias to **exit** is also provided, which deletes the interpreter but leaves the rest of the application running.

No information about the host file system is provided to the slave interpreter. Instead, all directories are represented by tokens that are looked up in the master interpreter by the aliased **source, load,** and **file** commands. Tokens appear in the slave as strings, as in **$p(:10:)**.

The **source** and **load** commands are restricted to only load packages from the *access path*. The access path defaults to be the same as the directories accessed by the master's **tcl_library** and **auto_path**. Files to be sourced or loaded should be in the form **[file join** *token filename*]. For **source**, *filename* is restricted to 14 characters or less, and cannot contain more than one dot (.) It must have a ".tcl" extension or be **tclIndex**.

The **file** command provides only the **dirname, join, extension, root, tail, pathname,** and **split** subcommands.

Syntax

::**safe**::**interpCreate** *?slave? ?options?*

::**safe**::**interpInit** *slave ?options?*

::**safe**::**interpConfigure** *slave ?option?*

::**safe**::**interpConfigure** *slave options*

::**safe**::**interpDelete** *slave*

::**safe**::**interpAddToAccessPath** *slave directory*

::**safe**::**interpFindInAccessPath** *slave directory*

::**safe::loadTk** *slave ?-***use** *windowId? ?-***display** *displayName?*

::**safe::setLogCmd** *command*

The arguments are as follows:

command
A command to evaluate to log messages from the **safe** package.
When *command* is invoked, the string to log will be appended as
an additional argument.

directory
A real directory name.

displayName
The name of the display on which to create the slave interpreter's
top level window. This option only works on UNIX systems.

NOTE: Conflicting -**windowId** and -**displayName** options will
likely generate a fatal error.

slave
The name of a slave interpreter.

windowId
A platform-dependent window ID or handle, or a Tk window path,
such as .tl1.f, that specifies the window to be used as the default
toplevel (.) window for the slave interpreter.

Options

The slave interpreter may be configured when created (with
interpCreate), when initialized (with **interpInit**), or later (with
interpConfigure). The following table lists valid options:

Option	Purpose
-**accessPath** *pathList*	Specifies the list of directories from which to **source** and **load** files. If -**accessPath** is not specified or if *pathList* is an empty list ({}), the slave will use the same directories as its master.

-deleteHook *command*	Specifies a command to evaluate in the master interpreter before deleting the slave. When *command* is evaluated, it will have the name of the slave appended as an additional argument. If **-deleteHook** is not specified, *command* defaults to {} (an empty list) and nothing is done when the slave is deleted.
-nested *boolean*	Specifies whether the slave may load packages into its slave interpreters. If **-nested** is not specified, *boolean* defaults to false and the slave may not load packages into its slaves.
-nestedLoadOk	An abbreviation for **-nested true**.
-noStatics	An abbreviation for **-statics false**.
-statics *boolean*	Specifies whether statically linked libraries may be loaded into the slave interpreter. If **-statics** is not specified, *boolean* defaults to true and static libraries may be loaded.

::safe::interpCreate *?slave? ?options?*

Creates a new slave interpreter with aliases for **source**, **load**, **file**, and **exit**, and configures it with *options*. If *slave* is omitted, **interpCreate** generates a new, unique name.

RETURNS   The name of the new slave interpreter.

::safe::interpInit *slave ?options?*

Initializes *slave* with *options*. *slave* is the name of an existing safe slave interpreter.

RETURNS   The name of the slave interpreter.

::safe::interpConfigure *slave ?option?*

Retrieves one or all options for *slave*.

RETURNS If *option* is specified, a two-element list containing the option name and its value, as in this example:

```
{-statics 1}
```

If *option* is not specified, a list of all options is returned, as in

```
{-accessPath {} -statics 1 -nested 0 -deleteHook {}}./0
```


::safe::interpConfigure *slave options*

Sets one or more options for *slave*. *options* lists one or more options and new values for them.

::safe::interpDelete *slave*

Deletes *slave* after calling the *deleteHook*, if any.

::safe::interpAddToAccessPath *slave directory*

Adds *directory* to *slave*'s access path.

RETURNS The token for the new entry in the access path.

::safe::interpFindInAccessPath *slave directory*

Retrieves the token for *directory* in *slave*'s access path.

RETURNS The token for *directory*.

ERROR Raises an error if *directory* is not in *slave*'s access path.

::safe::loadTk *slave* ?-use *windowId*? ?-display *displayName*?

Loads Tk into a safe interpreter.

RETURNS The name of the slave interpreter.

::safe::setLogCmd *command*

Specifies the command to be used to log interesting events in the
safe package. When *command* is invoked, a string will be
appended as an additional argument.

RETURNS The logging command (*command*).

Example

```
::safe::setLogCmd puts stderr
::safe::interpCreate foo -statics 1
::safe::loadTk foo
```

The **interpCreate** command results in the following output to
stderr:

```
NOTICE for slave foo : Created
NOTICE for slave foo : Setting accessPath=({C:/PROGRAM
FILES/TCL/8.1/TCL/lib/tcl8.1} {C:/PROGRAM
FILES/TCL/8.1/TCL/lib/tcl8.1/encoding} {C:/PROGRAM
FILES/TCL/8.1/TCL/lib/tcl8.1/opt0.4} {C:/PROGRAM
FILES/TCL/8.1/TCL/lib/tcl8.1/http2.0} {C:/PROGRAM
FILES/TCL/8.1/TCL/lib/tcl8.1/http1.0} {C:/PROGRAM
FILES/TCL/8.1/TCL/lib/tcl8.1/reg1.0} {C:/PROGRAM
FILES/TCL/8.1/TCL/lib/tcl8.1/msgcat1.0} {C:/PROGRAM
FILES/TCL/8.1/TCL/lib/tcl8.1/dde1.0} {C:/PROGRAM
FILES/TCL/8.1/TCL/lib} {C:/PROGRAM
FILES/TCL/8.1/TCL/lib/tk8.1} {C:/PROGRAM
FILES/TCL/8.1/TCL/lib/tk8.1/demos} {C:/PROGRAM
FILES/TCL/8.1/TCL/lib/tk8.1/images}) staticsok=1
nestedok=0 deletehook=()

NOTICE for slave foo : auto_path in foo has been set to
{$p(:0:)} {$p(:1:)} {$p(:2:)} {$p(:3:)} {$p(:4:)}
{$p(:5:)} {$p(:6:)} {$p(:7:)} {$p(:8:)} {$p(:9:)}
{$p(:10:)} {$p(:11:)}
```

scale

The **scale** command creates and manipulates widgets that may be
used to display numeric values or enter numeric values by direct
manipulation. (See also **scrollbar**.)

Scale Options

Scale widgets recognize the following standard widget options. (See the Appendix for a complete list of standard widget options and their meanings.)

activebackground	foreground	relief
background	highlightbackground	repeatdelay
borderwidth	highlightcolor	repeatinterval
cursor	highlightthickness	takefocus
font	orient	troughcolor

In addition, scale widgets recognize the following widget-specific options:

-bigincrement *increment*
Specifies the large increment for some scale operations. *increment* is a floating-point number. If *increment* is 0, the increment is set to 1/10 of the range of the scale, as specified with -**to** and -**from**. This is the default.

-command *command*
Specifies a command to call whenever the scale's value changes as a result of a widget command. When *command* is invoked, the current value of the scale will be appended as an additional argument.

-digits *integer*
Specifies the number of significant digits used when converting the scale's value to a string. If *integer* is less than or equal to 0, it is set so that every possible slider position (as determined from **resolution**) will have a different display string.

-from *minimum*
Specifies the minimum value of the scale. *minimum* is a floating-point number. This corresponds to the left end of a horizontal scale and the top of a vertical scale.

-label *string*

Specifies a constant string to be displayed by the scale. For horizontal scales, this is displayed just above the left end of the scale. For vertical scales, it is displayed just to the right of the top of the scale.

-length *distance*

Specifies the long dimension of the scale in screen units. For horizontal scales, this is the width of the scale. For vertical scales, it is the height.

-resolution *resolution*

Specifies the resolution of the scale as a real number. If *resolution* is greater than 0, the scale's value is always rounded to a multiple of *resolution*. If *resolution* is less than or equal to 0, no rounding occurs. *resolution* also affects placement of and values for tick marks and the endpoints of the scale. If **-resolution** is not specified, *resolution* defaults to 1.0.

-showvalue *boolean*

Specifies whether the current value of the scale should be displayed.

-sliderlength *distance*

Specifies the size of the scale slider in screen units.

-sliderrelief *relief*

Specifies the relief for the slider. Valid values are the same as for **-relief**. (See the Appendix for details.)

-state *state*

Specifies the state of the scale. *state* must be one of the following:

- **normal**   The slider is displayed using the **foreground** color and may be manipulated by the user.

- **active**   The slider is displayed using the **activebackground** color and may be manipulated by the user.

- **disabled**   The scale is displayed using the **foreground** color but cannot be activated or invoked by the user.

-tickinterval *interval*

Specifies the spacing between numeric labels below or to the left of the scale. *interval* is a floating-point number. If *interval* is 0.0, no labels are displayed. This is the default.

-to *maximum*
Specifies the maximum value of the scale. This corresponds to the right end of a horizontal scale and the bottom of a vertical scale.

-variable *varName*
Specifies the name of a global variable to link to the scale's value. When the variable changes, the scale's value will update. When the scale's value is manipulated, the variable will be set. The variable will be set in the global scope, but the name may include namespace qualifiers.

-width *distance*
Specifies the small dimension of the scale in screen units. For horizontal scales, this is the height; for vertical scales, it is the width.

Scale Commands

Scale widgets respond to the **cget** and **configure** standard widget commands. (See the Appendix for details.) In addition, scale widgets respond to the following widget-specific commands:

pathName **coords** *?value?*

pathName **get** *?x y?*

pathName **identify** *x y*

pathName **set** *value*

The arguments for scale widget commands are as follows:

value
A value for the scale.

x, y
Window coordinates within the scale widget.

pathName **coords** *?value?*
Retrieves the window coordinates of *value* within the scale. If *value* is not specified, the scale's current value is used.

RETURNS   A list of window coordinates, in the form {*x y*}.

pathName* get *?x y?
Determines the value in the scale that corresponds to the window coordinates (*x,y*). If *x* and *y* are omitted, the current position of the slider (as returned by the **coords** scale command) is used.

RETURNS   A real number indicating the current value of the scale.

pathName* identify *x y
Determines where (*x,y*) lies on the scale.

RETURNS   One of three values indicating the location of (*x,y*):

* **trough1**   The coordinates are in the trough, between the left or top end of the trough and the slider.

* **slider**   The coordinates are over the slider.

* **trough2**   The coordinates are in the trough, between the right or bottom end of the trough and the slider.

If the coordinates are not in the trough, an empty string is returned.

pathName* set *value
Sets the value of the scale to *value* if the scale is not disabled.

Default Bindings

Mouse Bindings

* Clicking with mouse button 1 in the trough moves the slider toward the mouse pointer and increments or decrements the scale's value by *resolution* to correspond to the new position. This auto-repeats as long as the mouse button is held down.

* Clicking with mouse button 1 in the trough with the CTRL key pressed moves the slider to the end of the trough, toward the mouse pointer, and updates the scale's value to correspond to the new position.

* Dragging the slider with mouse button 1 pressed moves the slider and changes the scale's value to correspond to the new position.

* Clicking with mouse button 2 in the trough sets the scale's value to the value corresponding to the position of the click.

Keyboard Bindings

* Pressing the LEFT ARROW or UP ARROW key moves the slider toward the **from** end of the scale by the value of *resolution*.

- Pressing the LEFT ARROW or UP ARROW key while pressing the CTRL key moves the slider toward the **from** end of the scale by the value of *bigincrement*.

- Pressing the RIGHT ARROW or DOWN ARROW key moves the slider toward the **to** end of the scale by the value of *resolution*.

- Pressing the RIGHT ARROW or DOWN ARROW key while pressing the CTRL key moves the slider toward the **to** end of the scale by the value of *bigincrement*.

- Pressing HOME moves the slider to the **from** end of the scale.

- Pressing END moves the slider to the **to** end of the scale.

Example

```
# A vertical scale with the larger value at the
# top
scale .s -from 100 -to 0 -orient vertical \
        -resolution .5 \
        -tickinterval 20 -label "Going up!" \
        -variable ::ns::var
```

Programmer's Tip: *Many of the default bindings on **scale** widgets are provided through procs. These procs include **tkScaleActivate**, **tkScaleButton2Down**, **tkScaleButtonDown**, **tkScaleControlPress**, **tkScaleDrag**, **tkScaleEndDrag**, and **tkScaleIncrement**. These commands are not of general interest and are not documented in this reference. The **bind**, **info args**, and **info body** commands can be used to explore the use and implementation of these commands.*

scan

The **scan** command parses a string into values. (See also **binary**; **format**.) It takes the following form:

scan *string formatString varName ?varName ... ?*

The arguments are as follows:

formatString
A string containing literal text and field specifiers indicating how each value should be parsed from *string*.

string
The string to parse.

varName
Name of a variable to set with data from *string* according to the specification in *formatString*.

Description

Scan processes *string* and *formatString* together from left to right using three rules:

- If the next character in *formatString* is a blank or a tab, the next zero or more adjacent whitespace characters in *string* are skipped.

- If the next character in *formatString* is a percent sign (%), the following characters in *formatString* are a *field specifier* that describes how to format data from *string* into the next named variable. (See the upcoming discussion of field specifiers for details.)

- Any other character in *formatString* must match the next character in *string*.

RETURNS   The number of fields processed, or -1 if the end of *string* is encountered before data is found matching the field specifiers in *formatString*.

ERROR   Raises an error if there are not enough *varName* values for the field specifiers in *formatString,* if *formatString* contains an invalid field specifier, or if more than one field specifier in *formatString* has an XPG3 position specifier referring to the same variable.

Field Specifiers

A field specifier consists of several parts, in the following order:

1. A discard specifier

2. An XPG3 position specifier

3. A maximum field width

4. A conversion character

All parts but the conversion character are optional.

Discard Specifier
If the first character after the % is an asterisk (*), the converted field is discarded rather than being assigned to one of the named variables.

XPG3 Position Specifier
The XPG3 format specifier consists of a decimal integer followed by a dollar sign ($). The number indicates which *varName* to set from this field. *varNames* are numbered starting with 1.

Programmer's Tip: *Because the dollar sign ($) is a special character to Tcl, formatStrings containing XPG3 position specifiers should be quoted with braces ({}) when specified in source code. However, such format strings will typically come from external repositories, such as message catalogs. (See the* **msgcat** *command entry for more information on message catalogs.)*

Without the optional XPG3 position specifier, **scan** matches *varNames* with field specifiers from left to right, in order. XPG3 format specifiers allow the *formatString* to override that order, with a goal of providing better localization support. (See the **format** command entry for a complete discussion of XPG3 specifiers.)

NOTE: An XPG3 position specifier must be present in either all of the field specifiers in *formatString* or none of them.

Maximum Field Width
The maximum field width specifies the most characters that the will be parsed from *string* to set the next variable. Fewer than that number of characters may be processed if a whitespace character or an invalid character is encountered in *string*. For example, **scan "123456789" "%12o%s" a b** stops processing for **a** when 8, an invalid octal digit, is seen.

Conversion Character
The conversion character is the only required part of the field specifier. Table 2-27 lists valid conversion characters and their effects.

NOTE: If the conversion character is anything other than **c** or **[**, whitespace characters in *string* are skipped before conversion begins.

Conversion Characters	Purpose
c	Converts a single character from *string* to its decimal equivalent. For example, **a** is converted to 97.
d	Converts decimal digits from *string* to an integer.
e, **f**, or g	Converts a floating-point number, possibly in scientific notation, to a Tcl floating-point number. These three conversions are interchangeable.
i	Converts characters from *string* to an integer. Characters are treated as for **expr**. For example, **0x20** is read as a hexadecimal number, and 32 is stored in the next variable.
n	Sets the next variable to the number of characters scanned from *string* so far. The next character to process from *string* does not change.
o	Converts octal digits from *string* to a decimal integer.
s	Copies characters to the next variable, up to the next whitespace character in *string* or the maximum field width.
u	Converts decimal digits from *string* to an unsigned decimal integer.
x	Converts hexadecimal digits from *string* to a decimal integer.
[*chars*]	Copies any of the listed *chars* to the next variable. A close bracket (]) is treated as one of the characters to copy if it's the first one in *chars*. Ranges of characters may be specified with a dash, such as **a-z**. A dash is treated as one of the characters to copy if it's the first or last one in *chars*.
[^*chars*]	Copies any characters not listed in *chars* to the next variable. A close bracket (]) is treated as one of the characters to exclude if it's the first one in *chars*. Ranges of characters to exclude may be specified with a dash, such as **a-z**. A dash is treated as one of the characters to exclude if it's the first or last one in *chars*.

Table 2-27. Scan Conversion Characters

Example

```
set fmt {%d %s %c}
set s [format $fmt 1 foo 97]
scan $s $fmt f1 f2 f3
```

scan differs from the ANSI C **sscanf** function in the following ways:

- **%p** conversions are not supported.
- **%c** conversions converts a single character, and no field width may be supplied.
- The **l**, **h**, and **L** modifiers are ignored.

The **scrollbar** command creates and manipulates scroll bar widgets that are used to control which part of other widgets, such as texts and canvases, are visible. (See also **canvas**; **entry**; **listbox**; **text**.)

Scroll Bar Overview

A scroll bar is used to display and control the view of scrollable widgets, such as texts and canvases, so that the view of those widgets needn't be large enough to display all of their contents at once. Scroll bars may be either horizontal (typically controlling the side-to-side movement of the controlled widget) or vertical (typically controlling the up-and-down movement of the controlled widget).

Scroll Bar Elements
A scroll bar includes two triangular buttons, one at each end, and a trough between them. A variable-sized slider, or *thumb*, sits in the trough. The view can be adjusted in various ways by using the mouse or the keyboard to manipulate directly the parts of the scroll bar.

The size of the thumb relative to the length of the trough indicates the amount of the controlled widget that is visible. For example, if a text widget is sized so that 20 of its 40 lines of text are visible, the thumb of its vertical scroll bar will be half the length of the trough.

The position of the thumb indicates what part of the controlled widget is visible. For example, if the first line of a text widget is visible, then the thumb of its vertical scroll bar is at the top of the trough.

The parts of the scroll bar, shown in Figure 2-3, have names that are used in some bindings and commands:

- **arrow1**   The top or left button
- **trough1**   The part of the trough between **arrow1** and **slider**
- **slider**   The movable rectangle in the trough
- **trough2**   The part of the trough between **slider** and **arrow2**
- **arrow2**   The bottom or right button

Scroll Bar Protocol

When a scroll bar is manipulated, it must communicate with the associated widget to control the widget's view. For example, when the user clicks the bottom arrow of a vertical scroll bar, the contents of the associated widget scroll up. Similarly, when the widget changes, it must communicate with the scroll bar so that the size and position of the thumb correctly portray the current view of the widget. For example, when lines are added to a text widget, the thumb should become smaller, to indicate that a smaller percentage of the text is visible.

The communication between a scroll bar and its associated widget is well-defined and consistent for all scrollable widgets. A scroll bar communicates with its associated widget by calling the widget's **xview** or **yview** command whenever the scroll bar is manipulated. This is configured by using the scroll bar's -**command** option. A scrollable widget communicates with its scroll bars by calling the scroll bar's **set** command whenever a change in the widget affects the view. This is configured using the widget's -**xscrollcommand** and -**yscrollcommand** options.

NOTE: Before Tk version 4, the protocol between scroll bars and scrollable widgets was different. This protocol is still supported for backward-compatibility, but it is deprecated.

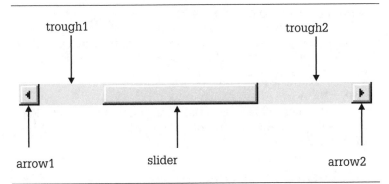

Figure 2-3.   Parts of a scroll bar

Scroll Bar Options

Scroll bar widgets recognize the following standard widget options. (See the appendix for a complete list of standard widget options and their meanings.)

activebackground	highlightcolor	repeatdelay
background	highlightthickness	repeatinterval
borderwidth	jump	takefocus
cursor	orient	
highlightbackground	relief	

In addition, scroll bar widgets recognize the following widget-specific options:

-activerelief *relief*
Specifies how the active element of the scroll bar will be displayed. *relief* may be **flat, groove, raised, ridge, solid,** or **sunken.** Nonactive elements are always displayed with **raised** relief.

NOTE: This option has no effect on Microsoft Windows systems.

-command *command*
Specifies the command to invoke when the scroll bar is manipulated. Typically, this is an **xview** or **yview** command for a scrollable widget, such as a text or a canvas widget.

-elementborderwidth *distance*
Specifies the width, in screen units, of the border drawn around
the two arrows and the slider ("thumb") within the scroll bar. If
distance is less than 0, the value of the **-borderwidth** option is
used. This is the default.

-width *distance*
Specifies the short dimension of the scroll bar, in screen units. For
vertical scroll bars, this is the width; for horizontal scroll bars, this
is the height.

Scroll Bar Commands

Scroll bar widgets respond to the **cget** and **configure** standard
widget commands. (See the Appendix for details.) In addition,
scroll bar widgets respond to the following widget-specific
commands:

> *pathName* **activate**
>
> *pathName* **activate** *element*
>
> *pathName* **delta** *deltaX deltaY*
>
> *pathName* **fraction** *x y*
>
> *pathName* **get**
>
> *pathName* **identify** *x y*
>
> *pathName* **set** *first last*

The arguments to the scroll bar widget commands are as follows:

deltaX, deltaY
The number of pixels to compute delta for.

element
A part of the scroll bar: **arrow1**, **slider**, or **arrow2**.

first, last
View coordinates to update the scroll bar with.

x, y
Scroll bar window coordinates, in pixels.

pathName activate
Determines the active element of the scroll bar.

RETURNS   The active element name, or an empty string if no
element is active.

pathName activate *element*
Makes *element* active and displays it with **activebackground** and
activerelief.

pathName delta *deltaX deltaY*
Determines how much the view must change to cause the slider to
move *deltaX* or *deltaY* pixels. *deltaX* is ignored for vertical scroll
bars, and *deltaY* is ignored for horizontal scroll bars.

RETURNS   A view coordinate.

pathName fraction *x y*
Determines the view coordinate for a position within the scroll bar.
x and *y* are window coordinates, in pixels. If (*x,y*) is outside the
trough, the closest point in the trough is used.

pathName get
Returns the list of arguments to the most recent scroll bar **set**
command.

pathName identify *x y*
Determines which scroll bar element, if any, is under (*x,y*). *x* and *y*
are window coordinates, in pixels.

RETURNS   The name of a scroll bar element, or an empty string if
no element is under (*x,y*).

pathName set *first last*
Sets the coordinates of the current view. *first* and *last* are view
coordinates. *first* should be less than *last*.

NOTE: Prior to Tk version 4, the scrolling protocol used different
view coordinates. In the old-style scrolling, the scroll bar **set**
command took four integer arguments: *totalUnits*, *windowUnits*,
firstUnit, and *lastUnit*. This form is still supported (set determines
which is being used by the number of arguments given) but should
not be used.

Default Bindings

Scroll bar widgets are created with bindings that make them behave as expected, consistent with the user interface conventions on each platform. Specifically:

Mouse Bindings

- Clicking mouse button 1 or 2 over **arrow1** causes the view of the associated widget to move left or up by one unit. This auto-repeats if mouse button 1 is held down.

- Clicking mouse button 1 or 2 over **arrow2** causes the view of the associated widget to move right or down by one unit. This auto-repeats if mouse button 1 is held down.

- Clicking mouse button 1 over **trough1** causes the view of the associated widget to move left or up by one page. This auto-repeats if mouse button 1 is held down.

- Clicking mouse button 1 over **trough2** causes the view of the associated widget to move right or down by one page. This auto-repeats if mouse button 1 is held down.

- Clicking mouse button 2 over **trough1**, **slider**, or **trough2** sets the view to the corresponding mouse position.

- Dragging the slider with mouse button 1 or 2 pressed adjusts the view of the associated widget to follow the slider. If the **-jump** option is true, the view is not redisplayed until the mouse button is released.

- Clicking mouse button 1 with the CTRL key pressed over **arrow1** or **trough1** causes the view of the associated widget to move to the extreme top or left.

- Clicking mouse button 1 with the CTRL key pressed over **arrow2** or **trough2** causes the view of the associated widget to move to the extreme bottom or right.

Keyboard Bindings

- In vertical scroll bars, pressing the UP ARROW key has the same effect as clicking with mouse button 1 over **arrow1**, and pressing the DOWN ARROW has the same effect as clicking with mouse button 1 over **arrow2**.

- In vertical scroll bars, pressing CTRL-UP ARROW has the same effect as clicking with mouse button 1 over **trough1**, and pressing CTRL-DOWN ARROW has the same effect as clicking with mouse button 1 over **trough2**.

- In horizontal scroll bars, pressing the LEFT ARROW key has the same effect as clicking with mouse button 1 over **arrow1**, and pressing RIGHT ARROW has the same effect as clicking with mouse button 1 over **arrow2**.

- In horizontal scroll bars, pressing CTRL-LEFT ARROW has the same effect as clicking with mouse button 1 over **trough1**, and pressing CTRL-RIGHT ARROW has the same effect as clicking with mouse button 1 over **trough2**.

- Pressing the PRIOR and NEXT keys has the same effect as clicking with mouse button 1 in **trough1** and **trough2**, respectively.

- Pressing HOME causes the view of the associated widget to move to the extreme top or left.

- Pressing END causes the view of the associated widget to move to the extreme bottom or right.

Example

```
proc scrolledText { w } {
    # A frame to hold the text and its scroll bars
    frame $w

    # Create the widgets. The text and scroll bars
    # can be created in any order.
    # A text showing 10 lines of 20 characters.
    # Wrapping is turned off to show the
    # horizontal scroll bar working
    text $w.text -width 20 -height 10  \
            -wrap none \
            -xscrollcommand [list $w.hsb set] \
            -yscrollcommand [list $w.vsb set]

    # The vertical scroll bar. When it changes,
    # it calls the text's yview command.
    scrollbar $w.vsb -orient vertical \
            -command [list $w.text yview]
    # The horizontal scroll bar. When it changes,
    # it calls the text's xview command.
    scrollbar $w.hsb -orient horizontal \
```

```
                -command [list $w.text xview]

   # Put them in an uneven 2x2 grid.  The top
   # left is the text, the top right is the
   # vertical scroll bar, the bottom left is
   # the horizontal scroll bar, and the bottom
   # right is empty.
   grid $w.text $w.vsb -sticky news
   grid $w.hsb           -sticky ew

   # Make sure only the text (in row 0, column 0)
   # resizes.
   grid columnconfigure $w 0 -weight 1
   grid rowconfigure $w 0 -weight 1

   return $w
}

scrolledText .f
pack .f -expand 1 -fill both
```

seek

The **seek** command sets the access position in an open channel.
(See also **fconfigure**; **open**; **socket**.) It takes this form:

  seek *channelId offset ?origin?*

The arguments are as follows:

channelId
Identifier for a channel, such as those channels returned by **open**
and **socket**.

offset
Integer offset relative to *origin* for new position.

origin
Base from which *offset* is measured. *origin* may be any of
the following:

- **start**   The new position will be *offset* bytes from the start of the data.
- **current**   The new position will be *offset* bytes from the current position in the channel.
- **end**   The new position will be *offset* bytes from the end of the data. If *offset* is positive, the new position is after the end of data.

If *origin* is not specified, it defaults to **start**.

Description

Buffered input on *channelId* is discarded, and buffered output for *channelId* is flushed before **seek** returns, even if *channelId* is configured to be unbuffered.

ERROR   Raises an error if the underlying device or file does not support seeking.

Example

```
# Insert a line into a file after a given number
# of lines
proc insertInFile { fileName insertAfter text } {
    # Open the file for reading and writing
    set fid [open $fileName r+]
    # Get the current contents
    set lines [split [read $fid] \n]
    # Figure out where to insert
    set position 0
    foreach line [lrange $lines 0 $insertAfter] {
        # Move over the line
        incr position [string length $line]
        # Move over the newline between lines
        incr position
    }
    # Seek to the place to insert and write the
    # new line
    seek $fid $position
    puts $fid $text
    incr $insertAfter
    # Put the rest of the file back
    foreach line \
```

```
        [lrange $lines $insertAfter end] {
    puts $fid $line
  }
  # Close the file
  close $fid
}
insertInFile someFile 3 "This is an inserted line"
```

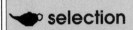 **selection**

The **selection** command manipulates the X Window selection, as
described in the *X Inter-Client Communication Conventions
Manual (ICCCM)*. (See also **clipboard**.) It takes the following forms:

selection clear *?*-**displayof** *window? ?*-**selection** *selection?*

selection get *?*-**displayof** *window?*
?-**selection** *selection? ?*-**type** *type?*

selection handle *?*-**selection** *selection? ?*-**type** *type?*
?-**format** *format? window command*

selection own *?*-**displayof** *window? ?*-**selection** *selection?*

selection own *?*-**command** *script? ?*-**selection**
selection? window

The arguments are as follows:

command
Command to evaluate to handle data.

format
The format the data should be stored in, such as **STRING**,
INTEGER, ATOM, or **PIXEL**. If -**format** is not specified, *format*
defaults to **STRING**.

NOTE: *format* is relevant only when data is to be accessed
by non-Tk applications. Tk converts all data to strings when
it is retrieved.

script
Script to evaluate when selection ownership changes.

selection
The selection to manipulate, such as **PRIMARY** or **CLIPBOARD**.
If -**selection** is not specified, *selection* defaults to **PRIMARY**.

type
The type of data being manipulated, such as **FILENAME**, **STRING**,
or **TIMESTAMP**. In other words, how the data should be
interpreted. If -**type** is not specified, *type* defaults to **STRING**.

window
The window whose display's selection should be manipulated. If
-**displayof** is not specified, *window* defaults to dot (.), the
application's default toplevel window.

selection clear
?-displayof *window? ?*-selection *selection?*

Clears *selection* on *window*'s display so that no window owns
the selection.

selection get *?*-displayof *window?*
?-selection *selection? ?*-type *type?*

Retrieves *selection* from *window*'s display as *type* data.

RETURNS   The data from the selection in the specified type.

selection handle
?-selection *selection? ?*-type *type?*
?-format *format? window command*

Associates *command* with *window*'s selection so that **selection
get** requests for *type* data from *selection* will be processed
by evaluating *command* and returning the data it provides to
the requestor.

When *command* is evaluated, two additional arguments are
appended: *offset* and *maxBytes*. *offset* is the offset within *selection*
for which data is requested, and *maxBytes* is the maximum

number of bytes to return. *command* will be invoked repeatedly until it returns fewer than *maxBytes* of data or raises an error.

If *command* is {} (an empty list), the existing handler for *selection*, *type*, and *command* is removed.

selection own *?*-displayof *window? ?*-selection *selection?*

Retrieves the widget path to the window in the current application, displayed on *window*'s display, which owns *selection*.

RETURNS A window path, or an empty string if no window matches the criteria.

selection own *?*-command *script? ?*-selection *selection? window*

Sets *window* as the owner of *selection* and notifies the current owner that it has lost ownership of *selection*. When *window* loses ownership (such as when a **selection own** command specifies another window), *script* will be evaluated to notify *window* that it has lost the selection ownership. If **-command** is not specified, *script* defaults to an empty list and no notification is done.

Example

```
# Set up to provide file contents as selection
# value
proc provideFile { fileName } {
    set fid [open $fileName r]
    selection own .
    selection handle . [list handleSelection $fid]
}
# Handle each part of the get request
proc handleSelection { fid offset maxBytes } {
    seek $fid $offset
    set data [read $fid $maxBytes]
    if {[string length $data] != $maxBytes} {
        close $fid
        selection clear
    }
```

```
        return $data
}
# Test it
pack [text .t -height 10 -width 20]
provideFile someFile
.t insert end [selection get]
```

2

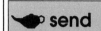 **send**

The **send** command executes a command in another Tcl application. (See also **dde**; **tk appname**; **winfo interps**.) It takes the following form:

> **send** *?options? app cmd ?arg arg ... ?*

The arguments are as follows:

app
Name of the application to evaluate *cmd*. This is initially set to the name of the script or executable containing the application, but can be set with **tk appname**.

arg
An argument to *cmd*.

cmd
Command to be evaluated by *app*.

The options are s follows:

-async
Does not wait for *cmd* to complete. **send** returns an empty string immediately, and the return value or error status of *cmd* is not available. This option is ignored if *app* is in the same process as the interpreter that invokes **send**.

-displayof *window*
Looks for *app*'s main window on *window*'s display.

--
The last option. The argument following this will be treated as *app* even if it starts with a - (dash).

Description

The **send** command enables Tcl applications to send commands to one another for evaluation. For example, a script running in one application can send commands to another as a macro replay feature in a Tcl-based application. The applications need not be in the same process.

send uses the X Windows server to communicate between interpreters, which opens a potentially serious security hole, because any application that connects to the X Window server can send any command to any application. Tk provides some small measure of security by rejecting incoming sends unless xhost-style access control is enabled and the list of enabled hosts is empty. This requires **xauth** or some other security provisions for applications. To completely disable communication via **send**, remove the **send** command with **rename send {}**. To reenable **send**, use **tk appname**.

RETURNS   The result of evaluating *cmd* and *args* in *app*.

ERROR   Raises an error if *cmd* raises an error in *app*.

Example

```
# Send a message to a logging process, if it is
# active
set apps [winfo interps]
if {[lsearch $apps myLogger] != -1} {
    send -async myLogger \
        trace "Something interesting happened in\
            [tk appname]"
}
```

Compatibility

send is available only on UNIX systems. **dde** provides similar functionality on Microsoft Windows systems.

set

The **set** command sets or queries the value of a variable. (See also **array**; **subst**.) It takes the following forms:

> **set** *varName*
>
> **set** *varName value*

The arguments are as follows:

value
The value to assign to *varName*.

varName
The name of the variable to manipulate.

Description

The **set** command sets or retrieves the value of a variable. If *varName* includes a namespace qualifier, the named variable is accessed in the specified namespace. If *varName* does not include a namespace qualifier, *varName* is accessed in the current scope unless **global** or **variable** has been used to bring a global or namespace variable in scope. When called outside any proc, an unqualified variable name refers to a global variable.

varName may take the form *name(index)*, which refers to the *index* element of the array *name*. *name* may include namespace qualifiers.

set *varName*

Retrieves the value of *varName*. This is the same as $*varName* and is useful for indirectly accessing a variable named by another variable.

RETURNS   The value of *varName*.

ERROR   Raises an error if *varName* does not exist.

set *varName value*

Assigns *value* to *varName*.

RETURNS The new value of *varName*.

Example

```
# Set some variables
set pi 3.14159
set names {heather jennifer}
# Two ways to set an array element
array set a { index1 foo }
set a(index1) foo
# Use indirection to access y
set x y
set y 1
puts "first, y is [set $x]"
set $x 2
puts "second, y is $y"
```

This script prints the following two lines:

```
first, y is 1
second, y is 2
```

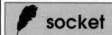

socket

The **socket** command opens a TCP/IP network connection. (See also **fconfigure**.) It takes the following forms:

> **socket** *?options? host port*

> **socket -server** *command ?*-**myaddr** *host? port*

The arguments are as follows:

command
A command to evaluate when a new client connects to *port*.
When *command* is evaluated, three additional arguments
will be appended:

- **channel**   The channel identifier of a new channel opened for communication with the client
- **address**   The network address of the client's host, in dotted-decimal form
- **port**   The client's port number

host
The host on which *port* is located. *host* may be a hostname (for example, somehost.example.com) or an IP address in dotted-decimal form (for example, 127.0.0.1). The reserved value **localhost** refers to the host on which the **socket** command is invoked.

port
The integer port number of the port to connect to (for client connections) or to listen on (for server connections).

socket *?options?* *host port*

Creates a new client connection to the server at *port* on *host*. *options* are as follows:

Option	Purpose
-myaddr *host*	Specifies the network address for the client side of the connection. *host* may be a hostname or an IP address in dotted-decimal notation. If **-myaddr** is not specified, *host* is chosen by the system network software. (This option is useful if the script is running on a host with multiple network interfaces.)
-myport *port*	Specifies the port number to use for the client side of the connection. *port* must be an integer. If **-myport** is not specified, a port is chosen by the system network software.

Option	Purpose
-async	Specifies that **socket** should return immediately, without waiting for the client socket to be connected. If the socket is configured for blocking mode, a **gets** or **flush** that is done on the socket before the connection is made will wait until the connection is completed or fails. If the socket is configured for nonblocking mode, a **gets** or **flush** done on the socket before the connection is made will return immediately, and **fblocked** will return 1.

RETURNS   A new channel identifier that is configured for reading and writing to the server.

ERROR   Raises an error if a connection to the server cannot be established.

socket -server
command ?-myaddr host? port

Creates a new server connection at *port*. *host* specifies the network address for the server side of the connection. *host* may be a hostname or an IP address in dotted-decimal notation. If **-myaddr** is not specified, the socket is bound to the special address **INADDR_ANY**, so that it can accept connections from any interface. This option is useful if the script is running on a host with multiple network interfaces.

NOTE: Tcl can accept new connections only when an event loop is active. This is always true in Tk-based interpreters. In **Tcl-based** interpreters, vwait may be used to enter an event loop.

RETURNS   A new channel identifier representing the server port. This channel <u>cannot</u> be used for I/O with **gets**, and so forth. Closing this channel stops the server from accepting more client connection requests without affecting existing connections.

Socket Configuration

The **fconfigure** command may be used to query several read-only options for a socket:

Option	Value Returned
-error	The current error status of the socket, or an empty string if no error has occurred.
-sockname	A list of three elements describing the socket, in the form {**address host port**}. In some cases where the hostname cannot be determined, the first and second elements may be the same.
-peername	A list of three elements describing the peer the socket is connected to, in the same form as is returned for **-sockname**. This option is not valid for server sockets (channel identifiers returned by **socket -server**).

2

Example

```
# A very simple client and server in the same
# script
proc genData { channel count } {
    puts $channel "$count foo bar baz"
    flush $channel
    incr count -1
    if { $count == 0 } {
        close $channel
        return
    } else {
        after 500 genData $channel $count
    }
}
# [fcopy] callback
proc cleanup { channel doneName args } {
    close $channel
    set ::$doneName 1
}
# [socket -server] callback
proc newClient {
    clientDoneName channel address port
} {
    fcopy $channel stdout \
        -command \
            [list cleanup $channel $clientDoneName]
}
# The server socket (creates new read socket).
# Let the system pick the port
```

```
set serverSocket \
        [socket -server \
                [list newClient clientDone] 0]
# Get the port from the socket
set sockname [fconfigure $serverSocket -sockname]
set port [lindex $sockname 2]
# The client (write) end of the socket
set clientSocket [socket localhost $port]
# Write some stuff on the write socket
genData $clientSocket 10
# Let the events run
vwait clientDone
# Close the server socket
close $serverSocket
```

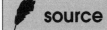

source

The **source** command reads Tcl commands from a file or resource and evaluates them. (See also **eval**.) It takes the following forms:

> **source** *filename*

> **source -rsrc** *resourceName ?filename?*

> **source -rsrcid** *resourceId ?filename?*

The arguments are as follows:

filename
Name of the file to process.

resourceId
Identifier of a TEXT resource to process.

resourceName
Name of a TEXT resource to process.

source *filename*

Reads and evaluates commands from *filename* until the end of the
file or until a **return** command is evaluated.

RETURNS   The value of the last command evaluated in *filename*.

ERROR   Raises an error if the script in *filename* raises an error.

source -rsrc *resourceName ?filename?*

Reads and evaluates commands from *resourceName* until the end
of the resource or until a **return** command is evaluated. If *filename*
is specified, Tcl looks for *resourceName* only in that file. If *filename*
is not specified, all open resource files are searched for
resourceName.

RETURNS   The value of the last command evaluated in
resourceName.

ERROR   Raises an error if the script in *resourceName* raises an error.

source -rsrcid *resourceId ?filename?*

Reads and evaluates commands from *resourceId* until the end of
the resource or until a **return** command is evaluated. If *filename* is
specified, Tcl looks for *resourceId* only in that file. If *filename* is not
specified, all open resource files are searched for *resourceId*.

RETURNS   The value of the last command evaluated in *resourceId*.

ERROR   Raises an error if the script in *resourceId* raises an error.

Example

```
source myProcs.tcl
```

Compatibility

The resource-based forms of **source** are only available on
Macintosh systems.

The **split** command splits a string into a list. (See also **join**.) It takes
the following form:

   split *string ?splitChars?*

The arguments are as follows:

splitChars
Which chars in *string* to split at. If *splitChars* is not specified, it
defaults to whitespace characters (blank, tab, and newline). If
splitChars is an empty string (" "), *string* is split between every two
characters.

string
The string to split.

RETURNS   A list made from splitting *string* wherever any
character in *splitChars* is found. The characters in *splitChars* are
not copied to the output.

Example

```
set string "the quick brown fox"
set list [split $string]
puts "The list <<$list>> has [llength $list]\
      elements"
set list [split $string ""]
puts "The list <<$list>> has [llength $list]\
      elements"
set list [split $string "o"]
puts "The list <<$list>> has [llength $list]\
      elements"
set string "foo/bar\\baz"
set list [split $string "\\/"]
```

```
puts "The list <<$list>> has [llength $list]\
    elements"
```

produces the output:

```
The list <<the quick brown fox>> has 4 elements
The list <<t h e { } q u i c k { } b r o w n { }
    f o x>> has 19 elements
The list <<{the quick br} {wn f} x>> has 3
    elements
The list <<foo bar baz>> has 3 elements
```

string

The **string** command performs string manipulations. (See also
glob.) It takes the following forms:

> **string bytelength** *string*
> **string length** *string*

> **string compare** *?-nocase? ?-length len? string1 string2*
> **string equal** *?-nocase? ?-length len? string1 string2*
> **string match** *pattern string*

> **string first** *string1 string2 ?index?*
> **string last** *string1 string2 ?index?*

> **string index** *string index*

> **string is** *class ?-strict? ?-failindex varname? string*

> **string map** *?-nocase? charMap string*

> **string range** *string first last*

> **string repeat** *string count*

> **string replace** *string first last ?newstring?*

> **string tolower** *string*
> **string totitle** *string*
> **string toupper** *string*

string trim *string ?chars?*
string trimleft *string ?chars?*
string trimright *string ?chars?*

string wordend *string index*
string wordstart *string index*

The arguments are as follows:

charMap
A list of keys and values to describe the mapping. *charMap* must
have an even number of elements, and is in the form {**key value
key value** ...}. Neither *key* nor *value* needs to be a single character.

chars
Characters to trim from the string.

class
A string class to test *string* against. Valid values are as follows:

Class	Value
alnum	Unicode letters and digits
alpha	Unicode letters
ascii	7-bit ASCII characters
boolean	String representations of a Boolean value, such as **true**, **off**, or **1**
control	Unicode control characters
digit	Unicode digits
double	A double-precision floating-point number recognizable by Tcl
false	String representations of a false Boolean value, such as **false**, **off**, or **no**
graph	Unicode printing characters, excluding space
integer	An integer recognizable by Tcl
lower	Unicode lowercase characters
print	Unicode printing characters, including space
punct	Unicode printing characters, excluding space and those matching the class **alnum**
space	Unicode space character
true	String representations of a true Boolean value, such as **true**, **on**, or **yes**
upper	Unicode uppercase characters

Class	Value
wordchar	Unicode alphanumerics (those matching the class **alnum**) and connectors (e.g., underscore)
xdigit	Hexadecimal digits (0-9, a-f, and A-F)

first, last, index
An index into the string. *index* takes one of the following forms:

Index	Value
int	An integer. 0 refers to the first character.
end	The last character of the string.
end-*int*	The character that is *int* characters from the end. For example, **end-1** refers to the *a* in "foo bar".

len
Number of characters to compare.

newstring
String to insert in place of removed text.

pattern
A **glob**-style pattern to match.

string1, string2, string
String to operate on.

varname
Variable to set with the index of the first character not matching the class.

string bytelength *string*

Determines the number of bytes used to represent *string* in internal UTF-8 format. Use **string length** to determine the number of characters in a string.

RETURNS   The number of bytes used by *string*, exressed as an integer.

string length *string*

Determines the number of characters in *string*.

NOTE: The value returned is not necessarily the size of the string in memory, due to the UTF-8 internal representation. Use **string bytelength** to get the size of the string in memory.

RETURNS A decimal integer.

string compare
?-nocase? ?-length *len? string1 string2*

Determines which string comes before the other in the collating sequence for the current locale. If the **-nocase** option is specified, case is ignored in the strings. If **-length** is specified, only the first *len* characters are compared. If *len* is negative, it is ignored.

RETURNS -1 if *string1* comes before *string2*; 0 if string1 and string2 are equal; 1 if *string1* comes after *string2*.

string match *pattern string*

Determines whether *string* matches the **glob**-style pattern *pattern*. *pattern* must match *string* except for the following special characters:

Character	Match
?	Any single character
*	Zero or more characters
[chars]	Any one of the characters in *chars*. *chars* may include a range of characters, such as **a-z**, which matches any character from *a* to *z*.
\x	*x*. For example, "\?" matches only a question mark, because the \ overrides the special meaning of ? in patterns.

RETURNS 1 if *string* matches *pattern*; 0 otherwise.

string equal ?-nocase? ?-length *len*? *string1 string2*

Determines whether two strings are equal. If the **-nocase** option is specified, case is ignored in the strings. If **-length** is specified, only the first *len* characters are compared. If *len* is negative, it is ignored.

RETURNS   1 if the strings are equal; 0 otherwise.

Example
```
# Test for string equality
if {[string equal $s1 $s2]} {
    puts "Strings are equal"
} else {
    puts "String are different"
}
```

Programmer's Tip: *Use* **string equal** *to test for string equality. It is more efficient and safer than* **expr**'*s equality tests.*

string first *string1 string2 ?index?*

Finds the first occurrence of *string1* in *string2*, starting at *index*. If *index* is not specified, it defaults to 0, the start of *string2*. For example, **[string first foo "foo bar foo bar"]** would return 0.

RETURNS   If *string1* exists in *string2*, the index of the start of the first occurrence of *string1* in *string2*; -1 otherwise.

string last *string1 string2 index*

Finds the last occurrence of *string1* in *string2*, starting at *index*. If *index* is not specified, it defaults to 0, the start of *string2*. For example, **[string last foo "foo bar foo bar"]** would return 8.

RETURNS   If *string1* exists in *string2*, the index of the start of the last occurrence of *string1* in *string2* after *index*; -1 otherwise.

string index *string index*

Returns the character at position *index* in *string*.

RETURNS   The character at *index* if *index* is between 0 and the length of *string*, inclusive. Otherwise, an empty string is returned.

string is *class* *?*-strict*?* *?*-failindex *varname?* *string*

Determines whether *string* is a member of *class*.

RETURNS   1 if *string* is a member of *class*; 0 otherwise. If **-strict** is specified, an empty string always returns 0; otherwise, an empty string matches all classes. If **-failindex** is specified and *string* does not match *class*, *varname* will be set to the index of the first character in *string* that does not match the class.

string map *?*-nocase*?* *charMap string*

For each *key*/*value* pair in *charMap*, replaces each instance of *key* in *string* with *value*. If the **-nocase** option is specified, case is ignored when looking for *key* in *string*.

RETURNS   The mapped string.

string range *string first last*

Copies a substring from *string*, starting at *first* to *last*. For example **[string range "foo bar" 4 end]** returns **bar**. If *first* is less than 0, it is treated as 0. If *last* is greater than the length of the string, it is treated as **end**.

RETURNS   The specified substring. If *first* is greater than *last*, an empty string is returned.

string repeat *string count*

Forms new string from *count* repetitions of *string*.

Example
```
puts [string repeat "-" 80]
```

string replace *string first last ?newstring?*

Replaces characters *first* through *last* in *string* with *newstring*. If *newstring* is not specified, it defaults to an empty string (" "), which accomplishes a deletion.

RETURNS A copy of *string* with *newstring* substituted. (*string* is unchanged.)

string tolower *string*

Converts all characters in *string* to lowercase.

RETURNS A copy of *string* in lowercase.

string totitle *string*

Converts the first character in *string* to uppercase and coverts all others to lowercase.

RETURNS A copy of *string* in title case.

string toupper *string*

Converts all characters in *string* to uppercase.

RETURNS A copy of *string* in uppercase.

string trim *string ?chars?*

Removes all characters in *chars* from the start and end of *string*.

RETURNS A copy of *string* with the specified characters removed.

Example

```
# Remove quotes, if present
set s [string trim $s "]
# Remove spaces, tabs, newlines, and carriage
# returns. s is unchanged, t gets the new value
set t [string trim $s]
```

string trimleft *string ?chars?*

Removes all characters in *chars* from the start of *string*.

RETURNS   A copy of *string* with the specified characters removed from the left end.

string trimright *string ?chars?*

Removes all characters in *chars* from the end of *string*.

RETURNS   A copy of *string* with the specified characters removed from the right end.

string wordend *string index*

Determines the index of the end of the word that includes the character at *index* in *string*. A word is a sequence of one or more letters, digits, and underscores. If *index* is less than 0, it is treated as 0. If *index* is greater than the length of *string*, it is treated as **end**.

RETURNS   A character index, expressed as an integer.

Example

The following script:

```
set s "foo bar"
for {set i 0} \
    {$i < [string length $s]} \
    {incr i} {
    puts "i:$i \
          start:[string wordstart $s $i] \
          end:[string wordend $s $i]"
}
```

produces the following output:

```
i:0   start:0   end:3
i:1   start:0   end:3
i:2   start:0   end:3
i:3   start:3   end:4
i:4   start:4   end:7
i:5   start:4   end:7
i:6   start:4   end:7
```

string wordstart *string index*

Determines the index of the start of the word that includes the character at *index* in *string*. A word is a sequence of one or more letters, digits, and underscores. If *index* is less than 0, it is treated as 0. If *index* is greater than the length of *string*, it is treated as the length of the string.

RETURNS   A character index, expressed as an integer.

Example

```
# Format one line of binary data
proc BinDumpLine { data lineLen } {
    for {set i 0} {$i < 256} {incr i} {
        set char [format %c $i]
        # Always compute the hexadecimal
        # representation
        set hexMap($char) "[format %02x $i] "
        # If the character isn't printable, show a
        # period
        if {! [string is print $char] } {
            set printMap($char) "."
        }
    }
    set l [expr {$lineLen * 3}]
    return "[format "%-*.*s" $l $l\
        [string map [array get hexMap] $data]] \
        [string map [array get printMap] $data]"
}
# Format a buffer of binary data on multiple lines
proc binDump { data } {
    set dataLen [string length $data]
    set lineLen 16
```

```
for {set i 0}\
    {$i < $dataLen}\
    {incr i $lineLen} {
    set line [string range $data $i \
                    [expr {$i+$lineLen-1}]]
    puts "[format %03d $i] :\
            [BinDumpLine $line $lineLen]"
    }
}
puts [binDump abcdefghijklmnopqrstuvwxyz]
```

 subst

The **subst** command performs limited substitutions on a string. (See also **eval**.) It takes the following form:

> **subst** *?-nobackslashes? ?-nocommands? ?-novariables?* *string*

The arguments are as follows:

string
The string to process.

The options are as follows:

-nobackslashes
Don't perform backslash substitution, such as expanding **\t** to a tab character.

-nocommands
Don't evaluate commands in brackets ([]) inside string.

-novariables
Don't substitute variable values.

RETURNS   The substituted string.

Example

The following script

```
set x foo
foreach option {-nobackslashes -nocommands \
            -novariables ""} {
    puts "$option\t[eval subst $option\
        {{$x\t[set x]}}]"
}
```

produces this output:

```
-nobackslashes    foo\tfoo
-nocommands       foo      [set x]
-novariables      $x       foo
          foo     foo
```

Programmer's Tip: string *will be evaluated by the Tcl parser before being passed to* **subst***. When passing a literal string to* **subst***, it is usually best to suppress evaluation by the parser by enclosing* string *in brackets (|}).*

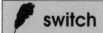

switch

The **switch** command executes one of several scripts based on a value. (See also **case**; **glob**; **regexp**; **string**.) It takes the following forms:

> **switch** *?options? string pattern body ?pattern body ... ?*

> **switch** *?options? string |pattern body ?pattern body ... ?|*

The arguments are as follows:

body
A script to evaluate if the corresponding *pattern* matches *string*. If *body* is -, the pattern uses the next specified body in the switch.

pattern
A pattern to test for a match. The last *pattern* may be **default**, in which case the corresponding body is executed if no other pattern matches *string*.

string
The value to match against each *patList*.

Options

-exact

string must match *pattern* literally; that is, [**string compare** *string pattern*] would return 0. This is the default if no option is specified.

-glob

Matches *string* against each *pattern* with the same rules as **string match**. This makes **switch** roughly equivalent to the obsolete **case** command.

-regexp

Matches *string* against each pattern with the same rules as **regexp**.

Programmer's Tip: *Only one of the three options should be specified. Specifying more than one option is not an error, but the results are uncertain. If string may start with a "-", you must specify "--" as the last option, to prevent errors.*

switch string *pattern body* *?pattern body ... ?*

Matches *string* against each *pattern*, in turn, and if a match is found, evaluates the corresponding *body*. Variable substitution is done on each *pattern* and *body*.

RETURNS   The value, if any, returned by evaluating *body*, or an empty string if no *pattern* matches *string*.

switch *string {pattern body* *?pattern body ... ?}*

Matches *string* against each *pattern*, in turn, and if a match is found, evaluates the corresponding *body*. The braces around the list of *pattern* and *body* pairs suppresses variable substitution, but allows for flexible and readable formatting of the *pattern* and *body*.

RETURNS   The value, if any, returned by evaluating *body*, or an empty string if no *patList* matches *string*.

Example

```
foreach arg $argv {
    # -- is needed because arg may start with -
    # Use exact matching, the default for switch
    switch -- $arg {
        default {
            puts "arg is \"default\""
        }
        -foo -
        -bar {
            puts "got -foo or -bar: \"$arg\""
        }
        default {
            puts "Couldn't match \"$arg\""
        }
    }
}
```

Programmer's Tip: *When a **switch** is formatted as in the
preceding example, it is tempting to put a comment before each
block to describe it. However, after string, **switch** must have an
even number of arguments or a list with an even number of
elements, and the text intended as comments is included in this
count. The following is wrong:*

```
# This is a bad switch command
switch -- $arg {
    # This is the foo case
    foo {
        doSomething
    }
}
```

*To make matters worse, this format will seem to work sometimes,
depending on the length and content of the text intended as a
comment. In the preceding example, **switch** sees patterns "#",
"is", "foo", and "foo" and bodies "This", "the", "case", and
"{doSomething}". The correct way to comment a **switch** is as
follows:*

```
switch -- $arg {
    foo {
    # This is the foo case
        doSomething
```

```
    }
}
```

*Here, the comment is buried in the body, where it is parsed
correctly.*

 tclLog

The **tclLog** command is used by the **-verbose** option of
pkg_mkIndex to log events during package indexing. (See also
pkg_mkIndex.) A default implementation is provided that writes to
stderr:

```
proc tclLog {string} {
    catch {puts stderr $string}
}
```

tclLog may be redefined to process *string* some other way.

Words

tcl_endOfWord, **tcl_startOfNextWord**, **tcl_startOfPreviousWord**,
tcl_wordBreakAfter, and **tcl_wordBreakBefore** determine where
words start and end based on regular expressions stored in the
global variables **tcl_nonwordchars** and **tcl_wordChars**.

Microsoft Windows considers spaces, tabs, and newlines to
be nonword characters, and anything else to be a word
character. UNIX considers only letters, numbers, and
underscores to be word characters, and considers anything
else to be a nonword character.

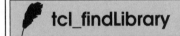

tcl_endOfWord

The **tcl_endOfWord** command determines where a "word" ends in a string. (See also **tcl_startOfNextWord**; **tcl_startOfPreviousWord**; **tcl_wordBreakAfter**; **tcl_wordBreakBefore**.) It takes the following form:

tcl_endOfWord *string start*

The arguments are as follows:

start
Index in *string* at which to start searching.

string
String to search for the end of a word.

RETURNS   The index of the first nonword character following the first word character after the *start* in *string*. -1 if there are no more end-of-word locations after *start*.

tcl_findLibrary

The **tcl_findLibrary** command searches in standard locations for a library script. It takes the following form:

tcl_findLibrary *basename version patch initScript enVarName varName*

The arguments are as follows:

basename
The base name of the library, such as "tk".

enVarName
Name of environment variable that holds the name of a directory to search for the library.

initScript
Initialization script to source when the library is found.

patch
The patch level for the library, such as "1".

varName
Name of a variable containing the directory the library is found in.

version
The version for the library, such as "8.1".

Description

tcl_findLibrary is a standard search procedure for use by extensions during initialization. It looks for a script library in several standard directories determined by its arguments and the **tcl_library** global.

If the variable named by *varName* is already defined, then $*varName*/$*initScript* is sourced. Otherwise, *initScript* is searched for in these directories, in the following order:

1. The directory named by the environment variable *enVarName*

2. In $basename$version under the Tcl library directory

3. Relative to the executable file:

   ../lib/$basename$version

   ../../lib/$basename$version

   ../library

   ../../library

   ../../$basename$version/library

   ../../../$basename$version/library

ERROR   Raises an error if *initScript* cannot be found or generates an error.

tcl_library

The **tcl_library** global variable is a string that contains the name of the directory containing the system library of Tcl scripts. If the environment variable **TCL_LIBRARY** exists, it is used to initialize **tcl_library**; otherwise, Tcl searches for the library scripts based on defaults compiled into the interpreter. This information is also available from the **info library** command.

The **tcl_patchLevel** global variable holds a string that describes the patch level of the current interpreter, such as "7.3p2" for the second patch release of version 7.3, or "8.1a1" for the first alpha release of version 8.1. This information is also available from the **info patchlevel** command.

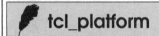

The **tcl_platform** global array describes the system on which the current interpreter is running. Tcl defines several elements that will always exist. Extensions and applications may define other elements.

Predefined elements of the **tcl_platform** array are the following:

Element	Contents
byteOrder	**littleEndian** or **bigEndian**.
machine	The instruction set for the system, such as **intel**, **PPC**, **68k**, etc.
os	The name of the operating system, such as **Win32s**, **Windows NT**, **MacOS**, **HP-UX**, etc.
osVersion	The version number of the operating system.
platform	One of **windows**, **macintosh** or **unix**.
user	The current user. On UNIX systems, this comes from the **USER** or **LOGNAME** environment variable. On Microsoft Windows and Macintosh systems, it comes from the **GetUserName** function.

NOTE: On Unix systems, **machine** is the value returned by `uname -m`, **os** is the value returned by `uname -s`, and **osVersion** is the value returned by `uname -r`.

tcl_precision

The **tcl_precision** global variable holds an integer that controls how many digits of precision are used when converting floating-point values to string representation. **tcl_precision** defaults to 12. A value of 17 is "perfect" IEEE floating-point representation, but it prevents rounding, so that some values may not appear correct and may be less useful. For example, with the default setting **[expr 2.0/5.0]** returns 0.4, but with **tcl_precision** set to 17, it returns 0.40000000000000002, which is precise but inaccurate.

All interpreters in a program share a single **tcl_precision** setting, and safe interpreters may not set it.

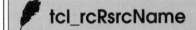

tcl_rcFileName

The **tcl_rcFileName** global variable holds the name of a user-specific reconfiguration (initialization) file. If this variable is set by the application initialization, this named file is sourced at startup, if it exists. In wish, the variable is set to ~/**.wishrc** on UNIX systems, and ~/**wishrc.tcl** on Microsoft Windows systems. Other Tcl-based applications may use other values.

tcl_rcRsrcName

The **tcl_rcRsrcName** global variable holds the name of a user-specific reconfiguration (initialization) TEXT resource. If this variable is set by the application initialization, this named file is sourced at startup, if it exists. In wish, the variable is set to "tclshrc".

NOTE: The **tcl_rcRsrcName** variable is valid only on Macintosh systems.

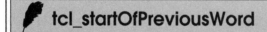

tcl_startOfNextWord

The **tcl_startOfNextWord** command determines where the next "word" starts in a string. (See also **tcl_endOfWord**; **tcl_startOfPreviousWord**; **tcl_wordBreakAfter**; **tcl_wordBreakBefore**.) It takes this form:

tcl_startOfNextWord *string start*

The arguments are as follows:

start
Index in *string* at which to start searching.

string
String to search for the start of a word.

RETURNS   The index of the first word character following a nonword character after *start* in *string*. -1 if there are no more start-of-word locations after the *start*.

tcl_startOfPreviousWord

The **tcl_startOfPreviousWord** command determines where the previous "word" starts in a string. (See also **tcl_endOfWord**; **tcl_startOfNextWord**; **tcl_wordBreakAfter**; **tcl_wordBreakBefore**.) It takes this form:

tcl_startOfPreviousWord *string start*

The arguments are as follows:

start
Index in *string* at which to start searching.

string
String to search for the start of a word.

RETURNS   The index of the first word character following a
nonword character before *start* in *string*. -1 is returned if there are
no more start-of-word locations before the *start*.

tcl_traceCompile

The **tcl_traceCompile** global variable holds an integer that controls
how much tracing information is printed to stdout when scripts are
compiled into internal bytecode representation. This variable is
used primarily to find suspected bugs in the Tcl compiler, and is
rarely used in practice. The following table shows valid values:

Value	Meaning
0	No tracing. This is the default.
1	Prints a one-line summary for each procedure or top level command.
2	Prints detailed listing of bytecodes during all compilations.

tcl_traceExec

The **tcl_traceExec** global variable holds an integer that controls
how much tracing information is printed to stdout as scripts are
executed. This variable is used primarily to find suspected bugs in
the Tcl compiler and interpreter, and is rarely used in practice. The
following table shows valid values:

Value	Meaning
0	No tracing. This is the default.
1	Prints a one-line summary for each procedure called.
2	Prints the command name and arguments for each Tcl command invoked.
3	Prints a detailed trace of each bytecode instruction.

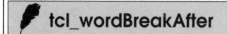

tcl_version

The **tcl_version** global variable holds a string that describes the revision level of the current interpreter, such as "7.3" for version 7.3, or "8.1" for version 8.1. (See also **tcl_patchLevel**.) This information is also available from the **info tclversion** command.

2

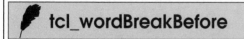

tcl_wordBreakAfter

The **tcl_wordBreakAfter** command determines where the next "word" break occurs in a string. (See also **tcl_endOfWord**; **tcl_startOfNextWord**; **tcl_startOfPreviousWord**; **tcl_wordBreakBefore**.) It takes this form:

> **tcl_wordBreakAfter** *string start*

The arguments are as follows:

start
Index in *string* at which to start searching.

string
String to search.

RETURNS   The index of the word boundary after *start* in *string*. -1 is returned if there are no more boundaries after *start*. The index returned refers to the second character of the pair that comprises a boundary.

tcl_wordBreakBefore

The **tcl_wordBreakBefore** command determines where the previous "word" break occurs in a string. (See also **tcl_endOfWord**; **tcl_startOfNextWord**; **tcl_startOfPreviousWord**; **tcl_wordBreakAfter**.) It takes the following form:

tcl_wordBreakBefore *string start*

The arguments are as follows:

start
Index in *string* at which to start searching.

string
String to search.

RETURNS   The index of the word boundary before *start* in *string*.
-1 is returned if there are no more boundaries after *start*. The
index returned refers to the second character of the pair that
comprises a boundary.

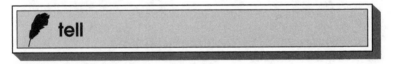

tell

The **tell** command reports the current position in a channel.
(See also **seek**.) It takes this form:

tell *channelId*

The following is the argument:

channelId
The channel to query.

RETURNS   An integer indicating the position within the channel,
or -1 if the channel does not support seeking.

Example

```
set fid [open someFile r]
# Read the first line
set line1 [gets $fid]
# Remember where the second line starts
set pos [tell $fid]
# Read the second and third lines
set line2 [gets $fid]
set line3 [gets $fid]
# Return to the start of line 2
```

```
seek $fid $pos
set line2 [gets $fid]
close $fid
```

2

The **text** command creates and manipulates text widgets.
(See also **entry**.)

Text Overview

The text widget provides a general-purpose textual widget that
supports displaying characters with various attributes (font, color,
and so forth) and editing the characters. A text logically consists of
a *view* and a *scroll region*.

The view is determined by the text *width* (*x* size) and *height*
(*y* size). It determines the part of the text that may be seen
without scrolling.

The scroll region extends the area of the text beyond the view.
Parts of the text outside the current view may be scrolled into
view with scroll bars attached to the text or with **xview**
and **yview** text commands.

The size of the text is specified in multiples of a font height and
character width. The locations of characters in the text are
specified with text indices that are a modified superset of those
used for **entry** widgets and text objects on a **canvas** widget.

The characters in a text widget are grouped into *logical lines*. Each
logical line is a sequence of zero or more characters followed by a
newline. A logical line may be wrapped onto multiple physical lines
in the text. The space before and after a logical line, and between

wrapped physical lines of a logical line, can be independently controlled. A logical line may be thought of as a paragraph, and the physical lines as lines within the paragraph.

NOTE: A text widget is never completely empty. A newly created text widget has a single newline character (in other words, a single paragraph with no text in it).

Text can be annotated with marks, tags, embedded windows, and embedded images.

Marks

Marks can be placed in the text. A *mark* associates a name with a location between two characters in the text. A mark name may be any string. A mark has *gravity*, which determines whether the mark is associated with the character to its left or to its right, and affects what happens to the mark when text is inserted. Deleting the text that includes a mark does not remove the mark; the mark remains and is associated with a new position, based on the gravity of the mark. The following are the two predefined marks:

- **insert**   Refers to the location of the text-insertion cursor—where text typed by the user will be inserted.

- **current**   Refers to the gap between characters closest to the current position of the mouse pointer.

These marks cannot be deleted.

Tags

Ranges of one or more characters can be tagged. Like binding tags for widgets, a text *tag* is a freeform text string. However, for ease of programming, a text tag should not include a space (" "), a plus sign ("+"), or a hyphen ("-"). A tag may be placed on multiple character ranges in a text (logically grouping the characters), and a character in a text may have multiple tags (making it a member of multiple groups). By default, the last tag applied to a character has priority over other tags on the same character, but the order may be manipulated.

NOTE: Mark names and tag names are managed separately, and a mark and a tag of the same name will not conflict with one another. However, when using the name in a text index, the mark takes precedence. (See the upcoming section, "Text Indices," for more information.)

A *tag* may carry with it options that override the defaults of the text widget (such as font, colors, and tabs), and additional formatting (such as margins, borders, and alignment). Options are applied starting with the text widget settings, proceeding through each tag from lowest priority (first applied) to highest priority (last applied). Thus, if a character has multiple tags, the option for the highest-priority tag takes precedence in any conflict, and if a high-priority tag does not provide some option, the value for that option carries through from lower-priority tags or from the widget settings.

Tcl scripts can be bound to events on tagged text to create hypertext links, context-sensitive pop-up menus, read-only ranges of characters, and many other features.

The only predefined tag is **sel**, which represents the currently selected characters. The background and foreground colors and the border width of the text widget are linked to the corresponding options of the **sel** tag; changing one of these options for the widget affects the **sel** tag, and vice versa. The **sel** tag cannot be deleted.

Embedded Windows

A text widget may contain one or more embedded windows. An *embedded window* is a Tk widget that is displayed in the text and treated as a single character. An embedded window may be referred to either by a text index indicating its position in the text or by its path name in the widget hierarchy.

Embedded windows move with surrounding characters as characters are inserted, deleted, scrolled, or wrapped (in response to resizing the text widget). If a range of characters that includes the embedded window is deleted, the window will be destroyed.

Embedded Images

A text widget may contain one or more embedded images. An *embedded image* is a reference to a Tk image that is displayed in the text and treated as a single character. An embedded image may be referred to either by a text index indicating its position in the text or by the image name assigned when the image was inserted in the text.

Embedded images move with surrounding characters as characters are inserted, deleted, scrolled, or wrapped (in response to resizing the text widget). If a range of characters that includes the embedded image is deleted, the copy of the image will be removed from the screen.

Text Options

Text widgets recognize the following standard widget options. (See the Appendix for a complete list of standard widget options and their meanings.)

background	highlightbackground	insertontime	selectborderwidth
borderwidth	highlightcolor	insertwidth	selectforeground
cursor	highlightthickness	padx	setgrid
exportselection	insertbackground	pady	takefocus
font	insertborderwidth	relief	xscrollcommand
foreground	insertofftime	selectbackground	yscrollcommand

In addition, text widgets recognize the following widget-specific options:

-height *lines*
Specifies the height for the widget, in lines. The line height is determined by the metrics of the font specified with **-font**. *height* must be an integer greater than 0.

-spacing1 *distance*
Specifies the amount of extra space to be left above each logical line. (See Figure 2-4.) *spacing1* is in screen coordinates. This option may be overridden by the **-spacing1** option in tags.

-spacing2 *distance*
Specifies extra space to be left between wrapped, physical lines of a logical line. *spacing2* is in screen coordinates. This option may be overridden by the **-spacing2** option in tags.

-spacing3 *distance*
Specifies extra space to be left below each logical line. *spacing3* is in screen coordinates. This option may be overridden by the **-spacing3** option in tags.

-state *state*
Specifies whether the contents of the widget can be edited. *state* may be either of the following:

- **normal**   Contents can be edited
- **disabled**   Contents cannot be edited

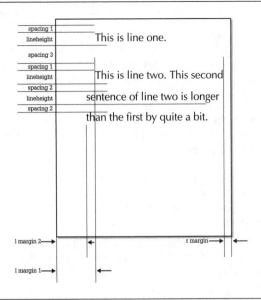

Figure 2-4. Line spacing in a text widget

-tabs *tablist*

Specifies tab stops for the text widget. *tablist* is a list of screen coordinates specifying the position of each tab. Each position may be followed by an alignment to indicate how text should be aligned at the tab. The alignment may be any of the following:

- **left** Tabbed text will be left-justified at the tab (that is, it will follow the tab position). This is the default if no alignment is specified.

- **right** Tabbed text will be right-justified at the tab (the tab will follow the last character in the text).

- **center** Tabbed text will be centered around the tab position.

- **numeric** Numeric text will have the decimal point placed at the tab position. Nonnumeric text will be right-justified at the tab position.

If there are more tabs in text's contents than have been configured with **-tabs**, Tk extrapolates additional tabs, using the spacing between the last two specified tabs and using the alignment of the last specified tab.

This option may be overridden by the -**tabs** option in tags.

-**width** *characters*
Specifies the width for the widget, in characters. The character
width is determined by the metrics of the font specified with -**font**.
If the font is proportionally spaced, the width of the character 0
(zero) is used.

-**wrap** *wraptype*
Specifies how to format logical lines into physical display lines.
wrap may be any of the following:

- **none**   Each logical line appears on one physical line in the text
  widget. If the logical line is longer than the text is wide, the
  remaining text is obscured to the right of the widget and may
  be scrolled into view.

- **char**   All the characters in the logical line will be displayed. If
  the logical line is longer than the text is wide, the text will be
  broken between characters and wrapped to a new display line,
  if necessary.

- **word**   All the characters in the logical line will be displayed. If
  the logical line is longer than the text is wide, the text will be
  broken between words and wrapped to a new display line, if
  necessary.

Text Commands

The text widget **mark** and **tag** commands are discussed in detail
in later sections. Text widgets also respond to the **cget** and
configure standard widget commands. (See the Appendix for
details.) In addition, text widgets respond to the following
widget-specific commands:

pathName **bbox** *index*

pathName **compare** *index1 op index2*

pathName **debug**
pathName **debug** *flag*

pathName **delete** *index1 ?index2?*
pathName **insert** *index string ?tagList string tagList ... ?*

pathName **dlineinfo** *index*

pathName **dump** *?dumpOptions? index1 ?index2?*

pathName **get** *index1 ?index2?*

pathName **index** *index*

pathName **scan mark** *x y*
pathName **scan dragto** *x y*

pathName **search** *?searchOptions? pattern index1 ?index2?*

pathName **see** *index*

pathName **xview**
pathName **xview** *viewoptions*
pathName **yview**
pathName **yview** *viewoptions*

The arguments are as follows:

dumpOptions, searchOptions, viewoptions
Command-specific options. See the following sections for details.

flag
A Boolean value.

index
A text index. (See the upcoming section on text indices for details.)

index1, index2
Text indices. If *index2* is not specified, it defaults to *index1*+1chars, so only one character is processed.

op
A relational comparison operator: <, <=, ==, >=, >, or !=.

pattern
The pattern to search for. The format and interpretation depends on *searchOptions*.

string
The string to insert into the text widget.

tagList
A list of text tags to add to the string.

x, y
Window coordinates to process.

Text Indices

Many text widget commands take one or more text indices as arguments. A *text index* is a list consisting of a base position and zero or more modifiers. The base position may take one of the following forms:

Index	Value
line.char	Character *char* in logical line *line* within the text. Lines in the text are numbered starting at 1. Characters in a line are numbered starting at 0. **1.0** refers to the first character in the widget. *char* may be **end** to refer to the newline character at the end of a line.
end	The character position just after the last newline in the text.
mark	The character position just after the mark named *mark*.
tag.**first**	The first character of the text tagged with *tag*, if any. This form raises an error if the text does not have any text with *tag*.
tag.**last**	The last character of the text tagged with *tag*, if any. This form raises an error if the text does not have any text with *tag*.
@x,y	The character at the point *(x,y)* relative to the upper-left corner of the text widget. If *(x,y)* lies outside of the text, this form refers to the first character in the line that is closest to *(x,y)*.
pathName	The position of window *pathName* embedded in the text. This form raises an error if *pathName* is not embedded in the text.
imageName	The position of image *imageName* embedded in the text. This form raises an error if *imageName* is not embedded in the text.

If the base index might match more than one of the preceding forms, the one earlier in the table is used. For example, if an embedded image has the same name as a mark, the mark is used.

Text index modifiers may take the following forms:

Modifier	Purpose
+ *count* **chars** - *count* **chars**	Moves forward or backward *count* characters in the text, moving to the next or previous logical line if necessary. If fewer than *count* characters are between the base index and the end or beginning of the text, this form moves to the end or beginning of the text. For example, **1.29-40chars+5chars** is equivalent to 1.5, because moving back 40 characters from 1.29 ends up at 1.0. **chars** may be abbreviated to **c**. Spaces around *count* are optional.
+ *count* **lines** - *count* **lines**	Moves to the same character position *count* logical lines forward or backward in the text. If fewer than *count* lines are between the base index and the last or first line of the text, this form moves to the last or first line of the text. If not enough characters are on the new line to remain at the same character position, the new position is at the end of the new line. **lines** may be abbreviated to l. Spaces around *count* are optional.
linestart	Moves to the start of the line containing the base index.
lineend	Moves to the end of the line containing the base index.
wordstart	Moves to the start of the word containing the base index. A "word" is a sequence of letters, digits, and underscores, or a single character that is not one of those.
wordend	Moves to the end of the word containing the base index.

Modifiers are used from left to right to update the base index and create a new base. For example, **2.13-1line-3chars** becomes **1.13-3chars**, and then **1.10**.

pathName bbox *index*
Retrieves the coordinates of a bounding box of the character at the specified text index. If the character is only partially visible, the bounding box describes just the visible part.

RETURNS A list of four window coordinates: {*x y w h*}, or {} (an empty list) if the characters are not visible.

pathName compare *index1 op index2*

Determines how *index1* relates to *index2*. For example, **compare {insert linestart} == 1.0** would determine whether the insertion cursor was in the first line of the text.

RETURNS 1 if *op* is true for *index1* and *index2*; 0 otherwise.

pathName debug

Determines whether internal consistency checks in the text widget are enabled.

RETURNS **on** if debugging is enabled; **off** otherwise.

pathName debug *flag*

Enables or disables internal consistency checks in the text widget. *flag* must be a Boolean value.

NOTE: This command controls the consistency check for all text widgets in the application.

pathName delete *index1 ?index2?*

Deletes the characters starting at *index1* to just before *index2*. If *index2* is at or before *index1*, no characters are deleted.

pathName insert *index string ?tagList string tagList ... ?*

Inserts *string* just before *index* in *pathName* with the tags in *tagList* applied to it. If no *tagList* is specified, *string* gets the tags common to the characters at *index*-1char and *index*.

pathName dlineinfo *index*

Retrieves information about the display line containing *index*.

RETURNS If the display line containing *index* is visible, a list of integer measurements, in pixels, in the form

{*x y w h base*}

where *x*, *y*, *w*, and *h* are the bounding box for the display line, and *base* is the distance from the top of the bounding box down to the baseline of the text.

If wrapping is turned off and the display line extends out of the view, the bounding box reflects the entire line, not just the visible part. If the display line containing *index* is not visible, an empty list is returned.

pathName dump ?dumpOptions? index1 ?index2?
Describes the character contents, marks, tags, and embedded windows in *pathName* from *index1* up to but not including *index2*. *dumpOptions* may include one or more of the following:

Option	Purpose
-all	Retrieves all information about the text. This is the default if no option is specified.
-command command	Invokes *command* for each set of data that would be returned for the dump. *command* will have three arguments appended when it is invoked: *key*, *value*, and *index*.
-mark	Retrieves information about marks.
-tag	Retrieves information about tags.
-text	Retrieves the character contents.
-image	Retrieves information about embedded images.
-window	Retrieves information about embedded windows.

RETURNS   A list in the following form:

{*key value index key value index ...*}

where *key* is one of the following:

- **text**   *value* is a text string that starts at *index* in *pathName*.
- **mark**   *value* is the name of a mark at *index* in *pathName*.
- **tagon**   *value* is the name of a tag that starts at *index* in *pathName*.
- **tagoff**   *value* is the name of a tag that ends at *index* in *pathName*.
- **window**   *value* is the path name of an embedded window (if -**window** was used to embed it) or an empty string (if -**command** was used to embed it). In the latter case, the **window** text widget command may be used to get information about the window.
- **image**   *value* is the name of an embedded image.

pathName get *index1 ?index2?*

Retrieves the characters from *index1* up to but not including *index2*.

RETURNS   The characters between *index1* and *index2*. Embedded windows and images are ignored.

Programmer's Tip: *When using a text widget as a file editor, be careful that you don't save the ever-present newline at index end. Use code such as **puts $fid [.t get 1.0 end-1c]**; otherwise, just loading and saving a file without changes will add a newline to the end of the file.*

pathName index *index*

Normalizes *index*. For example, **pathName index end** returns the line and character position of the last character in *pathName*.

RETURNS   A normalized text index in the form *line.char.*

pathName scan mark *x y*

Records *x* and *y* and the coordinates of the current view for use by future **scan dragto** text widget commands. This is usually bound to a mouse button press on the text.

pathName scan dragto *x y*

Adjusts the text view by ten times the difference between (*x,y*) and the coordinate of the last **scan mark** text widget command. This is usually bound to mouse motion events on the text and used to implement high-speed scrolling of the text within the view.

pathName search *?searchOptions?* pattern *index1 ?index2?*

Finds characters in *pathName* between *index1* and *index2* that match *pattern*. All the characters must be within one logical line.

If *index2* is specified, it must be at or between *index1* and the beginning of the contents (for backward searches) or the end of the contents (for forward searches). If *index2* is not specified, it defaults to *index1*, and the entire contents of *pathName* are searched; when the search reaches the beginning or end of the contents, it wraps to the end or beginning and continues.

searchOptions may include one or more of the following:

Option	Purpose
-forwards	Searches forward starting at *index1*. This is the default.
-backwards	Searches backward starting at *index1*.
-exact	Treats *pattern* as a literal string with no characters having special meaning. A range of characters in *pathName* matches *pattern* only if they match exactly. This is the default.
-regexp	Treats *pattern* as a regular expression according to the rules of **regexp**. A range of characters in *pathName* matches *pattern* if **regexp** would return 1.
-nocase	Ignores case when comparing *pattern* to *pathName* contents.
-count *varName*	Stores the number of characters in the match into *varName*.
--	Treats the next argument as *pattern* even if it starts with a dash.

RETURNS   If a match is found, the index of the start of the match; otherwise, an empty string.

pathName see *index*
Makes *index* visible. If *index* is visible, this command has no effect. If *index* is out of view, but close to the view, the view is changed so that *index* is just in view. If *index* is far out of view, the view is changed so that it is centered in the view.

Programmer's Tip: *After inserting new text at the bottom of a text widget,* **pathName see end** *will make sure that the last line is visible.*

pathName xview
Retrieves the current X view coordinate of the text.

RETURNS   A view coordinate list. These are the same values passed to scroll bars via the **-xscrollcommand** option.

pathName xview *viewoptions*
Sets the X coordinates of the text view. *options* may be any of the following:

Option	Purpose
moveto *fraction*	Adjusts the view so that *fraction* of the total width of the text is off the left of the view. *fraction* is a view coordinate.
scroll *number units*	Adjusts the view *number units*. *number* must be an integer. *units* is either of the following: **units** The view adjusts by *number* times the average character width for the text. **pages** The view adjusts by *number* times the width of the text, less a few characters. Negative values of *number* adjust the view to the right (making characters off the left of the view visible), and vice versa for positive values.

pathName **yview**

Retrieves the current Y view coordinate of the text.

RETURNS   A view coordinate list. These are the same values passed to scroll bars via the - **yscrollcommand** option.

pathName **yview** *viewoptions*

Sets the Y coordinates of the text view. *options* may be any of the following:

Option	Purpose
moveto *fraction*	Adjusts the view so that the character *fraction* through the contents is visible at the top of the view. *fraction* is a view coordinate.
scroll *number units*	Adjusts the view *number units*. *number* must be an integer. *units* is either of the following: **units** The view adjusts by *number* lines. **pages** The view adjusts by *number* times the height of the text, less two lines. Negative values of *number* adjust the view up (making characters off the top of the view visible), and vice versa for positive values.
?-**pickplace***?* *index*	Adjusts the view to make *index* visible. If -**pickplace** is not specified, *index* is placed at the top of the view. If -**pickplace** is specified, the view is adjusted as for the **see** text widget command.
number	Places line *number*+1 at the top of the view.

NOTE: The last two forms of **yview** mentioned here are obsolete and deprecated.

Marks

Text marks are manipulated with the **mark** text widget command, which takes the following forms:

> *pathName* **mark gravity** *markName*
>
> *pathName* **mark gravity** *markName* *direction*
>
> *pathName* **mark names**
>
> *pathName* **mark next** *index*
>
> *pathName* **mark previous** *index*
>
> *pathName* **mark set** *markName* *index*

The arguments are as follows:

direction
The gravity for the mark. *direction* must be **left** or **right**.

index
A text index.

markName
The name of the mark.

pathName mark gravity markName
Determines the gravity for *markName*.

RETURNS left or **right**.

pathName mark gravity markName direction
Sets the gravity for *markName* to *direction*.

pathName mark names
Determines what marks are currently set in *pathName*.

RETURNS A list of mark names.

pathName mark next index
Finds the next mark at or after *index* in *pathName*.

RETURNS   The name of the next mark, or an empty string if no
marks follow *index.*

pathName mark previous index
Finds the next mark at or before *index* in *pathName.*

RETURNS   The name of the previous mark, or an empty string if
no marks precede *index.*

pathName mark set markName index
Sets *markName* at *index* in *pathName.* If *markName* already exists
in *pathName,* it is moved to *index.*

pathName mark unset markName ?markName ... ?
Removes *markName* from *pathName.*

Tags

Text tags are manipulated with the **tag** text widget command,
which takes the following forms:

> *pathName* **tag add** *tagName index1 ?index2 index1 index2?*
> *pathName* **tag remove** *tagName index1 ?index2 index1*
> *index2 ... ?*

> *pathName* **tag bind** *tagName*
> *pathName* **tag bind** *tagName sequence*
> *pathName* **tag bind** *tagName sequence script*

> *pathName* **tag cget** *tagName option*
> *pathName* **tag configure** *tagName ?option? ?value? ?option*
> *value ... ?*
> *pathName* **tag delete** *tagName ?tagName ... ?*

> *pathName* **tag lower** *tagName ?belowThis?*
> *pathName* **tag raise** *tagName ?aboveThis?*

> *pathName* **tag names**
> *pathName* **tag names** *index*

> *pathName* **tag nextrange** *tagName index1 ?index2?*
> *pathName* **tag prevrange** *tagName index1 ?index2?*
> *pathName* **tag ranges** *tagName*

The arguments are as follows:

aboveThis, belowThis
The name of a tag to position the tag relative to.

index
A text index.

index1, index2
Text indices. If *index2* is not specified, it defaults to *index1*+1chars, and a single character is processed.

option
A text tag option name. Text tags may be configured with the following standard widget options. (See the Appendix for a complete list of standard widget options and their meanings.)

2

background	foreground
borderwidth	justify
font	relief

Tags may also override the following text-widget-specific options (refer to the earlier section "Text Options" for details):

spacing1	tabs
spacing2	wrap
spacing3	

In addition, text tags recognize the following tag-specific options:

Option	Meaning
-bgstipple *bitmap*	Specifies the bitmap to use when drawing the text background. If *bitmap* is an empty string, a solid fill is used (the default).
-fgstipple *bitmap*	Specifies the bitmap to use when drawing the text foreground. If *bitmap* is an empty string, a solid fill is used (the default).
-lmargin1 *space*	Specifies the space between the left side of the text window and the start of the first physical line of a logical line in the text. *space* is a screen coordinate. This option must be set for a tag on the first character of the logical line to take effect for the logical line.

Option	Meaning
-lmargin2 *space*	Specifies the space between the left side of the text window and the start of the second and subsequent physical lines of a logical line in the text. *space* is a screen coordinate.
-offset *space*	Specifies the vertical offset of the tagged characters' baseline from the rest of the line. A positive offset may be used for superscripts; a negative offset may be used for subscripts.
-overstrike *boolean*	Specifies that a horizontal rule will be drawn through the text.
-rmargin *space*	Specifies the minimum space between the right side of the text window and the end of each display line of a logical line in the text. *space* is a screen coordinate. This option must be set for a tag on the first character of the logical line to take effect for the logical line.
-underline *boolean*	Specifies that a horizontal rule will be drawn under the text.

NOTE: Figure 2-4, earlier in this section, shows the effect of *lmargin1*, *lmargin2*, and **rmargin**.

script
A script to execute when *sequence* is matched.

sequence
An event sequence as for the **bind** command, except that tagged text may respond only to keyboard and mouse events (such as **Enter**, **Leave**, and so forth) and to virtual events derived from keyboard and mouse events.

tagName
The name of the tag. May be any string, but should not include a space (" "), a plus sign ("+"), or a dash ("-").

value
A text tag option value.

pathName tag add *tagName index1 ?index2 index1 index2?*

Adds *tagName* to one or more ranges of characters.

pathName tag remove *tagName index1 ?index2 index1 index2 ... ?*

Removes *tagName* from the tags on characters from *index1* up to but not including *index2*.

pathName tag bind *tagName*

Lists the sequences with bindings for the specified tag.

RETURNS A list of all sequences with bindings for *tag*.

pathName tag bind *tagName sequence*

Retrieves the script bound to *sequence* on *tag*.

RETURNS The script bound to *sequence* on *tag*.

pathName tag bind *tagName sequence script*

Binds *script* to execute when the event *sequence* occurs on a character with *tag* in its list of text tags. Refer to the entry for **bind** for details on the format of *script*, substitutions performed on it when it is invoked, and the effects of **break** and **continue** within *script*.

If a character has more than one tag, the tags will be processed in order from lowest priority to highest priority, and one binding from each tag will be invoked. The binding that is invoked for each tag is the one that is most specific for the current event sequence. (Refer to **bind** for details.) If a binding on *pathName* (made with **bind**) also matches the sequence, the binding on *pathName* will be invoked after all tag bindings.

pathName tag cget *tagName option*

Retrieves *tagName*'s value for *option*. This is just like the **cget** widget command. (See the Appendix for details.)

pathName tag configure *tagName ?option? ?value? ?option value ... ?*

Manipulates *tagName*'s options. This is just like the **configure** widget command. (See the Appendix for details.)

pathName tag delete *tagName ?tagName ... ?*

Removes all information about *tagName* from *pathName*. This includes bindings and display options. Also removes *tagName* from all character ranges that are tagged with it.

pathName tag lower tagName ?belowThis?

Lowers tagName's priority so that it is lower than the tag belowThis. If belowThis is not specified, tagName's priority becomes the lowest of all tags.

pathName tag raise tagName ?aboveThis?

Raises tagName's priority so that it is higher than the tag aboveThis. If aboveThis is not specified, tagName's priority becomes the highest of all tags.

pathName tag names

Determines which tags are defined for pathName even if they are not currently associated with any characters.

RETURNS A list of tag names, in priority order, with the lowest-priority tag first.

pathName tag names index

Determines which tags are on the character at index.

RETURNS A list of tag names, in priority order, with the lowest-priority tag first.

pathName tag nextrange tagName index1 ?index2?

Searches forward from index1 for the first range of characters at or after index1 and before index2 that is tagged with tagName. If index2 is not specified, it defaults to **end**.

RETURNS If tagged text is found, a list of two text indices: the index of the first tagged character with tagName as a tag, and the index of the next character without tagName as a tag. Otherwise, an empty list is returned.

pathName tag prevrange tagName index1 ?index2?

Searches backward from index1 for the first range of characters before index1 and at or after index2 that is tagged with tagName. If index2 is not specified, it defaults to 1.0.

RETURNS If tagged text is found, a list of two text indices: the index of the first tagged character with tagName as a tag, and the index of the next character without tagName as a tag. Otherwise, an empty list is returned.

pathName tag ranges tagName

Determines which ranges of characters have been tagged with tagName.

RETURNS   A list in the following form

{*index1 index2 index1 index2 ...*}

where each pair of indices describes a different tagged range. *index1* is the first character in the range with *tagName*. *index2* is the first character after *index1* without *tagName*. If no characters have *tagName*, the list may be empty.

Embedded Windows

Embedded windows are manipulated with the **window** text widget command, which takes the following forms:

pathName **window cget** *index option*

pathName **window configure** *index ?option value ... ?*

pathName **window create** *index ?option value ... ?*

pathName **window names**

The arguments are as follows:

index
A text index.

option
An embedded window option from the following table:

Option	Purpose
-align *where*	Specifies where the window will be aligned if it is shorter than the line height of the surrounding text. *where* is one of the following: **top** Aligns the top of the window with the top of the line **center** Centers the window within the line height **baseline** Aligns the bottom of the window with the baseline of the line **bottom** Aligns the bottom of the window with the bottom of the line

Option	Purpose
-create script	Specifies a script that will be invoked to create the embedded window when it needs to be displayed but does not exist. script must create a new window and return its name. script is typically a Tk widget command invocation. For example, **button .t.b[incr count]**. This option has no effect if **-window** is specified.
-padx space	Specifies extra space to leave to the left and right of the window. space is in screen coordinates.
-pady space	Specifies extra space to leave above and below the window. space is in screen coordinates.
-stretch boolean	Specifies whether the window should be stretched to fill the line height if it is not as tall as the surrounding characters.
-window pathName	Specifies the name of a window to embed.

value
A value for an embedded window option.

pathName **window cget** *index option*
Retrieves the value of *option* for the window at *index*. This is just like the **cget** widget command. (See the Appendix for details.)

pathName **window configure** *index ?option value ... ?*
Manipulates options for the window at *index*. This is just like the **configure** widget command. (See the Appendix for details.)

pathName **window create** *index ?option value ... ?*
Creates a new embedded window at *index* in *pathName*.

pathName **window names**
Determines which windows are embedded in *pathName*.

RETURNS   A list of window path names.

Embedded Images

Embedded images are manipulated with the **image** text widget command, which takes the following forms:

pathName **image cget** *index option*

pathName **image configure** *index option ?value?*
?option value ... ?

pathName **image create** *index ?option value ... ?*

pathName **image names**

The arguments are as follows:

index
A text index.

option
An embedded image option from the following table:

Option	Purpose
-align *where*	Specifies where the image will be aligned if it is shorter than the line height of the surrounding text. *where* is one of the following:
	top Aligns the top of the image with the top of the line
	center Centers the image within the line height
	baseline Aligns the bottom of the image with the baseline of the line
	bottom Aligns the bottom of the image with the bottom of the line
-image *image*	Specifies the name of an image to embed. The image must have been previously created with the **image** command.
-name *imageName*	Specifies the name to give this instance of *image*. If **-name** is not specified, *imageName* defaults to *image*. If *imageName* already exists, a serial number in the form #*nn* is appended to make it unique.
-padx *space*	Specifies extra space to leave to the left and right of the image. *space* is in screen coordinates.
-pady *space*	Specifies extra space to leave above and below the image. *space* is in screen coordinates.

value
An embedded image option value.

pathName* image cget *index option
Retrieves the value of *option* for the image at *index*. This is just like the **cget** widget command. (See the Appendix for details.)

pathName* image configure *index option ?value?* *?option value ... ?
Manipulates options for the image at *index*. This is just like the **configure** widget command. (See the Appendix for details.)

pathName* image create *index ?option value ... ?
Creates a new embedded image at *index* in *pathName*.

RETURNS A unique identifier for the image.

***pathName* image names**
Determines which images are embedded in *pathName*.

RETURNS A list of image names.

Default Bindings

NOTE: If the text is disabled, the view can be adjusted and text can be selected, but no insertion cursor is displayed and <u>no</u> modification (for example, typing, cutting, or pasting, even with script commands, such as insert) is allowed.

Text widgets are created with bindings that make them behave as expected, consistent with the user interface conventions on each platform. Specifically:

Mouse Bindings

- Clicking mouse button 1 clears the selection and sets the insertion cursor just before the character under the mouse pointer.

- Double-clicking mouse button 1 selects the word under the mouse pointer and sets the insertion cursor to the beginning of that word.

- Triple-clicking mouse button 1 selects the line under the mouse pointer and sets the insertion cursor to the beginning of that line.

- Dragging with mouse button 1 pressed selects from the insertion cursor to the current position of the mouse pointer. The selection is expanded by characters, words, or lines, depending on how the selection was started (as described in the preceding paragraphs). If the mouse pointer crosses the left, right, top, or bottom side of the text, the text scrolls to reveal characters, if any, out of view on that side of the text.

- Dragging with mouse button 1 and the SHIFT key pressed expands the selection by characters, words, or lines, depending on how the selection was started (as described in the preceding paragraphs).

- Clicking mouse button 1 with the CTRL key pressed positions the insertion cursor without affecting the selection.

- Clicking mouse button 2 in the text pastes the selection (from another widget or the clipboard) at the position of the mouse pointer.

- Dragging with mouse button 2 pressed scrolls the characters in the text.

Keyboard Bindings

- Typing printable characters inserts those characters in the text at the insertion cursor.

The insertion cursor may be manipulated with the following keys:

- Pressing the LEFT ARROW or RIGHT ARROW key moves the insertion cursor left or right.

- Pressing the UP ARROW or DOWN ARROW key moves the insertion cursor up or down.

- Pressing the HOME key moves the insertion cursor to the beginning of the line.

- Pressing the END key moves the insertion cursor to the end of the line.

- Pressing PAGE UP or PAGE DOWN moves the insertion cursor up or down one page.

When moving the insertion cursor, the selection is affected as follows:

- If no modifier key is pressed, the selection is cleared and LEFT ARROW and RIGHT ARROW move the cursor by a single character.

- If the SHIFT key is pressed, the selection is expanded to follow the insertion cursor.

- If the CTRL key is pressed, LEFT ARROW and RIGHT ARROW move by words instead of characters.

- If the CTRL key is pressed, UP ARROW and DOWN ARROW move by logical lines instead of physical lines. For example, SHIFT-CTRL-LEFT moves the cursor one word toward the beginning of the entry and expands the selection to include that word.

- Pressing CTRL-PAGE UP or CTRL-PAGE DOWN adjusts the view left or right one page, respectively, without moving the insertion cursor.

- Pressing SELECT or CTRL-SPACEBAR sets the selection anchor to the position of the insertion cursor.

- Pressing SHIFT-SELECT or SHIFT-CTRL-SPACEBAR adjusts the selection to the current position of the insertion cursor. If there is no selection, the text from the anchor to the insertion cursor is selected.

- Pressing CTRL-/ selects all characters in the text.

- Pressing CTRL-\ clears the selection in the text.

- Pressing F16 (labeled COPY on some workstation keyboards) or CTRL-C copies the selection, if any, to the clipboard.

- Pressing F20 (labeled CUT on some workstation keyboards) or CTRL-X copies the selection, if any, to the clipboard and deletes it from the entry.

- Pressing F18 (labeled PASTE on some workstation keyboards) or CTRL-V inserts the contents of the clipboard at the position of the insertion cursor.

- Pressing DELETE deletes the selection, if there is one, or the character to the right of the insertion cursor if there is no selection.

- Pressing BACKSPACE deletes the selection, if there is one, or the character to the left of the insertion cursor if there is no selection.

NOTE: In addition to the preceding key bindings, text widgets support most emacs key bindings. For example, CTRL-A is equivalent to HOME, and CTRL-T transposes the two characters to the right and left of the insertion cursor.

Example

```
# Style settings
# Set up fonts
array set fonts {
    "font1" {-family Helvetica -size 18 \
            -weight bold }
    "font2" {-family Helvetica -size 16 \
            -weight bold -slant italic}
    "font3" {-family Helvetica -size 14 \
            -weight bold}
    "font4" {-family Helvetica -size 12 \
            -weight bold}
    "font5" {-family Helvetica -size 12 \
            -weight bold -slant italic}
    Normal  {-family Times -size 12}
}
# Set up indentation
# and styles (combinations of the font and indentations)
for {set level 1; \
        set increment [expr {1.0/3.0}]} \
    {$level < 6} \
    {incr level} {
    set indent "[expr {($level-1)*$increment}]c"
    set indents(indent$level) \
            [list -lmargin1 $indent \
                  -lmargin2 $indent]]
    set styles(Heading$level) \
            [list font$level indent$level]
}
set styles(Normal) [list Normal]
#-----------------------------------------------
# Style management
proc setStyle { text index style } {
    global styles
    foreach tag [.t tag names $index] {
      .t tag remove $tag [list $index linestart] \
                          [list $index lineend]
    }

    if {[string match "Heading*" $style]} {
        addButtons $text $index
```

```
    } else {
        delButtons $text $index
    }

    foreach tag $styles($style) {
        .t tag add $tag [list $index linestart] \
                       [list $index lineend]
    }
}
proc addButton { text command } {
    global bcount
    if {! [info exists bcount]} {
        set bcount 0
    }
    return [button .b[incr bcount] -text $text \
            -command $command]
}
proc addButtons { text index } {
    set start \
            [$text index [list $index linestart]]
    if {[catch {$text window configure $start}]} {
        $text window create $start \
                -create [list addButton ">" \
                              [list demote $text \
                                   current]]
        $text window create $start \
                -create [list addButton "<" \
                              [list promote $text \
                                   current]]
    }
}
proc delButtons { text index } {
    set start [$text index \
                [list $index linestart]]
    while {
          ! [catch {$text window configure $start}]
    } {
        $text delete $start
    }
}
proc level { text index } {
    set tags [$text tag names $index]
    set lindex [lsearch $tags font*]
    if {$lindex == -1} {
        set level -1
    } else {
        set fontTag [lindex $tags $lindex]
        regexp -- {font([0-9]*)} $fontTag \
                all level
    }
```

```
        return $level
}
proc promote { text index } {
    set level [level $text $index]
    if {$level > 1} {
        incr level -1
        setStyle $text $index Heading$level
    }
}
proc demote { text index } {
    set level [level $text $index]
    if {$level < 5} {
        incr level 1
        setStyle $text $index Heading$level
    }
}
#--------------------------------------------------
# Create the widgets
scrollbar .sb -command [list .t yview]
pack .sb -side right -fill y

text .t -height 15 -width 40 \
        -yscrollcommand [list .sb set] \
        -wrap word \
        -font $fonts(Normal)
pack .t -side left -fill both -expand 1

menu .popup -tearoff 0 \
        -postcommand [list postMenu .popup]
foreach style [lsort [array names styles]] {
    .popup add command -label $style
}
# Reconfigure the menu to act on the line the menu
# was posted over
proc postMenu { menu } {
    global styles
    set current [.t index current]
    foreach style [array names styles] {
        $menu entryconfigure $style \
                -command \
                [list setStyle .t $current $style]
    }
}
#--------------------------------------------------
# Create tags for the fonts
foreach font [array names fonts] {
    .t tag configure $font -font $fonts($font)
}
```

```
# Create tags for indentation
# eval is needed because each element of indents
# is a list
foreach indent [array names indents] {
    eval .t tag configure $indent \
            $indents($indent)
}
#-------------------------------------------------
# Bind the style management to the text widget
# Mouse events...
bind .t <ButtonPress-3> \
        [list tk_popup .popup %X %Y]
# Keyboard events...
bind .t <Control-KeyPress->> \
        [list demote .t insert]
bind .t <Control-KeyPress-<> \
        [list promote .t insert]
bind .t <Control-KeyPress-0>\
        [list setStyle .t insert Normal]
for {set level 1} {$level < 6} {incr level} {
    bind .t <Control-KeyPress-$level> \
            [list setStyle .t insert Heading$level]
}
#-------------------------------------------------
# Put in some sample text
foreach style [lsort [array name styles]] {
    .t insert end "$style\n"
    setStyle .t insert-1c $style
}
```

Programmer's Tip: *Many of the default bindings on text widgets are provided through procs. These procs include* **tkTextButton1**, **tkTextClosestGap**, **tkTextInsert**, **tkTextKeyExtend**, **tkTextKeySelect**, **tkTextNextPara**, **tkTextNextPos**, **tkTextNextWord**, **tkTextPaste**, **tkTextPrevPara**, **tkTextPrevPos**, **tkTextResetAnchor**, **tkTextScrollPages**, **tkTextSelectTo**, **tkTextSetCursor**, **tkTextTranspose**, *and* **tkTextUpDownLine**. *These commands are not of general interest and thus are not documented in this reference. The* **bind**, **info args**, *and* **info body** *commands can be used to explore the use and implementation of these commands.*

 time

The **time** command evaluates a script multiple times for performance testing. It takes the following form:

time *script ?count?*

The arguments are as follows:

count
How many times to evaluate *script*. If *count* is not specified, it defaults to 1. A high value, such as 10,000, is recommended for best results, since it will average out the effect of other processes running on the system.

script
Script to time.

RETURNS   A string in the following form:

xxx microseconds per iteration

Example

```
set s1 abcdefghijklmnopqurstuvwxyz?
set s2 abcdefghijklmnopqurstuvwxyz!
puts "Expr string compare [time {
    expr {$s1 == $s2}
} 100000]"
puts "Safe string compare [time {
    string compare $s1 $s2
} 100000]"
```

The **tk** command provides access to some miscellaneous Tk features that don't fit in other commands. (See also **send**; **wm**.) It takes the following forms:

> **tk appname**
> **tk appname** *appName*
>
> **tk scaling** *?-displayof* window?*
> **tk scaling** *?-displayof* window? number*

The arguments are as follows:

appName
Name to give the application. The name is used with **send** to communicate with the application.

number
A floating-point number specifying the number of pixels per point for *window*'s display. (A point is 1/72 of an inch.)

window
The window whose display should be accessed. If **-displayof** is not specified, *window* defaults to dot (.), the application's default toplevel window.

tk appname

Retrieves the name of the current application.

RETURNS   The application name.

tk appname *appName*

Sets the application name to *appName*. If *appName* is already used, a serial number in the form #*n* (where *n* is an integer) is added to make the name unique. *appName* should not start with a capital letter. If **send** has been disabled with **rename send** {}, this command reenables it.

RETURNS   The new name of the application. This may differ from *appName* if a serial number is needed for uniqueness.

tk scaling *?-displayof window?*

Retrieves the scale factor used by Tk when displaying to *window*'s display.

RETURNS   The number of pixels per point for the display, expressed as a floating-point number. For example, if the display had 72 dots per inch (dpi), the returned value would be 1.0. A 90 dpi display would have a scaling of 1.25.

tk scaling *?-displayof window? number*

Sets the scale factor used by Tk when displaying on *window*'s display.

Example

```
proc pixelToInch { pixels } {
    return [expr {$pixels / (72 * [tk scaling])}]
}
puts "100 pixels is [pixelToInch 100] inches\
    on display"
```

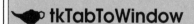 **tkTabToWindow**

The **tkTabToWindow** command updates the input focus. It takes this form:

    tkTabToWindow *window*

The argument is as follows:

window
The window to make current.

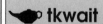 **tkwait**

The **tkwait** command waits for a window to become visible or be destroyed, or for a global variable to change. (See also **vwait**.) It takes the following forms:

    tkwait variable *varName*

    tkwait visibility *window*

    tkwait window *window*

The arguments are as follows:

varName
Name of a variable to wait for. If *varName* does not include namespace qualifiers, it is assumed to refer to a global variable.

window
Path to a window through the Tk widget hierarchy.

tkwait variable *varName*

Waits for *varName* to be modified. This form is equivalent to **vwait varName**.

tkwait visibility *window*

Waits for *window* to become visible. This is typically used to wait for a newly created window to become visible before continuing.

tkwait window *window*

Waits for *window* to be destroyed. This is often used to implement modal dialog boxes.

Example

```
# Create a new toplevel window
toplevel .modal
# Populate it
entry .modal.e -width 15 -textvariable e
button .modal.b -text OK \
        -command [list destroy .modal]
pack .modal.e .modal.b -side top
# Wait for the user to interact with it
tkwait window .modal
# Get the result
puts $e
```

🫖 tk_chooseColor

The **tk_chooseColor** command displays a dialog box for selecting a color. It takes this form:

> **tk_chooseColor** *options*

The options are as follows:

-initialcolor *color*
Specifies the color to start with. If **-initialcolor** is not specified, *color* defaults to the first color in the palette.

-parent *window*
Specifies that the dialog box should be a child of, and displayed on top of, *window*.

-title *title*
Specifies the title for the dialog box. If **-title** is not specified, *title* defaults to "Color".

RETURNS   If the user selects a color, the color's name or value; otherwise, an empty string.

Example

```
proc recolorButton { button } {
    set oldColor [$button cget -background]
    set newColor [tk_chooseColor
                    -initialcolor - $oldColor]
    if {[string length $newColor] != 0} {
        $button configure -background $newColor
    }
}
button .b -command [list recolorButton .b]
```

tk_chooseDirectory

The **tk_chooseDirectory** command displays a dialog box for selecting a directory or "folder" (often called a "directory browser"). (See also **tk_getOpenFile**; **tk_getSaveFile**.) It takes this form:

> **tk_chooseDirectory** *options*

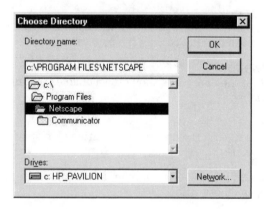

The options are as follows:

-initialdir *directory*
Specifies the directory to start in.

-mustexist *boolean*
Specifies whether the user must choose an existing directory. If *boolean* is false, the user may enter a nonexistent directory name. If *boolean* is true, only existing directories may be selected and returned. If **-mustexist** is not specified, *boolean* defaults to false.

-parent *window*
Specifies that the dialog box should be a child of, and displayed on top of, *window*.

-title *title*
Specifies the title for the dialog box. If **-title** is not specified, *title* defaults to "Choose Directory".

RETURNS   If the user selects a directory, the full path of the directory; otherwise, an empty string.

Example

```
set dir [tk_chooseDirectory -initialdir [pwd] \
        -mustexist 1]
if {[string length $dir] != 0} {
    cd $dir
}
```

Compatibility

The **tk_chooseDirectory** command is available only on Microsoft Windows systems.

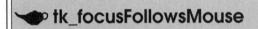

tk_focusFollowsMouse

The **tk_focusFollowsMouse** command creates bindings so that focus will be given to whatever window or widget the mouse pointer is in. It takes this form:

tk_focusFollowsMouse

Description

Many UNIX window managers implement a focus policy that requires a user to click in a window to set the input focus to that window. **tk_focusFollowsMouse** creates widget bindings so that within each toplevel of the current Tk application, the focus will follow the mouse pointer without clicking.

NOTE: There is no built-in way to revert to requiring a click in a widget to set focus.

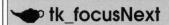

tk_focusNext

The **tk_focusNext** command determines the next widget in the focus, or tab order, for a toplevel window. (See also **tk_focusPrev**.) It takes this form:

> **tk_focusNext** *window*

The argument is as follows:

window
The window to start in.

Description

Many applications use the TAB and SHIFT-TAB keys to move between fields in a dialog box. Tk implements this by using **tk_focusNext** with a binding like the following:

```
bind all <Key-Tab> \
        [list tkTabToWindow [tk_focusNext %W]]
```

RETURNS   The next window in the focus order.

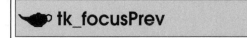

tk_focusPrev

The **tk_focusPrev** command determines the previous widget in the focus, or tab order, for a toplevel window. (See also **tk_focusNext**.) It takes this form:

> **tk_focusPrev** *window*

The argument is as follows:

window
The window to start in.

Description

Many applications use the TAB and SHIFT-TAB keys to move between fields in a dialog box. Tk implements this by using **tk_focusPrev** with a binding like the following:

```
bind all <Shift-Key-Tab> \
        [list tkTabToWindow [tk_focusNext %W]]
```

2

RETURNS   The previous window in the focus order.

The **tk_getOpenFile** and **tk_getSaveFile** commands, respectively, display a dialog box for selecting a file to open or save (often called a "file browser"). They take the following forms:

   tk_getOpenFile *options*

   tk_getSaveFile *options*

The options are as follows:

-defaultextension *extension*
Specifies the extension to add to the filename if the user does not specify one. This option is relevant only for **tk_getSaveFile** and is ignored on Macintosh systems.

-filetypes *filePatternList*
Specifies the files that should be displayed in the dialog box. *filePatternList* is a list of lists. Each sublist specifies one type of file and is in this form:

   typeName {extension ?extension ... ?} ?{macType ?macType ... ?}?

where the fields mean the following:

- *typeName*   A description of the type that will be displayed in the File types listbox
- *extension*   A file extension for *typeName*
- *macType*   A four-character Macintosh file type name

Here is an example:

```
"Hypertext Markup Language" {htm html HTM HTML} \
        {HTML}
```

NOTE: *macType* is required on Macintosh systems and is ignored on other systems, so it may be safely specified on all systems.

-initialdir *directory*
Specifies the directory to start in. If **-initialdir** is not specified, *directory* defaults to the current directory. On Macintosh systems, the General Controls control panel may override the application's default directory, in which case this option is ignored.

-initialfile *filename*
Specifies the filename to be displayed in the dialog box. This option is relevant only for **tk_getSaveFile**.

-parent *window*
Specifies that the dialog box should be a child of, and displayed on top of, *window*.

-title *title*
Specifies the title for the dialog box. This option is ignored on Macintosh systems.

RETURNS   If the user selects a file, the full path of the file; otherwise, an empty string.

Example

```
set fileName [tk_getOpenFile \
    -title "Open HTML file" \
    -filetypes {"Hypertext Markup Language" \
            {htm html HTM HTML} {HTML}}
if {[string length $fileName != 0]} {
    # ... do something with the file
}
```

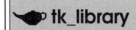

tk_library

The **tk_library** global variable is a string that contains the name of
the directory containing the system library of Tcl scripts for Tk. If
the environment variable **TK_LIBRARY** exists, it is used to initialize
tk_library; otherwise, Tcl searches for the library scripts based on
defaults compiled into the interpreter.

tk_messageBox

The **tk_messageBox** command displays a message and one or
more buttons with which the user can respond to the message.
(See also **message**.) It takes this form:

> **tk_messageBox** *options*

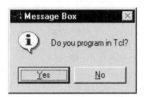

The options are as follows:

-default *name*
Specifies the symbolic name of the default button for the message
box. *name* may be **abort**, **retry**, **ignore**, **ok**, **cancel**, **yes**, or **no**.
These buttons may be displayed in various combinations, as
specified by the **-type** option. If **-default** is not specified, the first
button from the **-type** is the default.

-icon *iconImage*
Specifies the icon to be displayed with the message. *iconImage*
may be **error**, **info**, **question**, or **warning**. If **-icon** is not specified,
iconImage defaults to **info**.

-message *string*
Specifies the text for the message. If **-message** is not specified, *string* defaults to an empty string.

-parent *window*
Specifies that the dialog box should be a child of, and displayed on top of, *window*.

-title *title*
Specifies the title for the dialog box. If **-title** is not specified, *title* defaults to an empty string.

-type *type*
Specifies the buttons to be displayed in the dialog box. If **-type** is not specified, *type* defaults to **ok**. *type* may be **abortretryignore**, **ok**, **okcancel**, **retrycancel**, **yesno**, or **yesnocancel**.

RETURNS   The symbolic name of the button that the user has pressed. (Refer to **-default** for a list of button names.)

ERROR   Raises an error if the default button is not in those specified by *type*.

Example

```
if { $changes } {
    set choice [tk_messageBox \
                    -title "Unsaved changes" \
                    -message "Save changes?" \
                    -icon question \
                    -type yesnocancel]
    switch -- $choice {
        yes {
            SaveFile
        }
        cancel {
            return
        }
        no {
            # Fall through to exit
        }
    }
}
exit
```

🪔 tk_optionMenu

The **tk_optionMenu** command creates an option menu button and associated menu to allow selection of one of several values. (See also **menu**; **tk_popup**.) It takes this form:

> **tk_optionMenu** *pathName varName value ?value ... question*

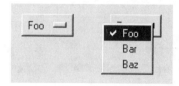

The arguments are as follows:

pathName
The path to the menu button through the widget hierarchy.

value
A value to display in the option menu.

varName
Name of the variable to hold the current selection from the menu.

Description

The option menu consists of radio button entries that share *varName* as their variable. Additional entries may be added as long as they are radio button entries that share the same variable.

RETURNS   The name of the associated menu. This may be used to reconfigure the menu, e.g., to change the items listed on it.

Example

```
# Create the option menu. One item is required
set optMenu [tk_optionMenu .options choice temp]
# Add some menu magic
$optMenu configure \
        -postcommand [list postMenu $optMenu]
```

```
proc postMenu {menu args} {
    puts [info level 0]
}
# Remove the placeholder
$optMenu delete 0
# Add some real items
for {set i 0} { $i < 10} {incr i} {
    $optMenu add radiobutton -label "Item $i"
            -variable choice
}
# Clean up the button and global value
$optMenu invoke 0
```

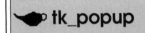 **tk_patchLevel**

The **tk_patchLevel** global variable holds a string that describes the patch level of Tk, such as "7.3p2" for the second patch release of version 7.3, or "8.1a1" for the first alpha release of version 8.1.

tk_popup

The **tk_popup** command displays a pop-up menu at a specified location on the screen. (See also **menu**; **tk_optionMenu**.) It takes this form:

tk_popup *menu x y ?entry?*

The arguments are as follows:

entry
Index of the entry in *menu* that should be displayed at (*x,y*). If *entry* is not specified or is an empty string, the first entry in *menu* is used.

menu
The name of an existing menu to be displayed.

x, y
Screen coordinates, in pixels, where the menu should be displayed.

Example

```
# Create a text widget
text .t -width 10 -height 5
# Configure mouse button three to display a pop-up
# menu at the mouse location.
bind .t <Button-3> [list tk_popup $menu %X %Y]
```

2

tk_strictMotif

The **tk_strictMotif** global variable controls whether Tk attempts to follows Motif look and feel standards as closely as possible. It is 0 by default, and may be set to 1 so that Tk more closely follows Motif standards. This variable is only meaningful on UNIX systems.

tk_version

The **tk_version** global variable holds a string that describes the revision level of Tk, such as "7.3" for version 7.3, or "8.1" for version 8.1. (See also **tk_patchLevel**.)

toplevel

The **toplevel** command creates and manipulates windows.

Toplevel Options

Toplevel widgets recognize the following standard widget options. (See the Appendix for a complete list of standard widget options and their meanings.)

borderwidth	highlightthickness
cursor	relief
highlightbackground	takefocus
highlightcolor	

In addition, the toplevel widgets recognizes the following widget-specific options:

-background *color*
Specifies the background for the window, as for other widgets (see the Appendix), except that if an empty string is specified, the toplevel widget will be transparent.

NOTE: Transparent backgrounds are unreliable, and do not always refresh properly as a window is moved.

-class *class*
Specifies the class for the window. The class is used when querying the option database and for event bindings.

-colormap *colormap*
Specifies the color map to use for the toplevel. *colormap* may be **new** or the name of another Tk window. If **new** is specified, a new color map is created for the window and its children. If a window name is specified, it must be on the same display as the new toplevel, and the new toplevel will share the color map of that window.

NOTE: -colormap is meaningless on Microsoft Windows systems.

-container *boolean*
Specifies whether the toplevel will be used as a container for another window. If *boolean* is true, the toplevel should not have any children other than the embedded window.

-height *distance*
Specifies the height of the toplevel, in window coordinates.

-menu *menu*
Specifies a menu widget to be used as the toplevel's menu bar.

-screen *screen*
Specifies the screen on which to display the toplevel. If -**screen** is not specified, the toplevel is displayed on the same screen as the application's default toplevel, ".".

-use *windowId*
Specifies the window ID of another window to contain the new toplevel.

-visual *visual*
Specifies the visual information for the toplevel. If -**visual** is not specified, the toplevel will use the default visual information for its screen.

NOTE: -**visual** is meaningless on Microsoft Windows systems.

-width *distance*
Specifies the width of the toplevel, in window coordinates.

NOTE: The **class**, **colormap**, **screen**, **use**, and **visual** options can be set only when the toplevel widget is created, and can't be set with the **configure** widget command.

Toplevel Commands

Toplevel widgets respond to the **cget** and **configure** standard widget commands. (See the Appendix for details.) Toplevels have no widget-specific commands.

Default Bindings

Toplevel widgets have no default bindings. They are not intended to be interactive.

Example

```
toplevel .tl1 -container true
toplevel .tl2 -use [winfo id .tl1]
button .tl2.b -text "Click me!"
pack .tl2.b
```

trace

The **trace** command monitors variable accesses. It takes the
following forms:

> **trace variable** *varName ops command*
>
> **trace vdelete** *varName ops command*
>
> **trace vinfo** *varName*

The arguments are as follows:

command
Command to evaluate when one of *ops* occurs for *varName*.
When *command* is evaluated, three additional arguments
will be appended:

- **name1** The name of the variable
- **name2** If *name1* refers to an array, the index to the array;
  otherwise, name2 is an empty string
- **op** The operation that occurred (**r**, **w**, or **u**)

ops
Operations on *varName* to monitor. *ops* is a string of one or more of
the following characters:

- **r** Evaluates *command* when *varName* is read (accessed)
- **w** Evaluates *command* when *varName* is written (set)
- **u** Evaluates *command* when *varName* is unset (deleted)

varName
Name of the variable to monitor.

Description

When a variable is accessed, set, or deleted, all relevant traces on the variable are invoked in the reverse order they were created (in other words, the last trace first) until one raises an error. When an array element is traced, a trace on the whole array is invoked before the trace on the individual element.

Programmer's Tip: *While the name may suggest a debugging aid,* **trace** *is very useful in general for data-driven applications. For example, a trace can be used to respond to a radio button variable changing, by enabling or disabling another part of a dialog box.*

command is evaluated in the context that the variable was operated on. If *command* invokes a proc, the proc may access the variable via **upvar** or **uplevel**.

NOTE: **name1** and **name2** are from the context of the variable operation and may not match the name of the variable when the trace was created. For example, if a local variable is linked to a global variable via **upvar** and then set, a write trace will receive the name of the local variable in **name1** and **name2**.

While *command* is executing, read and write traces are suspended, so accessing or setting the traced variable will <u>not</u> result in read and write traces being evaluated. Unset traces remain in effect.

Read traces are invoked <u>before</u> the value has been returned to satisfy the variable access. If *command* modifies the traced variable, the value set by *command* will be returned.

Write traces are invoked <u>after</u> the value has been set but before the assignment is complete. If *command* modifies the traced variable, the value set by *command* will prevail. This can be used to implement read-only variables.

Unset traces are invoked <u>after</u> the variable has been unset. The variable no longer exists, and traces on it have been removed. When an unset trace on a local variable is invoked because the proc containing the variable returns, the trace is invoked in the context of the calling proc.

trace variable *varName ops command*

Schedules *command* to be invoked when *ops* are performed on *varName*.

trace vdelete *varName ops command*

Removes *command* from the list of traces to invoke when *ops* are performed on *varName*.

NOTE: This command does <u>not</u> raise an error if no such trace exists.

trace vinfo *varName*

Lists the traces on *varName*.

RETURNS   A list of lists containing all the traces on *varName*, in this form:

{{*ops command*} {*ops command*} ...}

The first element of the list is the last trace created, and the first one to be invoked.

Example

```
# Make a variable read-only
# Note: varName is expected to have namespace or
# global qualifiers, such as ::someVar
proc ReadOnlyTrace {
    varName value name1 name2 op
} {
    set $varName $value
    # Unsetting removes traces. Put it back.
    if {[string equal $op u]} {
        trace variable $varName wu \
              [lrange [info level 0] 0 2]
    }
    error "readonly"
}
```

```
# Set the initial value BEFORE setting up the
# trace
set myStatic 1
# Make it readonly
trace variable myStatic wu \
        [list ReadOnlyTrace ::myStatic $myStatic]
```

2

```
# Do something when a radio button changes
# Some widgets
radiobutton .rb1 -variable v(rb) -value 1 \
        -text One
radiobutton .rb2 -variable v(rb) -value 2 \
        -text Two
radiobutton .rb3 -variable v(rb) -value 3 \
        -text Three
text .trace -width 5 -height 5
pack .rb1 .rb2 .rb3 .trace -side top
# Trace the radio buttons' variable
# Pass the name as an arg to the trace routine so
# we don't have to reconstruct from name1 and
# name2
set traceCmd [list traceRb .trace v(rb)]
trace variable v(rb) w $traceCmd
# Set up to remove the trace when the text is
# destroyed
bind .trace <Destroy> \
        [list trace vdelete v(rb) w $traceCmd]
# The proc to do the trace
proc traceRb { text varName name1 name2 op } {
    $text insert end "[set ::$varName]\n"
}
# Set the first value (AFTER setting the trace)
set v(rb) 1
```

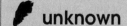

unknown

The **unknown** command tries to find undefined commands. (See also **auto_load**; **package**.) It takes this form:

> **unknown** *cmdName* ?*arg arg ... ?*

The arguments are as follows:

arg
An argument to *cmdName*.

cmdName
The undefined command to search for.

Description

When a Tcl interpreter is asked to evaluate a command that is
"unknown" (not yet defined), it looks for a command named
unknown to attempt to find the command. If **unknown** is not
found, the interpreter raises an error. If **unknown** is found, it is
invoked with the unknown command and its arguments.

Tcl provides a default implementation of **unknown**. Applications
can define their own replacement as long as it conforms to the
following prototype:

```
proc unknown { cmdName args } {
}
```

and returns *cmdName*'s value, if found, or raises an error if
cmdName is not found or raises an error.

The default **unknown** command does the following:

- If the global variable **auto_noload** is <u>not</u> defined, calls
  auto_load to attempt to load the command. If that succeeds,
  the command is executed and its value is returned.

- If the global variable **auto_noexec** is <u>not</u> defined, calls
  auto_execok to see whether *cmdName* is an external
  executable. If so, **exec** is used to execute *cmdName* with its
  arguments, and the result is returned.

- Determines whether *cmdName* has been invoked interactively
  at the global scope. If so, determines whether *cmdName* looks
  like a shell history invocation, and, if so, processes it as a
  history invocation.

- Determines whether *cmdName* is a unique abbreviation
  (prefix) for a Tcl command, and, if so, invokes that command.

RETURNS   The result of evaluating *cmdName*.

ERROR Raises an error if *cmdName* cannot be found or raises an error.

unset

The **unset** command deletes one or more variables. (See also **set**.) It takes this form:

> **unset** *varName ?varName varName ... ?*

The argument is as follows:

varName
The name of the variable to unset.

ERROR Raises an error if *varName* refers to a variable that does not exist.

Example

```
# Unset a simple variable
if {[info exists a]} {
    puts "a was $a"
    unset a
}
# Create an array
array set b {
    index1 value1 index2 value2 index3 value3
}
# Unset one element
unset b(index2)
# b has two elements now, get rid of both
unset b
```

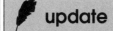
update

The **update** command allows the application to get "up to date." (See also **after**.) It takes this form:

update *?idletasks?*

The argument is as follows:

idletasks
Only processes idle callbacks, not events (such as file events)
or errors.

Description

Generally, Tcl and Tk are single-threaded, and no events are
processed during other computations. To allow events, such as
user interactions, to be processed during long computations,
update may be called.

Example

```
set counter 0
entry .e -textvariable counter
pack .e
for {set counter 1} \
      {$counter < 100} \
      {incr counter} {
    # Without this update, the display would never
    # show the intermediate values
    update idletasks
    after 1000
}
```

uplevel

The **uplevel** command evaluates a script in a different context on
the execution stack. (See also **eval**; **info level**; **namespace eval**;
upvar.) It takes this form:

   uplevel *?level? script*

The arguments are as follows:

level

Which level of the call stack to find the context for evaluating *script*. *level* may be an integer (specifying the number of levels up the call stack from where **uplevel** is invoked) or an integer preceded by a number sign (#) (specifying the absolute level down the call stack from the global scope). If *level* is not specified, it defaults to 1, which evaluates *script* in the context of the caller of the current proc.

script

The script to evaluate.

NOTE: **uplevel** includes an implicit **eval**, so script will be evaluated twice: first by the Tcl parser and then by **uplevel**.

Description

Each time a proc or **namespace eval** is invoked, a new context is created and added to the execution stack. This context contains the values of arguments and local variables, and other housekeeping information. **uplevel** allows a proc to evaluate code in the caller's context or in the global scope. The former is useful for implementing new control structures in Tcl. (This is demonstrated in the **repeat** example under the **return** command entry.)

The effect of **uplevel** is to make seemingly nonexistent the stack contexts between the proc that invokes **uplevel** and the target context. For example, consider a scenario in which proc A calls proc B, which in turn calls proc C, which uses **uplevel** to invoke D. In this scenario, if *level* is 1, #2, or defaulted, then D appears to be invoked from B. If *level* is 2 or #1, then D appears to be invoked from A. If *level* is 3 or #0, then D appears to be invoked in the global scope.

RETURNS   The value of *script*.

ERROR   Raises an error if *script* raises an error.

Example

```
# A proc with a complex API
proc complex {
    arg1 arg2 switch1 switch2 arg3 args
} {
```

```
    # ...do something complex...
}
# A simple way to invoke it with a bunch of
# defaults.
# The [uplevel] makes sure that arg1 and args are
# handled in the context of the proc that calls
# [simple]; that is, [complex] can't tell that
# [simple] exists.
# The [list] is important in case arg1 has
# embedded spaces, which would be removed by the
# [eval] implicit in [uplevel].
proc simple { arg1 args } {
    return [uplevel 1 \
        [list complex $arg1 foo -bar -baz stuff] \
        $args]
}
```

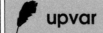

upvar

The **upvar** command links a local variable to a variable in another context. (See also **info level**; **namespace eval**; **upvar**.) It takes this form:

> **upvar** *?level? otherVar myVar ?otherVar myVar ... ?*

The arguments are as follows:

level
Which level of the call stack to find *otherVar*. *level* may be an integer (specifying the number of levels up the call stack from where **uplevel** is invoked) or an integer preceded by a number sign (#) (specifying the absolute level down the call stack from the global scope). If *level* is not specified, it defaults to 1, which finds *otherVar* in the context of the caller of the current proc.

NOTE: If *level* is 0, *myVar* becomes an "alias" for *otherVar* in the current context.

myVar
The name of the local variable used to access *otherVar*.

otherVar
The name of a regular variable, array variable, or array element.

NOTE: If *otherVar* refers to an array element, manipulating
myVar will not trigger traces on the array containing that element.
Traces on the element that *myVar* refers to will be triggered.
An important special case of this is that if *otherVar* is an element
of the global env array, then changes will not be passed on to new
subprocesses correctly.

Description

upvar allows a proc to manipulate a variable in the caller's context
or in the global scope. All arguments to Tcl procs are passed by
value, but call-by-reference can be achieved by passing a variable
name and using **upvar** to access or update the named variable in
the caller's scope.

NOTE: **unset myVar** unsets *otherVar* and leaves *myVar* as a
reference to a nonexistent variable in another context. Setting
myVar then creates *otherVar* in the target context.

ERROR   Raises an error if *myVar* names an already-existing
variable in the current context. (If *myVar* was previously used in
another **upvar**, it is associated with the new *otherVar*.)

Example

```
# A proc with a call-by-reference argument
proc foo { arrName } {
    # A local name for the array
    upvar 1 $arrName a
    # See if the array exists yet.
    if {[info exists a]} {
        puts "$arrName existed with [array size a]\
            elements"
        unset a
    }
    # Set some elements of a
    set a(1) something
    set a(3) "something else"
}
# Tell [foo] to set the array b
foo b
```

```
# Print the array elements
parray b

# "pop" a value off the front of a list like the
# TclX command
proc lvarpop { listName } {
    upvar $listName list
    set first [lindex $list 0]
    set list [lrange $list 1 end]
    return $first
}
# Try it
set l [list a b c d e]
set first [lvarpop l]
puts "$first was at the start of $l"

# Dump a variable with less typing
#     puts "someLongVarName is $someLongVarName"
# becomes
#     dumpVar someLongVarName
proc dumpVar { varName } {
    upvar $varName var
    puts "$varName is $var"
}
```

Programmer's Tip: *global is a special case of* **upvar**.
Specifically, **upvar #0 foo foo** *is equivalent to* **global foo**.

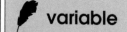

variable

The **variable** command creates and initializes namespace
variables. (See also **global**; **namespace**.) It takes this form:

> **variable** *name ?value? ?name value ... ?*

The arguments are as follows:

name
The name of the variable to create. *name* may include namespace
qualifiers, to indicate what namespace it should be created in. If no

namespace qualifiers are present, the current namespace is used. *name* may not refer to an array element.

value
The initial value to assign to *name*.

Description

variable is typically used inside **namespace eval** to initialize a namespace, like this:

```
namespace eval foo {
    variable Foo
}
```

However, **variable** may be called outside a namespace, and *name* may contain namespace qualifiers indicating what namespace the variable is to be evaluated in.

name may be an array, but it can't be initialized with *value*. After *name* is created with **variable**, it may be set like other variables:

```
variable foo
set foo(bar) baz
```

Programmer's Tip: *global is a special case of* **variable**. *Specifically,* **variable ::foo** *is equivalent to* **global foo**. *However,* **global** *does not provide for an initial value. A common error is to convert code that uses* **global** *as follows:*

```
global foo bar baz
```

to use **variable** *like this:*

```
variable foo bar baz
```

This creates variables named **foo** *and* **baz**, *and initializes* **foo** *with the value* **bar**.
It is best to reference only one variable with **global** *and* **variable** *commands. Thus, the first of the preceding examples becomes:*

```
global foo
global bar
global baz
```

This rendition translates directly and correctly to use **variable**.

vwait

The **vwait** command processes events while waiting for variable to be set. (See also **tkwait variable**.) It takes this form:

> **vwait** *varName*

The argument is as follows:

varName
Name of a variable to wait for. If *varName* does not include namespace qualifiers, it is assumed to refer to a global variable.

Description

vwait may be used by Tcl scripts to allow events to be processed to handle file I/O, timers, and so forth. This is equivalent to **tkwait variable**, which is not available in interpreters without Tk.

ERROR   Raises an error if no events handlers are scheduled, because **vwait** would wait forever.

Example

```
# Let events happen for 5 seconds
after 5000 [list set done 1]
vwait done
```

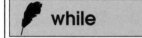

while

The **while** command evaluates a script repeatedly as long as a condition is unsatisfied. (See also **for**; **foreach**.) It takes this form:

> **while** *condition script*

The arguments are as follows:

condition
The end condition for the loop. *script* will be evaluated until **expr condition** returns True.

NOTE: *condition* should almost always be protected by braces ({}). Otherwise, it will be evaluated only once (by the Tcl parser) and *script* will either never execute (if *condition* is initially false) or will execute forever (if *condition* is initially true).

2

script
The script to evaluate.

Description

If *script* calls **continue**, the rest of this evaluation of *script* is skipped and *condition* is tested again. If *script* calls **break**, the rest of this evaluation of *script* is skipped, *condition* is not evaluated again, and **while** returns.

ERROR   Raises an error if *script* raises an error.

Example

```
set i 0
while {$i < 10} {
    puts "i:[incr i]"
}
```

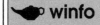 **winfo**

The **winfo** command retrieves information about a window. (See also **tk**; **wm**.) It takes the following forms:

> **winfo atom** *?-***displayof** *window? name*
> **winfo atomname** *?-***displayof** *window? id*
>
> **winfo cells** *window*
>
> **winfo children** *window*
> **winfo parent** *window*
> **winfo toplevel** *window*

winfo class *window*

winfo colormapfull *window*

winfo containing *?-***displayof** *window? rootX rootY*

winfo depth *window*

winfo exists *window*

winfo fpixels *window distance*
winfo pixels *window distance*

winfo geometry *window*

winfo height *window*
winfo width *window*

winfo id *window*
winfo pathname *?-***displayof** *window? id*

winfo interps *?-***displayof** *window?*

winfo ismapped *window*
winfo viewable *window*

winfo manager *window*

winfo name *window*

winfo pointerx *window*
winfo pointerxy *window*
winfo pointery *window*

winfo reqheight *window*
winfo reqwidth *window*

winfo rgb *window color*

winfo rootx *window*
winfo rooty *window*

winfo screen *window*
winfo screencells *window*
winfo screendepth *window*
winfo screenheight *window*
winfo screenwidth *window*
winfo screenmmheight *window*
winfo screenmmwidth *window*
winfo screenvisual *window*

winfo server *window*

winfo visual *window*
winfo visualid *window*
winfo visualsavailable *window* *?includeids?*

winfo vrootheight *window*
winfo vrootwidth *window*
winfo vrootx *window*
winfo vrooty *window*

winfo x *window*
winfo y *window*

The arguments are as follows:

color
A color name or number.

id
An X server atom integer identifier.

name
The name of an X server atom.

number
A distance, in screen coordinates.

rootX, rootY
Screen coordinates to access.

window
The path to a window through the Tk widget hierarchy.

winfo atom *?-displayof window? name*

Retrieves the atom ID for *name* on *window*'s display. If **-displayof** is not specified, *window* defaults to ".". If *name* does not exist, it is created.

NOTE: This command is meaningless on Microsoft Windows and Macintosh systems.

RETURNS   The atom ID for *name*, expressed as an integer.

winfo atomname *?-displayof window? id*

Retrieves the name of the atom number *id* on *window*'s display. If **-displayof** is not specified, *window* defaults to ".".

NOTE: This command is meaningless on Microsoft Windows and Macintosh systems.

RETURNS   The name of atom *id*.

ERROR   Raises an error if atom *id* does not exist.

winfo cells *window*

Retrieves the number of cells in *window*'s color map.

RETURNS   The number of cells, expressed as an integer.

winfo children *window*

Determines *window*'s children.

RETURNS   A list of *window*'s children in the order of their creation. The elements of the list include the full path to the children through the widget hierarchy.

winfo parent *window*

Retrieves the name of *window*'s parent, similar to the way in which **file dirname** returns the name of the directory containing a file. The parent of any window created with **toplevel** is ".". The parent of "." is an empty string.

RETURNS   The name of *window*'s parent.

winfo toplevel *window*

Determines the toplevel window that contains *window*.

RETURNS   The name of the toplevel window.

winfo class *window*

Retrieves *window*'s class. For widgets, such as buttons and menus, this is determined by the widget type. For example, a button is of class **Button**. For containers, such as frames and toplevels, this may be set by the **-class** option when the container is created.

RETURNS   The class string for *window*.

winfo colormapfull *window*

Determines whether *window*'s color map is full.

RETURNS   1 if the last attempt to allocate a new color has failed and no colors have been frees since; 0 otherwise.

winfo containing
?-displayof *window?* rootX rootY

Determines the window on *window*'s display that contains the screen coordinates (*rootX*,*rootY*). If **-displayof** is not specified, *window* defaults to ".".

RETURNS   The full path to the highest window in the stacking order that contains (*rootX*,*rootY*).

If no Tk window includes (*rootX*,*rootY*), an empty string is returned.

winfo depth *window*

Determines the number of bits per pixel for *window*.

RETURNS   The number of bits, expressed as an integer.

winfo exists *window*

Determines whether *window* exists.

RETURNS   1 If *window* exists; 0 otherwise

winfo fpixels *window distance*

Determines how many pixels take up *distance* in *window*. (See also **tk scaling**; **winfo pixels**; and the **canvas canvasx** and **canvasy** commands.)

RETURNS   The number of pixels, expressed in floating-point form.

winfo pixels *window distance*

Determines how many pixels take up *distance in window*. (See also **tk scaling**; **winfo fpixels**; and **the canvas canvasx** and **canvasy** commands.)

RETURNS   The number of pixels, expressed as an integer.

winfo geometry *window*

Determines the size and position of *window*.

RETURNS   A string in the form *width***x***height***+***x***+***y*, where all dimensions are screen coordinates, in pixels.

winfo height *window*

Determines the height of *window*. Just after creation, all windows have a height of 1. This height is updated by the geometry manager (for example, **pack**) after the next update. The **update** command can be used to force and update before querying the height, or **winfo reqheight** can be used to retrieve *window*'s requested height.

RETURNS   The height of *window* in pixels, expressed as an integer.

winfo width *window*

Determines the width of *window*. Just after creation, all windows have a width of 1. This width is updated by the geometry manager (for example, **pack**) after the next update. The **update** command can be used to force and update before querying the width, or **winfo reqwidth** can be used to retrieve *window*'s requested width.

RETURNS The width of *window* in pixels, expressed as an integer.

winfo id *window*

Determines the platform-specific integer window identifier for *window*. (See also **toplevel**; **winfo pathname**.) On UNIX systems, this is the X Windows identifier. On Microsoft Windows systems, this is the HWND. On Macintosh systems, this is a Tk-internal value.

RETURNS A hexadecimal string.

winfo pathname *?-displayof window? id*

Retrieves the path through the Tk widget hierarchy to the window on *window*'s display whose ID is *id*. (See also **winfo id**.) If **-displayof** is not specified, *window* defaults to ".".

RETURNS The path to window *id*.

ERROR Raises an error if *id* is not a window in the current Tk application.

winfo interps *?-displayof window?*

Retrieves a list of other Tk-enabled interpreters using *window*'s display. (See also **send**.) If **-displayof** is not specified, *window* defaults to ".".

RETURNS An unordered list of interpreter names.

NOTE: This command always returns an empty list on Microsoft Windows and Macintosh systems.

winfo ismapped *window*

Determines whether *window* is displayed.

RETURNS 1 if *window* is visible; 0 if it is iconified or hidden.

winfo viewable *window*

Determines whether *window* is displayed.

NOTE: This command differs from **ismapped** insofar as **ismapped** tests only the specified window, whereas **viewable** tests that the window and all of its ancestors are displayed. In practice, no difference exists between the two commands, and **ismapped** may be slightly more efficient.

RETURNS 1 if *window* is visible; 0 if it is iconified or hidden.

winfo manager *window*

Determines the geometry manager responsible for *window*.

RETURNS The name of the geometry manager (**pack** or **grid**, for example). If *window* is embedded in another widget, the container widget's creation command (**canvas**, for example) is returned.

winfo name *window*

Retrieves *window*'s name within its parent widget, similar to the way in which **file tail** returns the name of a file within its directory. For example, **winfo name .f1.b1** returns "b1". The name of the application's default toplevel window is the application name. Thus, **winfo name .** returns the same value returned by **tk appname**.

NOTE: For **winfo name** to succeed, window must exist.

winfo pointerx *window*

Retrieves the X screen coordinate of the mouse pointer on *window*'s screen.

RETURNS   The x screen coordinate of the mouse pointer, in pixels, if the pointer is on *window*'s display; -1 otherwise.

winfo pointerxy *window*

Retrieves the X and Y screen coordinates of the mouse pointer on *window*'s screen.

RETURNS   A list containing the x and y screen coordinates of the mouse pointer, in pixels, if the pointer is on *window*'s display; otherwise, {-1 -1}.

winfo pointery *window*

Retrieves the Y screen coordinate of the mouse pointer on *window*'s screen.

RETURNS   The y screen coordinate of the mouse pointer, in pixels, if the pointer is on *window*'s display; -1 otherwise.

winfo reqheight *window*

Retrieves the requested height for *window*. (See also **winfo height**.)

RETURNS   *window*'s height in pixels, expressed as an integer.

winfo reqwidth *window*

Retrieves the requested width for *window*. (See also **winfo width**.)

RETURNS   *window*'s width in pixels, expressed as an integer.

winfo rgb *window color*

Determines the red, green, and blue components of *color* in *window*.

RETURNS   A list of three values, in the form {*r g b*}. For example, **winfo rgb . orange** might return {**65280 41984 0**}.

winfo rootx *window*

Determines the X screen coordinate of the *window* on the screen. (See also **winfo x**; **winfo vrootx**.) If *window* has a border, this is the position of the outside of the border.

RETURNS   The number of pixels, expressed as an integer.

winfo rooty *window*

Determines the Y screen coordinate of the *window* on the screen. (See also **winfo y**; **winfo vrooty**.) If *window* has a border, this is the position of the outside of the border.

RETURNS   The number of pixels, expressed as an integer.

winfo screen *window*

Determines the name of the screen on which *window* is displayed.

RETURNS   A screen name, in the form *displayName.screenIndex*.

winfo screencells *window*

Determines the number of cells in the default colormap for *window*'s screen.

RETURNS   The number of cells, expressed as an integer.

winfo screendepth *window*

Determines the number of bit per pixel on *window*'s display.

RETURNS   The number of pixels, expressed as an integer.

winfo screenheight *window*

Determines the height of *window*'s screen, in pixels. (See also **winfo vrootheight**.)

RETURNS   The height of *window*'s screen in pixels, expressed as an integer.

winfo screenwidth *window*

Determines the width of *window*'s screen, in pixels. (See also **winfo vrootwidth**.)

RETURNS The width of *window*'s screen in pixels, expressed as an integer.

winfo screenmmheight *window*

Determines the height of *window*'s screen, in millimeters.

RETURNS The height of *window*'s screen in millimeters, expressed as an integer.

NOTE: This value depends on configuration information that is often not set correctly, and thus is less reliable than **screenheight**.

winfo screenmmwidth *window*

Determines the width of *window*'s screen, in millimeters.

RETURNS The width of *window*'s screen in millimeters, expressed as an integer.

NOTE: This value depends on configuration information that is often not set correctly, and thus is less reliable than **screenwidth**.

winfo screenvisual *window*

Determines the default visual class for *window*'s screen.

RETURNS One of the following class values: **directcolor**, **grayscale**, **pseudocolor**, **staticcolor**, **staticgray**, or **truecolor**.

winfo server *window*

Determines the name and version of the display server for *window*'s screen.

RETURNS A platform-specific value. On UNIX systems, this is a string in the form "X*major*R*minor vendor vendorVersion*". On

Microsoft Windows systems, returns a string in the form
"**Windows** *major.minor vendorVersion API*". For example, for build
1381 of Microsoft Windows NT 4, the returned value would be:

```
"Windows 4.0 1381 Win32"
```

winfo visual *window*

Determines the visual class for *window*.

RETURNS   One of the following class values: **directcolor,
grayscale, pseudocolor, staticcolor, staticgray**, or **truecolor**.

winfo visualid *window*

Determines the ID of the visual class for *window*.

RETURNS   The visual class identifier, expressed as an integer.

winfo visualsavailable
window ?includeids?

Retrieves a list of available visuals.

RETURNS   A list of lists. If **includeids** is not specified, each
element is of the form {*class bitsperpixel*}. If **includeids** is specified,
each element is of the form {*class bitsperpixel id*}.

winfo vrootheight *window*

Determines the height of *window*'s root window. If *window* is
displayed in a "room" or "workspace," such as those provided by
the Common Desktop Environment on UNIX, this is the height of
the workspace. Otherwise, it is the height of *window*'s screen.
(See also **winfo screenheight**.)

RETURNS   The height of *window*'s root window in pixels,
expressed as an integer.

winfo vrootwidth *window*

Determines the width of *window*'s root window. If *window* is displayed in a "room" or "workspace," such as those provided by the Common Desktop Environment on UNIX, this is the width of the workspace. Otherwise, it is the width of *window*'s screen. (See also **winfo screenwidth**.)

RETURNS   The width of *window*'s root window in pixels, expressed as an integer.

winfo vrootx *window*

Determines the X screen coordinate of the *window* in its root window. If *window* is displayed in a "room" or "workspace," such as those provided by the Common Desktop Environment on UNIX, this is the position in the workspace. Otherwise, it is the position on *window*'s screen. (See also **winfo x**.) If *window* has a border, this is the position of the outside of the border.

RETURNS   The number of pixels, expressed as an integer.

winfo vrooty *window*

Determines the Y screen coordinate of the *window* in its root window. If *window* is displayed in a "room" or "workspace," such as those provided by the Common Desktop Environment on UNIX, this is the position in the workspace. Otherwise, it is the position on *window*'s screen. (See also **winfo y**) If *window* has a border, this is the position of the outside of the border.

RETURNS   The number of pixels, expressed as an integer.

winfo x *window*

Determines the X coordinate of *window* in its parent. If *window* has a border, this is the position of the outside of the border.

RETURNS   The number of pixels, expressed as an integer.

winfo y *window*

Determines the Y coordinate of *window* in its parent. If *window* has a border, this is the position of the outside of the border.

RETURNS   The number of pixels, expressed as an integer.

The **wm** command allows interaction with the window manager. (See also **winfo**.) It takes the following forms:

wm deiconify *window*
wm iconify *window*
wm state *window*
wm withdraw *window*

wm frame *window*
wm overrideredirect *window* *?flag?*

wm group *window* *?leader?*
wm transient *window* *?master?*

wm iconbitmap *window* *?bitmap?*
wm iconmask *window* *?bitmap?*
wm iconwindow *window* *?pathName?*

wm title *window* *?title?*
wm iconname *window* *?newName?*
wm iconposition *window* *?x y?*

wm aspect *window* *?minNumer minDenom maxNumer maxDenom?*
wm geometry *window* *?newGeometry?*
wm grid *window* *?baseWidth baseHeight widthInc heightInc?*
wm maxsize *window* *?width height?*
wm minsize *window* *?width height?*
wm resizable *window* *?wSettable hSettable?*

wm positionfrom *window* *?who?*
wm sizefrom *window* *?who?*

wm protocol *window ?name? ?script?*
wm client *window ?hostname?*
wm command *window ?command?*
wm colormapwindows *window ?windowList?*
wm focusmodel *window ?focusType?*

The arguments are as follows:

baseWidth, baseHeight
The number of grid units represented by the *window*'s current width and height.

bitmap
A bitmap specification. (For details, see the discussion of the **-bitmap** option in the Appendix.)

command
Command line to invoke *window*'s application.

flag
A Boolean value, such as **on**, **0**, **false**, and so forth.

focusType
The focus model used by *window*. *focusType* may be **passive** or **active**. (See **wm focusmodel** for details.)

height
The height for *window*. If *window* is gridded, *height* is in grid units; otherwise, it's in pixels.

hostname
The name of the host on which *window*'s application is running.

leader
The leader of a window group.

master
A toplevel window.

maxNumer, maxDenom
Numerator and denominator of the maximum aspect ratio for *window*.

minNumer, minDenom
Numerator and denominator of the minimum aspect ratio for *window*.

name
Specifies the protocol to respond to. *name* must be one of
WM_DELETE_WINDOW, **WM_SAVE_YOURSELF**, or
WM_TAKE_FOCUS.

newGeometry
A specification of *window*'s size and position, in this form:

$$=w\text{x}h\pm x\pm y$$

The leading equal sign (=), and the size (*w*x*h)* or position (±*x*±*y*),
may be omitted.

If *window* is gridded, *w* and *h* are in grid units; otherwise, they are
in pixels. *x* and *y* are screen coordinates, in pixels. If *x* is positive, it
specifies the distance from the left edge of the screen to the left
edge of *window*'s border; if *x* is negative, it specifies the distance
from the right edge of the screen to the right edge of *window*'s
border. If *y* is positive, it specifies the distance from the top edge of
the screen to the top edge of *window*'s border; if *y* is negative, it
specifies the distance from the bottom edge of the screen to the
bottom edge of *window*'s border.

newName
String to be displayed with the icon when *window* is minimized.

script
Script to invoke in response to a protocol message.

title
A string for *window*'s title bar.

who
Specifies who requested *window*'s position. *who* must be **user** or
program.

width
The width for *window*. If *window* is gridded, *width* is in grid units;
otherwise, it's in pixels.

widthInc, heightInc
The number of pixels per grid unit. When resized, *window*'s
width will be restricted to integer multiples of *widthInc*, and its
height will be restricted to integer multiples of *heightInc*.

window
The name of a Tk toplevel window.

windowList
List of windows with private color maps. (See **wm colormapwindows** for details.)

wSettable, hSettable
Booleans which control whether the width or height of the window is changeable.

x, y
Screen coordinates for *window*'s icon.

wm deiconify *window*

Displays *window* as a normal window, not an icon.

wm iconify *window*

Displays *window* minimized (as an icon).

wm state *window*

Determines the current display state of *window*. Returns one of the following values:

- **icon**   *window* is an icon window for another window
- **iconic**   *window* has been iconified
- **normal**   *window* is displayed on the screen
- **withdrawn**   *window* is not on the screen as a window or an icon

wm withdraw *window*

Removes *window* from the display.

wm frame *window*

Retrieves the window handle for the frame around *window*, if there is a frame; otherwise, retrieves *window*'s window handle.

RETURNS   An integer window handle, in hexadecimal form.

wm overrideredirect *window* *?flag?*

Determines whether *window* will be managed or ignored by the window manager. If *flag* is true, the window manager ignores *window*, which means, among other things, that *window* will not have a frame, title bar, and so forth. This is useful for splash screens and similar special-purpose windows.

If *flag* is specified, it must be a Boolean value that will control the handling of *window*. If *flag* is not specified, this command returns 0 or 1 to indicate the current state of *window*.

wm group *window ?leader?*

Manipulates *window*'s window group. Some window managers manage windows in groups so that they all can be iconified or restored simultaneously.

NOTE: This command has no effect on Microsoft Windows systems.

If *leader* is specified as a valid toplevel window, this command adds *window* to *leader*'s group of windows. If *leader* is specified as an empty string, it removes *window* from any window group. If *leader* is not specified, the leader of *window*'s group, if any, is returned.

wm transient *window ?master?*

Controls the transient property of *window*. Some window managers treat "transient" windows, such as pull-down menus, specially.

If *master* is specified as the name of a toplevel window, *window* is marked as a transient slave of *master*. If *master* is specified as an empty string, any indication that *window* is a transient slave is removed. If *master* is not specified, this command returns the name of the toplevel master, if any, for *window*.

wm iconbitmap *window ?bitmap?*

Manipulates the bitmap for *window*'s icon.

NOTE: This command has no effect on Microsoft Windows systems.

If *bitmap* is specified as a valid bitmap, this command sets *window*'s icon bitmap. If *bitmap* is specified as an empty string, it removes *window*'s icon bitmap. If *bitmap* is not specified, then the current bitmap icon, if any, is returned.

Programmer's Tip: *iconbitmap has no effect on Microsoft Windows and Macintosh systems. For Microsoft Windows, get Leo Schubert's* **winico** *extension, available in the Tcl Resource Center at* **www.scriptics.com**.

2

wm iconmask *window ?bitmap?*

Manipulates the mask bitmap for *window*'s icon.

NOTE: This command has no effect on Microsoft Windows systems.

If *bitmap* is specified as a valid bitmap, this command sets *window*'s icon's mask bitmap. If *bitmap* is specified as an empty string, it removes *window*'s icon's mask bitmap. If *bitmap* is not specified, it then the current icon mask bitmap, if any, is returned.

wm iconwindow *window ?pathName?*

Manipulates *window*'s icon window. When *window* is iconified, *pathName* will be displayed as its icon. When *window* is restored, *pathName* will be removed from the display.

NOTE: This command has no effect on Microsoft Windows systems, and is not supported by all UNIX window managers.

If *pathName* is specified as a valid toplevel window, it is set as *window*'s icon window. If *pathName* is specified as an empty string, the icon window for *window*, if any, is removed. If *pathName* is not specified, *window*'s icon window, if any, is returned.

wm title *window ?title?*

Manipulates *window*'s title. If *string* is specified, sets *window*'s title to *string*. If *string* is not specified, returns *window*'s current title.

wm iconname *window ?newName?*

Manipulates *window's* icon name. (See also **wm title**.) If *newName* is specified, sets *window's* icon's name. If *newName* is not specified, returns *window's* icon's name.

wm iconposition *window ?x y?*

Manipulates *window's* icon's position. If *x* and *y* are specified as integers, sets them as the requested position of *window's* icon. If *x* and *y* are specified as an empty string, removes the icon position request from *window*. If *x* and *y* are not specified, returns the previously requested icon position, if any.

wm aspect *window ?minNumer minDenom maxNumer maxDenom?*

If *minNumer*, *minDenom*, *maxNumer*, and *maxDenom* are specified as integers, they are passed to the window manager, which should enforce that the *window's* aspect ratio (width/height) is between *minNumer*/*minDenom* and *maxNumer*/*maxDenom*.

NOTE: This command has no effect on Microsoft Windows systems.

If *minNumer*, *minDenom*, *maxNumer*, and *maxDenom* are specified as empty strings, any previously existing restrictions on *window's* aspect ratio are removed. If no arguments are specified, the current restrictions on aspect ratio are returned as a list that is either empty (if no restrictions were in place) or in the form {*minNumer minDenom maxNumer maxDenom*}.

wm geometry *window ?newGeometry?*

If *newGeometry* is specified, sets the size and/or position of *window*. If *newGeometry* is not specified, returns the size and position of *window* in the form *w*x*h*+*x*+*y*.

wm grid *window ?baseWidth baseHeight widthInc heightInc?*

If *baseWidth*, *baseHeight*, *widthInc*, and *heightInc* are specified
as integers, they are passed to the window manager, which
should enforce that the *window*'s width is in integer multiples
of *widthInc*, and that *window*'s height is in integer multiples
of *heightInc*.

NOTE: This command has no effect on Microsoft Windows systems.

If *baseWidth*, *baseHeight*, *widthInc*, and *heightInc* are specified as
empty strings, any previously existing restrictions on *window*'s
size are removed. If no arguments are specified, the current
gridding restrictions are returned as a list that is either empty (if no
restrictions were in place) or in the form {*baseWidth baseHeight
widthInc heightInc*}.

wm maxsize *window ?width height?*

Specifies the maximum size of *window*. If *width* and *height* are
specified, sets the maximum width and height for *window*. If
width and *height* are not specified, returns the maximum width
and height.

NOTE: This command has no effect if resizing has been disabled
with **wm resizable**.

wm minsize *window ?width height?*

Specifies the minimum size of *window*. If *width* and *height* are
specified, sets the minimum width and height for *window*.
If *width* and *height* are not specified, returns the minimum
width and height.

NOTE: This command has no effect if resizing has been disabled
with **wm resizable**.

wm resizable *window* *?wSettable hSettable?*

Determines whether *window* may be resized by the user.
If *wSettable* and *hSettable* are both specified as Boolean values,
they determine whether the width and height of *window* may
be changed. If *wSettable* and *hSettable* are not specified, this
command returns a list of two Boolean values indicating which
dimension may be changed.

wm positionfrom *window* *?who?*

Indicates to the window manager the source of window position
requests. Some window managers ignore programmatic requests
and honor only user requests. If **wm positionfrom** is not called, Tk
sets the source to **user** whenever **wm geometry** is called. If *who* is
specified as **user** or **program**, this command sets the position
source. If *who* is specified as an empty string, it removes the
current position source. If *who* is not specified, it returns the
current position source.

wm sizefrom *window* *?who?*

Indicates to the window manager the source of window size
requests. Some window managers ignore programmatic requests
and honor only user requests. If **wm positionfrom** is not called, Tk
sets the source to **user** whenever **wm geometry** is called. If *who* is
specified as **user** or **program**, this command sets the size source. If
who is specified as an empty string, it removes the current size
source. If *who* is not specified, it returns the current size source.

wm protocol *window* *?name? ?script?*

Manages handlers for window protocol requests. If *name* and *script*
are both specified and *script* is not an empty string, binds *script* to
be invoked whenever *window* receives a *name* protocol message.
name is also added to *window*'s **WM_PROTOCOLS** property.

If *name* and *script* are both specified and *script* is an empty string,
it removes the binding *name* for *window* and removes *name* from
window's **WM_PROTOCOLS** property. If *name* is specified and
script is not, it returns the script bound to *name* protocol messages

for *window*. If neither *name* nor *script* is specified, it returns a list of protocol messages with bindings for *window*.

NOTE: Tk has a default binding to **WM_DELETE_WINDOW** that destroys window. This binding is <u>not</u> indicated by **wm protocol .
WM_DELETE_WINDOW**.

Example
```
proc confirmExit { w } {
    set response [tk_messageBox \
        -message "Really Exit?" \
        -type okcancel]
    if {[string equal $response "ok"]} {
        destroy $w
    }
}
wm protocol . WM_DELETE_WINDOW \
        [list confirmExit .]
```

wm client *window ?hostname?*

If *hostname* is specified, sets *hostname* as *window*'s **WM_CLIENT_MACHINE** property and returns an empty string. Otherwise, it returns the current value of the **WM_CLIENT_ MACHINE** property.

wm command *window ?command?*

Manipulates *window*'s **WM_COMMAND** property, which specifies a command needed to invoke *window*'s application. If *command* is specified as a nonempty list, it is stored in the property. If *command* is specified as an empty list, the property is deleted. If *command* is not specified, returns the current value of the property.

wm colormapwindows
window ?windowList?

Manipulates *window*'s **WM_COLORMAP_WINDOWS** property, which specifies the order in which private color maps will be used. *windowList* lists descendants of *window* in the Tk widget hierarchy in priority order. If *window* is not in *windowList*, it is added to the end. The private color maps for descendants will be used starting from the first element of *windowList* to the last element as long as more color maps are available on *window*'s display.

If *windowList* is specified, it is stored in the property. If *windowList* is not specified, this command returns the current value of the property.

wm focusmodel *window ?focusType?*

Manipulates the focus model for *window*. An **active** focus model means that the window can claim the focus for itself and its descendants even if the focus is in an another application. A **passive** model means that the application will wait for the window manager to give it focus, as appropriate (the default).

If *focusType* is specified, this command sets the focus model for *window*. If *focusType* is not specified, it returns the current focus model for *window*.

Compatibility

Most **wm** commands are designed for specific interactions with X Windows window managers and have little or no meaning on Microsoft Windows or Macintosh systems. Most are harmless, but ineffective, in those environments.

On UNIX, window managers tend to be finicky, and may or may not honor property settings, window groups, and so forth. Only experimentation with various window managers can determine how they will react.

Part 3
Appendix

Tk includes a number of basic widgets for user interaction. Other systems call these user interface elements *controls* or *gadgets*. The appearance of widgets is controlled by *options* that may be set when a widget is created and/or configured later. The following sections describe the commands used to create widgets, the commands used to configure widget options, the common widget options, and the values of those options.

Setting Options

Generally, all widgets have useful defaults for their options, so for each particular widget, you need to set only those options for which you want to override the default setting. Options may be specified in several ways and at different times:

- In X Windows resources (on UNIX systems)
- In the option database (using the **option** command)
- When a widget is created (with the widget creation command)
- During the lifetime of the widget (with the widget's **configure** command)

For information on the X Windows resource database, consult your system documentation. The option database is described in the entry for the **option** command.

NOTE: The database name and class for an option that is needed for the X Windows resource and **option** can be determined by using the **configure** widget command. (See the following section for more information.)

Options that are not set explicitly (when the widget is created or, later, with **configure**) take default values. Default values come from several sources, which are processed in the following order:

- Each widget has a built-in default for each option.

- On UNIX systems, option values found in the X Window resource database override built-in defaults.

- Values stored in the option database with **option** override built-in defaults and X Window resource values.

Programmer's Tip: *Some options have static effect and control the widget's appearance until* **configure** *is used to change their value. For example, colors are static options. Other options have dynamic effect, setting up an association that allows the widget to change as events in Tk occur. For example, setting the* **-textvariable** *option for an entry causes the entry widget to display the current value of the specified variable as the variable changes.*

Creating Widgets

Each instance of a Tk widget is created with a widget creation command. The general form of a widget creation command is:

> *cmd pathName ?option value ...?*

The individual elements are as follows:

- **cmd**   The widget creation command: **button, canvas, checkbutton, entry, frame, label, listbox, menu, menubutton, message, radiobutton, scale, scrollbar, text,** or **toplevel.**

- **pathName**   The path to the new widget through the Tk widget hierarchy. *pathName* must not exist when the widget creation command is invoked.

- **option**   A valid option for the widget to be created. Each *option* must be valid for the type of widget being created.

- **value**   The value for *option* for the new widget. Each *value* must be valid for the corresponding *option*.

Not all widgets support all options. (See the individual widget creation commands for a list of options for each widget.) The following sections discuss the options that are common to various widgets.

Any number of options and their values may be specified, as in this example:

```
button .b -text "OK" -command exit \
        -background red -foreground white
```

This command creates a new red-and-white button as a child of the main toplevel window (.), puts "OK" in its label, and invokes the command **exit** when the button is clicked.

Once a widget is created, its options may be queried with the **cget** widget command and queried and set with the **configure** widget command.

The **cget** widget command retrieves the current value of a single widget option. It takes the following form:

    pathName **cget** *option*

The arguments are as follows:

option
The name of the option to retrieve.

pathName
The path through the widget hierarchy to the widget to query.

RETURNS
The current value of *option* for *pathName*.

ERROR
Raises an error if *option* is not a valid option for *pathName*.

Example

```
set background [.b cget -background]
```

The **configure** widget command manipulates widget options. It takes the following forms:

pathName **configure**

pathName **configure** *option*

pathName **configure** *option value ?option value ...?*

The arguments are as follows:

option
The name of the option to retrieve.

pathName
The path through the widget hierarchy to the widget to query.

value
The value for *option*.

pathName configure

Retrieves a list of all options for *pathName* and their values.

RETURNS   A list of lists. Each sublist is in one of two forms, having either two or five elements. A two-element list represents an abbreviation for an option name. The list takes this form:

{*abbreviation fullOptionName*}

Here is an example:

```
{-bd -borderwidth}
```

A five-element list represents an option and its value. The list takes this form:

{*fullOptionName dbName dbClass defaultValue currentValue*}

The individual elements are as follows:

- **fullOptionName**   The full option name, as specified when configuring the widget on the command line
- **dbName**   The name of the option in the option database
- **dbClass**   The class of the option in the option database

- *defaultValue*   The default value for the option, effective if the option isn't set when the widget is created or reconfigured
- *currentValue*   The current value for the option

pathName configure *option*

Retrieves the values for an option for *pathName*.

RETURNS   A five-element list in the same form as the sublists returned by *pathName* **configure**.

pathName configure *option value ?option value ...?*

Sets one or more option values for *pathName*.

Example

```
# Create a button with default values
button .b
# Set some options
.b configure -text "Hello" -command [list puts Hello]
```

Option Types

anchor

One of the four corners of a rectangle (specified with compass points), or the middle of the rectangle. Valid values are **n**, **ne**, **e**, **se**, **s**, **sw**, **w**, **nw**, and **center**.

NOTE: The **pack** and **grid** geometry managers use compass directions to specify widget anchoring. A widget may stick to any or all sides of a geometry manager's parent, so **new**, for example, specifies that the widget should stick to the north, east, and west sides. When used for Tk widget options, anchors may take only one of the nine values listed for *anchor*.

bitmap

The name of a file, or built-in or user-defined bitmap from the
following table:

Form	Meaning
@*fileName*	The name of a file containing a bitmap description in standard X Windows format
name	The name of a bitmap defined previously with a call to **bitmap**
error	A circle with a diagonal line across it
gray75	A checkerboard pattern where three out of four bits are on
gray50	A checkerboard pattern where every other bit is on
gray25	A checkerboard pattern where one out of every four bits is on
gray12	A pattern where one-eighth of the bits are on, consisting of every fourth pixel in every other row
hourglass	An hourglass symbol
info	A large letter *I*
questhead	The silhouette of a human head, with a question mark in it
question	A large question mark
warning	A large exclamation point

In addition, the following predefined names are available only on
Macintosh systems:

Name	Description
accessory	A desk accessory
application	A generic application icon
caution	A triangle with an exclamation point
cdrom	A CD-ROM icon
document	A generic document
edition	The edition symbol
floppy	A floppy disk
folder	A generic folder icon
note	A face with balloon words
pfolder	A locked folder

Name	Description
preferences	A folder with prefs symbol
querydoc	A database document icon
ramdisk	A floppy disk with chip
stationery	Document stationery
stop	A stop sign
trash	A trash can

boolean

A string representing a logical true or false. Valid values are **0**, **1**, **true**, **false**, **on**, **off**, **yes**, and **no**.

color

A color name or RGB specification. Color names are defined in the X Windows server's color database. Over 700 color names are defined, including many "natural" names (such as **blue** and **lightgreen**) and many "designer" names (such as **lemon chiffon** and **tomato**).

NOTE: No way exists to ask Tk for a list of these colors from a script. However, you can find these names in the source distribution, in the file xcolors.c in Tk's xlib directory.

An RBG specification starts with a number sign (#) and includes 4, 8, 12, or 16 bits for each color (specified as 1 to 4 hexadecimal digits). Valid forms are *#RGB*, *#RRGGBB*, *#RRRGGGBBB*, and *#RRRRGGGGBBBB*. If fewer than 16 bits are specified, each value is padded with 0's to make it a 16-bit value. For example, **#31a273** is the same as **#3100a2007300**.

command

A Tcl command that may have additional arguments appended to it before being invoked. For example, the **-xscrollcommand** option sets the command to invoke to scroll a widget horizontally. When the scroll command is invoked, the lower and upper limits of the view are appended. The following example shows a possible implementation of a scroll command. Note that the list passed as a value for the **-xscrollcommand** option does not include the *lower* and *upper* arguments to the proc.

```
proc scrollCommand { w lower upper } {
    puts "Widget $w should show $lower to $upper\
          of the horizontal range"
}
text .t -xscrollcommand [list scrollCommand .t]
```

cursor

A cursor specification in one of the following forms:

> *name ?fgcolor? ?bgcolor?*
>
> *@source mask fgcolor bgcolor*
>
> *@source fgcolor*

NOTE: Only the first form is supported on Microsoft Windows and Macintosh systems.

The fields are as follows:

name
A cursor name from those listed in Table 3-1 (courtesy of D. Richard Hipp). In addition, Macintosh systems support the cursor names **ibeam, crosshair, watch, plus,** and **arrow,** and will load cursor resources of the types **crsr** (color) and **CURS** (black and white) by the name of the resource. The application and all of its open dynamic libraries' resource files will be searched for the named cursor. If conflicts exist, color cursors are always loaded in preference to black-and-white cursors.

fgcolor, bgcolor
The foreground and background colors for the cursor. If only *fgcolor* is specified, *bgcolor* defaults to being transparent. If neither color is specified, *fgcolor* defaults to **black** and *bgcolor* defaults to **white**.

source
The name of a file containing the source bitmask for the cursor, in the form described for **bitmap**.

mask
The name of the file containing the mask bitmask for the cursor, in the form described for **bitmap**. If *mask* is not specified, it defaults to *source* and the background of the cursor is transparent.

↗	arrow	gobbler	⇓	sb_down_arrow
⊤	based_arrow_down	gumby	↔	sb_h_double_arrow
⊥	based_arrow_up	hand1	⇐	sb_left_arrow
⇀	boat	hand2	⇒	sb_right_arrow
	bogosity	♡ heart	⇑	sb_up_arrow
◪	bottom_left_corner	▣ icon	⇕	sb_v_double_arrow
◪	bottom_right_corner	▨ iron_cross	shuttle
↓	bottom_side	▸ left_ptr	sizing
⊥	bottom_tee	⊢ left_side	✳ spider
▣	box_spiral	⊢ left_tee	spraycan
▲	center_ptr	leftbutton	☆ star
○	circle	⌐ ll_angle	⊙ target
	clock	⌐ lr_angle	+ tcross
	coffee_mug	✗ man	top_left_arrow
✚	cross	middlebutton	top_left_corner
✳	cross_reverse	mouse	top_right_corner
+	crosshair	pencil	top_side
⊕	diamond_cross	♟ pirate	⊤ top_tee
●	dot	+ plus	trek
⊡	dotbox	? question_arrow	⌐ ul_angle
↕	double_arrow	right_ptr	umbrella
↗	draft_large	→⊢ right_side	⌐ ur_angle
↗	draft_small	⊣ right_tee	watch
▨	draped_box	rightbutton	✗ X_cursor
♺	exchange	⊞ rtl_logo	I xterm
✛	fleur	sailboat	

Table 3-1.   Cursor Names

distance

A floating-point number followed by an optional one-character unit specifier from the following table:

Letter	Units
none	Pixels
c	Centimeters
i	Inches
m	Millimeters
p	Points (1 point = 1/72")

font

The font to use.

image

The name of an image created with **image**.

integer

An integer number in one of several formats: decimal (e.g., **255**), octal (e.g., **0177**), or hexadecimal (e.g., **0xff**).

justification

left, **right**, or **center**.

milliseconds

An integer number of milliseconds. For example, 1500 is 1.5 seconds.

orientation

horizontal or **vertical**.

relief

A 3-D effect for a widget. Valid values are **raised**, **sunken**, **flat**, **ridge**, **solid**, and **groove**.

script

One or more complete Tcl commands that will be evaluated as provided, without additional arguments appended. Contrast this with **command** type options. For example, the -**command** option of button widgets sets a script that is evaluated when the button is invoked:

```
button .b -command {
    someCommand arg1 arg2
    otherCommand arg3 arg4
}
```

varname

3

A variable name, possibly with namespace qualifiers. For example, **myVar** or **myNameSpace::var**.

Options

NOTE: Option names can be abbreviated to a unique prefix. For example, -**activeba** is sufficient to distinguish -**activebackground** from -**activeborderwidth**. However, abbreviating option names makes code harder to read and is not recommended.

-activebackground *color*

Specifies the background color for the widget when it is *active*, such as the background color for a button while the mouse pointer is over it. The definition of "active" varies from platform to platform.

-activeborderwidth *distance*

Specifies the width of the 3-D border around active elements. This has an effect only if -**relief** is not **flat**.

-activeforeground *color*

Specifies the foreground color for the widget when it is *active*, such as the foreground color of a button while the mouse pointer is over it.

-anchor *anchor*

Specifies how information in the widget (such as characters in a text item) is to be displayed.

-background *color*

Specifies the normal background color for the widget.

-bitmap *bitmap*

Specifies the bitmap to display in the widget.

-borderwidth *distance*

Specifies the width of the 3-D border around normal elements. This has an effect only if **-relief** is not **flat**. **-borderwidth** may be abbreviated to **-bd**.

-cursor *cursor*

Specifies the shape of the mouse pointer when it's over the widget and any of its children who do not have a nondefault cursor set. If *cursor* is an empty list ({}), the default cursor is restored.

-disabledforeground *color*

Specifies the foreground color to use when the widget is disabled. If *color* is an empty string, disabled elements are drawn with the normal foreground color, but with a stipple pattern that makes them appear dimmer.

-exportselection *boolean*

Specifies whether the widget exports its selection to the system clipboard (such as the X Windows selection). Only one of all the widgets in an application with -**exportselection** enabled can have a selection set at one time.

-font *font*

Specifies the font for text in the widget.

-foreground *color*

Specifies the normal foreground color for the widget.

-highlightbackground *color*

Specifies the color for the focus highlight when the widget does not have input focus. This option has an effect only if -**highlightthickness** is positive.

-highlightcolor *color*

Specifies the color of the focus highlight when the widget has input focus. This option has an effect only if -**highlightthickness** is positive.

-highlightthickness *distance*

Specifies the size of the input focus highlight around the widget.

-image *image*

Specifies an image to draw in the widget. For widgets that have both -**image** and -**bitmap** options, such as buttons, -**image** typically overrides -**bitmap** and only *image* is displayed in the widget.

-insertbackground *color*

Specifies the background color for the area under the text-insertion cursor.

-insertborderwidth *distance*

Specifies the size of the border to be drawn around the insertion cursor.

-insertofftime *milliseconds*

Specifies the amount of time the insertion cursor is off during each blink cycle.

-insertontime *milliseconds*

Specifies the amount of time the insertion cursor is on during each blink cycle.

-insertwidth *distance*

Specifies the width of the text-insertion cursor.

-jump *boolean*

Specifies how new values for widgets with sliders, such as scales and scroll bars, are reported to the rest of the application. If **-jump** is disabled (*boolean* is false), values are continuously reported as the slider is dragged (the default). If **-jump** is enabled, the new value is reported only when the slider is released, and the value appears to jump.

-justify *justification*

Specifies the justification for text in the widget.

-orient *orientation*

Specifies the direction of the long dimension for widgets such as
scroll bars and scales. For example, a scroll bar that controls
moving the contents of text up and down is usually shown
vertically along the side of the text, and thus *orientation* is **vertical**.

-padx *distance*

Specifies extra space between the left and right edges of the
widget and its contents.

-pady *distance*

Specifies extra space between the top and bottom edges of the
widget and its contents.

-relief *relief*

Specifies the 3-D effect to be used for the widget. This option has
no effect if **-borderwidth** is 0.

-repeatdelay *milliseconds*

Specifies how long a button or key, such as an arrow in a scroll bar,
must be depressed before its action begins to repeat.

-repeatinterval *milliseconds*

Specifies how often the action is repeated for a button or key that
remains depressed.

-selectbackground *color*

Specifies the background to use when drawing selected items in
the widget.

-selectborderwidth *distance*

Specifies the width of the 3-D border drawn around selected items in the widget. The relief for selected items is always **raised**. In some widgets, such as listboxes, space is always allowed for the selection border, even around nonselected items.

-selectforeground *color*

Specifies the foreground color to use when drawing selected items in the widget.

-setgrid *boolean*

Specifies whether the widget controls the resizing of its toplevel window to be consistent with its natural size requirements. For example, a toplevel window containing a text widget with **-setgrid** enabled would be constrained to resizing so that an integer number of lines of full characters are displayed in the text widget.

-takefocus *focus*

Specifies if or when the widget will take the keyboard focus during keyboard traversal. The default Tk bindings include procs bound to TAB and SHIFT-TAB to move between widgets. These procs use the **-takefocus** option for a widget to decide whether it gets focus, according to the following table:

Focus	Meaning
0	The widget will never take keyboard focus.
1	The widget takes focus if it is viewable.
{}	The widget is skipped if it is disabled, has no key bindings, or is not viewable.
command	*command* is evaluated with the widget name appended to it. *command* should return 0, 1, or an empty string. The actions in the preceding table entries are taken based on that result.

-text *string*

Specifies the string to display in the widget, such as the text on a button. The appearance of the string will depend on other options, including -**anchor** and -**justify**.

-textvariable *varname*

Specifies the variable whose contents will be displayed in the widget. The appearance of the string will depend on other options, including -**anchor** and -**justify**.

NOTE: For widgets which recognize a -**textvariable** option but not a -**text** option, -**text** will be interpreted as a unique prefix of -**textvariable** so **entry** .e -**text foo** creates an entry which gets its display value from a variable named foo rather than displaying the text "foo".

-troughcolor *color*

Specifies the color of the area around the slider in widgets such as scales and scroll bars.

-underline *integer*

Specifies which character in a string to underline. The first character is 0. This is used by the keyboard binding procs for menu widgets, to determine the navigation keys for a menu. For example, a File menu entry is typically configured with the options -**label File -underscore 0**, to make F the accelerator key for the File option.

-wraplength *distance*

Specifies the length of the longest line of text to display in the widget. If *distance* is less than or equal to 0, no wrapping is done and text is broken only at newline characters.

-xscrollcommand *command*

Specifies the command to evaluate when the view of the widget is
moved horizontally. Typically, this is **scrollbar set**, where *scrollbar*
is the path through the Tk widget hierarchy of a horizontal scroll
bar associated with the widget. When *command* is invoked, the
lower and upper bounds of the view are appended as additional
arguments.

-yscrollcommand *command*

Specifies the command to evaluate when the view of the widget
is moved vertically. Typically, this is **scrollbar set**, where *scrollbar*
is the path through the Tk widget hierarchy of a vertical scroll
bar associated with the widget. When *command* is invoked,
the lower and upper bounds of the view are appended as
additional arguments.

INDEX

Index **539**